Genocide In Our Time

An Annotated Bibliography with
Analytical Introductions

RESOURCES ON CONTEMPORARY ISSUES

RESOURCES ON CONTEMPORARY ISSUES

Richard A. Gray
Series Editor

Devoted to topics that address important social, economic, political, and environmental concerns, RESOURCES ON CONTEMPORARY ISSUES is a new bibliographic series that guides the reader to the most significant literature available on these subjects. Every book in this series is designed for use:
    in academic, public, and high school libraries
    by public policy makers–government officials, legislators, lobbyists, etc., and
    by professionals and specialists–e.g., journalists or economists–interested in the
    related subjects.
Librarians, teachers, students, policy makers, and others will find them useful not only as a means of organizing the literature of the topic, but also as a framework for understanding the complexity of the issue.

RESOURCES ON CONTEMPORARY ISSUES is one of the few bibliographic series to consistently provide analytical introductions–background text which explains the significance of the topic and provides a context in which to understand the citations assigned to each chapter. Each volume contains 800 to 1,000 annotated citations, a glossary, a chronology of events, and author and title indexes.

Other volumes in this series:

The American Farm Crisis
Protectionism
South Africa
Sandinista Nicaragua Part 1: Revolution, Religion, and Social Policy
Sandinista Nicaragua Part 2: Economy, Politics, and Foreign Policy

This series is available on standing order.

For information call or write:

The Pierian Press
P.O. Box 1808
Ann Arbor, MI 48106
(800) 678-2435
Fax (313) 434-6409

Genocide In Our Time

An Annotated Bibliography with
Analytical Introductions

by

Michael N. Dobkowski
Professor of Religious Studies
Hobart and William Smith Colleges

and

Isidor Wallimann
Lecturer in Sociology
School of Social Work in Basel
and the Institute of Sociology
University of Bern, Switzerland

RESOURCES ON CONTEMPORARY ISSUES

Pierian Press
Ann Arbor, Michigan
1992

DEDICATION

To **Raphael Lemkin**
(1901-1959)

International lawyer, scholar, activist, and principal drafter of the 1958
U.N. Convention for the Prevention and Punishment of Genocide.

To **Monik Dobkowski, Bronia and David Kalt**,
who survived the Holocaust and to their daughter, **Susan Castle**.

Their enduring example of courage, dignity, and generosity of spirit
is an inspiration.

And to **all survivors**,

In gratitude for the lessons you continue to teach us all.

ISBN 0-87650-280-X

Copyright © 1992, The Pierian Press
All Rights Reserved

No part of this publication may be reproduced or transmitted
in any form or by any means electronic or mechanical,
including photocopying, recording or by any information
storage and retrieval system, without permission in writing
from Pierian Press

Printed and bound in the United States of America.
Cover art by: Brian Rooney

The Pierian Press
Box 1808
Ann Arbor, Michigan 48106
1-800-678-2435

Table of Contents

Table of Contents v
Preface x
General Introduction to the Topic xii
   by **Michael Dobkowski** and **Isidor Wallimann**

Chapter 1: Ethnocide   1

by **Alison Palmer**

The distinction between ethnocide and genocide, which is clear in principle, is often unclear and imprecise in practice. A successful ethnocide can leave a broken-spirited people who have relinquished the will to live. An imperial culture can use a variety of means to destroy a technologically inferior one. It can destroy a subject culture's ecology, its traditional economy, its forms of political and social organization, and its religion. Techniques of destruction range from a seemingly mild belittlement of the subject culture's values to overt oppression. Perhaps the most brutal methods used are transmigration of dominant peoples into the subject culture's geographic domain and the abduction of the subject culture's infants and children from that domain.

Ethnocide and Genocide Contrasted 1
Ethnocide and Development 2
Organizations to Protect Indigenous Peoples 2
Forms of Ethnocide 2
The Question of Intent 4
Interactions of Ethnocide and Genocide 5
Ethnogenesis 5
Annotated Bibliography 7

Chapter 2: The Holocaust   23

by **Michael Dobkowski**

The Holocaust, the paradigmatic genocide, was a product of the convergence of a technically efficient, well-educated and cultured bureaucracy, and barbaric intentionality. The Holocaust was a paper-shuffling genocide in that those who planned the operations of extermination for the most part never saw the "final solution" as an accomplished fact. The bureaucratization of genocide profoundly desensitized the bureaucrats who carried it out. A necessary prelude to genocide was the Nazis' barbaric program to dehumanize the Jew, to transform him into the Other, into a parasite, into an object of derision.

Then the outbreak of war in 1939 foreclosed opportunities for expulsion of the Jews from Europe and set the stage for the Holocaust which was carried out primarily on the conquered lands of Eastern Europe and the Soviet Union.

Bureaucracy and Barbarism 23
Intentionalism Versus Functionalism 24
Was the Holocaust Unique? 24
The Paper-Shuffling Genocide 24
The Banality of Evil 25
The Milieu of Anti-Semitism 25
War Made Genocide Possible 25
The Challenge We Face Today 26
Annotated Bibliography 27
   General Works 27
   Theoretical and Historical Works 29
   The Ghetto Experience 32
   Concentration Camps 33
   Survivor Accounts 34
   Rescue 36
   The Indifference of the World 37
   Jewish Resistance 40
   Selected Fiction 40
   Representations and Reflections on the Holocaust ... 42
   Religious Implications 43

Chapter 3: The Issue of the Holocaust as a Unique Event 47

by **Alan Rosenberg** and **Evelyn Silverman**

If the Holocaust was a truly unique event, then it lies beyond our comprehension. If it was not truly unique, then there is no unique lesson to be learned from it. Viewed solely from the perspective of its uniqueness, the Holocaust must be considered either incomprehensible or trivial. A contexualist analysis, on the other hand, finds that it was neither "extra historical" nor just another atrocity. It is possible to view the Holocaust as unprecedented in many respects and as an event of critical and transformational importance in the history of our world. Using this method, we can determine the ways in which the uniqueness question both helps and hinders our quest for understanding of the Holocaust.

Comparability or Uniqueness 48
Three Principal Options 48
Explicating the Uniqueness Question 49
What Constitutes Uniqueness? 50
Contextualists 51
The *Historikerstreit* 51
Intention Versus Methodology 52
Interpretive Grids 52
Conclusion 53
Annotated Bibliography 55

Chapter 4: The Victims Who Survived 67

by **Sidney M. Bolkosky**

Studies of survivors' testimonies that concentrate on the ability of the afflicted to find meaning in suffering are at best problematic in the face of the overwhelming force of Holocaust testimonies. To many of those who survived, survival was not a triumph but an unbearable burden. "Nothing can ever be good again" and "All my happiness is gone for ever" are recurring motifs in their testimonies. The lives of survivors are forever haunted by images, sounds, and smells that contain ominous questions about survival and about guilt for having survived. "Why me?" and "Why was I saved?" appear in the testimonies over and over again. As Elie Wiesel phrased it, the question is not "to be *or* not to be" but rather "to be *and* not to be." One woman, a survivor of Auschwitz, compared herself to a hollow tree: "still alive but empty inside." The appended diary by Agi Rubin embodies these themes of despair, guilt, and inner emptiness.

Annotated Bibliography 72
   Major Titles 72
   Briefly Annotated Titles 74
Appendix: The Diary, by **Agi Rubin,**
   with commentary by **Sidney Bolkosky** 76

Chapter 5:
The Armenian Genocide: Revisionism and Denial 85

by **Rouben Adalian**

The Turkish government has adopted three lines of argument to convince the world that nothing out of the ordinary happened to the Armenians during the years 1915-1923. Three theses have been advanced: the denial thesis; the revisionist thesis; and the justification thesis. The three theses can in turn be divided among six categories of authors as follows: participants, apologists, rationalizers, revisionists, disinformers, and distorters. In the years since 1923 several factors have contributed to the world's acquiescence in the Turkish program of denial and revisionism. First, Turkey became respectable as the Turkish Republic under Kemal Attaturk; second, Turkey joined the United Nations as a charter member in 1945; and third, Turkey joined the North Atlantic Treaty Organization in 1952.

Post-War Unsettlement 85
Sidebar: The Armenian Genocide: 1915-1923:
    An Introduction 86
    Annotated Bibliography for Sidebar 88
Eastern Armenia Under Communism 88
Abdications and Retributions 89
Turkey Reformed 89
Armenians in Diaspora 90
Turning Points 90
Defining the Armenian Experience 91
The Arguments 92
The Authors 92
Conclusion 93
Annotated Bibliography for Main Article 95
    The Participants 95
    The Apologists 96
    The Rationalizers 97
    The Revisionists 99
    The Disinformers 101
    The Distorters 103

Chapter 6: The Ukrainian Famine 107

by **Lyman H. Legters**

In the mind of Stalin, the problem of the Ukrainian peasants who resisted collectivization was linked with the problem of Ukrainian nationalism. Collectivization was imposed on the Ukraine much faster than it was on other parts of the Soviet Union. The resulting hardship in the Ukraine was deliberately intensified by a policy of unrelenting grain procurement. It was this procurement policy that transformed hardship into catastrophe. Famine by itself is not genocide, but the consequences of the policy were known and remedies were available. The evidence is quite powerful that the famine could have been avoided, hence the argument turns on Stalin's intentions.

Lenin's New Economic Policy 108
"Primitive Accumulation" 108
Collectivization 109
Peasantry and Nationality 109
Unrelenting Grain Procurement 109
Terror-Famine 110
The UN Definition of Genocide 110
Annotated Bibliography 111
    Briefly Annotated Works 115

Chapter 7: Genocide and Modern War

by **Eric Markusen**

It is the governments of the world that either carry out or condone genocide, modern war, and other forms of mass killing. Although genocide and warfare are often regarded as distinctly different phenomena, there are in fact a number of important connections and commonalities between them, among which are several psychosocial facilitating factors. Markusen gives special attention to three of these: dehumanization of the victims, the systematic use of euphemistic language in describing the violence that is inflicted on victims, and bureaucratic organization of the overall effort. These three factors are of approximately equal importance in the waging of both wars and genocides. "The scale of man-made death is the central moral as well as material fact of our time."

In the light of this fact, it is particularly unfortunate that the energy and resources devoted to understanding and preventing mass killing have been negligible.

Introduction	117
The Violence of the Twentieth Century	117
Structural Violence	119
The Preparations for Nuclear Omnicide	120
Genocide and Modern War as Forms of Governmental Mass Killing	121
Genocide	121
Modern (Total) War	122
Connections and Commonalities Between Genocide and Modern War	124
Modern War Expedites Genocide	124
Blurring of the Line Between War and Genocide	124
Psychosocial Facilitating Factors Common to Both Genocide and Modern War	125
Conclusions	126
Annotated Bibliography	131
The Murderousness of the Twentieth Century	131
Genocide	133
Modern War	136
Nuclear Omnicide	139
Commonalities and Connections between Genocide and Modern War	143

Chapter 8: Early Warning, Intervention, and Prevention of Genocide

by **Israel W. Charny**

The record of governments on the prevention of, or intervention in, genocide has always been very poor. Even those states that can be called the bastions of democracy, such as the United States and Israel, have deeply tarnished records. In part to counterbalance the performance of governments, it is urgently necessary to make individuals far more aware than they have been of their responsibility to guard against the intrusion of attitudes that promote genocide. Charny analyzes various key indicators that new genocidal threats may be taking shape. Governments should immediately give their support to several international initiatives for the prevention of genocide, such as the creation of an International Genocide Bureau or a World Genocide Tribunal.

The Foreseeability of Genocide	149
No Cooperation with Mass Killers	150
The Record of Governments Is Very Poor	150
Ugly Behaviors in the Bastions of Democracy	150
The U.S. and Pol Pot	151
The U.S., Israel, and China	151
Israel, the U.S., and the Armenian Genocide	151
The Responsibility of Individuals	151
The Courage to Withstand One's Own Nation	152
Proposal for a World Genocide Early Warning System Foundation	152
Early Warning Processes	154
Other Proposals for Preventing Genocide	156
International Alert	156
Conclusions	156
Annotated Bibliography	158

Appendix   167

Appendix: Chronology of Genocide
   by **Michael Dobkowski** 167

Indexes   169

Author Index 169

Title Index 175

PREFACE:

In the course of preparing this volume, we have incurred many debts, some of which we are able to acknowledge publicly. We are particularly grateful to the contributors for the prompt submission of their chapters and the high quality of their work. To those who offered editorial advice, we give special thanks. The editors, of course, assume final responsibility for the text.

The staff members of the libraries we used were unfailingly helpful in making materials available. We would like to offer special thanks to the reference staff of the Hobart and William Smith Colleges Library who took an interest in this project and helped in ways that were far beyond the library walls.

To colleagues and students in our respective institutions who have provided an intellectual environment that was conducive to productive work, many thanks. We are grateful for their interest and support, particularly our students. It made this book possible and necessary. A special acknowledgment to Richard A. Gray, Senior Editor at Pierian Press, who contributed many useful suggestions and criticisms. The volume is better for his efforts.

Credit for typing goes to Sharon Elder and Pati Mattice.

We would like to thank Karen Gabe Dobkowski for all of her assistance, encouragement, and good humor. She has been instrumental in helping us think and feel about genocide. Her valuable comments and at times her direct and heartfelt way of putting things have influenced our thinking here. And to Batsheva, Jonathan, Tamar, and all children for being never-ending sources of joy and hope. In the end, it is for them that we do this work.

Finally, we provide, in alphabetical order, a brief biographical sketch of each of the contributors to this volume.

Rouben Adalian, Ph.D., is Director of Academic Affairs at the Armenian Assembly of America in Washington, DC.

Sidney M. Bolkosky is Professor of History at the University of Michigan-Dearborn. He is the author of *Harmony and Dissonance: Voices of Jewish Identity in Detroit, 1914-1967 (1991)* and co-author with Betty Allias and David Harris of *Life Unworthy of Life: A Holocaust Curriculum* (1987).

Israel W. Charny is the Executive Director of the Institute on the Holocaust and Genocide in Jerusalem and Associate Professor of Psychology at the Bob Schapell School of Social Work at Tel Aviv University in Tel Aviv, Israel. He is the author of *How Can We Commit the Unthinkable? Genocide: The Human Cancer* (1982) and the editor of *Genocide: A Critical Bibliographic Review* (Vol 1, 1988) and (Vol 2, 1991).

Michael N. Dobkowski is Professor of Religious Studies at Hobart and William Smith Colleges in Geneva, New York. He is the co-author, with Isidor Wallimann, of *Towards the Holocaust: The Social and Economic Collapse of the Weimar Republic* (1983), *Genocide and the Modern Age: Etiology and Case Studies of Mass Death* (1987), and *Radical Perspectives on the Rise of Fascism in Germany, 1919-1945* (1989).

Lyman H. Legters, Professor Emeritus of Russian and East European Studies at the University of Washington, is a senior fellow of the William O. Douglas Institute and director of its project, States and Societies in East-Central Europe. He edited the institute's volume, *Western Society after the Holocaust* (1983). His latest book is *Eastern Europe—Transformation and Revolution, 1945-1991* (1992).

Eric Markusen is Associate Professor of Sociology and Social Work at Southwest State University, Marshall, Minnesota. He is the co-author, with Robert Jay Lifton, of *The Genocidal Mentality: Nazi Holocaust and Nuclear Threat* (1990).

Alison Palmer is a doctoral candidate at the London School of Economics and Political Science, London, England.

Alan Rosenberg teaches philosophy at Queens College of the City University of New York. He is the author and co-author of a number of articles on the Holocaust and co-editor of *Echoes from the Holocaust: Philosophical Reflections on a Dark Time* (1988).

Agi Rubin is a survivor of the Holocaust from Munkacs in Carpetho-Ruthenia who now lives in Southfield, Michigan.

Evelyn Silverman is a reference librarian and subject bibliographer at the Benjamin S. Rosenthal Library of Queens College of the City University of New York.

Isidor Wallimann is a Lecturer in Sociology at the School of Social Work in Basel, and at the Institute of Sociology, University of Bern, Switzerland. He is the co-editor, with Michael Dobkowski, of *Towards the Holocaust, Genocide and the Modern Age* and *Radical Perspectives on the Rise of Fascism in Germany, 1919-1945*. He is the author of *Estrangement: Marx's Conception of Human Nature and the Division of Labor* (1981).

General Introduction To The Topic

by **Michael Dobkowski** and **Isidor Wallimann**

The "progress" of the twentieth century has been constant along its journey of horrors—from the massacre of the Armenians, to the planned famine in the Ukraine, to the Holocaust, to the killing fields of Cambodia. The enormity of the genocidal horrors of our century is indicated by our almost schizophrenic attitude toward it. We move between attitudes of despair on one hand and denial or avoidancy on the other. These attitudes are actually mirror images of each other. They both seek to deny reality by avoiding any responsibility for the need to understand the phenomenon so that we can avoid repeating it again and again. Our first obligation, therefore, is to face it squarely.

If genocide is the destruction of a national, ethnic, racial, or religious group, the study of genocide is the attempt to understand this phenomenon, both in its genesis and prevention. Far too great and too grave has the suffering caused by genocide been for it to be ignored. Far too many resources—scientific and other—are spent to destroy rather than to enhance life. The study of genocide can only have one goal—and its very object of investigation demands that it be to preserve and to promote human life. All else would be perverse. Therefore, any scientific effort to study genocide is bound to combine both theory and action—is bound to be praxis; praxis designed to change the conditions that have led to genocide in the past, or could do so in the future. It is, and must be, change-oriented interpretation and theorizing, action-oriented scholarship.

Massive human suffering caused by people is not unique to genocide. In fact, much more suffering and death are and have been inflicted worldwide in ways that technically are not called genocide. Millions may have died from genocide in recent history. But hundreds of millions succumbed as a result of human induced starvation or war. What, then, makes the study of genocide so important, so compelling? What should make genocidal killing a more important object of study than the killing through war or anonymous economic mechanisms—particularly if more lives could potentially be preserved by studying the latter? Clearly, there is no reason why the study and prevention of genocide should have precedence over the study and prevention of other processes that are equally or even more destructive of human lives. Rather, what has emerged may be seen as a division of labor among like-minded scholars holding similar values, nurturing similar hopes, and working with similar intentions: to prevent the destruction of life, to create life-enhancing social conditions.

Scholars have been more concerned with the study of war, poverty, and disease than with the study of genocide. However, since the genocidal destruction of life cannot be clearly dissociated from other but equally destructive processes, any study of genocide must also be informed by and connected to all other efforts to understand and to prevent the mass destruction of human lives. Therefore, a scientific praxis to understand and prevent poverty, disease and war will also directly enhance the understanding and prevention of genocide.

The term "genocide" was coined against the aftermath of World War II, indicating that the study of genocide, as we know it today, is about fifty years old. The motivation to focus specifically on genocide—as opposed to other life-destroying processes—may greatly vary from one individual to another. However, the twentieth century experience with genocide is still too deeply engraved in societal consciousness; the pain of survivors and relatives of victims is still too vivid; the remaining injustice suffered by members of various ethnic groups is still too deep for it not to have had an effect on the scholarly community and some of its practitioners.

To say that the term "genocide" and the effort to study and prevent it is new implies that the phenomenon itself may be recent to human history. In other words, processes that destroy groups on the basis of their religion, race, ethnicity, or nationality may be correlates of modernity and the tremendous social differentiation, that is, the hierarchically and horizontally highly segmented society that characterizes it. By implication, then, genocide would not be expected to occur in societies with little social differentiation.

Indeed, when consulting the historical wisdom on this point, it appears that the first mass killings where genocide might have been involved occurred in societies with sufficient differentiation to be classified as agricultural societies. All previous human history—agricultural societies emerged only about 6,000 years ago—did not seem to know genocide although lives were destroyed in warfare.

Mass Warfare

In essence, the phenomenon of mass warfare is connected with civilization. It is possible only within conflict situations peculiar to civilized societies. Although human beings have possessed the technical skills to create weapons such as axes, clubs, and spears for about 25,000 years, it appears that the species did not deliberately make weapons in order to wage war until the emergence of Neolithic man. In fact, no weapons specifically designed to be used against other human beings have been found that can be dated before the emergence of Neolithic man—founder of agriculture—in approximately 10,000 B.C.E. This is not to suggest that earlier humans did not sporadically kill other humans with hunting tools, rocks, and other such items. Early humans were aggressive and often violent. Yet organized mass violence was not yet part of human behavior.

Ritualistic Practices in Warfare

The institution of mass warfare occurred during the crucial stages of the transition to civilization. Archaeological and anthropological evidence suggests that it can be found in the later neolithic period. The first identifiable weapons are found in communal sites used by societies with a mixed economy of hunting and agriculture. It is in this period that we also find the first evidence of fortified settlement, perhaps the most telling evidence of warlike activity. The conflicts of Neolithic man were definitely rule-governed group activities: they involved genuine weapons for warfare and were the focus of time and resources. Yet they were not "modern" because they had very limited objectives beyond the fighting itself. The warfare was often accompanied by ritualistic practices, with attention given to the rites of death and there was no interest in conquest of the opponent's territory. Neolithic warfare therefore did not function as a coercive of political imposition. It is only with the emergence of the city-state as a social entity that we see the ingredients of mass warfare of genocidal proportions. With the rise of the city-states and significant social differentiation, there emerged forces and institutions that made mass warfare an essential feature of intercity policies. In Mesapotamia and Egypt around 4,000 to 3,000 B.C.E., we find the first real evidence of potentially genocidal war. In the "cradle of civilization," cities were walled in and fortified from the very beginning and a regular army emerged as a new social organization.

Ritually Uncontrolled Killing

To the extent that history can only be appropriated through records in one form or another, the aforementioned conclusion may be unwarranted. Nevertheless, since archeology or oral history have produced no evidence to the contrary, for all practical purposes we can accept it as a valid inference. Furthermore, modern anthropological records of hunting and gathering or horticultural societies seem to indicate that in minimally differentiated societies even warfare is ritually controlled to minimize human loss. Genocide, on the other hand, is an event that potentially knows no limit short of the total annihilation of the group and is, if anything, a ritually *uncontrolled* killing process. Lastly, the available records on agricultural societies lead us to suspect that genocide may for the first time have occurred in this social formation. Written language itself is to be found only in relatively differentiated societies where it primarily serves as a device to administer society and to integrate it politically and economically. Social formation with less differentiation, such as hunting and gathering and horticultural societies, had no need for such means. Therefore, the very sources that inform us of mass killing are the product of increased social differentiation, a condition also associated with events of genocide.

Genocide and Social Differentiation

To define genocide as the destruction of religious, ethnic, racial, or national groups is to presuppose a social organism sufficiently differentiated to include one or more of the above groups. While the history of social differentiation spans thousands of years, the notion that social life is subject to ever more pronounced differentiation primarily arose in the nineteenth century. To the extent that agricultural societies did perceive themselves to be differentiated, differentiation was seen as rather static. However, once the agricultural mode of production—based on local self-sufficiency—was penetrated by exchange and market relations transforming local into ever wider universal social interactions and dependencies, the stage was set for social differentiation to accelerate at a hitherto unknown speed and to reach an unforeseeable complexity.

Vertical and Horizontal Segmentation

The phenomenally increased—and still increasing—vertical and horizontal segmentation of society was particularly noticeable in the ninteenth century and numerous scholars of the period articulated it irrespective of their political persuasion. Vertical segmentation is characterized by hierarchies of status, class, power, and authority, whereas horizontal segmentation consists of the social and industrial division of labor. Suddenly, nation states appeared as major political power centers with administrative units that increasingly subsumed diverse ethnic, religious, and racial groups and incorporated previously independent administrative units under its rule. Bureaucracy and market systems were greatly expanded and elaborated to serve as primary means of co-ordination. As they operated to hold together what differentiation threatened to break apart, they themselves accelerated social differentiation.

Reification

The division of labor in a general societal and a narrower economic sense—linking the most varied human groups, social classes, political units, and continents often in antagonistic fashion—grew into an ever more elaborate, impenetrable web, one increasingly difficult to comprehend. Social organization, social interaction, production, and distribution have taken on lives of their own, have become reified. Human beings could no longer regulate, control, shape, and reshape these forces but rather were dominated by them. While individuals increasingly lost control and comprehension of the mechanisms and the world they created, the ever increasing division of labor—coerced by market forces—brought forth ever more powerful and efficient means of production and destruction, ever more anonymous, distant, and powerful centers of administration, decision making, and conflict management; for every increase in social differentiation in the division of labor is social change implying a conflict laden re-alignment of interest and power relations.

We need not be concerned here with the unproductive academic dispute whether social life is at all possible without reification or whether there could be a world in which human agency never produces unintended consequences. What demands our full attention, however, is the observation—and the insight—that reification has assumed intolerable, catastrophic proportions. Many developments, but particularly the life-destroying processes of which genocide is just one of the more important examples, make this evident.

Those who coined the terms "alienation" and "estrangement" were not inspired by the quest for a world without any reification and unexpected consequences to human action. Rather, they had the vision of a world in which—although human action may produce unexpected consequences—humanity could free itself from the fateful position of the sorcerer's apprentice, and would be capable of intervening, of correcting mistakes and of avoiding socially induced suffering and catastrophes. They rejected a world in which humanity is the plaything of processes run amuck, the victim of forces and power relations that annihilate. They knew that human history is for the most part characterized by the very absence of massive life destruction and the knowledge that humanity is capable of consciously shaping its history, of controlling the means and relations of production and destruction.

Modernity

Genocide is only one of many manifestations to show that a social formation and the associated social relations have gone berserk. So has modernity, world society with a differentiation so excessive as to prohibit a sufficient understanding of its web and processes, highly coercive to both individuals and groups and, thus, all too often defying intervention. If genocide is characterized by uncontrolled state power, so is modernity; if it is made possible because of segmented individuals who do their jobs as part of a coercive division of labor and who no longer see where and how they are connected to the social whole, so is modernity; if it requires technical and administrative thoroughness and efficiency, so does modernity; if it is massively destructive to life, so is modernity; if it is directed against certain national, religious, ethnic, or racial groups, modernity has brought them forth, has forcibly taken them into its confinement—and often pitted one against the other in the course of social differentiation.

Seen against the background of modernity, of modern processes and forces of production and destruction, events of genocide may no longer be construed as unique occurrences only. Because they also manifest a pattern deeply embedded in modernity, we must conceptualize them as integral parts of modernity. Granted, we are horrified by them and are still unable to comprehend the genocidal events in the twentieth century, particularly the Holocaust. Why are we not equally dazzled by the even larger potential of destruction already in place? Why not by the military machinery ready to administer the looming nuclear omnicide? Why not at the millions who anonymously perish of hunger right before our eyes due to our universally anonymous market forces and power relations? Can all this be comprehended at all? Can modernity be comprehended? Should we not be dazzled by modernity, instead of by some selective phenomena produced by it? Should we not go to the root cause both in our cognition and action, in praxis? By seeing genocide embedded in modernity, we do not mean to take a purely determinisitic point of view. Even with modernity as a given, genocide only occurs under specific circumstances. History, place, ideology remain important. The historicity of particular genocides remains important. However, modernity is still a necessary, if not a sufficient, condition for genocide to occur. Furthermore, by placing the emphasis on anonymous life destruction processes in modernity, we also imply an expansion of the United Nations convention of genocide—that no explicit human agency may be required. For instance, the structural violence exercised by market forces determining production and distribution alone is generally known to kill millions and could also assume genocidal qualities.

Clearly, from our perspective, genocide is a part, and must be studied in the context, of modernity. As a phenomenon, it is but one element among, or a subset of, other life annihilation processes. Processes killing millions by starvation may also be genocidally directed at specific national, ethnic, racial, or religious groups. In imperialism's thrust for ever greater market penetration and brutal conquest of other at least minimally exchange-oriented and differentiated societies, it causes many groups to suffer ethnocide while it exposes others to genocide. In war's massive destruction of lives, some national, ethnic, racial, or religious groups may suffer total or near total extinction. Omnicide alone would blur all differentiation in modernity's human-induced destruction of life.

The Study of Genocide

What is it, then, that specifically characterizes the study of genocide? First, it is the acquisition of knowledge not for its own sake but to prevent modernity's tremendous destruction of life. Second, it is the effort to improve our understanding of all life-annihilation processes inherent in modernity. Third, it is the effort to learn more about the circumstances under which modernity's life destruction processes tend to focus on specific groups in events known to us as genocide. For instance, what are the circumstances under which wars or life-annhilating economic or political conflicts genocidally turn against ethnic, racial, religious, or national groups, or when do conflicts involving such groups tend to escalate into genocides? Fourth, it is the effort to develop means to prevent genocide. Such means must simultaneously be developed on two levels. On the structural level, means and strategies must be found for the increased social control over spheres that have become reified and taken on lives of their own. On another level, intervention techniques must be developed for situations that threaten to escalate into genocide.

The Present Volume

While they touch on many of the issues discussed above, the contributors to this volume elaborate on them and cover additional terrain. The typology and history of mass killing and genocide in themselves are unable to convey the emotional hurt and suffering that victims must have endured. The perspective of survivors alone can convey to us, aside from other insights they can give based on their direct observations, what this horrible experience has meant for them and how they were psychologically and physiologically affected during and after the event. Bolkosky confronts us with one Holocaust survivor's account and supplements it with the relevant historical background. The immediacy of the survivor's account gives us some entry into the emotional and psychological realm of survivorship and helps us to experience it in ways that objective historical scholarship cannot.

The work of Markusen, Legters, and Palmer focuses on phenomena that are not classically defined as genocide but, since they show many points of intersection, are highly important to the study of genocide. Thus Palmer explores numerous policies towards ethnic minorities worldwide and shows their overt and covert ethnocidal dimensions, while, in the Ukrainian case chosen by Legters, the issue is one of demarkation. Should the Ukrainian famine be viewed as a case involving an economic catastrophe, as a political conflict, as ethnocide, as mass killing, or as genocide? How were these dimensions connected or could they have been? Linkages are also the theme of Markusen's investigation, which looks at the possible connections between modern war and genocide, particularly as it concerns the nature of modern war and its social, psychological, and organizational foundations in modernity. Aspects of the latter are also used by Dobkowski and by Rosenberg and Silverman in their analyses of the Holocaust. Dobkowski views the Holocaust as the paradigmatic genocide. It introduced an unprecedented technological mass killing. It represents a kind of ultimate confrontation with death, faceless and unmediated. Rosenberg and Silverman further demonstrate the criteria under which the Holocaust can be viewed as a unique event.

Adalian describes in detail the methods by which the Turkish genocide against the Armenians has been covered up, excused, and denied. Simultaneously, we obtain a good account of the event itself, including some of its causes and consequences. Finally, the manner and dynamic in which the Armenian genocide has been articulated, relativized, and denied can serve in the development of intervention strategies and early warning systems such as those that Charny proposes in his essay.

CHAPTER 1

ETHNOCIDE

by **Alison Palmer**

The distinction between ethnocide and genocide, which is clear in principle, is often unclear and imprecise in practice. A successful ethnocide can leave a broken-spirited people who have relinquished the will to live. An imperial culture can use a variety of means to destroy a technologically inferior one. It can destroy a subject culture's ecology, its traditional economy, its forms of political and social organization, and its religion. Techniques of destruction range from a seemingly mild belittlement of the subject culture's values to overt oppression. Perhaps the most brutal methods used are transmigration of dominant peoples into the subject culture's geographic domain and the abduction of the subject culture's infants and children from that domain.

Ethnocide occurs when the culture of a people is destroyed, and the continued existence of the group as a distinct ethnic identity is thereby threatened. The physical destruction of the people is not necessary, but it often occurs simultaneously. Ethnocide has been particularly virulent against indigenous minorities under processes of colonial expansion, state development programs, and nation-state building. Despite being a worldwide phenomenon, it has only recently been acknowledged by academics and international agencies. Ethnocide is rarely successful, however, and cultural resurgence of the oppressed group is a common consequence.

Ethnocide and Genocide Contrasted

In its most simple form, the term ethnocide refers to the destruction of a culture. It is conceptually distinct from genocide, which is the intention to physically destroy a people, and while both are often pursued simultaneously, ethnocide, unlike genocide, can be achieved without the death of the people concerned. In a great many cases, however, the distinction between the two is less clear, and successful ethnocide can leave a broken-spirited people who have relinquished the will to live.

Although the practice of ethnocide is historically and geographically widespread, the term itself is not widely used. There are a number of reasons for this. One reason has been the tradition among anthropologists and ethnographers of academic objectivity while they study the changes that traditional cultures have undergone due to contact with state policies or with modern and different cultures. The subject of their study has often been ethnocide, yet, because they have assumed the stance of impartial observer, they have been unwilling to speak out and condemn the destruction they have witnessed. A number of less emotive concepts have been used in place of ethnocide, such as acculturation—the modification of a culture as it comes into contact with a dominant culture; deculturation and detribalization—the breakdown of tribal social cohesion, and increasing participation of the individuals within a wider society; and assimilation—the absorption of a people into a dominant culture while requiring that their specific cultural distinctiveness be left behind. The concepts themselves deny the negative and destructive processes involved in such change.

Academics have also had recourse to theories which stress the natural progression of all societies as they develop, modernize, and industrialize. These theories assume that outmoded cultures are "primitive," "backward" and "underdeveloped," in which the people are denied admirable human qualities and are often likened to animal-like states. The solution for these anachronistic cultures is understood to be the inclusion of the people into the modernizing culture of the state and its forms of organization: the destruction of pre-modern cultures has been considered inevitable.[1]

Ethnocide and Development

A second reason why the concept is not widely used is that ethnocide is usually pursued, or is covertly condoned, by a state under wider policies of development, modernization, or nation building. It is not in the interests of the developers or of the state for their actions to be labelled as ethnocidal. Measures taken to prevent this include outright denial of the consequences of their actions, preventing knowledge of their activities from leaking out to a critical public by prohibiting entry to the region, making special provisions for the people in question which look good on paper but not in practice, and cloaking their activities under more acceptable terms such as assimilation into the national culture.

Organizations to Protect Indigenous Peoples

Another reason for the new emphasis on ethnocidal situations has been the growth of international organizations such as Survival International, Cultural Survival, and the International Work Group on Indigenous Affairs, which campaign to raise public awareness of the plight faced by many indigenous peoples, and to support their struggles for cultural and physical survival. A number of recently published international symposiums and declarations by concerned academics and specialists have added voice to the international condemnation of ethnocidal projects. Examples of these are the Declaration of Barbados, 1971, and the UNESCO Conference on Ethnic Development and Ethnocide, San Jose, 1981.

Although there is growing public awareness of ethnocides being carried out against indigenous people, it is important to remember that it also occurs in modern states against minority cultures, such as against the Ukrainians in the USSR, the Hungarians in Rumania, and the Kurds in Turkey and Iraq.

Forms of Ethnocide

The destruction of cultural identity can refer to the destruction of artistic artifacts, intellectuals, artists, religious icons, and others; and in a wider sociological sense, it can mean the destruction of a group's social organization. This can take many forms. The following are some of the most recurrent ones:

a) The eco-system which forms the basis of a people's social and economic system is destroyed. For example, the construction of the Kautokeino dam in the Norwegian tundra destroyed the fragile reindeer pastoralism upon which Saami culture is based and resulted in a considerable loss of Saami identity.[2] Another form, deforestation, has occurred in Sarawak, and has changed the indigenous peoples' swidden farming, causing the disintegration of their societies.[3]

b) People are forced into new forms of economic organization which, though they commonly fail, divide societies, establish different bases of prestige and authority, and incur starvation, debt, and exploitation. One of the two most common reasons for economic reorganization is to permanently settle a population whose traditional economy rotates seasonally over a large area. Permanent settlements increase the ability to control a population, to minimize resistance organizations, and to enable large areas of land to be taken for development projects. The second reason is to include previously excluded people within the dominant economy, so that they may be used as a cheap form of labor. For example, in the late nineteenth and early twentieth centuries, Australian Aborigines were included in white society as cattle-station hands and as domestic servants.

c) Traditional forms of authority and political organization are purposefully destroyed or undermined. This is often linked to economic reorganization, such as in the Amazon region of Peru where the cohesion of Indian communities has been fragmented as individuals are tempted away by the promise of a piece of land which they can own themselves.[4] Also, individuals with knowledge or wealth connected to the "new" economy can assume greater prestige and power than the traditional political figures, as happened in the traditional politico-religious hierarchies of the Aguacatan Indians of Guatemala.[5] The authority of religious leaders is commonly targeted, as in Guatemala where shamans are being annihilated by hired killers.[6]

d) Projects are established to include a people within the state's homogenizing cultural identity while their culture is excluded. Two means of achieving this are commonly pursued. In states where a minority culture is more or less integrated, their culture is denied expression as state education instructs students in the state's official language and the suppressed culture is written out of history. Mother-tongue publications and even traditional naming of children may also be forbidden. An example is the "Rumanianization" policies against the Hungarian minority in Rumania from 1948.[7] The other form is the "civilization" of indigenous peoples deemed by the state to be "primitive" and "backwards." This includes forsaking oral traditions and often their own language in favor of learning to read and write; donning western-style clothes; adopting western-style codes of morality; adopting a different work ethic; and replacing traditional religious and belief systems for the state religion.

e) The most active religious ethnocidal programs in recent history have been policies of Christianization. These were forcefully pursued in European colonization from the fifteenth century when the Spanish Conquistadors landed at Santo Domingo in 1492; they continue today, particularly in South America. The relationship between the religious missions and the state is not fixed; it is variable, subject to the extent to which their objectives are compatible. For example, the Council of the Catholic missions in the Brazilian Amazona condemned a state policy launched in the 1970s to remove the protected status of certain Indian groups and organized successful protest against the government.[8] The Protestant Summer Institute of Linguistics, on the other hand, receives state support as it operates as mediator between the indigenous people and state development projects in a large number of states.[9] In nineteenth century Australia, state funding for missionary projects was gradually decreased due to the missions' failure to produce sufficient numbers of transformed Aborigines.

f) Working closely with the methods outlined in the above two forms is the denial of a culture's distinct identity or reality by the dominant culture. In Venezuela, for example, the "Indian problem" has been "solved" by the official declaration that there are no Indians, but all are Venezuelans. Similarly in Ecuador, the separate identity of the Quicha Indians is negated as they are officially categorized in the general mestizo ethnic group.[10] A different form of denial is the manufacture of cultural stereotypes that become the dominant language by which a people is known. For example, degrading and simplistic stereotypes of North American Native Peoples form the basis of white knowledge of these separate cultures, denying their reality and history and exerting considerable influence on policy making in Indian affairs.[11]

g) Transmigration is another means by which ethnocide might be achieved. This refers to state policies which transfer large numbers of people from the dominant culture into a region where the minority culture that already inhabits the area is demographically overwhelmed. The minority culture then becomes a minority in its own land. This has occurred in Tibet where hundreds of thousands of Chinese have been relocated throughout the Tibetan provinces, on short-term but financially rewarding employment contracts.[12] It is also the policy of Indonesia, where Javanese peasants have been transferred to Irian Jaya and Balinese farmers to East Timor.[13] Transmigration is usually accompanied by some of the other measures already discussed to forcibly repress the minority culture.

h) In some situations children of the minority culture have been systematically abducted to be brought up within the dominant culture. The premise of abduction is that the younger the children are, the less they will have been exposed to the culture of their parents and the easier it will be for them to forget it and to learn a new culture. Consequently, even babies are taken. In this way, it is hoped that the removal of future generations will prevent the continued survival of the minority culture as a distinct group. This was a widespread state policy in Australia during the first half of this century when children, particularly those with some degree of white ancestry, were kidnapped and placed in Christian missions or in white homes to be raised as servants. Such was the fear of forcible separation from their children that many parents denied to themselves their own and their children's Aboriginality.[14] In Tibet, thousands of children have been forcibly sent to China for secondary education, which is taught in Chinese. For the children, this means seven years of forced exile and isolation from their own culture.[15]

i) A final form of cultural destruction that might be included is ideological colonialism in which any cultural expressions—using culture in both senses—which predate or oppose the particular state ideology are purged. The most obvious of these have occurred in communist regimes, such as in Tibet, where the Buddhist religion, its buildings, books, statues, monks, and nuns were systematically victimized and destroyed by the Chinese communists as expressions of anti-Chinese Tibetan nationalism, and where the traditional economic organization was forcibly reorganized and redistributed. Within China itself, in Peking, pre-communist buildings, statues, and other "symbols of Old China" were destroyed so that a new "symbol of socialist China" might be constructed.[16] In Cambodia also, the era of the communist Khmer Rouge, 1975-1979, systematically destroyed all elements of modern, pre-communist lifestyles, such as middle classes, health personnel, urban dwellers, techniques and implements of modern technology, and forms of social organization based upon the family group.[17] In some of these cases it might be plausible to apply the term "autoethnocide" (ie., ethnocide against one's own people in a similar sense to how) "autogenocide" is used by the United Nations in reference to Cambodia.

The "other side" of these ethnocidal measures is often the establishment of special reserves or camps for the displaced people. This is a widely practiced policy and may, under certain conditions, act as a prelude to genocide (see below). The transference of people to reserves can be both voluntary, as with the hill tribes of Thailand, where the state administration encourages Hmong settlement in the lowland camps but does not force it[18]; or forcible, such as in Paraguay, where the Ache Indians are hunted and often killed and the remnant rounded up and forced into camps, which are usually isolated and guarded. For the Ache there is no hope of escape. Conditions are unsanitary and there is very little medical aid or food; violence, sexual abuse, starvation, and death are common place and the living are reduced to states of abject despondency with little will or strength to survive.[19]

The Question of Intent

The crime of ethnocide has not been established in international law in the same way that genocide was established by the 1946 United Nations Convention. The question of the intentions of those causing ethnocide remains a crucial issue however, since Article II(e) of the United Nations Convention—"Forcibly transferring children of the group to another group"—includes a specific form of ethnocide within its area of jurisdiction. In at least this form, then, establishing the intentions behind the transfer of children can determine whether or not the action can be punished by international law. This may set a precedent for other forms of ethnocide to become embodied in international law as criminal activities. The establishment of ethnocide as an international crime is the second reason why "intent" is important: the consolidation of a solid body of documentation which clearly demonstrates the intentional destruction of distinct cultural groups will add weight to this demand. At present ethnocidal activities are roughly included in a range of international covenants such as the International Covenant on Economic, Social and Cultural Rights (1976) but these can lack specificity and are not necessarily legally binding.[20]

While many cases of ethnocide have clearly been intended to destroy the distinct cultural identity of a specific group of people, others are less clear. The rapid expansion of state development projects might, at times, not intend to bring cultural destruction since planning commonly alludes to vast tracts of empty wilderness. The use of this myth is not satisfactory, however; sufficient data clearly document the necessary small population-to-area ratio that is necessary for many indigenous cultures to survive in a fragile ecosystem. By resorting to the "empty wilderness" myth, policy decisionmakers consciously override the existence of those inhabiting the land, and ignore the destructive effects of their policies; they also impose a particular set of laws on land ownership that are clearly not recognized by the indigenous people, whose own traditional laws are negated.

Another example is the intentions of many missionaries which in some cases have been not so much destructive as salvational, hoping to raise "Satan-worshipers" to a higher spiritual and civilized level of humanity. The establishment of reserves, supposedly to protect the physical and cultural survival of a people, is another difficult area in which to gauge intentions. The reality of the reserves can serve to expose their destructive consequences, as Richard Arens forcefully demonstrated in his tour of four reservations at the request of the Paraguayan state.[21] Despite all of this, policymakers might continue to declare that their intentions were honorable.

A further reason why the intentions behind any policy are considered is that change is endemic to all societies. It is important to establish where change has been generic, coming from within the society itself; where it has been forcibly imposed from outside of the community; and where people have welcomed change brought about by contact with outside cultures as a means to rid themselves of outmoded or unwanted internal forms of organization—a form of chosen adaptation. Only the second type of change can be considered ethnocidal.

Interactions of Ethnocide and Genocide

While the definitions of genocide and ethnocide may be relatively distinct, in practice they often confusingly interact. It is helpful to distinguish the main forms that this interaction might take.

a) Ethnocide might be a more viable alternative to genocide. If the objective of policy is to remove a people whose continued traditional lifestyle is considered to be an obstacle to some larger aim, such as a development project, a number of solutions are possible (e.g., ethnocide, genocide, or expulsion). Due to insufficient analyses of cases, it is not yet possible to clearly establish which conditions are necessary for the pursuit of these different options. One factor which might be influential in the choice of ethnocide rather than genocide is the extent to which international spotlights are focused upon the situation. International pressure does not necessarily result in a change of policy, yet it may be sufficient in some cases to encourage a change from overt genocidal policies to more covert ethnocidal ones under the protective guise of "assimilation" or "reservations."

A second possible factor is that, once the "obstacle" has been removed through physical destruction, ethnocidal policies might be continued against the survivors for whom no "use" can be found to ensure their continued powerlessness and dissolution. This may have been the case in Queensland, Australia, during the late nineteenth century where isolated reserves were established for the dispirited and abused Aborigines who had survived the violent onslaught of frontier expansion. From these survivors, whose traditional lifestyles and communities had been destroyed, those who were not integrated into the dominant white economy were randomly and forcibly transferred to the reserves where it was assumed they would naturally die out as a race.[22] The example highlights a third possible factor—the extent to which the population of an unwanted culture can be incorporated, albeit often forcibly, into the dominant economy.

b) Ethnocide might act as a prelude to genocide. Certainly genocidal Nazi policies were augmented at the Wannsee Conference in 1942. Prior to this, Jews, Gypsies, and other targeted groups were subjected to ethnocidal practices. During Kristallnacht, synagogues were set ablaze the length of Germany. Families and communities were torn apart and deprived of their means of livelihood as they were redistributed throughout Europe or confined in isolated ghettoes.[23] In early colonial Australia, assimilationist policies towards the Aborigines were initially encouraged, yet their continued failure fueled impatience and encouraged frontiersmen to use violence as a means to end the Aborigine obstacle.

c) Ethnocide and genocide might be pursued simultaneously. This is perhaps the most common form of interaction for several reasons. First, little discrimination may be made in the means of removing the "obstacle" culture and both are seen as effective and complementary measures. In some cases, certain segments of a population might be spared from genocide if they are thought to be useful and are subject to ethnocidal policies. For example, far greater numbers of women and young girls found on the Ache reservations in Paraguay have been attributed to their use as sexual chattels for camp guards.[24] Second, ethnocidal policies commonly result in genocide—they are a means of achieving the physical destruction of a people. The destruction of the ecosystem on which a society depends often leads to starvation, as do failed attempts to force economic reorganization upon a people with insufficient resources. People removed to reservations face death from starvation, lack of sanitation or medical support, and violence; having survived total disruption of their lives and grief from physical separation from loved ones, they also commonly lose the will to live and see death as a welcome release.[25]

Ethnogenesis

In spite of the widespread enactment of ethnocide throughout the globe, a number of peoples facing cultural destruction have reasserted their distinct identities and successfully struggled against the policies which oppress them. This counter resurgence is a widespread phenomenon which has gained momentum from international voluntary and statutory agencies, such as the International Work Group on Indigenous Affairs and Cultural Survival; from the church in a number of cases such as the Jesuit church in Paraguay[26,27]; and from the establishment of pan-identities to fight a common struggle, such as the Pan-Andean Indians.[28] Significantly, younger people who have directly experienced assimilationist policies are rejecting the values and lifestyles of the dominant cultures, and are fighting for a future in the traditional culture of their people.[29,30]

Given the extent to which ethnogenesis occurs, it seems sensible to conclude that, while ethnocidal policies are relatively easy to pursue, it is less easy for them to succeed. The apparent optimism that this suggests has a considerable negative side; ethnocide is a less successful means than genocide to achieve the objective of removing a distinct cultural identity.

NOTES

1. Elias Seville-Casas, ed., *Western Expansion and Indigenous Peoples* (The Hague: Mouton, 1977), 33-36.

2. Robert Paine, *Dam a River, Damn a People?* (Copenhagen: International Work Group on Indigenous Affairs, 1982), 94.

3. Evelyne Hong, *Natives of Sarawak: Survival in Borneo's Vanishing Forests* (Malaysia: Institute Masyarakat, 1987).

4. Richard Chase Smith, *The Dialectics of Domination in Peru* (Cambridge, MA: Cultural Survival, Inc., 1982), 83.

5. Douglas E. Brintall, *Revolt Against the Dead* (New York and London: Gordon and Breach, 1979).

6. Norman Lewis, *The Missionaries* (London: Arrow Books, 1988), 59.

7. *Witness to Cultural Genocide. First-Hand Reports on Rumania's Minority Policies Today* (New York: American Transylvania Federation, Inc. and the Committee for Human Rights in Rumania, n.d.).

8. Sue Branford and Oriel Glock, *The Last Frontier; Fighting Over Land in the Amazon* (London: Zed Books, 1985).

9. Soren Hvalkof and Peter Aaby, eds., *Is God an American?* (Copenhagen: International Work Group on Indigenous Affairs and Survival International, 1981).

10. Norman E. Whitten, Jr., *Sacha Runa: Ethnicity and Adaptation of Ecuadorian Jungle Quicha* (Urbana, Chicago, and London: University of Illinois Press, 1978).

11. Raymond William Stedman, *Shadows of the Indian* (Norman: University of Oklahoma Press, 1982).

12. Vanja Kewley, *Tibet, Behind the Ice Curtain* (London: Grafton Books, 1990).

13. Carmel Budiardjo and Liem Soei Liong, *The War Against East Timor* (London: Zed Books, 1984). Also Carmel Budiardjo and Liem Soei Liong, *West Papua: The Obliteration of a People* (Thornton Heath, England: Tapol, n.d).

14. Sally Morgan, *My Place* (London: Verago, 1987).

15. Tibet Support Group, *UK Fact Sheet* (February 1989).

16. Tiziano Terzani, *Behind the Forbidden Door* (London and Sydney: Unwin, 1987), 25, 57.

17. David Albin and Marlowe Hood, *The Cambodian Agony*, (Armonk, New York, and London: M.E. Sharpe, 1987).

18. Nicholas Tapp, *The Hmong of Thailand* (London: Anti-Slavery Society, 1986).

19. Mark Munzel, *The Ache Indians: Genocide in Paraguay* (Copenhagen: International Work Group on Indigenous Affairs, 1973).

20. Julian Burger, *Report from the Frontier* (London and Cambridge, MA: Zed Books and Cultural Survival, 1987), 262-283.

21. Richard Arens, *The Forest Indians in Stroessner's Paraguay: Survival or Extinction* (London: Survival International, 1978).

22. Jan Roberts, *Massacres to Mining* (Victoria, Australia: Dove Communications, 1981).

23. Martin Gilbert, *The Macmillan Atlas of the Holocaust* (New York: Macmillan, 1982).

24. Munzel.

25. Richard Arens, ed., *Genocide in Paraguay* (Philadelphia: Temple University Press, 1976).

26. Munzel.

27. Branford and Glock.

28. Whitten.

29. Robert Davis and Mark Zannis, *The Genocide Machine in Canada* (Montreal: Black Rose Books, 1973).

30. Susana B.C. Devalle, *Multi-Ethnicity in India: The Adivasi Peasants of Chota Nagpur and Santal Parganas* (Copenhagen: International Work Group on Indigenous Affairs, 1980).

Chapter 1: Annotated Bibliography

Readers are advised to consult the many publications of international agencies such as the International Work Group on Indigenous Affairs, Survival International, Cultural Survival, the Minority Rights Group, and the Anti-Slavery Society. The following represent a small selection from a vast wealth of literature on cultural destruction.

* 1.1 *
Ablin, David, and Marlowe Hood, eds. *The Cambodian Agony*. Armonk, NY, and London: M.E. Sharpe, Inc., 1987. ISBN 0-87332-421-8.

The Ablin and Hood collection of papers emanating from the Conference on "Kampuchea in the 1980's," held at Princeton University in 1982, considers the legacy Cambodia inherited from almost a decade of war and violence. Of particular interest are the chapters by May Ebihara, which includes analysis of the destruction of key basic social institutions—'the family, village, and *wat*' (p.23)—by the Khmer Rouge, their replacement by rural communities, and the result this had upon individual status; and David R. Hawk, which considers the violations of international human rights in Democratic Kampuchea, 1975-1979, and the physical and cultural destruction waged against minority ethnic groups and religious practices, particularly Buddhism.

* 1.2 *
Ahmad, Eqbal. "The Public Relations of Ethnocide." *Journal of Palestine Studies* 12:3 (1983): 31-40.

Israel established the Kahan Commission of Inquiry to investigate the massacres of Shatila and Sabra camps for Palestinian refugees in West Beirut in 1982. Ahmad assesses the commission's recommendations. He emphasizes two elements: 1) the commission represents a historical pattern in which key figures are absolved of direct responsibility by a judicial system that is ideologically bound to its political counterpart; and 2) this pattern is enthusiastically endorsed by representatives of Western public opinion. Ahmad argues that "this pattern does not merely hold; rather, it is now extended to cover up a policy of ethnocide"; he outlines connections between mass violence and extermination, dispersal and expulsion, and ethnocide in Israeli policies as attempts to "solve" the "Palestinian problem" in the occupied territories.

* 1.3 *
"Ocean Mining and Cultural Genocide in Guam." *Journal of Contemporary Asia* 9:1 (1979) 107-116.

Institutionalized racism in United States-controlled Guam has led to the cultural oppression of the indigenous Chamorro people. The article specifically refers to the Pacific Daily News (PDN), Guam's single newspaper, and its links via corporate finance to United States proposals to exploit the mineral wealth in the oceans of Micronesia. Reference is also made to ethnocide and genocide in Guam since the onset of colonialism in 1521. The conclusion is optimistic: Chamorro nationalists successfully forced the PDN to reverse its English-only language policy in the 1970s.

* 1.4 *
Arens, Richard. *The Forest Indians in Stroessner's Paraguay: Survival or Extinction?* SI Document Series no. 4. London: Survival International, 1978.

A short supplement to Arens' 1976 publication, this document tells of the author's own visit to Indian reservations at the invitation of the Paraguayan state. The Minister of Defence is cited as stating official policy to be the integration of the Indians, understood by the author to mean instant "sedentarization," causing suffering and death. Four camps are visited, three of which compound the processes of deculturation outlined in *Genocide in Paraguay*, and which reveal the consequences of ethnocide—"abject depression" and "psychic death" (p.3). The fourth reserve, which did not pursue a policy of enforced sedentarization, was found to be devoid of these symptoms. A short section is included on a subsequent conference at the Ministry of Defence which shows the official response to be denunciation of allegation of genocide and slavery. The report concludes that ethnocide and genocide against the Indians is the "final solution" to those obstacles to the state's plan of deforestation.

* 1.5 *
Arens, Richard, ed. *Genocide in Paraguay*. Philadelphia: Temple University Press, 1976. LC 76-5726. ISBN 0-87722-088-3.

Arens has assembled and edited a disturbing and important collection of papers by leading experts on the genocidal and ethnocidal oppression of the Ache Indians by the Paraguayan state. Aches held captive on the government reservation were denied their traditional music and religion, adequate food, and medical services; their language was discouraged; and many were forced into slavery, particularly young girls who were used for sex.

Arens' introduction discusses the role of the international press and the American media; the federal government in particular is condemned for failing to publicize either the Ache's plight or American involvement. Paraguayan officials have persistently denied allegations of atrocities.

The paper by Norman Lewis draws attention to the destructive missionary endeavors which received state endorsement. Chaim F. Shatan discusses the destruction of the Ache from a psychological perspective and refers to his previous analysis of Vietnam veterans. He also suggests the "rehumanization" of the Ache. Monroe C. Beardsley includes ethnocide within the United Nations' definitions of genocide while also recognizing it a crime in itself, often as a prelude to genocide. The obverse of ethnocide—the right to participate in one's own culture—is considered as a basic human right.

* 1.6 *

Barabas, Alicia, and Miguel Bartolomé. *Hydraulic Development and Ethnocide: The Mazatec and Chinantec People of Oaxaca, Mexico*. IWGIA Document no. 15. Copenhagen: International Work Group on Indigenous Affairs, 1973.

The authors have written a coherent examination of the policies by the Mexican federal government and regional development agencies to incorporate two indigenous ethnic groups into "the nationalist capitalist system of production and consumption." They argue that this is achieved through "the elimination of their economic semi-independence and cultural identity." (p.2). The construction of hydraulic dams in 1949 and in the 1970s demanded the resettlement of Indians into zones of ethnic heterogeneity and changed economies.

Discrimination and intentional social disorganization ensued. Nationalist policy denied the Indian traditional heritage of cultural pluralism so that "the policy of the *indigenistas* as carried out by the National Indigenista Institute (was)... explicitly directed towards the destruction of indigenous cultures and the integration of ethnic minorities into the lowest and most exploited stratum of the national structure." (p.18) Brief mention is made of an emergent messianic movement which has united the Chinantec and strengthened their traditional cultural affinity in the face of oppression.

* 1.7 *

Berglund, Staffan. *The National Integration of Mapuche*. Stockholm: Almqvist and Wiksell International, 1977. ISBN 91-22-00130-1.

Berglund questions the implementation of national integrationist policies in Chile and the subsequent abuse of human rights between 1970 and 1973. His study is based on comparative field work among Mapuche Indians and rural laborers and smallholders, and larger collective agricultural units which have undergone relatively successful organizational and economic reform. It is not confined to cultural considerations and includes economic and socio-political spheres. Part I examines these spheres within contemporary Mapuche society and includes quantitative data. Chapters 9 and 10 trace the history of Chilean integrationist policies from 1813 and land reform legislation from the 1960s. Part II concentrates upon national integration, defined as "a process in which reallocation of resources and power in favor of the majority is the main issue." (p.39) Given this, the question of maintaining Mapuchean identity is inextricably linked to the question of land use and their relation with other land users. Berglund concludes that only class solidarity with other exploited, non-Mapuchean sectors can achieve their continued cultural existence and socio-political rights.

* 1.8 *

Bodley, John H., ed. *Tribal People and Development Issues*. Mountain View, CA: Mayfield Publishing Company, 1988. ISBN 0-87484-786-9.

Bodley includes in this edited collection case studies and policy documents and assessments from the mid-nineteenth century onwards. The purpose of the volume is to understand the assumptions policy decision makers have made towards tribal groups. The central question it addresses is why development policy affecting indigenous peoples has such scant regard for their basic human rights and survival. The collection is intended to extend the main themes outlined in Bodley's 1972 publication, *Victims of Progress*. Case studies are taken mainly from Amazona, the Arctic, Australia, Melanesia, South East Asia, and Africa. The 39 papers in the book are necessarily short and serve as appetizers for subsequent study, yet their selection and arrangement provide a comprehensive and varied portrayal of central elements in the global history of tribal destruction and exploitation. This is a useful introductory book, particularly for students of development and human rights issues.

* 1.9 *

Bodley, John H. *Victims of Progress*. 3d ed. Mountain View, CA: Mayfield Publishing Company, 1990. ISBN 0-87484-945-4.

In an important and useful publication, Bodley directly addresses the issues of ethnocide and genocide against indigenous peoples of the world under the ethnocentric dogma of industrialized civilization. The success of his book lies in his systematic coverage of all the major topics and angles of destruction, using a full range of historical and more contemporary cases to clearly illustrate each point. Chapter 10, which has been completely rewritten for this edition, argues that ethnocide is the result of a dominant realist philosophy among politicians and religious and scientific leaders over a 150-year period. Realist philosophy assumed the inevitable extinction of tribal groups, or their integration into "civilized" society. The approach recognizes that indigenous people could not survive rapidly encroaching industrialization—yet their demise and disappearance warns us that global technological, social, and political advance needs to be balanced with humane considerations if cultures, societies, and world ecosystems are to have a future. It is a crucial political question since ethnocide has been the outcome of political decisions devoid of human rights. The appendixes include a number of international declarations and human rights programs.

* 1.10 *
Branford Sue, and Oriel Glock. *The Last Frontier; Fighting over Land in the Amazon*. London: Zed Books Ltd., 1985. ISBN 0-86232-395-9; 0-86232-396-7 pa.

In a personalized account that is colored with numerous detailed examples, the authors investigate development problems in the Brazilian Amazon region. They deal mainly with the struggle by peasant farmers against powerful landowners, but also consider the purposes behind the state's transmigration policy, and its effect upon the indigenous landowners. Anti-Indian sentiment is found to be more overt among local landowners and politicians. Anger is focused upon Indian land occupation and is founded upon irrational hatred and ignorance of Indian culture. It is articulated in demands for the seizure of Indian lands and for their conformity to non-Indian work ethics.

An attempted state project of the 1970s to emancipate Indians with sufficient contact with national society was condemned by CIMI—the missionary council of the Catholic Church—as a deliberate policy of cultural extermination. It aimed to remove the protected status of Indian land ownership and was to be followed by the enforced division of land into family plots. The project was dropped in 1979 due to successful opposition. Space is also given to the activities of the strong Indian movement which operates at local and national levels.

* 1.11 *
Brintnall, Douglas E. *Revolt Against the Dead*. New York, London, and Paris: Gordon and Breach, 1979. LC 79-1528. ISBN 0-677-05170-0.

Brintnall examines the transformation of the Aguacatan Indians of Guatemala, based on field work done in the 1970s. The study reveals a complex picture of interrelations in which deliberate exogenous destruction of traditional religious hierarchies occurs within a wider matrix of modernization, largely determined by the Aguacatan themselves. While these religious hierarchies suffered demolition under the Christianization policies of missionaries, particularly the Summer Institute of Linguistics, their destruction also instigated changes within the Indian groups, such as the abolition of traditional political structures and intergroup antagonisms, which increased the possibility for the Indians to pursue their new, liberationist, economic directives. This was a case of cultural destruction and integration rather than assimilation.

* 1.12 *
Budiardjo, Carmel, and Liem Soei Liong. *The War Against East Timor*. London: Zed Books Ltd., 1984. ISBN 0-86232-228-6.

The authors analyze the war that has raged in East Timor since late 1975 against the expanding Indonesian state. The rationale for the study was the emergence of new information following a lull in the late 1970s, which challenged the assumption that the Timorese resistance had been successfully squashed. The authors purpose was to provide a "basis for renewed solidarity with the victims of Indonesian aggression." (p.xvii) It utilizes a range of documentary sources from the resistance movement, overseas aid organizations, the Indonesian press, and leaked 1982 instructions to Indonesian troops on "counter-insurgency operations." Many of these are presented in the second section of the book. Allegations of genocide and violence are made and Chapter 5 is specifically concerned with the program of Indonesianization pursued since 17 July 1976 after the adoption by the Indonesian Parliament of the Bill of Integration. The imposition of Indonesian political and social structures under military control rendered East Timorese second class citizens, constantly suspected of disloyalty to the Indonesian state. Similarly, the systematic, forced transition from traditional agriculture to plantations, and the transmigration of Balinese farmers to the region, had caused landlessness, forcible confinement in camps, famine, and increasing reliance upon relief agencies. Special attention has been paid to the massive construction of a standardized Indonesian educational system devoid of Timorese culture and history.

* 1.13 *
Budiardjo, Carmel, and Liem Soei Liong. *West Papua: The Obliteration of a People*. Thornton Heath, England: Tapol, n.d. ISBN 0-9506751-1-3.

A publication of Tapol, the British organization concerned with the dissemination of information and defense of human rights in Indonesia, this book focuses on the military occupation of Irian Jaya, on the transmigration policy to settle one million Javanese in tribal areas, and on the Papuan resistance of the OPM, the Free Papua Movement. A consequence of Javanese settlement has been the dispossession of Papuan homelands with the subsequent disruption of existing social structures and cultural destruction as displaced Papuans become urban fringe-dwellers, and are exposed to attempts to modernize them. The "*Koteka* operation" in the early 1970s against the Dani is singled out as the "most systematic of these attempts." A major factor in the violence of administering transmigration and modernizing programs is that it lies in the hands of the military. Papuans are portrayed as both primitive and a potential threat to Indonesian territorial defense against Papua New Guinea, warranting military intervention. Indonesian education omits all reference to Papuans and their culture. A further consequence of transmigration has been the upheaval of the ecological balance necessary for Papuan shifting horticulture, resulting in famine.

* 1.14 *
Burger, Julian. *Report from the Frontier*. London and Cambridge, MA: Zed Books, Ltd. and Cultural Survival Inc., 1987. ISBN 0-86232-391-6 (Zed).

In this readily accessible book, Burger explores the present-day situation of indigenous people under threat from development projects, and their struggles for physical and cultural survival. The rapid rate of development is based upon two myths—that the land is wild and empty, and that it promises under-used resources that will solve state economic and political problems. The author includes a large number of cases spread throughout the world. Ethnocide is identified as the "one overwhelming and universal menace to indigenous peoples," while "assimilation into industrial society has brought few benefits and many hardships" as they become "part of the growing mass of landless and underemployed poor." (p.31) One chapter is dedicated to a discussion of governmental and international action and concludes that since governments are usually involved in the violation of human rights, "they pay little heed to the international instruments to which they are signatories. There is no guarantee, therefore, that the declaration of principles or any subsequent convention concerning the rights of indigenous peoples will have any meaningful impact..." (p.269).

* 1.15 *
The Chittagong Hill Tracts. Indigenous Peoples and Development Series, no. 2. London: The Anti-Slavery Society, 1984. ISBN 0-900918-19-5.

In the Chittagong Hill Tracts in eastern Bangladesh, a war is being waged between the Shanti Bahini Peace Force of the indigenous hill people and Bangladeshi troops sent to the area by Dhaka to enforce state development plans. These plans to economically reorganize the Tracts into permanent, settled, and individually owned farms, and to construct the Kaptai Dam using large sums of foreign aid have attracted tens of thousands of Bengalis into the area. The consequence has been the destruction of tribal traditional shifting cultivation, dispossession of tribal lands and villages, economic exploitation, starvation, debt, violence, and the upheaval of traditional socio-political community organization. The tribal view of the onslaught is "at best, 'exploitation' but more commonly...ethnocide verging on genocide" (p.7), as recurrent massacres, arrests, and tortures coincide with Muslim troop violence aimed specifically at the tribal Buddhist religion.

* 1.16 *
Colchester, Marcus, ed. *An End to Laughter*. London: Survival International, 1985. ISSN 0308-2857.

The 1985 annual report from Survival International presents articles concerning the destruction wrought upon tribal peoples by projects for economic development under the ambit of nation-state building in India, Namibia, Nicaragua, and Latin America. The value of this collection lies in its demonstration that the form of destruction is specific to each case and is determined by a greater number of factors than are immediately apparent. The removal of people from their traditional lands appears as a common cause of cultural destruction—a threat faced by over two million people in central India due to the construction of hydroelectric dams in Maharashtra and Madhya Pradesh. Also included is a brief report on the ethnocidal policies of the Pinochet regime in Chile as experienced by the Mapuche Indians, and a collection of correspondence between Survival International and the World Bank which successfully halted a project that threatened the cultural survival of 6,700 Indians in West Central Amazona in Brazil.

* 1.17 *
Colletta, Nat J. "Folk Culture and Development: Cultural Genocide or Cultural Revitalization?" *Convergence* 10:2 (1977): 12-19.

Colletta challenges the orthodox perspective on development which views traditional cultures as antipathetic to economic advancement. A wide variety of examples are used to demonstrate that, contrary to conventional approaches, indigenous cultural forms can be adapted to achieve change. Development and modern state formation, it is argued, do not necessitate the destruction of existing cultures.

* 1.18 *
Conquest, Robert. *The Great Terror, A Reassessment*. London, Sydney, Auckland, and Johannesburg: Hutchinson, 1990. ISBN 0-09-174293-5.

In Chapter 10 of this work, a new edition of his 1968 publication, Conquest concentrates specifically upon the purge of cultural and scientific representatives and institutions of previous or "counter" ideologies. The intelligentsia, universities, and publishers were all targeted and widespread arrests, interrogations, and torture ensued. Conquest refers to this era as "a holocaust of the things of the spirit." (p.307) He also examines the horror of labor camps as ideological re-education centers for ideologically unsound peasants and intellectuals. The author's 1968 book was widely acknowledged to be the only authoritative historical work on the the Ukraine during the Stalinist era of the 1930s. See also 6.2.

* 1.19 *
Conquest, Robert. *The Harvest of Sorrow: Soviet Collectivization and the Terror-Famine*. London, Melbourne, Auckland, and Johannesburg: Hutchinson, 1986. ISBN 0-09-163750-3. Another edition: New York and Oxford: Oxford University Press, 1986. LC 86-2437. ISBN 0-19-504054-6.

Conquest analyzes Stalinist policies in the Ukraine between 1929 and 1933. He identifies two distinct processes—dekulakization and collectivization policies from 1929-1932; and imposed famine and ethnocide during 1932-1933, which attacked Ukrainian culture, intelligentsia, and religion. Ukrainian nationalism was singled out as the problem demanding resolution. Conquest makes use of a wide range of evidence to substantiate claims, including testimonies from survivors. This is a scholarly work from a highly respected authority. See also 6.3.

* 1.20 *
Dargyay, Eva K. *Tibetan Village Communities: Structure and Change*. Warminster, England: Aris and Phillips Ltd., 1982. ISBN 0-85668-151-2.

Dargyay's socio-anthropological study of small rural communities in Gyantse district is based upon interviews with Tibetan refugees in India and Switzerland in the 1970s. The Chinese occupation has brought about "the destruction of the traditional Tibetan culture," "alienation," and "flight." (p.4) Dargyay's reconstruction of traditional village life serves as a measure for change in the post-invasion period, which is examined in the final chapter.

* 1.21 *
Davis, Robert, and Mark Zannis. *The Genocide Machine in Canada*. Montreal: Black Rose Books, 1973. LC 75-306912. ISBN 0-919618-04-9.

Two journalists point the finger at those involved in perpetrating the cultural destruction of Indian and Inuit peoples in Arctic Canada under the general claim of development. Theirs is a lively book which locates the impact of Canadian and foreign state and private enterprises upon the native peoples, within a wider discussion of the United Nations Convention on Genocide. The limitation of the latter is identified and suggestions made for a more applicable, preventative approach to the issue. Ethnocidal policies aimed specifically at children forcibly transplant them to an alien educational system which denies their own culture. Recent ethnogenesis among the youth is noted.

* 1.22 *
Davis, Shelton H. *Victims of the Miracle*. Cambridge, London, New York, and Melbourne: Cambridge University Press, 1977. LC 77-5132. ISBN 0-521-21738-5.

In one of the first studies to do so, Davis draws attention to the fate of the Amazonian Indians under Brazilian economic development. He provides students of development and human rights with a thorough grounding in Brazilian Indian policy. The imposition of national and multi-national economic programs has disregarded these aspects of Brazilian law, and has had far-reaching consequences for indigenous and non-indigenous peoples everywhere. Davis' book is an extension to the arguments of Darcy Ribeiro on the central role of economic and political policy in the increasing physical and cultural extinction on Amazonian tribes, published in 1957, 1962, and 1970.

* 1.23 *
Devalle, Susana B.C. *Multi-Ethnicity in India: The Adivasi Peasants of Chota Nagpur and Santal Parganas*. IWGIA Document no. 41. Copenhagen: International Work Group on Indigenous Affairs, 1980.

In a clearly presented argument, Devalle examines the contemporary economic and cultural oppression of the Adivasis population of India, particularly those in Bihar state. As the original inhabitants, the tribal identity of the Adivasis presents a problem to the creation of an integrated Indian identity by means of Sanskritization and Westernization policies. Two cultural and one economic solutions are identified: 1) the gradual replacement of traditional culture, particularly language and religion, through education—that is, detribalization; 2) a Rousseauian "noble savage" idealism purporting to isolate and preserve tribal groupings assumed to be stagnant; and 3), specific tribal development programs to integrate "inherently backwards" Adivasis into a larger, capitalist oriented, economic plan. All three seek to eliminate Adivasis culture and identity by denying Adivasis reality and any political or economic autonomy. Consequently, the centuries-long struggle of the Adivasis against their exploitation has recently been strengthened as they articulate for their own autonomous state and seek pantribal unity in agrarian resistance to imposed capitalist development, and to defend their own cultures and identities.

* 1.24 *
Dorstal, W., ed. *The Situation of the Indian in South America*. Geneva: World Council of Churches, 1972.

The Symposium on Inter-Ethnic Conflict in South America acted as a critical consultation to the World Council of Churches. All contributors to this volume are anthropologists or ethnographers with direct experience working with South American Indians. They address not only the role of church missions in the region but also political, industrial, and educational spheres. Their papers are confined to Indian groups which are less well documented.

A general introduction looks at the history of colonization in South America and argues that current cultural pluralism is a structural consequence of this history. Within this, Indian populations are subjected to economic exploitation under internal colonialism which is denied by the state's dominant sectors. Policies of Indian acculturation towards national integration center around "native problems (such as 'laziness', or being 'depraved' or 'inferior', which)…are (assumed to be)…essentially rooted in cultural differences, in the backwardness or inadequacy of the cultural norms of the natives in comparison with the dominant culture of the nation as a whole." (pp.25-26) This false perception of Indian reality perpetuates the disruption of meaningful integration. The collection ends with an interesting assortment of information, demographic data, critical bibliographies and the Declaration of Barbados for the Liberation of Indians resulting from the symposium.

This is a highly useful book which condenses many of the main threats specific to each South American state within a single volume. It is a collection of papers first presented at the Symposium on Interethnic Conflict in South America in January 1971 in Barbados at the behest of the World Council of Churches program to Combat Racism.

* 1.25 *
Elder, James F. *On the Road to Tribal Extinction: Depopulation, Deculturation, and Maladaptation among the Bartak of the Phillipines*. Berkeley, Los Angeles, and London: University of California Press, 1987. LC 87-1861. ISBN 0-520-06046-6.

Elder's careful study of the demise of Batak identity is based upon extensive fieldwork between 1966 and 1981 on Palawan Island in the Philippine archipelago. The author's knowledge of the entire population and his detailed collection of data, which includes two extensive censuses set eight years apart, are invaluable to his focus upon internal changes in culture and social organization due to contact with migrating lowland Filipino farmers. A useful introduction discusses theoretical models for analyzing change in indigenous cultures and ethnocide, and challenges the widely used "victims of progress" model which is overly simplistic and resorts to stereotypes. The final chapter compares the case study with a number of tribal societies that successfully adapted to modernization forces. It leads to the conclusion that the Bataks' failed adaptation is due to the loss of their specific ethnic identity through the erosion of their culture and their language. The study focuses upon internal change rather than state policy.

* 1.26 *
Edwards, Coral, and Peter Read, eds. *The Lost Children*. Sydney, Auckland, New York, Toronto, and London: Doubleday, 1989. ISBN 0-86824-384-1.

This unusual and important book has developed from the work of Link-Up (NSW), an organization formed to confront problems arising from a particularly insidious form of ethnocide, or indeed genocide. From the early twentieth century until the 1960s, Australian state policies systematically abducted Aboriginal children assumed to have mixed-race heritage and placed them in missionary and educational institutions, with foster families or as cheap or unpaid labor for whites. The objective was to force their adoption of white culture, thereby significantly eradicating Aboriginal culture. It was assumed that full-blooded Aborigines would naturally and quickly die out. It was hoped that this combination would solve the "Aborigine problem." The book contains testimonies from thirteen people born after 1950 who fought for reunification with their families and to reclaim their Aboriginal identity. They represent only a fragment of the picture, since the editors estimate that in contemporary Australia "there may be one hundred thousand people of Aboriginal descent who do not know their families or communities….some do not even know they are of Aboriginal descent." (p.ix)

* 1.27 *
Ervin, Alexander M. "A Review of the Acculturation Approach in Anthropology with Special Reference to Recent Change in Native Alaska." *Journal of Anthropological Research* 36 (1980): 49-70.

In this interesting paper, Ervin concentrates upon the methods adopted by a threatened population to preserve its own identity. A process of transculturation has occurred among Alaskan Native leaders who made use of new access to positions of power and influence made possible by processes of assimilation and acculturation into the dominant American society, but did so in order to successfully maintain and strengthen their traditional ethnic and socio-cultural identity. The case study is contextualized within a theoretical discussion of acculturation approaches to ethnology.

* 1.28 *
Fisher, Robin, and Kenneth Coates, eds. *Out of the Backyard; Readings on Canadian Native History*. Ontario: Copp Clark Pitman Ltd., 1988. ISBN 0-7730-4-767-0.

Fisher and Coates have assembled a stimulating collection of articles on the history of contact of Europeans with Indian and Inuit peoples. The range of arguments and the diversity of both historical periods and peoples considered make this an important work. While one paper specifically looks at the physical destruction of the island Beothuck people, a number of others consider the cultural ramifications of contact. What emerges is a multidimensional picture of destruction and cultural adaptation in which native power is seen to be a persistent and compelling force in the determination of contact history. The value of this collection is its revelation of the complexity of contact which challenges a unilinear process of the wholesale destruction of native cultures. It implies that ethnocide can be a subtle process.

* 1.29 *
Gailey, Christine Ward. "Categories without Culture: Structuralism, Ethnohistory and Ethnocide." *Dialectical Anthropology* 8:3 (1983): 241-250.

Gailey's paper is an academic warning of the shortcomings of a structuralist approach to understanding the perpetuation of ethnic cultures over time. She argues that a structuralist perspective can result in a form of academic blindness which excludes other possible interpretations of cultural change wrought by contact with early European colonialism, such as ethnocide.

* 1.30 *
Gilbert, Martin. *The Macmillan Atlas of the Holocaust*. New York: Macmillan, 1984. ISBN 0-306-80218.

Gilbert's useful and interesting book provides detailed information on the Nazi deportations of European Jews throughout the occupied territories. It brings to the fore the chaos of Nazi policy. Much of the book is given to maps of the journeys and is accompanied by a useful and upsetting text.

* 1.31 *
Goodman, Michael Harris. *The Last Dalai Lama*. London: Sidgwick and Jackson, 1986. ISBN 0-283-99367-7.

Goodman's work is a biography of His Holiness the Fourteenth Dalai Lama. Although much of the book covers the pre-1950 period, a substantial section is dedicated to the sustained efforts to preserve Tibetan identity and culture despite the force of Chinese oppression. The difficulties of success are vividly explained and the changing forms of Chinese destruction are explored in detail. The contradictions between Tibetan rights under the Chinese constitution and their brutal fate under Chinese rule, are highlighted in Chapter 16, where barbarous examples are cited to demonstrate how Articles 11, 88, 89, and 96 have been broken. It is a highly readable account, chronologically ordered with much detail.

* 1.32 *
Hauptman, Laurence M. *The Iroquois Struggle for Survival*. Syracuse: Syracuse University Press, 1986. ISBN 0-8156-2349-6.

Hauptman's book is a rare study of Iroquois nationalism from World War II to 1973 and the takeover at Wounded Knee. From the 1940s, retrogressive policy in the Bureau of Indian Affairs severely threatened the continuation of Iroquois culture in favor of programs for their total assimilation into white culture. A large part of the book reconstructs the continuing struggles between Iroquois representatives and United States policies.

* 1.33 *
Hernandez, Deborah Pacini. *Resource Development and Indigenous People*. Occasional Paper no. 15. Cambridge, MA: Cultural Survival, Inc., 1986. LC 85-143558.

Hernandez evaluates the impact of the El Cerejon coal strip mining project in northern Colombia upon the indigenous Guajoros which "may indeed result in their extinction as a culture." (p.3) The report assesses the early phase of development, its planning, and Guajiro response. A number of recommendations are made to mitigate some of the detrimental effects of the project, including redistributing portions of land royalties to Guajiro communities, initiating ecological improvement schemes, and the development of health and educational centers which would include cultural programs to reassert Guajiro culture.

* 1.34 *
Hong, Evelyne. *Natives of Sarawak: Survival in Borneo's Vanishing Forests*. Malaysia: Institut Masyarakat, 1987. ISBN 967-9966-03-8.

Hong analyzes the impact of land development, logging schemes, and the construction of hydroelectric dams upon the indigenous people of Sarawak and upon their subsequent resistance. The erosion of indigenous land rights, changes in forest laws and logging have destroyed traditional farming and ancestral sites.

Economic and ecological damage and malnutrition threaten the survival of the people. Cultural alienation and urbanization have occurred, specifically among the young, through the introduction of Western education, values and lifestyles. There is fear that traditional society will "fail to reproduce itself." (p.211) The book calls for state protection of the cultural identity of these people.

* 1.35 *
Hvalkof, Soren, and Peter Aaby, eds. *Is God an American? An Anthropological Perspective of the Missionary Work of the Summer Institute of Linguistics*. IWGIA Document no. 43. Copenhagen and London: International Work Group on Indigenous Affairs and Survival International, 1981. ISBN 87-980717-2-6.

The Hvalkof and Aaby collection of anthropological papers critically examines the role of the American Summer Institute of Linguistics (SIL)—the largest organization of Protestant missionaries—among tribal groups throughout the world and particularly in Latin America. The first chapter introduces the reader to the development of SIL and stresses the equivocal position of missionaries working as mediators between Indians and expanding state development and military projects. The main thrust of SIL is to save indigenous and peasant people from Satan by translating the Bible into their respective languages, a policy recognized by the contributors as a form of cultural imperialism causing ethnocide. The remaining chapters amplify these themes with specific reference to local communities.

* 1.36 *
Independent Commission on International Humanitarian Issues. *Indigenous Peoples*. London: Zed Books Ltd., 1987. ISBN 0-86232-759-8.

This work is a concise introduction to the main issues which threaten the survival of indigenous peoples today. The last section on international and national action considers the roles of governments, large finance corporations and industries, the United Nations, and other agencies.

* 1.37 *
Kewley, Vanja. *Tibet: Behind the Ice Curtain*. London: Grafton Books, 1990. ISBN 0-246-13594-8.

Kewley's book is a compelling eye witness account of a Western journalist's clandestine investigation of Chinese genocide and ethnocide in Tibet. Personal impressions are supported by historical data to produce a well-rounded and informed perspective on the continuing Chinese policies of oppression. The crux of the book is the extensive interviews held with Tibetans who directly suffered under Chinese brutality, which Kewley compares to Nazi policies of the Holocaust. Ethnocidal policies, which continue to date, have been pursued coterminously with policies of genocide. The persistent policy of demographic relocation of Chinese into Tibet is another grave threat to the culture's survival. The dearth of data from the region, which is under extreme Chinese control, adds to the significance of the book.

* 1.38 *
Kliot, N. "Accommodation and Adjustment to Ethnic Demands: The Mediterranean Framework." *The Journal of Ethnic Studies* 17:2 (1989): 45-70.

The author discusses trends of cultural and political oppression of ethnic groups within Mediterranean states in a general paper that covers vast ground. Consequently it precludes the sophisticated analysis that would result from more detailed examination of cases.

* 1.39 *
Legters, Lyman H. "'The American Genocide.' Pathologies of Indian-White Relations." *Policy Studies Journal* 16:4 (1988): 768-777.

In his short, provocative discussion of the concept of genocide, Legters seeks to extend its definition to include debilitating forms of mass destruction other than "the deliberate extermination of human life" alone. (p.770) He suggests that ethnocide—cultural genocide—be included under the term, referring to the histories of the Native American peoples.

* 1.40 *
Lewis, Norman. *The Missionaries*. London: Arrow Books Ltd., 1989. ISBN 0-09-959960-0.

Lewis' book consists of personal reminiscences of his encounters with missionary work among indigenous peoples, mainly in Latin America. He reveals the savage and relentless destruction caused by the North American fundamentalists.

* 1.41 *
Lizot, Jaques. *The Yanomami in the Face of Ethnocide*. IWGIA Document no. 22. Copenhagen: International Work Group on Indigenous Affairs, 1976.

The author lived among the Yanomami of the Upper Orinoco in Venezuela during the period of 1968-1975. In this work, he takes a short and direct look at the detrimental effects of missionary work on these people. Lizot argues that the missionaries are almost totally ignorant both of the complexity of the Yanomami traditional lifestyle and of the disastrous effects of their intervention. The economy, the social organization, enforced schooling at an isolated missionary institution, and health are singled out as areas where this is most evident. He attributes a decreasing population to malnutrition and disease, both inculcated by whites. Lizot proposes that integration of the Yanomami into the national life is possible if the richness of their traditions is respected and included under the ambit of cultural pluralism.

* 1.42 *

Markus, Andrew. *Governing Savages*. Sydney, Wellington, London, and Boston: Allen and Unwin, 1990.

Governing Savages is a highly readable account of official policies towards Australian Aborigines in the Northern Territory in the first half of this century. Three chapters introduce the main perspectives with which white settlers viewed Aborigines, while Chapters 4-11 each concentrate on a wide range of different institutions. Perhaps the most illuminating aspect of the book is the complexity of attitudes held by both individuals and institutions towards Aborigines, echoed in respective policies aimed at "solving" "the problems" that Aborigines represented to white invaders. Of these problems, the question of where people of mixed race were to fit into society was the most vexed. Ethnocidal policies were here resolutely pursued by a number of missionaries, more tentatively by various government representatives.

* 1.43 *

Mattingley, Christobel, ed. *Survival in Our Own Land*. Adelaide: Wakefield Press, 1988. ISBN 0-85904-048-8.

Aborigines from the Nunga, Pitjantjatjara, and Arynyamathanha communities speak of their history and experiences under white rule from 1836. Much of the volume is given to the question of cultural identity, as traditional customs were prohibited through European religious and educational institutions, and labor exploitation. The ways in which different people resisted and successfully reasserted their own identity are celebrated. This is an unusual and interesting book which tells Australian history from the perspective of some of its original inhabitants.

* 1.44 *

McLoughlin, William G. *Cherokees and Missionaries, 1789-1839*. New Haven, and London: Yale University Press, 1984. LC 83-11759. ISBN 0-300-03075-4.

McLoughlin examines the complexity of relations between the Cherokee nation, missionaries, and the United States state and federal governments during the period of the first United States Indian policy. The policy intended to acculturate all 125,000 Indians east of the Mississippi within fifty years with the aim of their becoming "full and equal citizens" of America. Missionaries were integral to this policy, yet they became increasingly estranged from support for state policies over the issue of forced removals. From 1828 they developed gradual respect for Cherokee qualities. McLoughlin takes issue with previous attempts to explain Native American cultural destruction by recourse to a single economic cause; he also argues that, despite attempts, the Cherokee culture was not destroyed but transformed.

* 1.45 *

McNeely, Jeffrey A., and David Pitt, eds. *Culture and Conservation*. London, Sydney, and Dover: Croom Helm, 1985. ISBN 0-7099-1321-4.

The editors have assembled a collection of papers on a topic often overlooked in development projects. Their book covers a diversity of projects situated throughout the world and deals with questions of vital importance such as the contribution indigenous peoples can make to development and conservation in terms of knowledge, practice, and participation in decision making and planning. Although this volume does not address the question of ethnocide, its importance lies in its clear demonstration that there is a viable alternative to those who argue that ethnocide is an unavoidable consequence of development.

* 1.46 *

Milner, Clyde A. *With Good Intentions: Quaker Work among the Pawnees, Otos, and Omahas in the 1870s*. Lincoln, and London: University of Nebraska Press, 1982. LC 81-16238. ISBN 0-8032-3066-4.

Milner offers a comparative study of the interactions between state assimilation policies administered by the Hicksite Quaker group, and the Pawnee, Oto, and Omaha Native American societies during the 1870s. Its usefulness lies in its comparative approach, which highlights the complexity of relations between and within these groups, and between different Indian societies of the Great Plains. Milner explores how these interactions affected Quaker endeavors which, despite "good intentions," failed in their civilizing mission, largely because of the inadequacy of their powers of enforcement. Unfortunately, the failure did not leave Indian cultures intact but formed the thin-edge-of-the-wedge, preparing the ground for increasing government programs which undermined their traditional economic, social, and cultural lifestyles.

* 1.47 *

Moody, Roger, ed. *The Indigenous Voice*. Vols. 1 and 2. London and Copenhagen: Zed Books Ltd. and International Work Group on Indigenous Affairs, 1988. ISBN 0-86232-305-3 (Zed); 0-86232-518-8 (Zed pa.).

Moody has compiled a two-volume anthology of extracts from indigenous people, speaking of their own plight and fight against genocide and ethnocide resulting from development and colonialism. The material is arranged thematically, and each chapter gives voice to a wide range of struggles throughout the world. This allows the reader to draw out similarities in protest and in processes of destruction. Volume 1 concentrates upon forms of oppression while Volume 2 focuses upon ethnic cultural and political revivals. Although no conclusions are drawn to tie the material together, these volumes provide students of human rights and development with an invaluable and extensive range of primary data. It is a challenging, unique collection which speaks straight from the heart.

* 1.48 *
Morgan, Sally. *My Place*. London: Virago, 1987. ISBN 0-85210-199-7.

In her autobiographical account of her realization of Aborigine identity, Morgan personalizes the consequences of Australian state policies of child abduction and forced assimilation. *My Place* is a valuable contribution.

* 1.49 *
Munzel, Mark. *The Ache Indians: Genocide in Paraguay*. IWGIA Document no. 11. Copenhagen: International Work Group on Indigenous Affairs, 1973.

Munzel's detailed report outlines the plight of the Ache Indians of Paraguay. Their situation in the early 1970s, as witnessed by the author, is set in a historical context of war against the Ache since colonization. The authorities condone manhunts and massacres. The forced removal of Ache to reserves has been the solution to the problem of violence from the early 1960s. Ache held captive on the reserves are subject to white administrative abuse, such as sexual exploitation, theft of food relief, violence, and the continued sale of young children to Paraguayans as a source of cheap labor. Disease and death are commonplace and there are no sanitary facilities or preventative medical supplies. Ache culture is demonstrably suppressed, resulting in demoralization, loss of identity, and a perception of self as neither Ache nor human, but as "half-dead." Munzel makes clear that this is not a policy of modernization but the work of specific individuals who receive indirect state support. His report names names while he notes the sympathetic role of the Jesuits.

* 1.50 *
Neterowicz, Eva M. *The Tragedy of Tibet*. Washington, DC: The Council for Social and Economic Studies, 1989. ISBN 0-930690-22-2.

In a slim volume, the author introduces the reader to the current abuses in Tibet by Chinese imperialists. Since their invasion in 1950, the Chinese "have conducted a systematic persecution against the Tibetan people and their culture and religion" (p.7) in order to prevent uprisings of Tibetan nationalism. The author's briefly traced history of invasion and oppression culminates in an outline of the situation since 1987. The three main methods used to destroy Tibetan identity are the division of Tibet into separately administered and renamed provinces; "brutal suppression" by the military of expressions of Tibetan culture; and the transmigration of huge numbers of Chinese into Tibet. International, particularly United States, concern is noted.

* 1.51 *
Newson, Linda A. *Indian Survival in Colonial Nicaragua*. Norman, OK, and London: University of Oklahoma Press, 1987. LC 86-40078. ISBN 0-8061-2008-8.

Indian Survival is a detailed study of cultural survival, deculturation and cultural integration, and transformation among Nicaraguan indigenes under Spanish colonization. Two Indian cultural types are identified—chiefdoms and tribes—which were separated geographically. The main forces of civilization and Christianization were missionaries, although Spanish administration exerted some influence on the "Western fringe" of colonization. A substantial part of the book is given to processes of deculturation, particularly Chapter 3 and Section 4, covering the period 1522-1720. Population decline due to famine, disease, and infanticide had negative repercussions upon the structure of Indian society, as did the Spanish destruction of existing forms of political organization and the exploitative grant system and the missions. Comparison is made to other South American states.

* 1.52 *
Ohland, Klaudine, and Robin Schneider, eds. *National Revolution and Indigenous Identity*. IWGIA Document no. 47. Copenhagen: International Work Group on Indigenous Affairs, 1983.

Ohland and Schneider have edited a collection of papers on the conflict between the Nicaraguan Sandinistas and the Miskitos, an indigenous people of the Atlantic Coast who demonstrated their resistance to policies of national integration by supporting the anti-Sandinista insurgency mounted from Honduras in 1982. The high fatalities inflicted on both sides prompted large scale flight into Honduras and resulted in forcible resettlement of the remaining seven to eight thousand. As a result of this drastic change in socio-economic organization, the Miskito traditional way of life has been severely threatened. The collection seeks to illustrate the complexity of relations between the Miskitos and Sandinistas which led to this situation.

* 1.53 *
Olson, James S., and Raymond Wilson. *Native Americans in the Twentieth Century*. Provo, UT: Brigham Young University Press, 1984. LC 83-21009. ISBN 0-8425-2141-0.

Olson and Wilson analyze Native American culture and government policies since the 1880s with particular emphasis on the twentieth century. Native Americans are referred to as survivors of "centuries of cultural genocide inflicted upon them by non-Native Americans." (p.x) A distinction is made between European "Indian haters" who "denied even the humanity of Native Americans," and who pursued vigorous near-genocidal policies, and "liberal assimilationists" bent on destroying their culture. It is the policies and legislation that arose out of the latter which forms the focus of the book. The land issue is identified as one root cause of assimilationist policies.

* 1.54 *
Ortiz, Roxanne Dunbar. *Indians of the Americas*. London: Zed Books, n.d. ISBN 0-86232-201-4.

The theme of this book is the question of nation-state building, self-discrimination, and human rights in relation to the Indians of the American continent. It is divided into four parts, dealing with Indian movements and supportive international agencies from the 1970s; theoretical analysis of Indians and the "national question," referring to state policies, Indian and pan-Indian nationalists, particularly Guatemala; an examination of the Navajo and Sioux Indian movements; and a case study of the Miskutu in Nicaragua. Ortiz' scholarly book addresses theoretical and methodological issues in the study of a complex subject.

* 1.55 *
Paine, Robert. *Dam a River, Damn a People?* IWGIA Document no. 45. Copenhagen: International Work Group on Indigenous People, 1982.

In a a well organized pamphlet, Paine deals with a difficult issue—the effect that the construction of a hydroelectric dam in Kautokeino county in the Norwegian tundra will have for the settlers and pastoral Saami culture. Since its inception in the 1970s, the project has consistently failed to acknowledge the full consequences of the dam for the Saami. Paine argues that the oversimplistic official approach is based upon the unavailability of information and upon the neglect of that data which were readily accessible. Part II seeks to counter the official 1980 Court of Appraisal denial of detrimental consequences. The author concludes that the project will incur the loss of Saami identity, as they become "more Norwegian" and so, "less Saami." (p.94) The work is relevant to the study of ethnocide since it raises the question of intent. Despite declared State intentions to protect Saami culture, denial and ignorance have produced the converse effect.

* 1.56 *
Permanent Peoples' Tribunal Session of the Philippines. *Philippines, Repression and Resistance*. Pilipino: KSP, 1981.

This is an unusual collection of testimonies extracted from the cases brought before the Permanent Peoples' Tribunal, 30 October-3 November 1980, against the Marcos and the United States governments of "economic, political, military and cultural repression" of the Filippino and Bangsa Moro people. (p.6) The verdict of the Tribunal includes condemnation "in the most rigorous terms (of)...the program of displacement and physical extinction that is now being waged by the Marcos regime against the Bangsa Moro people..." (p.227) The greater part of the book provides testimonies for the Filipino case: of particular note are those on cultural repression which look at the threat to the cultural survival of minority groups from state development projects such as damming and logging. A shorter section is dedicated to the Bangsa Moro case.

* 1.57 *
Price, David. *Before the Bulldozer*. Cabin John, MD: Seven Locks Press, 1989. LC 88-675683. ISBN 0-932020-67-4.

In 1980, Price was invited by the World Bank to work as a consultant to an imminent project to construct a gravel road through Nambiquara lands in Brazil. This is the story of his involvement with the Nambiquara, from graduate anthropologist, through FUNAI (the National Indian Foundation), to World Bank representative on behalf of the Nambiquara. He chronicles the various inroads of imposing cultures upon the Nambiquara, and includes the ignorance and racism of the local peasantry, the sometimes well-intended projects of FUNAI to "pacify" the "wild" Indians (pp.11-12), and the World Bank projects. Price stresses the powerlessness of the Nambiquara.

* 1.58 *
Ramos, Alicida R., and Kenneth Taylor. *The Yanomami in Brazil*. IWGIA Document no. 37. Copenhagen: International Work Group on Indigenous Affairs, 1979.

Ramos and Taylor highlight the threatened cultural and physical destruction of the Yanomami Indians in the 1970s. Their book is divided into three sections which critically examine development projects of highway construction, mining and agriculture, and consider the proposal for a Yanomami Indian Park. The park is urged as an humanitarian step suitable for ecological preservation, for sustained protection of the

Yanomani, and as preparation for "successful contact with the national society." (p.136)

* 1.59 *
Read, Peter. *A Hundred Years War*. Canberra: Australian National University, 1988. ISBN 0-08-034405-4.

In a highly accessible account, Read examines the contact between the Wiradjuri Aborigines of New South Wales and European missionaries and government officials from 1883. Read makes excellent use of conventional historical material and a large amount of information gained from Wiradjuri Koori to understand how the policies of the Aboriginal Protection Board affected a small Aboriginal population of about one dozen major family groups. The thrust of the policies was to destroy Aboriginal culture and to "change the blacks into whites." (p.xvi) The text, divided into four temporal "cycles," demonstrates that the consequences of the policies were at times unintended, yet Read draws attention to the problematic question of official intent, its common concealment, and the differences between written and applied policies. Read charts the gradual awakening of Aboriginal identity, dating it to have taken root in the 1930s.

* 1.60 *
Retboll, Torben, ed. *East Timor, Indonesia and the Western Democracies*. IWGIA Document no. 40. Copenhagen: International Work Group on Indigenous Affairs, 1980.

Retboll's collection of transcribed documents demonstrates "Indonesian atrocities in East Timor," "the responsibility of the Western democracies," and "the cover-up in the Western mass media." (preface) They are introduced by a letter from Professor Noam Chomsky to the United Nations General Assembly in 1978.

* 1.61 *
Reynolds, Henry. *Dispossession*. Sydney, Wellington, London, and Boston: Allen and Unwin, 1989. ISBN 0-04-370182-5.

This revised edition of *Aborigines and Settlers*, published in 1972, presents a collection of documentary excerpts from nineteenth and early twentieth century European sources to explore the complexities of Aboriginal-white relations during the period of colonization. The material is well organized: each chapter addresses a different aspect of contact which is clearly introduced and explores the variety of issues involved. The book is edited by a leading authority and is an invaluable compilation of primary data which are useful to specialists and to the general reader.

* 1.62 *
Roberts, Jan. *Massacres to Mining*. Victoria, Australia: Dove Communications, 1981. ISBN 0-85924-171-8.

Massacres to Mining is an impassioned but brief study of white assimilation policies and violence against Aborigines of Australia from 1788 to the present. It serves as a good introduction to understanding colonialism in Australia and clearly demonstrates that attempts to destroy Aboriginal culture have not ended. Despite the fact that it covers all of Australia, Roberts avoids excessive generality by the constant use of specific examples which ground the themes in concrete reality. The author includes recent attempts by different Aboriginal communities to reclaim their identity and their land.

* 1.63 *
Sahaydak, Maksym. *Ethnocide of Ukrainians in the U.S.S.R. An Underground Journal from the Soviet Ukraine, Spring 1974*. Baltimore, Paris, and Toronto: Smoloskyo Publishers, 1976. ISBN 0-914834-00-3.

The uncensored Issue 7-8 of the nationalist journal, *The Ukrainian Herald*, contains two articles, the second specifically concerned with ethnocide. An impassioned, partisan, and informative analysis of Russification policies within Ukraine uses demographic data to demonstrate that the genocidal and ethnocidal Kremlin policies were systematic solutions to expressions of Ukrainian nationalism from 1917. Forced migration and discrimination in economic, educational, cultural, and political spheres are emphasized as the main areas of ethnocidal policies. Language, rather than blood, is identified to be the psychological and cultural criteria for national identity: the replacement of Ukrainian by Russian as the medium of instruction in education, science, and the media is stressed. Contradictions between Kremlin internationalist policy statements and practices are drawn out, and it is concluded that "The heart of the matter is that Ukraine is a colony." (p.94)

* 1.64 *
Sevilla-Casas, Elias, ed. *Western Expansion and Indigenous Peoples*. The Hague, Paris: Mouton Publishers, 1977. ISBN 90-279-7510-8.

This collection of papers was first presented in Session 643 at the IXth International Congress of Anthropological and Ethnological Sciences on cultural and physical destruction of indigenes. Geographically focused upon Central and Latin America, the volume is divided into three sections which cover theoretical issues, the period of colonization, and the present day. A theoretical paper by John H. Bodley, "Alternatives to Ethnocide," discusses anthropological definitions of the term and the problematic role of anthropologists in exposing or disguising ethnocidal processes. Integration of indigenes into state political systems and cultural autonomy are discussed as possible alternatives to ethnocide. It also includes a wide number of case studies.

* 1.65 *
Smith, Richard Chase. *The Dialectics of Domination in Peru*. Occasional Paper no. 8. Cambridge, MA: Cultural Survival, Inc., 1982.

Smith's paper is a clearly presented, critical assessment of the Pichis-Palcazu Special Project, a vast one-billion dollar state development and colonization project in central Peru. The project, which included an objective to resettle 150,000 people into the area from overcrowded Lima, overlooked the 8,000 indigenous Amuesha and Campa people in officially recognized Native Communities, and between 5,000 to 8,000 other settlers living in the region. Much of the publication vocalizes the struggle for Indian rights and discusses the viability of alternatives to specific parts of the project, such as road building, and of the integration of Indians into the national economy. The report ends with an optimistic discussion of autonomous development as a possible alternative for both the survival of Indian societies and for nation-building.

* 1.66 *
Stedman, Raymond William. *Shadows of the Indian*. Norman, OK: University of Oklahoma Press, 1982. LC 82-40330. ISBN 0-8061-1822-9.

Stedman examines the portrayal of Indians in American popular culture. The foreword states that "It is an interesting and important book, interesting because of the vividness of the images..., important because those images still dominate national Indian policy."(p.ix) Added to this, *Shadows of the Indian* is important since it takes the reader through one clear form of cultural destruction that denies Indian cultures, histories, and realities, and continues with a form that replaces it, the limited number of stereotypes which have been constructed by whites. Finally Stedman's book is interesting since it considers a much neglected area of destruction whose pervasive insidiousness is masked by the deceptions of media paraphernalia.

* 1.67 *
Tapp, Nicholas. *The Hmong of Thailand*. Indigenous Peoples and Development Series, no. 3. London: The Anti-Slavery Society, 1986. ISBN 0-900918-17-9.

The Hmong are a tribal people of northern Thailand whose culture "now stands at the crossroads between violent change and total destruction." (p.9) In a short document, Tapp briefly outlines traditional Hmong social organization and their history of persecution under the Han Chinese until the late 1880s. He then discusses contemporary problems of opium economy; government welfare and development programs; the establishment of assimilationist refugee camps in the lowlands; deforestation; tourism, which "is contributing to the erosion of Hmong culture and cultural values." (p.52); and the lack of rights accorded to the Hmong, the majority of whom are denied citizenship.

* 1.68 *
Terzani, Tiziano. *Behind the Forbidden Door*. London and Sydney: Unwin Paperback, 1987. ISBN 0-04-951026-6.

Terzani examines the destruction of Chinese cultures since the Cultural Revolution, whose purpose was "to eliminate the vestiges of the past and to destroy the old culture in order to create a new one." (p.181) The author was expelled from China in 1984 for his outspoken criticism of Chinese policies and for pushing his journalistic enquiries into areas forbidden to outsiders. The author's examination is colourful and insightful.

* 1.69 *
Thornton, Russell. "History, Structure and Survival: A Comparison of the Yuki (Ukmno'm) and Tolowa (Hush) Indians of Northern California." *Ethnology* 25:2 (1986): 119-130.

Thornton concisely summarizes the decimation and survival of two populations of American Indians from 1850 to the present day. Differences in the contact history of the Yuki and the Tolowa people with whites are illustrated. Factors suggested to explain why the larger Yuki population suffered a continual decrease which eventuated in their complete dissolution as a distinct tribal unit, while the smaller Tolowa community witnessed a resurgence from approximately mid-twentieth century, are 1) the impact of the different rates of decimation upon tribal social organization; 2) different experiences on reservations; and 3) different forms of social organization, particularly marriage, kinship systems, and patterns of residence. The main conclusion is the suggestion "that the maintenance of the "group boundaries" of an American Indian tribe ultimately determines its survival." (p.129)

* 1.70 *
Treece, David. *Bound in Misery and Iron: The Impact of the Grande Carasjas Program on the Indians of Brazil*. SI Document n.s. 4. London: Survival International, 1987. ISBN 0-946592-01-3.

Treece's book is an angry report on the massive Greater Carajas program which is wreaking ecological, cultural, and social destruction upon an area of Brazil the size of France and Britain combined, and which presents urgent humanitarian and ecological problems for the world. The rapid pace of the project has displaced thousands of the eight million people who traditionally live in the region. Treece focuses upon the imminent threat to the 13,000 tribal people of the area who, despite having legal protection, suffer economic, social, cultural, and physical destruction from contact with non-Indian society as officials waive their legislative responsibilities. The role of the major investors—the World Bank and the EEC—is criticized for lack of serious consultation with Indians and irresponsibility over human rights. Treece argues that recognition of tribal land rights is the only way to ensure their physical and cultural survival.

* 1.71 *
Turnbull, Colin. *The Mountain People*. London: Jonathan Cape, 1973. ISBN 0-224-00865.

In a personalized account of an anthropologist's field study among the small Ik community in the mountainous regions bordering Uganda, Sudan, and Kenya, Trumbull describes the distressing psychological damage experienced by an entire community who suffered rapid and drastic change of socio-economic organization, which created unstable social relations, famine, total despondency, neglect of sanitation, and death. The concluding recommendations reek of despair and offer no real hope for either survival or salvation. Trumbull has written a chilling, detailed study of wide significance for those concerned with the experience of collective social and psychological death rather than with official policies.

* 1.72 *
UNESCO. *Informe Final: Reunion de Expertos sobre Etnodesarrollo y Etnocidio en America Latina, 7-11 de Diciembre de 1981; FLACSO, San Jose, Costa Rica. N. SS-82 / WS / 32*. Paris: UNESCO, 12 July 1982.

This is the final report of the UNESCO Conference of San Jose on Ethnic Development and Ethnocide in Latin America, held in December 1981.

* 1.73 *
Valkeapaa, Nils-Aslak. *Greetings from Lappland*. London: Zed Press, 1983. ISBN 0-86232-155-7.

Valkeapaa describes the current plight of the indigenous Saami in Nordic countries which are normally so progressive on human rights issues. The Saami author identifies four main threats: development projects; the military, as the region is used as a base for tens of thousands of NATO forces; tourism, which ridicules and denigrates Saami culture; and state education, which imposes Western values and languages. The book includes struggles of the Saami to retain their land and culture. The direct and magical style invites the reader into the lived culture; it also includes factual and more academic information and discussion.

* 1.74 *
Walter, Lynn. *Ethnicity, Economy and the State in Ecuador*. Aalborg, Denmark: Aalborg University Press, 1981. LC 82-209680. ISBN 8773071390.

Walter's short paper on the integration of Indians into mainstream Ecuadorian life was presented at the Aalborg University Center. Attempts to forge a homogenous Ecuadorian identity concomitantly with state development projects deny the existence of distinct Indian cultures and identities and seek their assimilation. In the words of Guillermo Rodriquez Lara, a former president, "'There is no more Indian problem...we all become white men when we accept the goals of the national culture'." (p.23)

* 1.75 *
Whitten, Norman E., Jr. *Sacha Runa: Ethnicity and Adaptation of Ecuadorian Jungle Quicha*. Urbana, Chicago, and London: University of Illinois Press, 1976. LC 75-28350. ISBN 0-252-00553-8.

Whitten has written an indepth ethnographic analysis of the Canels Quicha, the native peoples of Pastza and Tena provinces of Ecuador. The focus lies in the effect upon the Indians of state nationalism as agrarian reform and cultural homogenization. These deny Quicha identity and officially subsume them under the general national category of mestizo. Paradoxically, processes of homogenization have re-emphasized ethnic boundaries: ethnogenesis and pan-Andean identities have been promoted. The government denies ethnocidal consequences of state nationalism and considers it an outcome of international petroleum company exploitation during the 1960s. Whitten warns of a possible future genocide of the Quicha, whose situation is precarious.

* 1.76 *
Witness to Cultural Genocide. First-Hand Reports on Rumania's Minority Policies Today. New York: American Transylvanian Federation, Inc. and the Committee for Human Rights in Rumania, n.d.

The articles, letters, and memoranda of personalized accounts in this collection describe Rumanian policies towards the Hungarian minority in Transylvania. They speak of the oppression and torture of Hungarian intellectuals who were conceived of as a threat to Rumanian dominance of Transylvania before the 1989 revolution and of the widespread discrimination against Hungarian language, education, health, employment, and housing. The crux of the problem lies in Transylvania's troublesome history of annexation to Hungary and Rumania. The Hungarian minority were identified as a potential irredentist nationalist threat. Paper I discusses post-1968 policies within the context of international legal codes and suggests a gradual program of "psychological torture...and genocide." (p.20) Paper II focuses on educational, artistic, and religious institutions.

* 1.77 *
World Bank. *Economic Development and Tribal Peoples*. Washington, DC: World Bank, Office of Environmental Affairs, 1981. LC 82-11192. ISBN 0-8213-0010-5.

The World Bank's Office of Environmental Affairs examines the need to re-think its policy on funding development projects which often have devastating effects upon tribal peoples. The proposals argue that there should be a gradual inclusion of isolated tribal groups into the national society and that tribal peoples should benefit economically from World Bank assisted projects. Section 3 considers the "Prerequisites for Ethnic Identity and Survival" in terms of land, health, and cultural autonomy.

CHAPTER 2

THE HOLOCAUST

by **Michael Dobkowski**

The Holocaust, the paradigmatic genocide, was a product of the convergence of a technically efficient, well-educated and cultured bureaucracy, and barbaric intentionality. The Holocaust was a paper-shuffling genocide in that those who planned the operations of extermination for the most part never saw the "final solution" as an accomplished fact. The bureaucratization of genocide profoundly desensitized the bureaucrats who carried it out. A necessary prelude to genocide was the Nazis' barbaric program to dehumanize the Jew, to transform him into the Other, into a parasite, into an object of derision. Then the outbreak of war in 1939 foreclosed opportunities for expulsion of the Jews from Europe and set the stage for the Holocaust which was carried out primarily on the conquered lands of Eastern Europe and the Soviet Union.

The attempt by the Nazis and their collaborators to systematically exterminate the Jewish people and most of the Romanies, or Gypsies, during World War II, commonly termed the Holocaust or *Shoah* in Hebrew, has come to be viewed as the paradigmatic genocide. Adolf Hitler's Third Reich exploited all the advantages of modern technology and bureaucratic organization to transport Jews from the far reaches of Europe to various concentration and killing sites, including ghettos in Eastern Europe and specially constructed extermination camps in occupied Poland where the Jews were starved, subjected to inhumane living conditions, ravaged by disease, shot in mass numbers, and executed in gas chambers as quickly and efficiently as possible. By the time the war was over in 1945, almost six million Jews and several hundred thousand Gypsies had been annihilated. Although not every victim was Jewish, the principal goal of the Nazi plan was to rid Europe, if not the world, of Jews. Mass murder is nothing new, of course. We have seen many tragic examples in history. But genocide is a crime against humanity because it negates human value as such. When the administration of death becomes a bureaucratic procedure, when killing and efficiency are the only values left, then clearly we are faced with something more than the age-old disregard for life.

Bureaucracy and Barbarism

This combination of technological and bureaucratic mass murder and barbaric intentionality has raised serious questions about the notion of progress; the capacity of human beings to engage in evil and goodness; and the nature of individual and group responsibility.[1] The fact that many of the planners and perpetrators of the Nazi Holocaust were well-educated and cultured only adds to the centrality of the phenomenon. Three of the four Einsatzgruppen that were responsible for killing approximately one million Jews in the East by shooting were commanded by Ph.D.s. Twenty-three doctors at Auschwitz selected well over a million Jews to the gas chambers. The engineers, architects, jurists, bureaucrats, teachers, chemists, and others who were involved in designing the camps, furthering racist propaganda and segregation, expropriating Jewish property, subverting the rule of law, transporting the victims to the death camps, manufacturing the Zyklon B gas, and directing and profiting from slave labor were central, not incidental, parts of the killing process. And this all occurred in the twentieth century, in the middle of Europe, the font of modernism and culture. The Holocaust is, therefore, of utmost importance since it occurred in this century and was perpetrated by people who, at least ostensibly, were nurtured in Western civilization and values.

Intentionalism Versus Functionalism

In the last several years, debate has emerged among historians about how and why the Nazis came to pursue the Final Solution. Was it a premeditated policy or did the general circumstances of the war or other social and economic forces serve as a catalyst to propel it? The "intentionalists" see Hitler as the driving force of Nazi policy and find a high degree of consistency and order in Nazi anti-Semitic policy. "The War Against the Jews," as Lucy Dawidowicz called it, was from a very early point the goal of the Nazis.[2] They discern a rather direct road from the anti-Semitic policies of the 1930's to genocide in the 1940s. The "functionalists," in contrast, view the Third Reich as a maze of competing groups, personalities, and rival bureaucracies. Hitler is portrayed as a leader who certainly despised the Jews, but who preferred to delegate authority and who intervened on the Jewish question only occasionally. Annihilation policies were improvised and emerged out of the chaotic system itself. The road to Auschwitz was "twisted."[3]

Was the Holocaust Unique?

The debate between the "intentionalists" and the "functionalists" revolves essentially around another controversial question of whether the Holocaust should be viewed as a unique event or as merely the latest, possibly the most heinous, example of inhumanity in history. If the Holocaust should prove to be unique, the factors that make it so can be drawn upon for a better understanding of not only the Holocaust but also other examples of mass death. It has been argued that the Holocaust is unique because of its scope; the unprecedented involvement of the legal and administrative apparatus; the horrible treatment meted out to the individuals to be annihilated; the ideological passion of the killers; the concerted ideological and religious campaign directed against the victims; the degree of intentionality of the killers and the planners of the Final Solution; the varied physical and psychological techniques used to reify the intended victims; and the bureaucratic and technological aspects of the mass death.

The Paper-Shuffling Genocide

In order to understand how thousands of intellectuals, students, scientists, jurists, religionists, and bureaucrats were able to cross the moral barrier that made massacre in the millions possible, it is necessary to consider the dehumanizing capacities of bureaucracy in modern political and social organizations. In the Nazi state, or more specifically in the S.S. offices in Berlin, the Reich Security Main Office, an inconspicuous series of offices in an even more inconspicuous building, on the Prinz Albrechtstrasse, and the S.D. headquarters around the corner on the Wilhemstrasse, bureaucrats like Adolph Eichmann manipulated numbers on paper and shuffled those papers to other officials, and a few hundred miles away countless tens of thousands were condemned to a brutal death. They never had to, and often never did, see the results of their paper-shuffling genocide.[4]

Bureaucratic murder was seen in clearest relief on 20 January 1942 at the Wannsee Conference which was called by Hermann Goring and presided over by Reinhard Heydrich, head of the S.D., to coordinate the process of annihilation within the S.S., to enlist the help of other state agencies, and most importantly to extend the process of annihilation throughout German-occupied Europe. The fifteen men who gathered around the table of the elegant villa in a posh Berlin suburb overlooking the Grosser Wannsee lake for their eighty-five minute meeting, interrupted occasionallly for light refreshment and drink, included high level functionaries from the S.S., the S.D., and the Gestapo who were old hands at the process of extermination. The other participants came from the Ministry of the Interior, the Ministry of Justice, the Foreign Office, the Party Chancellery, the Reich Ministry for the Occupied Eastern Territories, the Office of the Four-Year Plan, and the Office of the Governor General of Poland. The government officials were senior civil servants beneath the cabinet level, and eight of the fifteen held doctorates. Under the mask of geniality and old-boy friendships and a *gemütlich* atmosphere, the most chilling discussion took place sealing the fate of millions of Jews.

Heydrich reviewed the history of the campaign against the Jews. He then listed the numbers of Jews believed to be alive in each European country, from several hundred in Albania to over five million in the Soviet Union, totalling more than eleven million. All were to be included in the Final Solution.

The Banality of Evil

Everyone in attendance had long since stopped thinking of Jews as human beings. No one, therefore, raised objections to the fundamental policy of exterminating the Jewish people. The issues discussed were logistical and public relational; occasionally interagency rivalries surfaced. According to the official record of the meeting, more time was spent on the problem of the part-Jews —*Mischlinge*—than any other issue. What occurred at that meeting was a demonstration of the bureaucratization of the Nazi Holocaust, of the banality of evil at work, re-inforced by the collective legitimation of a group mentality.[5]

Raul Hilberg, Hannah Arendt, Richard Rubenstein, Robert Jay Lifton, Zygmunt Bauman, Berel Lang, and others have noted that in order to make it possible to kill the Jews, mechanisms and institutions were created that blocked traditional concepts of individual morality and responsibility.[6] Psychologically, people must not be allowed to feel guilt when they destroy others. Here is where the concerted ideological anti-Semitism comes into play; here is the importance of the campaign that turned the Jew into the Other, into a parasite, an object of derision, that caused the Jew to be reduced to shaven heads and tatooed arms and then *to refuse to be consumed by gas and fire*.

The Milieu of Anti-Semitism

The campaign against the Jews came out of a milieu that nurtured anti-Semitism. Anti-Semitism had been one of the cardinal elements of Hitler's world view from the very outset. It also informed much of the political rhetoric of National Socialism during its formative stage. Nazi ideology saw in the Jews a universal devilish element threatening the integrity and mission of the German nation or *Volk*. In Hitler's mind, the threat the Jews posed formed the matrix of his ideology. As "Semites" they were a foreign race mongrelizing the Germanic stock of the nation; as democrats, they weakened the ability of the nation to express itself through a "national" leader and "idea"; as Marxists and Socialists, they were dedicated to the defeat of Germany; as Jews, they were interested in domination; and so on.[7] The point is, by placing Jews at the center of what threatened Germany and Europe, Nazism was able to harness people's energy and direct it in a particular direction. They dehumanized the Jews and stripped them of any human qualities. This was the necessary ideological prelude to a genocidal policy that turned idea into genocidal reality.

The transformation came soon after Hitler, shaped by the pseudo-messianic concept of saving humanity from the Jews, was invested with power. Anti-Semitism now became official state policy. German Jews were publicly reviled, beaten, boycotted, delegitimized, expelled from the professions, and expropriated. As Hannah Arendt, Richard Rubenstein and others have pointed out, when Jews lost their citizenship rights, when they became surplus populations with no rights and protected by no one, they became susceptible to genocide. *Kristallnacht*, on 9-10 November 1938, capped this first orgy of violence and discrimination with the destruction of nearly four hundred synogogues, thousands of Jewish businesses and institutions, and countless physical assaults and large-scale arrests. At least ninety-one Jews were killed and thirty thousand Jewish males were incarcerated in Dachau, Buchenwald, and Sachsenhausen concentration camps. This was the prelude to the Final Solution in Europe. The murder program went largely unopposed because of the pervasive, moderate anti-Semitism that was a part of European culture and that prepared the way and then prevented effective resistance.

War Made Genocide Possible

The outbreak of war in September 1939 foreclosed opportunities for expulsion of Jews at the same time that it brought millions of additional Jews in Eastern Europe and the Soviet Union under German authority. It also provided the conditions that made genocide possible. The conquest of Poland was followed by the brutal ghettoization and relocation of Polish Jewry as part of the policy of extermination. As mobile death squads, Einsatzgruppen, fanned out along the eastern front, spreading havoc and death, attention behind the lines was given to ghettoization which would ultimately send hundreds of thousands of Jews to the slave labor and death camps in occupied Poland and the Greater Reich. Those who were capable of working were put to work in the ghettos, albeit under intolerable conditions calculated to kill as many as possible through starvation, cold, and disease. The Nazis set up *Judenräte*, or Jewish councils, responsible for overseeing the daily activities in the ghetto and providing some infrastructure of services. These councils were desperate and beleaguered institutions that generally attempted to ameliorate the suffering of the victims but were the inevitable, if unwilling, pawns of the oppressors. In the end, the vast majority of Europe's Jews perished, though not without resistance. The story of Jewish resistance is one of hope and unbelievable courage against overwhelming odds. The Jews were no match for the state power and well-oiled military machine of the Nazis. Resistance, in a pure military sense, was doomed to failure.

Many Jews died in the ghettos, but not quickly enough. The Nazis felt more radical solutions were needed. Before 1941, a network of concentration camps was established in areas occupied by the Nazis. These camps, like Dachau, Buchenwald, Bergen-Belsen, and Sachsenhausen, were horrific places that held opponents of the regime and served as slave labor depots. Nevertheless, unlike the annihilation camps, the concentration camps were not necessarily part of the systematic program of annihilation. Many thousands died there, but many others managed to work and survive.

In contrast, the annihilation camps were built in Poland near the largest concentrations of Jews in Europe and the ghettos, in close proximity to railroads and near populations that might be considered indifferent to the fate of the Jews. The first to be put into operation was Chelmno or Kulmhof in December 1941. It was followed by Belzec in March 1942, Sobibor in May 1942, Treblinka in July 1942, and Maidanek in August 1942. Fewer than 100 Jews survived the camps at Chelmno, Belzec, Sobibor, and Treblinka. More than 1.5 million Jews and some 50,000 Gypsies were murdered in those places.[8]

The methods of annihilation varied. At first, mobile gas vans were used to asphyxiate the victims. Technical people at Reich Security Main Office headquarters designed a tightly closed truck with the cab sealed off from the freight section. They converted Saurer truck chassis into vans with closed compartments that could hold about eighty people. The carbon monoxide exhaust was diverted into the compartment. Chelmno, about forty miles northeast of Lodz, experimented with them first on 8 December 1941. In the spring, the same method was used at Belzec, Sobibor, and Treblinka. Here, too, diesel engines were used but in fixed installations. The same was initially true of the largest killing center, Auschwitz in Eastern Upper Silesia, where between 1 1/2 and 2 1/2 million people died. At Auschwitz, as later in Maidanek near Lublin, a crystalline form of hydrogen cyanide that turned gaseous when exposed to the air was used for the killing. This chemical, marketed as a disinfectant and manufactured by a Frankfurt firm called Degesch, went by the trade name Zyklon B. The first experiments with Zyklon B were conducted on 3 September 1941 at Auschwitz on some six hundred Russian POWs and another 250 sick prisoners from the camp hospital. Systematic operations began in January 1942. Transports from all over Europe brought Jews to Auschwitz. Soon, gas chambers disguised as shower rooms were installed as were cremataria, with forty-six ovens in all. They had a capacity to burn from 12,000 to 20,000 bodies a day. Tens of thousands of other victims were burned in open air pits.

It is impossible to know precisely how many Jews died during the Holocaust. Somewhere between 5.1 and 5.9 million Jews perished—nearly two-thirds of European Jewry and one-third of the Jews in the world lost their lives. In addition to this human tragedy that grips our sensibilities and shocks our sense of values, there is also the cultural, intellectual, and religious tragedy of the destruction of European Jewry, a world, a way of life, that can never be replaced. In the end, millions participated in and assented to this policy: those who knew it was happening but let it continue, as well as those who contributed to it more directly. Even the Allies did not make rescue of the Jews a priority. They all carry a share of the responsibility for this genocidal event.

The Challenge We Face Today

We are at a crucial turning point with respect to the level of sensitivity and awareness of the importance of the Holocaust. There may have been a time not very long ago when one could assume a degree of common understanding of the Holocaust and common feeling for its victims, but no such consensus exists today. The problem is that the further events fade into the past, the more the construction of convenient truth grows and is perfected. Time is an enemy of the Holocaust. More and more shrill voices insist it never happened. Worse yet may be those who want to relativize the Holocaust or to universalize and trivialize it by theorizing that Hitler had good reason to fear the Jews or that Nazi atrocities were not unusual and must be seen in the light of Soviet atrocities and the political standards of the period. This tendency to deny or to minimize the veracity and uniqueness of the Holocaust is likely to increase with German unification. With the passage of time, the past loses its truth unless its most pointed lessons are continually reiterated and underscored. That is the challenge we face today.

NOTES

1. See Zygmunt Bauman, *Modernity and the Holocaust* (Ithaca: Cornell University Press, 1989); George Kren and Leon Rappaport, *The Holocaust and the*

Crisis of Human Behavior (New York: Holmes & Meir, 1980); and Richard Rubenstein, *The Cunning of History: The Holocaust and the American Future* (New York: Harper & Row, 1975).

2. Lucy Dawidowicz, *The War Against the Jews, 1933-1945* (New York: Holt, Rinehart and Winston, 1975).

3. Karl Schleunes, *The Twisted Road to Auschwitz* (Urbana: University of Illinois Press, 1971).

4. See Rubenstein, 22-35.

5. Hannah Arendt, *Eichmann in Jerusalem: A Report on the Banality of Evil* (New York: The Viking Press, 1965).

6. Raul Hilberg, *The Destruction of the European Jews*, 3 vols. rev. ed. (New York: Holmes & Meier, 1985); Rubenstein; Robert Jay Lifton, *The Nazi Doctors* (New York: Basic Books, 1986); Bauman; and Berel Lang, *Act and Idea in the Nazi Genocide* (Chicago: University of Chicago Press, 1990).

7. Gerald Fleming, *Hitler and the Final Solution* (Berkeley: University of California Press, 1982).

8. Yitzhak Arad, *Belzec, Sobibor, Treblinka: The Operation Reinhard Death Camps* (Bloomington: Indiana University Press, 1987).

Chapter 2: Annotated Bibliography

GENERAL WORKS

* 2.1 *
Braham, Randolph L. *The Politics of Genocide*. 2 vols. New York: Columbia University Press, 1980. LC 80-11096. ISBN 0-231-05208-1 (vol. 1); 0-231-04388-0 (vol. 2).

The Hungarian Jewish community remained relatively untouched until the Spring of 1944 when the Nazis began deportations to Auschwitz; Adolf Eichmann played a pivotal role in the process. Braham shows that many Hungarians assisted the Nazis. This is the definitive study of the Holocaust in Hungary.

* 2.2 *
Dawidowicz, Lucy. *The War Against the Jews, 1933-1945*. New York: Holt, Rinehart and Winston, 1975. LC 74-15470. ISBN 0-03-013661-0.

In what is probably the most widely read work on the Holocaust, Dawidowicz argues that World War II was a two-fold war. The Nazis had conventional objectives such as territory, power, and wealth. They also unleashed a "war against the Jews" motivated by ideology and anti-Semitism. Hitler intended the genocide and World War II provided an effective vehicle to accomplish it. A useful appendix indicates the fate of the Jews, country by country.

* 2.3 *
Fleming, Gerald. *Hitler and the Final Solution*. Berkeley: University of California Press, 1982. LC 83-24352. ISBN 0-520-05103-3.

Fleming bases his position on material from British, American, and Soviet archives. He makes a strong case for the thesis that Hitler was instrumental in planning and implementing the "Final Solution." He refutes revisionists like David Irving who argues for Hitler's limited knowledge of and participation in the genocide.

* 2.4 *
Gilbert, Martin. *The Holocaust: A History of the Jews of Europe during the Second World War*. New York: Holt, Rinehart and Winston, 1986. LC 85-5523. ISBN 0-03-062416-9.

A distinguished British historian, using documents and survivor accounts, describes the Holocaust from the perspective of the victims. He provides detailed accounts of the suffering as well as the valor of the Jews.

* 2.5 *
Heller, Celia Stopnicka. *On the Edge of Destruction*. New York: Schocken, 1980. LC 76-22646. ISBN 0-231-03819-4.

In a scholarly sociological analysis of the social, political, and economic situation of Polish Jews between the world wars, Heller develops the context to explain why Polish Jews fared so badly during the Holocaust. Her discussion of Polish anti-Semitism is particularly informative.

* 2.6 *
Hilberg, Raul. *The Destruction of the European Jews*. 3 vols. Rev. ed. New York: Holmes & Meier, 1985. LC 83-18369. ISBN 0-8419-0832-X (set). Originally published in 1961.

In one of the most important works written on the Holocaust, Hilberg provides a masterly analysis and synthesis of the mechanism of genocide, including the bureaucratic process. He proposes the notion of the "machinery of destruction" that developed in stages, the result of decisions taken by countless decision makers. The bureaucrats were not operating on a different moral plane. Hilberg is also unsparing in his critique of Jewish passivity. He claims that the Jews displayed an almost complete lack of resistance. They complied easily to most decrees. At times they even moved ahead of the Germans in what he calls "anticipatory compliance." Critics point out that Hilberg relied excessively on German sources and was remarkably thin in his discussion of the inner world of diverse Jewish communities.

* 2.7 *
Koonz, Claudia. *Mothers in the Fatherland: Women, the Family, and Nazi Politics*. New York: St. Martins, 1987. LC 86-13815. ISBN 0-312-54933-4.

Koonz examines the role of women in Nazi Germany and the effects that Nazism had on the family and women generally. She argues that Nazism's attitudes toward women and gender were second only to racism in structuring the new German society and defining its enemies. She also focuses on the women's movement in Germany, women resisters, and the fate of Jewish women.

* 2.8 *
Lanzmann, Claude. *Shoah: An Oral History of the Holocaust*. New York: Pantheon, 1985. LC 85-16760. ISBN 0-394-55142-7.

This is the complete text of Lanzmann's 9 1/2 hour film, which consists of interviews with victims, perpetrators and bystanders as well as selected documents. The film is particularly insightful on the role and attitudes of the non-Jewish Poles, which he found to be quite hostile to Jews.

* 2.9 *
Marrus, Michael R., and Robert O. Paxton. *Vichy France and the Jews*. New York: Basic Books, 1981. LC 80-70307. ISBN 0-465-090005-2.

Marrus and Paxton argue that collaboration with the Nazis went particularly far in France. Vichy officials not only persecuted Jews as ordered by the Nazis, but initiated their own anti-Semitic policies and agendas. By 1942 Vichy had banned Jews from engaging in certain professions and expropriated Jewish property. For many Vichy officials, the roundup and deportation of about 75,000 Jews that began in 1942 were simply a continuation of a program deemed by many to be in the French national interest.

* 2.10 *
Mayer, Arno J. *Why Did the Heavens Not Darken?* New York: Pantheon Books, 1988. LC 88-42621. ISBN 0-394-57154-1.

Mayer places what he terms "Judeocide" in the broad context of anti-Semitism and the specific setting of the Nazis' war against Bolshevism. He argues that the latter was more important than the former in Nazi plans to exterminate the Jews. Nazi Germany did not begin its "systematic" mass murder of the Jews, Mayer believes, until its crusade against Bolshevism ran aground in 1942. Mayer's book is a massive synthesis of scholarship.

* 2.11 *
Mendelsohn, Ezra. *The Jews of East Central Europe Between the World Wars*. Bloomington: Indiana University Press, 1983. LC 81-48676. ISBN 0-253-33160-9.

Mendelsohn offers an ambitious study of the demographic, socioeconomic, and cultural condition of East Central European Jewry before World War II. He concludes that the Jews in this region faced a crisis by 1939. The economic base was severely eroded and democracy was under challenge. While there was little anti-Semitism in Yugoslavia, Bulgaria, and the Baltic states, the large Jewish populations of Poland, Rumania, and Hungary experienced great difficulty.

* 2.12 *
Reitlinger, Gerald Roberts. *Final Solution*. New York: Barnes, 1953. LC 53-13001.

Reitlinger, a British historian, provides one of the earliest scholarly books on the Holocaust. He documents the evolution of the events and policies that led to the Final Solution.

* 2.13 *
Schleunes, Karl. *The Twisted Road to Auschwitz*. Champaign: University of Illinois Press, 1971. LC 74-102024.

Schleunes demonstrates how contradictory the Nazi policies and aims concerning the Jews occasionally were. He believes this confusing situation lasted until 1938, when a more coherent anti-Jewish policy was formulated. Until then, competing interests in the Nazi hierarchy led to confusion and lack of coordination. It was only after the outbreak of war, when Hitler felt secure in his power, that he helped formulate the "final solution."

* 2.14 *
Yahil, Leni. *The Holocaust*. New York: Oxford University Press, 1990. LC 89-27750. ISBN 0-19-504522-X. First published in Hebrew in 1987.

Yahil provides a sweeping analysis of the Holocaust. Although she bases her work primarily on secondary sources, the author skillfully synthesizes this material to provide one of the most comprehensive and readable one volume histories of the Holocaust.

THEORETICAL AND HISTORICAL WORKS

* 2.15 *
Arendt, Hannah. *Eichmann in Jerusalem: A Report on the Banality of Evil*. New York: The Viking Press, 1965. LC 64-25532.

Arendt originally wrote this assessment of the Eichmann trial for the *New Yorker*. Her conclusions prompted a debate on the nature of evil and on the role of the Jews, particularly the Jewish councils, in the destruction of the Jewish people. The book became a center of much controversy, chiefly due to her notion of the banality of evil and her criticism of Jewish leadership. The Nazis could not have been as effective without the cooperation of the victims. For Arendt there was no special Jewish predilection for passivity. Rather, Jewish reactions were part of the moral collapse the Nazis caused in European society. Her analysis is flawed by its lack of attention to the historicity of the events described.

* 2.16 *
Bauman, Zygmunt. *Modernity and the Holocaust*. Ithaca: Cornell University Press, 1989. LC 89-7274. ISBN 0-8014-2397-X.

Bauman provides an original set of reflections on racism, extermination, rationality, individual responsibility in criminal societies, and the sources of obedience and resistance. Bauman rejects the tendency to reduce the Holocaust to an episode in Jewish history or to see it as unique. Rather, he argues that it is rooted in the very nature of modern society. The Holocaust reveals the negative side of instrumental rationality and shows how this principle can generate moral indifference on a massive scale.

* 2.17 *
Bettelheim, Bruno. *The Informed Heart: Autonomy in a Mass Age*. Glencoe, IL: The Free Press, 1960. LC 60-13776.

Imprisoned in Dachau and Buchenwald in the late 1930s, Bettelheim drew on that experience to develop a theory of survival. He stresses the notion of individual autonomy and sense of self. The Nazis set out to dehumanize their victims, to break down their autonomy. Bettelheim asserts that prisoners in the camp exhibited child-like behavior, identified with the SS, and fell into an "anonymous mass" without social organization. Critics have contended that his psychological models derive from his own experiences of camp life and may not apply to the even more brutal and genocidal regimes introduced a few years later.

* 2.18 *
Breitman, Richard. *The Architect of Genocide: Himmler and the Final Solution*. New York: Alfred A. Knopf, 1991. LC 90-52956. ISBN 0-394-56841-9.

Breitman argues that Himmler, the head of the S.S., was the true architect of the Holocaust. Although Hitler conceived the idea, set the tone of the regime and issued the decisive orders, it was Himmler who worked out the design and implementation. Breitman describes how military and diplomatic factors, economic restraints, the opportunities provided by war, and the pressures of "scientific" research affected the timing and scope of the Holocaust.

* 2.19 *
Chalk, Frank, and Kurt Jonassohn. *The History and Sociology of Genocide: Analyses and Case Studies*. New Haven: Yale University Press, 1990. LC 89-27381. ISBN 0-300-04446-1.

The authors present over two dozen cases of genocide from antiquity to the present, expanding the U.N. definition to include political and social groups. They classify genocides according to the motives of the perpetrators; to eliminate a real or potential threat; to spread terror among real or potential enemies; to acquire wealth; and to implement an ideology. In the twentieth century, the ideological genocides have become the most important type.

* 2.20 *
Chorover, Stephen L. *From Genesis to Genocide*. Cambridge, MA: MIT Press, 1979. LC 78-21107. ISBN 0-262-03068-3.

The author investigates the use of technology to control human behavior. He explores the evolution of the Eugenics movement; the origins of Nazi racist theories in late nineteenth century Europe and America; and the way these theories merged with social, political, and cultural conditions in Germany in the 1930s to make genocide possible.

* 2.21 *
Dwork, Deborah. *Children with a Star*. New Haven: Yale University Press, 1991. ISBN 0-300-05054-2.

Dwork bases her study on hundreds of oral histories conducted with survivors who were children in the Holocaust, as well as on a wide documentation including diaries, letters and photos. She expands the definition of resistance by examining the activities of people—primarily women—who helped Jews. By focusing on children, the most vulnerable members of the community, she demonstrates how European society functioned during the war years. This study clarifies the horror of the Nazi genocide and those who assisted it.

* 2.22 *
Fein, Helen. *Accounting for Genocide: National Responses and Jewish Victimization during the Holocaust*. New York: Free Press, 1979. LC 75-53085. ISBN 0-02-910220.

Using social science techniques, Fein attempted to determine why Jewish death rates were so high in some countries and relatively low in others. She examined such variables as the extent of SS control; the character of the local government; the level of anti-Semitism; the location of the country; the amount of warning time; and the size and influence of the Jewish community. She found that in those countries where Jews were viewed as inhabiting the same "universe of moral obligation," resistance to Nazism was greatest. In nine of the twenty-two states or regions occupied by or allied to Germany, fewer than fifty percent of the Jews were killed.

* 2.23 *
Frankl, Viktor E. *Man's Search for Meaning: An Introduction to Logotherapy*. New York: Simon & Schuster, 1963, 1984. LC 84-10520. ISBN 0-671-24422-1.

A psychiatrist survivor attributes his survival to the development of a philosophy which focuses on the meaning of life. That philosophy led Frankl to formulate an existential theory of psychiatric practice which he calls "logotherapy." According to logotherapy, we can discover the meaning of life in three different ways: by creating a work or doing a deed; by experiencing something or encountering someone; and by the attitude we take toward unavoidable suffering. In the Nazi concentration camp, the third way remained an option even in the worst situations because Frankl believes we retain control of our attitudes toward our own suffering. For this reason, he rejects the Bettelheim thesis that those who became more like their tormentors had the best chance of living.

* 2.24 *
Friedman, Philip. *Roads to Extinction: Essays on the Holocaust*. Philadelphia: Jewish Publication Society, 1980. LC 79-89818. ISBN 0-8276-0170-0.

One of the pioneers of Holocaust history, Friedman, a Polish-Jewish survivor and historian, devoted himself, until his death in 1960, to the study of the Holocaust. In this collection of his major essays, he examines the Holocaust from two points of view: that of German policy and that of Jewish reaction. One long essay is on the annhilation of Lvov's Jews, which he witnessed; another deals with Ukranian-Jewish relations under the Nazis.

* 2.25 *
Hartman, Geoffrey, ed. *Bitburg in Moral and Political Perspective*. Bloomington: Indiana University Press, 1986. LC 85-45960. ISBN 0-253-34430-1.

Hartman includes a comprehensive group of essays on the moral and political implications of the Bitburg affair. President Reagan's visit to the cemetery where Waffen SS lie buried and the general reaction to the controversy suggest that we may have reached a point of saturation with regard to Holocaust issues. The book includes Theodore W. Adorno's previously unpublished analysis of moral dilemmas generated by the Holocaust and Saul Friedlander's essay on the "new revisionism."

* 2.26 *
Jaspers, Karl. *The Question of German Guilt*. Trans. from the German by E.B. Ashton. New York: Capricorn Books, 1961. Originally published in Germany in 1947 as *Die Schuldfrage, ein Beitrag zur deutschen Frage*.

One of modern Germany's most distinguished philosophers, tackles the issue of German guilt. He develops four categories of guilt: criminal guilt, political guilt, moral guilt and metaphysical guilt. Criminal guilt is the result of crimes having been committed. Jurisdiction lies with the courts. Political guilt involves the actions of leaders and the citizenry. Jurisdiction lies with the victors. Moral guilt emerges from the responsibility of each person for all his or her deeds. Jurisdiction rests with the individual's conscience. Metaphysical guilt derives from the co-responsibility every human being shares for evil in the world. Jaspers' definitions may be too restrictive, thus absolving too many of the guilty.

* 2.27 *
Kren, George M., and Leon Rappaport. *The Holocaust and the Crisis of Human Behavior*. New York: Holmes & Meier, 1980. LC 79-23781. ISBN 0-8419-0544-4.

The authors argue for the singular nature of the Holocaust by focusing on the Holocaust universe of the death camps—the systematic dehumanization of the victims; the technology of mass death; and the bureaucratic organization on a wide scale. From the perspective of the "ash-darkened prisms" of post-Holocaust sensibility, they analyze how and why the three pillars of Western civilization—law, religion, and science—failed to prevent the Holocaust.

* 2.28 *
Lang, Berel. *Act and Idea in the Nazi Genocide*. Chicago: The University of Chicago Press, 1990. LC 89-37320. ISBN 0-226-46868-2.

In a series of philosophically sophisticated essays, Lang rigorously examines the relationship between act and idea. He argues that the events of the Nazi genocide compel reconsideration of such fundamental moral concepts as individual and group responsibility, the role of knowledge in ethical decisions, and the conditions governing the relation between guilt and forgiveness. He also analyzes the questions of how we write about the Nazi genocide; issues of memory and institutionalization; and the teaching of the Holocaust. Lang rejects Robert J. Lifton's notion of doubling. The divided self is not divided at all, he says. It is constructed by the Nazis in order to avoid admitting what a unified self would have to admit—the knowledge of evil.

* 2.29 *
Lifton, Robert J., and Erik Markusen. *The Genocidal Mentality: Nazi Holocaust and Nuclear Threat*. New York: Basic Books, 1990. LC 79-23781. ISBN 0-8419-0544-4.

The authors draw parallels between the Nazi Holocaust and Lifton's concept of nuclearism, focusing on the "disassociative process" which permits individuals to avoid knowing the meaning or consequences of their own actions.

* 2.30 *
Lifton, Robert Jay. *The Nazi Doctors: Medical Killing and the Psychology of Genocide*. New York: Basic Books, 1986. LC 85-73874. ISBN 0-465-04905-2 pa.

Lifton argues that there was a special affinity between Nazism and a perverted medical outlook he calls the "Nazi biomedical vision." Drawing heavily on eugenic ideas, the Nazi doctor viewed the German nation as a biological organism which was threatened by a kind of collective illness, the source of which was the Jews. How could physicians trained as healers become killers? They did so through "doubling," forming a second, relatively autonomous self—a process enhanced by the Nazi vision of a racially pure German people. There is a dialectic between the two selves. The Nazi doctor needed the Auschwitz self in order to function in an environment so opposed to his previous ethical principles. At the same time he needed his prior self in order to continue to see himself as a humane individual. Chapters on Drs. Joseph Mengele and Eduard Wirths are quite revealing. See also 7.27.

* 2.31 *
Marrus, Michael R. *The Holocaust in History*. Hanover, NH: Brandeis University Press, 1987. LC 87-6291. ISBN 0-87451-425-8.

Marrus skillfully integrates the historiography of the Holocaust into the general developments of historical scholarship. He examines the issues of uniqueness; the debate between intentionalists and functionalists; the role of the allies, the victims, Jewish resistance, and bystanders; and the issue of rescue. His is a comprehensive, useful assessment of the vast historical scholarship on the Holocaust.

* 2.32 *
Miller, Judith. *One by One, by One: Facing the Holocaust*. New York: Simon & Schuster, 1990. ISBN 0-671-64472-6.

Miller attempts to analyze and interpret how the Holocaust affects the peoples and governments of West Germany, Austria, France, the Netherlands, the USSR, and the United States. She argues that, although each country experienced the Holocaust differently, all use the same techniques to consciously and unconsciously shape their memories—denial, trivialization, rationalization, shifting of blame.

* 2.33 *
Rubenstein, Richard L. *The Age of Triage: Fear and Hope in an Overcrowded World*. Boston: Beacon Press, 1983. LC 82-9407. ISBN 0-8070-4376-1.

Rubenstein analyzes the socioeconomic and cultural forces of modernity that produce surplus populations and that lead to genocidal tendencies. The situation of Europe's Jews became progressively more hopeless as the economies of Western and Eastern Europe were modernized. He believes that there is a direct relationship between the rationalization of agriculture, the creation of surplus populations, and the potential for genocide.

* 2.34 *
Rubenstein, Richard L. *The Cunning of History: The Holocaust and the American Future*. New York: Harper & Row, 1975. LC 75-9334. ISBN 0-06-067013-4.

In this brief but highly suggestive book, Rubenstein argues that the Holocaust was the result of structural and institutional factors prevalent in Western civilization. He places the Holocaust on a continuum that begins in the Judeo-Christian tradition, continues in slavery, and ends in the faceless, mindless bureaucracy of the twentieth century. Genocide is most likely to occur when people refuse to extend the benefits and protection of their societies to strangers. Genocide is the ultimate expression of absolute rightlessness.

* 2.35 *
Sereny, Gita. *Into That Darkness: An Examination of Conscience*. New York: Vintage, 1983. LC 82-40049. ISBN 0-394-71035-5.

Sereny provides one of the most revealing and insightful portraits of a Nazi. The book is based on interviews with Franz Stangl, the commandant of Treblinka, held while he was in prison in 1971. Stangl is morally blind to the crimes he committed.

THE GHETTO EXPERIENCE

* 2.36 *
Adelson, Alan, and Robert Lapides, eds. *Lodz Ghetto: Inside a Community under Siege*. New York: Viking Press, 1989. LC 89-40167. ISBN 0-670-82983-8.

Based on Lucjan Dobroszycki's rich archive of ghetto materials, this book is an elaboration of his *Chronicle of the Lodz Ghetto*. It is made up of diaries, photographs and other documents, including speeches by Judenrat head Mordecai Chaim Rumkowski. The section on Rumkowski supports the view that he acquiesced in the Nazi liquidation of the Lodz Ghetto.

* 2.37 *
Arad, Yitzchak. *Ghetto in Flames*. New York: Ktav, 1981. LC 80-50198. ISBN 0-87068-753-0.

Arad, who was to become the chair of the board of directors of Yad Vashem, chronicles the destruction of the ghetto of Vilna. His account covers Vilna from 1941 to 1944.

* 2.38 *
Baker, Leonard. *Days of Sorrow and Pain*. New York: Macmillan, 1978. LC 77-28872. ISBN 0-02-506340-5.

Baker examines the career of Rabbi Leo Baeck, the leading liberal Jewish theologian and Rabbi in Germany, who decided to stay with his people and was sent with them to Theresienstadt, where he was an inspiration. Baker also examines the umbrella organization for German Jews from mid-1939 on that was the counterpart of the East European Judenrate—the Reichsvereinigung, or National Union of Jews in Germany. He suggests a complicated picture of complicity and resistance, of acquiescence and struggle.

* 2.39 *
Bor, Josef. *The Terezin Requiem*. New York: Avon, 1978. LC 79-396915.

Raphael Schächter was a young orchestra conductor, imprisoned in the Terezin concentration camp. Schächter was determined to perform Verdi's Requiem at the camp, feeling that it captured the fate and hope of his people. Despite overwhelming odds, he succeeded. It is an inspiring story of human dignity and determination.

* 2.40 *
Dobroszycki, Lucjan, ed. *Chronicle of the Lodz Ghetto, 1941-1944*. New Haven: Yale University Press, 1984. LC 84-3614. ISBN 0-300-03208-0.

Lodz was the second largest ghetto. It originally contained 163,000 people with deportees continually being added from elsewhere. When the war ended, 877 Jews were left. The Department of Archives in the ghetto worked to record everything that went on. Dobroszycki, a survivor of the ghetto, provides the introduction and analysis of these excerpts from the archives.

* 2.41 *
Gutman, Yisrael. *The Jews of Warsaw, 1939-1943: Ghetto, Underground, Revolt*. Bloomington: Indiana University Press, 1982. LC 81-47570. ISBN 0-253-33174-9.

In order to understand the Warsaw Ghetto uprising, Gutman looks beyond the ghetto itself to consider the broader character of Jewish public life as it took shape during the occupation and ghettoization periods. A survivor of the uprising, he argues that the Poles could have done more, particularly the Armia Krajowa, the Home Army. Once the uprising began in the spring of 1943, the Jews were supported by the relatively weak and poorly armed Communist resistance, the Armia Ludowa, but were brutally opposed by the Polish Right.

* 2.42 *
Hilberg, Raul, Stanislaw Staron, and Josef Kermisz, eds. *The Warsaw Diary of Adam Czerniakow*. New York: Stein and Day, 1979. LC 78-9272. ISBN 0-8128-2523-3.

The diary begins in 1939 when Czerniakow became the head of the Warsaw Judenrat and ends abruptly on 23 July 1942, the day of his death. Czerniakow gives historical information and records the day-to-day problems of a Jewish bureaucrat trying to function under intolerable circumstances. His diary entries show him to have been a courageous man crushed by the terrible burdens he faced. He took his life in the summer of 1942 rather than give orders for deportations.

* 2.43 *
Jagendorff, Siegfried. *Jagendorf's Foundry: Memoir of the Romanian Holocaust, 1941-1944*. Ed. by Aron Hirt-Manheimer. New York: Harper Collins, 1991. LC 90-55540. ISBN 0-06-016106-X.

In the fall of 1941, Romania exiled an estimated 150,000 Jews to Moghiliev-Podolski in the Occupied Soviet Ukraine. The 56-year-old Siegfried Jagendorf was among the deportees. He took control of the Jewish ghetto and established a hospital, a soup kitchen, and orphanages. With a hand-picked team of Jewish professionals and craftsmen, Jagendorf restored a foundry that became the center of an effort that would save over 10,000 lives. In this memoir, skillfully edited and commented on by Hirt-Manheimer, Jagendorf chronicles the daily struggles of the deportees and how they were saved.

* 2.44 *
Kaplan, Chaim. *Scroll of Agony*. New York: Macmillan, 1965. LC 64-12533.

Kaplan, a Hebrew school principal who lived in Warsaw and died not long after deportations began in 1942, chronicles daily activities in the Warsaw Ghetto from September 1939 to August 1942. It is a record of persecution, the Nazi conquest of Poland, the relationship of the Jews with their Polish neighbors, and the internal life of the ghetto.

* 2.45 *
Korczak, Janusz. *Ghetto Diary*. New York: Schocken Press, 1978. LC 78-398298.

In this diary, a courageous Warsaw pediatrician and head of a Jewish orphanage reveals his thoughts and feelings. What emerges is a picture of a man of compassion and dignity who stayed in the ghetto with his charges. He has become a symbol of selfless devotion.

* 2.46 *
Ringelblum, Emmanuel. *Notes from the Warsaw Ghetto: The Journal of Emmanuel Ringelblum*. New York: Schocken Press, 1975. LC 74-10147.

Ringelbaum's *Journal* is an invaluable source on the organization, religious life, and human side of the ghetto. The notes, which go up to the uprising in 1943, reveal, in powerful and poignant detail the impact of the war on the daily life and fate of the ghetto Jews. It is one of the classic works on the Holocaust, written by a perceptive social historian.

* 2.47 *
Tory, Avraham. *Surviving the Holocaust: The Kovno Ghetto Diary*. Ed. by Martin Gilbert. Cambridge, MA: Harvard University Press, 1990. ISBN 0-674-85811-5.

Tory's diary is an account of life and death in the ghetto of Kovno, Lithuania, from June 1941 to January 1944. It incorporates his collection of official documents, Jewish council reports and original photographs and drawings made in the ghetto. He shows the determination of the Jews to sustain their community in the midst of terror.

* 2.48 *
Trunk, Isaiah. *Judenrat: The Jewish Councils in Eastern Europe under Nazi Occupation*. New York: Macmillan, 1972. LC 70-173692.

Trunk attempts to deal with the perplexing problem of the Jewish councils under Nazi occupation. He focuses on the conditions, external and internal, under which they performed and their motivations and results. Unlike Arendt, who was quick to generalize, Trunk relies on detail and nuance. He emphasizes that the context was constant terror, death, and intimidation. Some Councils supported resistance and others opposed it. Some were run well and democratic; others were corrupt and class-ridden.

* 2.49 *
Tushnet, Leonard. *The Pavement of Hell*. New York: St. Martin's Press, 1975. LC 73-87395.

Tushnet studied the behavior of the leaders of the Judenrat of Warsaw, Lodz, and Vilna, using archival material and interviews with survivors. The conclusions concerning these men are still controversial. Tushnet believes Czerniakow, Rumkowski, and Gens were men who had good intentions with very limited options. Criticism of them should be tempered by the context.

CONCENTRATION CAMPS

* 2.50 *
Abzug, Robert H. *Inside the Vicious Heart: Americans and the Liberation of Nazi Concentration Camps*. New York: Oxford University Press, 1985. LC 84-27252. ISBN 0-19-503597-6.

Allied soldiers liberated concentration camps at Buchenwald, Dachau, Bergen Belsen, Mauthausen, Ohrdruf, and Nordhausen, and other sites. Abzug attempts to assess their impact on the liberating soldiers. He captures their emotions—a combination of shock, anger, shame, guilt, disgust, and fear. He also attempts to understand the immediate and long-range consequences of their discoveries on the public mind.

* 2.51 *
Arad, Yitzchak. *Belzec, Sobibor, Treblinka: The Operation Reinhard Death Camps*. Bloomington: Indiana University Press, 1987. LC 85-45883. ISBN 0-253-34293-7.

Between 1942 and 1943, under the code name Operation Reinhard, more than 1 1/2 million Jews were gassed in the concentration camps of Belzec, Sobibor, and Treblinka, located in Nazi-occupied Poland. There were less than 200 Jewish survivors. Arad describes these camps with meticulous detail—their physical layouts, the process of extermination, the revolts and escapes, the day-to-day lives of those spared immediate deaths.

* 2.52 *
Borkin, Joseph. *The Crime and Punishment of I. G. Farben*. New York: Pocket Books, 1979. ISBN 0-671-82755-3.

Founded in 1925, I. G. Farben was a huge chemical conglomerate in Germany. During the Nazi era, Farben mobilized to support the war. Building and operating the slave-labor camp at Auschwitz, it was responsible for the deaths of thousands of prisoners. About 35,000 slaves were used at Auschwitz. Over 25,000 died. I. G. Farben derived huge profits from its subsidiary, DEGESH, which manufactured Zyklon B, the gas used to annihilate hundreds of thousands of people in Auschwitz's gas chambers. Borkin chronicles this tragic tale and the relatively light punishment meted out to its chief executives. As the cold war intensified, it apparently was in American interests to have a strong Germany as a buffer to the Soviets. Hence the leniency of the courts.

* 2.53 *
Des Pres, Terrence. *The Survivor: An Anthology of Life in the Death Camps*. New York: Oxford University Press, 1976. LC 75-25468.

In a landmark study and analysis of the phenomenon of the survivor, Des Pres interprets survivor memoirs, by such authors as Chaim Kaplan, Alexander Donat, Primo Levi, Gerda Klein, Elie Wiesel, and others. He chronicles both the inhuman suffering and the inspiring dignity of the survivor. He argues that there is a "system" to survival, the existence of a biological-ethical imperative to survive. The memoirs he cites provide an immediacy to the experience and immerse the reader in the emotional horror of the camps.

* 2.54 *
Feig, Konnilyn. *Hitler's Death Camps: The Sanity of Madness*. New York: Holmes & Meier, 1979. LC 81-140. ISBN 0-8419-0675-0.

Hitler's Death Camps is a well-documented history of the nineteen major collection and annihilation camps used by the Nazis against the Jews. Notwithstanding the horror of these places, they operated efficiently and all too effectively. This was their "sanity." Feig also examines the indifference of the Allies and the Polish government in exile.

* 2.55 *
Ferencz, Benjamin B. *Less Than Slaves: Jewish Forced Labor and the Quest for Compensation*. Cambridge, MA: Harvard University Press, 1979. LC 79-10690. ISBN 0-674-52525-6.

Ferencz describes the complicity of major German firms in the Holocaust, particularly on the issue of slave labor and their refusal to accept either legal or moral responsibility for their crimes. Ferencz also analyzes the post-war trials of the major actors and why they received such light sentences.

* 2.56 *
Pawelczynska, Anna. *Values and Violence in Auschwitz: A Sociological Analysis*. Berkeley: University of California Press, 1979. LC 76-3886. ISBN 0-520-03210-1.

The author, a Polish sociologist and survivor of Auschwitz, brings social science insights and techniques to an examination of the sociology of survival in Auschwitz. She discusses the effect of differences in social background on survival. She challenges Bettelheim's theory that those who identified with their aggressors were best able to survive. She found, instead, that inmates who shared and who maintained their humanity defied camp conditions. She corroborates Viktor Frankl's insight that individuals were not powerless to affect their fate. Survival for some purpose and having a vision of life after the camps were useful coping mechanisms.

SURVIVOR ACCOUNTS

* 2.57 *
Delbo, Charlotte. *None of Us Will Return*. Boston: Beacon Press, 1968. LC 68-20635.

Delbo, a non-Jewish survivor of Auschwitz and other concentration camps, provides a powerful, stark account of her experiences.

* 2.58 *
Donat, Alexander. *The Holocaust Kingdom: A Memoir*. New York: Schocken, 1978. LC 77-89067.

In one of the more powerful and insightful Holocaust memoirs, Donat, a Polish Jew, tells how he and his wife and son survived the Warsaw Ghetto and Maidanek. His memoir, though notable for its restraint, provides extensive details of his experiences. There is the anguish of self-doubt as Donat reflects on the meaning of life and death.

* 2.59 *
Fenelon, Fania. *Playing for Time*. New York: Atheneum, 1977. LC 77-5502. ISBN 0-689-10796-X.

The author was a member of the Women's Orchestra in Auschwitz for eleven months. Her book provides revealing descriptions of this aspect of camp life.

* 2.60 *
Flinker, Moshe. *Young Moshe's Diary*. New York: Board of Jewish Education, 1971. LC 70-287609.

Like Anne Frank, Flinker kept a diary of his Holocaust experiences. The Flinkers were Orthodox Jews who lived in Holland. They fled to Belgium where they lived until they were betrayed by an informer. The family was sent to Auschwitz where the parents and their eighteen-year old son, Moshe, were killed. In this reflective diary, the gifted Moshe struggles with questions of Jewish suffering and God's justice. He engages in a theodicy which rivals some of the most probing examinations. While he questions divine justice, he pleads for his people. He is also consumed by guilt because he is not sharing in their suffering.

* 2.61 *
Frank, Anne. *The Diary of a Young Girl*. New York: Doubleday, 1952. LC 52-6355. First published in 1947 in Holland under the title *Het Achterhuis*.

A young Jewish girl, with her parents and sister, hid in an attic in Amsterdam for more than two years during which time she kept a diary. The diary tells of her fears, frustrations, hopes, her growing into young womanhood. It is very perceptive and poignant, providing her responses to the wonder of growing up and to the terror of being a Jew in Nazi Europe. She has become the symbol of the Jewish tragedy for the non-Jewish world. This is perhaps the most widely known of all the Holocaust books.

* 2.62 *
Hillesum, Etty. *An Interrupted Life: The Diaries of Etty Hillesum*. New York: Pantheon, 1983. LC 83-47750. ISBN 0-394-53217-1.

Hillesum, a highly educated and assimilated Dutch Jew was a remarkable young women who kept her journals from 1941-43. Her entries are intimate and frank. The Holocaust enters obliquely. She notes the appearance of a German soldier, the suicide of a professor, the relentless proliferation of restrictions. We see her transformation from a pleasure-seeking young woman into a person capable of confronting deep moral and religious questions. The diary ends in September 1943 on her deportation to Auschwitz where she died.

* 2.63 *
Klein, Gerda. *All but My Life*. New York: Hill & Wang, 1957. LC 57-12226.

Gerda Klein was fifteen when the Nazis invaded her native Poland. In her powerful narrative, she speaks of friendship and cooperation among the victims, the struggle to survive, and the horrors of the camps. It ends on the positive note of liberation and the journey to rebuild a shattered life.

* 2.64 *
Leitner, Isabella. *Fragments of Isabella: A Memoir of Auschwitz*. New York: Crowell, 1978. LC 78-4766. ISBN 0-690-01779-0.

This is a brief, sometimes angry memoir of a Hungarian Jewish survivor who was in her teens when transported to Auschwitz with her five siblings and mother. She is slow to forgive the Germans.

* 2.65 *
Leitner, Isabella. *Saving the Fragments: From Auschwitz to New York*. New York: New American Library, 1985. LC 85-8815. ISBN 0-453-00502-0.

Leitner continues her story with the liberation. She tells of her journey, with her two surviving sisters, to the United States where they are reunited with their father.

* 2.66 *
Levi, Primo. *If This Is a Man*. Trans. from the Italian by Stuart Woolf. New York: Orion, 1959. LC 59-13327. Reprinted as *Survival in Auschwitz*. New York: Collier, 1961.

In one of the best-known of the Holocaust memoirs, Levi describes the absurd routines of the camp, how the black market worked, the struggle of survival. He has insightful comments about memory and falsification, friendship and human weakness, and the power of language. He is as interested in how human beings react to unspeakable torment as in what influences the tormentor. He argues forcefully against the simplification of the experience.

* 2.67 *
Muller, Filip. *Eyewitness Auschwitz*. Briarcliff Manor, NY: Stein & Day, 1979. LC 78-66257. ISBN 0-8128-2601-9.

In one of the most disturbing of Holocaust memoirs, the author depicts the life of a *Sonderkommando* who witnessed first-hand the horrors inside the crematoria and gas chambers. He somehow managed to survive as a *Sonderkommando* for three years and tells about his experiences in unbelievable detail. It makes for horrifying reading.

* 2.68 *
Nomberg-Przytyk, Sara. *Auschwitz: True Tales from a Grotesque Land*. Chapel Hill: University of North Carolina Press, 1985. LC 84-17386. ISBN 0-8078-1629-9.

This is a painful and powerful memoir of the author's experiences in Auschwitz. In this book, which she wrote twenty years after her liberation, she not only records unimaginable atrocities but also richly describes human dignity and courage. With understatement, she depicts a world where cruelty co-existed with nobility, indifference with compassion. As an attendant in Dr. Josef Mengele's hospital, Nomberg-Przytyk observed him closely and gives a detailed description of his activities.

* 2.69 *
Wells, Leon. *The Death Brigade*. New York: Schocken Press, 1978. ISBN 0-89604-000-3. First published as *The Janowska Road*.

Wells was a youth in Lvov, Poland, when the Germans put him on the Death Brigade whose task was to destroy any traces of mass executions at the Janowska concentration camp. Among the most moving accounts is the narration of the death of his entire family. He also describes the collaboration of the Ukranian peasants with the Germans. This is one of the most revealing Holocaust texts.

RESCUE

* 2.70 *
Bierman, John. *Righteous Gentile*. New York: Viking, 1981. LC 80-52465. ISBN 0-670-74924-9.

Raoul Wallenberg, the "righteous gentile," was the Swedish diplomat who helped rescue from 30,000 to 100,000 Hungarian Jews. The first part of the book chronicles Wallenberg's life, particularly his activities in Budapest from July 1944 to his disappearance in January 1945. The second half deals with what is believed to have happened to him in the Soviet Union. Bierman is critical of the Swedish, U.S., Hungarian, and Israeli governments for not adequately pursuing the search for him.

* 2.71 *
Flender, Harold. *Rescue in Denmark*. New York: McFadden-Bartell, 1964. NUC 72-18668.

At great risk to themselves, the Danish people initially hid the Jews and helped them flee to Sweden. Flender suggests that the traditions of Danish democracy were the key here.

* 2.72 *
Friedman, Philip. *Their Brothers' Keepers*. New York: Crown Publishers, 1957. LC 57-8773.

Friedman examines Christians who helped Jews, such as Archbishop Stepanic in Croatia, Jesuit Father Pierre Chaillet, Raoul Wallenberg, and Anna Simaite in Lithuania.

* 2.73 *
Geis, Miep, with Alison Leslie Gols. *Anne Frank Remembered*. New York: Simon & Schuster, 1987. LC 86-25991. ISBN 0-671-54721-2.

Geis was one of the people who helped hide the Frank Family. Her story fills in the gaps left by Anne's diary, not only by providing information on events outside the time frame of the diary, but on events outside the world of the Annex, thus putting the diary into historical perspective.

* 2.74 *
Hallie, Philip. *Lest Innocent Blood Be Shed*. New York: Harper & Row, 1979. LC 77-11825. ISBN 0-7181-1831-6.

Hallie chronicles the remarkable story of how the entire village of Chambon-sur-Lignon, dominated by two charismatic Protestant pastors, saved several thousand Jews from the Nazis and the Vichy police. Hallie emphasizes the importance of moral action and leadership. People do have a choice.

* 2.75 *
Michaelis, Meir. *Mussolini and the Jews: German-Italian Relations and the Jewish Question in Italy*. Oxford: Oxford University Press, 1978. LC 78-40260. ISBN 0-19-822542-3.

Michaelis argues that anti-Semitism in Italy was muted because Jews were relatively well-integrated. The fascists and Mussolini were not really committed to the persecution of the Jews and that is primarily why so few died.

* 2.76 *
Oliner, Samuel P., and Pearl M. Oliner. *The Altruistic Personality: Rescuers of Jews in Nazi Europe*. New York: The Free Press, 1988. LC 87-33223. ISBN 0-02-923830-7.

The Oliners undertook the massive Altruistic Personality Project to understand why thousands would risk their lives to save Jews. Drawing on the data from this study and over 700 interviews with rescuers and nonrescuers, they found that those who intervened shared several characteristics, including a deep-seated empathy developed in childhood. They also discovered that many rescuers were influenced by the examples set by others including friends, church, and community groups. Rescuers felt a sense of responsibility for the oppressed and believed their actions could make a difference. It is carefully researched and wonderfully written and contains an engrossing collection of episodes of altruism.

* 2.77 *
Rosenfeld, Harvey. *Raoul Wallenberg, Angel of Rescue*. New York: Prometheus Press, 1982. LC 81-86333. ISBN 0-87975-177-0.

Rosenfeld is editor of *Martyrdom and Resistance*, the longest running periodical devoted to the Holocaust. His is a balanced and scholarly treatment of Wallenberg's career and postwar disappearance.

* 2.78 *
Tec, Nechama. *Dry Tears: The Story of a Lost Childhood*. New York: Oxford University Press, 1984. ISBN 0-19-503500-3.

In a compelling account, the young Tec describes how she survived in Nazi-occupied Poland by living with Polish gentiles. She presents the ordeal from the perspective of an adult who is now a professor of sociology at the University of Connecticut.

* 2.79 *
Tec, Nechama. *In the Lion's Den: The Life of Oswald Rufeisen*. New York: Oxford University Press, 1990. ISBN 0-19-503505-X.

Tec vividly recounts the story of Rufeisen, a Jew who passed as a Christian in Nazi-occupied Poland, and risked his life to save hundreds of other Jews. Eventually discovered, Rufeisen escaped and found shelter in a convent, where he converted to Catholicism.

* 2.80 *
Tec, Nechama. *When Light Pierced the Darkness: Christian Rescue of Jews in Nazi-Occupied Poland*. New York: Oxford University Press, 1986. ISBN 0-19-503643-3.

With data taken from published accounts, archival records and personal interviews, Tec studies the Poles who rescued Jews. She found that the rescuers tended to be individualists, self-reliant and have a broad commitment to stand up for the helpless. They were unassuming and did not begin their rescue activities with much pre-meditation. The introduction provides an excellent overview of rescue activities.

* 2.81 *
Yahil, Leni. *The Rescue of Danish Jewry: Test of a Democracy*. Trans. by Morris Gradel. Philadelphia: Jewish Publication Society, 1969. LC 69-19039. ISBN 0-8276-02324-4.

Yahil recounts the position of the Jewish community in Denmark, the daring rescue operations, and the important contribution made by many Swedish people. She clarifies certain legends that developed around Denmark's King Christian X. For instance, he indeed supported Jews but did not wear a yellow star. Yahil contends that the Danes were so forthright in rescue due to their deep-seated democratic tradition.

* 2.82 *
Zuccotti, Susan. *The Italians and the Holocaust: Persecution, Rescue and Survival*. New York: Basic Books, 1987. LC 86-47738. ISBN 0-465-03622-8.

Zuccotti chronicles and analyzes the extent of Italian opposition to the deportation and murder of Italian Jews. She provides the historical, cultural, and political context for the relative tolerance enjoyed by Italian Jews. Because anti-Semitism was not a major factor in Italian society, there was little sympathy for the mass murder of the Jews. About eighty-five percent of the 45,000 Jews in Italy during the German occupation survived because non-Jewish Italians were willing to help them even if the Pope resolved not to be involved. Many of the 6,800 who were killed were betrayed by informers. This is the best study of the subject.

THE INDIFFERENCE OF THE WORLD

* 2.83 *
Abella, Irving, and Harold Troper. *None Is Too Many*. New York: Random House, 1983. LC 83-42864. ISBN 0-394-53328-3.

The authors tell the tragic story of Canada's refusal to assist Jewish refugees because of pettiness, misunderstanding, and anti-Semitism. Only 4,000 Jews were admitted into Canada during this period.

* 2.84 *
Bauer, Yehuda. *American Jewry and the Holocaust*. Detroit: Wayne State University Press, 1981. LC 80-26035. ISBN 0-8143-1672-7.

Bauer traces the activities of the American Jewish Joint Distribution Committee (JDC). JDC acted as best it could, Bauer concludes, to assist Europe's threatened Jews.

* 2.85 *
Bauer, Yehuda. *Flight and Rescue*. New York: Random House, 1970. LC 74-85602.

Bauer offers a well-documented account of the organized escape of Eastern European Jews from 1944-48. Almost 300,000 Jews who survived the Holocaust began to move out of Eastern Europe in the last months of the war. The movement was known as *Brichah* (flight, in Hebrew), the name of the organization formed in Palestine to co-ordinate the effort.

* 2.86 *
Baumel, Judith Tydor. *Unfulfilled Promise: Rescue and Resettlement of Jewish Refugee Children in the United States 1934-1945*. Juneau, AK: The Denali Press, 1990. LC 90-32118. ISBN 0-938737-21-X.

Baumel analyzes the role of the U.S. government, voluntary agencies, the general and Jewish communities, and public opinion in the rescue and resettlement of approximately one thousand unaccompanied Jewish children who came to the United States from 1934-45. She discusses their adjustment to American society as well as the anti-Semitism and apathy they encountered.

* 2.87 *
Dinnerstein, Leonard. *America and the Survivors of the Holocaust*. New York: Columbia University Press, 1982. LC 81-15443. ISBN 0-231-04187-4.

In a disturbing study, Dinnerstein reveals the callous attitude of America towards the victims of the Holocaust. He discusses anti-Semitism in Congress and in the military occupation forces. Jewish victims often fared worse than their German oppressors. The U.S. State Department also made it difficult for Jews to obtain visas.

* 2.88 *
Falconi, Carlo. *The Silence of Pius XII*. London: Faber, 1970. LC 73-564569. ISBN 0-571-09147-4. Boston: Little Brown, 1970. LC 78-79360.

Falconi, a Papal historian, defends Pius. He didn't speak out because he was more fearful of communism; he understood the Catholics were not ready to risk their lives for Jews; and most important, because of his concern for protecting the church in Europe. Falconi stresses that Pius XII's policy was not a break with his predecessor, Pius XI, who said nothing when antisemitic laws were passed in Germany in 1933-35. Personally, Pius XII helped save many Jewish lives.

* 2.89 *
Feingold, Henry L. *The Politics of Rescue: The Roosevelt Administration and the Holocaust, 1939-1945*. New Brunswick, NJ: Rutgers University Press, 1970. LC 75-127049. ISBN 0-8135-0664-6. Reprint. New York: Holocaust Library, 1980.

In a pathbreaking study, Feingold investigates what Franklin Roosevelt, the Congress, the State Department, and other agencies did, and did not do, during the Holocaust to rescue Jews. He indicts a number of key people, perhaps none more than Assistant Secretary of State Breckenridge Long, who set up roadblocks to rescue attempts. This is a book about official indifference to the plight of the Jews.

* 2.90 *
Friedlander, Saul. *Pius XII and the Third Reich*. New York: Alfred Knopf, 1966. LC 66-10029.

Friedlander makes a strong case for Pius' attitude favoring Germany. What the Pope feared most was a communist takeover of Europe. That accounts for his relative silence and inactivity. Friedlander concurs with Falconi's evaluation that the Pope's response to Nazi Germany was conditioned by fear of communism, his Germanophilia and his desire to perpetuate the influence of the church. Pius believed that this was more possible in totalitarian states of the right than of the left.

* 2.91 *
Friedman, Saul S. *No Haven for the Oppressed*. Detroit: Wayne State University Press, 1973. LC 72-2271. ISBN 0-8143-1474-0.

Friedman argues that U.S. policy was basically indifferent to the plight of Jewish refugees. He describes the impact of the Depression, isolationism and F.D.R.'s unwillingness to challenge the Congress as the principal factors involved. He also characterizes the relationship between Rabbi Stephen S. Wise, the President of the American Jewish Congress, and F.D.R. as a "partnership in silence."

* 2.92 *
Gilbert, Martin. *Auschwitz and the Allies*. New York: Holt, 1981. LC 80-28911. ISBN 0-03-059284-4.

Gilbert relates the tragic story of allied unwillingness to recognize or acknowledge the Nazi genocide. Most of this reluctance was deliberate, Gilbert found. He isolates individuals like Anthony Eden and B. Long, who failed to pass on vital information. Others who were part of this "conspiracy of silence" were John J. McCloy, Assistant Secretary of War, and Sir A.W.G. Randall of England's Refugee Section.

* 2.93 *
Hochhuth, Rolf. *The Deputy*. Trans. by Richard and Clara Winston. New York: Grove, 1964. LC 64-13776. Originally published in Germany as *Der Stellvertreter*.

Hochhuth is responsible for raising the disturbing question of the Vatican's complicity in the Holocaust. Produced in 1963, this play created an uproar in both Europe and America with its claims concerning the unwillingness of Pius XII to speak out against Roman Catholic atrocities after having been personally apprised of the existence of extermination camps. The hero is a Roman Catholic priest who tries to fight the Vatican's lack of involvement.

* 2.94 *
Laqueur, Walter, and Richard Breitman. *Breaking the Silence*. New York: Simon & Schuster, 1986. LC 86-1931. ISBN 0-671-54694-5.

Gerhard Riegner, the representative of the World Jewish Congress in Switzerland, was one of the first to alert the West to the Nazi genocide. This book reveals that his source was Edward Schulte, a prominent German businessman in touch with Allied Intelligence.

* 2.95 *
Laqueur, Walter. *The Terrible Secret: Suppression of the Truth about Hitler's "Final Solution."* Boston: Little, Brown, 1980. LC 80-26613. ISBN 0-316-51474-8.

Laqueur reviews the many paths by which information seeped out of Nazi-occupied Europe. The Polish underground played a pivotal role here, notwithstanding the presence of anti-Semitism among the Polish leadership. He discusses the distinction between "knowing" and "believing." Laqueur concludes that the neutral nations such as Switzerland, Sweden, and Turkey, as well as the Vatican and the International Red Cross were almost fully aware of the plight of the Jews.

* 2.96 *
Lewy, Guenter. *The Catholic Church and Nazi Germany*. New York: McGraw-Hill, 1964. LC 64-21072.

Lewy largely corroborates Hochhuth's allegations. He points to the Church's paranoical fear of Bolshevism and traditional anti-Semitism as factors that led the Vatican to silence criticism of the Nazis. On the positive side, Lewy acknowledges Catholics who saved Jews.

* 2.97 *
Lipstadt, Deborah E. *Beyond Belief: The American Press and the Coming of the Holocaust, 1933-1945*. New York: The Free Press, 1985. LC 85-16243. ISBN 0-02-919160-2.

Lipstadt analyzes how the American press treated the Holocaust. She shows how the press persistently ignored the scope and significance of the developing tragedy. Editors remained skeptical and journalists often toned down their stories. She raises the distinction between knowledge and understanding.

* 2.98 *
Morse, Arthur D. *While Six Million Died: A Chronicle of American Apathy*. New York: Random House, 1968. LC 68-141031.

In one of the first studies criticizing American complicity in the Holocaust, Morse accuses American officials and elements in the American-Jewish community of not taking the plight of European Jews seriously enough. Because he relies only on published sources, some of which are untrustworthy, Morse makes some errors in fact and interpretation. He finds a combination of political expediency, isolationism, indifference, and raw anti-Semitism behind American apathy.

* 2.99 *
Penkower, Monty N. *The Jews Were Expendable: Free World Diplomacy and the Holocaust*. Urbana: University of Illinois Press, 1983. LC 82-17490. ISBN 0-252-00747-6.

In a well-researched study of international indifference to the plight of the Jews, Penkower contends that saving the Jews was not a priority since it did not directly contribute to victory. His chapters on the relative silence of the International Red Cross and the failure to rescue the Jews of Hungary are excellent.

* 2.100 *
Porat, Dina. *The Blue and the Yellow Stars of David: The Zionist Leadership in Palestine and the Holocaust, 1939-1945*. Cambridge, MA: Harvard University Press, 1990. ISBN 0-674-07708-3.

Porat investigates how and when the Zionist leadership in Palestine fully understood that European Jewry was facing annihilation; what rescue plans were developed; and why they were so ineffective. She essentially exonerates the Zionists.

* 2.101 *
Ross, Robert W. *So It Was True: The American Protestant Press and the Nazi Persecution of the Jews*. Minneapolis: University of Minnesota Press, 1980. LC 80-196. ISBN 0-8166-0948-9.

In a thoroughly documented study of fifty-two Protestant periodicals from 1933-45, Ross shows that hundreds of articles and editorials dealt with what was happening to the Jews. The Christian press provided all the details but was not forceful enough in protesting.

* 2.102 *
Wasserstein, Bernard. *Britain and the Jews of Europe, 1939-1945*. London: Oxford University Press, 1979. LC 79-40406. ISBN 0-19-822600-4.

The British did very little to help European Jewry. Anti-Semitism in the Foreign Office was a considerable factor as was its sensitivity to Arab feelings in Palestine. Most importantly, within the context of a total war effort, aid to the Jews of Europe was seen as a low priority.

* 2.103 *
Wyman, David S. *The Abandonment of the Jews: America and the Holocaust, 1941-1945*. New York: Pantheon, 1984. LC 84-42711. ISBN 0-394-42813-7.

F.D.R. and Congress failed to act. F.D.R. felt that action on behalf of Jews meant trouble politically. Members of Congress were negligent, as were Christian churches, the media, the Zionists and some prominent Jews. Wyman's concluding suggestions regarding what might have been done to save Jews are very suggestive. His is the best book on the subject.

* 2.104 *
Wyman, David S. *Paper Walls*. Amherst, MA: University of Massachusetts Press, 1968. LC 74-26913.

Wyman notes three principal reasons why the U.S. granted only 150,000 visas to Jews fleeing Europe from 1938-41: unemployment in the U.S., Nativism, and anti-Semitism.

JEWISH RESISTANCE

* 2.105 *
Ainsztein, Reuben. *Jewish Resistance in Nazi-occupied Eastern Europe*. New York: Harper & Row, 1975. LC 74-1759. ISBN 0-06-4900030-4.

Ainsztein explodes the myth of Jewish passivity. There was significant Jewish resistance in the ghettos, in the forests of Poland and Russia, and even in the concentration camps. This occurred despite the overwhelming force and terror of the Nazis. He also strongly criticizes the Poles and Soviets for not doing more to help the Jews.

* 2.106 *
Mark, Ber. *Uprising in the Warsaw Ghetto*. New York: Schocken, 1975. LC 74-26913.

It took the Nazis longer to quell the Warsaw uprising than it had taken them to defeat entire countries. The revolt lasted from mid-April to May in 1943 and, although it failed, it did have important consequences. The Jewish struggle spurred renewed efforts by the Poles and it became a symbol of Jewish resistance. The author, a Polish historian, has twice revised this work.

* 2.107 *
Eckman, Lester, and Chaim Lazar. *The Jewish Resistance*. New York: Shengold, 1977. LC 77-84749. ISBN 0-88400-050-8.

Eckman and Lazar recount the history of the Jewish partisans in Lithuania and White Russia. They provide details of physical resistance against enormous odds. Thousands of Jews fought in mixed units, under Soviet control, and in Jewish partisan units. The authors document Ukranian anti-Semitism as well.

* 2.108 *
Suhl, Yuri, ed. *They Fought Back: The Story of Jewish Resistance in Nazi Europe*. New York: Schocken, 1975. LC 74-26766.

In this anthology of thirty-four essays and eyewitness accounts dealing with the issue of resistance, the editor develops the contention that there was significant resistance against the Nazis despite few weapons, a hostile native population, and little experience with armed conflict.

SELECTED FICTION

* 2.109 *
Appelfeld, Aharon. *The Age of Wonders*. Boston: David R. Godine, 1981. LC 81-47318. ISBN 0-87923-402-4.

Appelfeld, a noted Israeli author, tells this story from the point of view of a ten-year-old boy named Bruno whose parents are assimilated Jewish intellectuals. Both of Bruno's parents despise the Jewish middle class. They also refuse to consider the possibility that the growing anti-Semitism in Austria could affect them. They are wrong.

* 2.110 *
Appelfeld, Aharon. *Badenheim 1939*. Boston: David R. Godine, 1980. LC 80-66192. ISBN 0-87923-342-7.

In this short, sparse novel, Appelfeld has written an understated, but powerful, metaphorical piece on impending doom. The novel is set in a resort town near Vienna where a group of cultured Jews are brought in the spring of 1939. Something is wrong. Finally they all board the boxcars that will take them to their fate.

* 2.111 *
Appelfeld, Aharon. *Tzili: The Story of a Life*. New York: Dutton, 1984. LC 83-24991. ISBN 0-14-007058-3.

Tzili, a young Jewish girl, is the subject of neglect and ridicule because she is considered "simple-minded." With the onset of war, she is left to fend for herself while her family flees. Her wandering, suffering, and abandonment can serve as a metaphor for all Jews.

* 2.112 *
Borowski, Tadeusz. *This Way to the Gas, Ladies and Gentlemen*. New York: Viking, 1967. LC 67-21889.

A non-Jewish survivor of Auschwitz describes the conditions in the death camps with remarkable understatement. This work is among the best short fiction on the Holocaust because Borowski is able to penetrate into the minds of the participants and witnesses.

* 2.113 *
Grossman, David. *See Under: Love*. New York: Farrar Straus Giroux, 1989. ISBN 0-374-25731-0.

In 1959 a nine-year-old Israeli boy concludes, from the murmuring of his parents that the "Nazi beast" is living in their cellar. As a child he sets out to tame it; as an adult he attempts to come to terms with it by creating mythic tales. This extraordinary, mythic novel about the Holocaust by a gifted young Israeli novelist is rich in symbolism.

* 2.114 *
Heyen, William. *Erika: Poems of the Holocaust*. New York: The Vanguard Press, 1977, 1984. LC 83-14671. ISBN 0-8149-0875-6.

Heyen is the son of a German who emigrated to America in 1928 and the nephew of a Nazi flyer shot down in the Soviet Union. He tries in these poems to discover how deeply he is attached to his German heritage and how far he must repudiate it.

* 2.115 *
Heyen, William. *The Swastika Poems*. New York: The Vanguard Press, 1977. LC 76-39729. ISBN 0-8149-0780-6.

Heyen continues to develop the aforementioned themes and conflicts.

* 2.116 *
Chodziesner, Gertrud. *Dark Soliloquy*. Trans. and with an introduction by Henry A. Smith. New York: Seabury, 1975. LC 75-2239. ISBN 0-8164-9199-2.

These lovely poems, sensitive yet powerful, were written during the Holocaust. The author, also known as Gertrud Kolmar, died at Auschwitz. Her poetry portends and laments the impending doom. Years before the Holocaust took place, she described the lonely, helpless position of the Jew in a world deaf to their cries for justice.

* 2.117 *
Sachs, Nelly. *O the Chimneys*. New York: Farrar, Strauss, 1967. LC 67-27518.

Sachs, the Nobel laureate of 1966, turns to the Bible, Jewish history, and Kabbalistic sources to provide a background for her Holocaust poetry. Born in Germany, she escaped to freedom in Sweden. Her poetry is consumed by sadness and loneliness.

* 2.118 *
Spiegelman, Art. *Maus: A Survivor's Tale*. New York: Pantheon, 1986. LC 86-42642. ISBN 0-394-74723-2.

Spiegelman, a cartoonist, uses this medium in a highly original fashion to tell the story of his father, Vladek, and his mother, Anja, both survivors of Auschwitz. The Jews are mice, the Nazis are cats, the Poles are pigs, the French are frogs, and the Americans are dogs. The animal characters create a distancing effect that allows the reader to follow the fable without being numbed by the inhuman horrors. In 1968 Anja committed suicide and the book ends with Artie calling his father a murderer for having destroyed Anja's memoirs without even reading them. It is very perceptive on relationships between survivors and their children.

* 2.119 *
Spiegelman, Art. *Maus II: A Survivor's Tale and Here My Troubles Began*. New York: Pantheon, 1991. ISBN 0-679-40641-7.

The first volume introduced readers to Valdek Spiegelman, a survivor of the Holocaust, and his son, a cartoonist trying to come to terms with his father, his father's experiences, guilt, and other feelings. The sequel moves from the barracks of Auschwitz to the bungalows of the Catskills. Spiegelman describes perceptively the traumas of survival against the background of a son's tortured relationships with his father. Spiegelman avoids sentimentalizing his tale. He writes with relentless honesty, sparing neither his father nor himself. He has found an original art form to add to what we know of the Holocaust experience. He won a Pulitzer Prize in 1992.

* 2.120 *
Wiesel, Elie. *Dawn*. Trans. from the French by Frances Frenayer. New York: Hill and Wang, 1961. LC 61-8461.

Wiesel is the best-known of all writers on the Holocaust. In this sequel to *Night*, a young survivor, now living in occupied Palestine, shifts from victim to executioner as he is ordered to kill a British hostage. Wiesel received the Nobel Peace Prize in 1986.

* 2.121 *
Wiesel, Elie. *Night*. Trans. from the French by Stella Rodeway. New York: Avon, 1969. LC 72-33106. First published in Yiddish in 1958.

Night is undoubtedly one of the most powerful and effective treatments of the Holocaust. As witness to the Holocaust, Wiesel remains firmly within the Judaic tradition of criticizing God for inaction. He emphasizes the centrality of memory.

* 2.122 *
Wiesenthal, Simon. *The Sunflower*. New York: Schocken, 1976. LC 75-35446. ISBN 0-8052-3612-0.

The first part of the book is an autobiographical moral tale about the issue of forgiveness. A dying German officer asks a Jewish prisoner for forgiveness. The Jew remains silent. The second part is a symposium of responses to the Jew's silence and the issue of forgiveness, by prominent theologians and philosophers.

REPRESENTATIONS AND REFLECTIONS ON THE HOLOCAUST

* 2.123 *
Alexander, Edward. *The Resonance of Dust*. Columbus: Ohio State University Press, 1979. LC 79-15515. ISBN 0-8142-0303-5.

Alexander analyzes the works of Sachs, Wiesel, Singer, Kovner, Bellow, and Kaplan. He explores the various themes that emerge in this literature including questions of memory and identity. What constraints are imposed on authors or readers of Holocaust literature? Is the Holocaust capable of literary representation?

* 2.124 *
Blatter, Janet, and Sybil Milton. *Art of the Holocaust*. New York: Rutledge Press, 1981. LC 81-5895. ISBN 0-8317-0418-7.

Blatter and Milton reproduce more than 350 works of art created by artists in ghettos, in hiding, or in the concentration camps. The authors' comments help to place them in historical perspective. The works reproduced in this collection reflect the spiritual resistance and courage of the artists.

* 2.125 *
Braham, Randolph L., ed. *Reflections of the Holocaust in Art and Literature*. New York: East European Monographs, 1990. LC 89-62260. ISBN 0-88033-965-9.

The contributors to this volume analyze the literary and artistic productions of people like Wiesel, Samuel Beckett, Samuel Pisar, and Aaron Zeitlin.

* 2.126 *
Costanza, Mary S. *The Living Witness; Art in Concentration Camps and Ghettos*. New York: Free Press, 1982. LC 81-70859. ISBN 0-02-906660-3.

Costanza has searched out and analyzed some of the most impressive Holocaust art. The art she found gives evidence of courage, moral and cultural resistance, and the desire of artists to depict through their art the horrors that they had witnessed and experienced.

* 2.127 *
Ezrahi, Sidra Dekoven. *By Words Alone: The Holocaust in Literature*. Chicago: University of Chicago Press, 1980. LC 79-56908. ISBN 0-226-23335-9.

Dealing with works written after the Holocaust, Ezrahi discusses the language of the Holocaust, documentation as art and the literature of survival. She attempts to define a Jewish "lamentation tradition" and examines certain authors from that perspective.

* 2.128 *
Fine, Ellen S. *Legacy of Night: The Literary Universe of Elie Wiesel*. Albany: State University of New York Press, 1982. LC 81-14601. ISBN 0-87395-589-7.

Fine considers the themes and literary approach that dominate Wiesel's writings. She carefully describes and analyzes Wiesel's commitment to memory, witnessing, Jewish identity, and the faith-doubt dialectic. Hers is one of the most insightful of analyses of Wiesel's work.

* 2.129 *
Green, Gerald. *The Artists of Terezin*. New York: Hawthorn, 1969. LC 69-16020.

The author of the television production "Holocaust" presents an account of the artists of Terezin with numerous reproductions of their work. He focuses on people like Otto Ungar, Bedrich Fritta, and Leo Haas.

* 2.130 *
Heinemann, Marlene. *Gender and Destiny: Women Writers and the Holocaust*. Westport, CT: Greenwood Press, 1986. LC 86-367. ISBN 0-313-24665-3.

Heinemann analyzes six works on the Holocaust by women writers including Charlotte Delbo. She addresses the difference in male and female "understandings" of the Holocaust.

* 2.131 *
Insdorf, Annette. *Indelible Shadows: Film and the Holocaust*. New York: Vintage Books, 1983. LC 82-48892. ISBN 0-394-71464-4.

After studying seventy-five films on the Holocaust, Insdorf asks whether this genre can be successful in treating a subject of such moral magnitude. She argues that there can be no unmediated testimony in film. Included are chapters on Hollywood and the new German guilt.

* 2.132 *
Knopp, Josephine Z. *The Trial of Judaism in Contemporary Jewish Writing*. Urbana: University of Illinois Press, 1975. LC 74-18319. ISBN 0-252-00386-1.

Knopp investigates Jewish writing after the Holocaust and concludes that Judaism is reaffirmed through the emergence of a moral code she calls "mentshlekhayt," which is central to the Jewish tradition.

* 2.133 *
Langer, Lawrence L. *The Holocaust and the Literary Imagination*. New Haven: Yale University Press, 1975. LC 75-8443. ISBN 0-300-1908-4.

Langer analyzes selective literary works around the theme of the aesthetic problem of reconciling normalcy with horror. He points out the inadequacies of language to cope with the problem of presenting the Holocaust to readers. Words like "suffering," "tragedy," and "dignity" are just inadequate.

* 2.134 *
Langer, Lawrence L. *Holocaust Testimonies*. New Haven: Yale University Press, 1991. ISBN 0-300-04966-8.

Langer's is the first sustained analysis of the unique ways in which oral testimony of survivors has contributed to our understanding of the Holocaust. Drawing on the Fortunoff Video Archives for Holocaust Testimonies at Yale University, Langer shows how oral testimonies complement historical material by providing the human dimension. He offers a critical analysis of the distinctions between written and oral testimony. Oral testimony is distinguished by the absence of literary mediation. See also 4.6.

* 2.135 *
Langer, Lawrence L. *Versions of Survival: The Holocaust and the Human Spirit*. Albany: State University of New York Press, 1982. LC 81-14560. ISBN 0-87395-583-8.

Langer analyzes theories of survival developed by Bettelheim, Frankl, and Des Pres. He focuses on the writing of Wiesel, Kolmar, and Sachs and argues against the literary or moral unity in Holocaust literature. He also challenges the notion that there is a prototypical survivor, or simple theory of survival by focusing on the interpretation of Holocaust memoirs and the "versions of survival" they illuminate. See also 4.7.

* 2.136 *
Morse, Jonathan. *Word by Word: The Language of Memory*. Ithaca, NY: Cornell University Press, 1990. LC 89-23931. ISBN 0-8014-2383-X.

The Holocaust is the central event in the history of language in the twentieth century, because one of its intended effects was the destruction of all memory of itself. This goal was partially achieved since survivors and others have had to use language that can never replicate the totality of the experience.

* 2.137 *
Rosenfeld, Alvin H. *A Double Dying: Reflections on Holocaust Literature*. Bloomington: Indiana University Press, 1980. LC 79-3006. ISBN 0-253-13337-8.

Rosenfeld argues that the literature of atrocity should be read on moral as well as artistic grounds. Using this perspective, he finds the literature of Wiesel, Levi, and Borowski, for example, to be effective while Styron's *Sophie's Choice* he finds inauthentic.

* 2.138 *
Young, James E. *Writing and Rewriting the Holocaust*. Bloomington: Indiana University Press, 1988. LC 87-35791. ISBN 0-253-36716-6.

Young examines how historical memory and understanding are created in Holocaust diaries, memoirs, fiction, poetry, drama, films, video testimony, and memorials. He is one of the first to critique how Holocaust memory is constructed and performed in video testimonies and memorial sites.

RELIGIOUS IMPLICATIONS

* 2.139 *
Berkovits, Eliezer. *Faith after the Holocaust*. New York: Ktav, 1973. LC 72-6256.

An Orthodox Jewish theologian interprets the Holocaust using classical rabbinic categories. He concludes that Christianity and Western civilization, not God, are responsible for the Holocaust. He argues for the theological necessity of the State of Israel.

* 2.140 *
Berkovits, Eliezer. *With God in Hell: Judaism in the Ghetto and Deathcamps*. Rockaway Beach, NY: Hebrew Publishing Co., 1979. ISBN 0-88482-937-5.

Berkovitz examines the behavior of religious Jews during the Holocaust and argues for the resiliency of the pious and the authentic and against complicity. He looks at the depths of their faith even in extremity.

* 2.141 *
Cargas, Harry James. *Shadows of Auschwitz: A Christian Response to the Holocaust*. New York: Crossroad, 1990. ISBN 0-8245-1030-5.

Cargas, a major contemporary Christian thinker, reflects on what the Holocaust means for Christians and Christianity. He argues that it is the greatest tragedy for Christians since the Crucifixion. Will there be a resurrection for Christianity after the Holocaust? Only if it confronts its role in the tragedy in a forthright manner.

* 2.142 *
Cohen, Arthur. *The Tremendum*. New York: Crossroads Books, 1981. LC 81-52. ISBN 0-8245-0006-7.

In a bold, theological reflection on the Holocaust, Cohen treats theological evil resulting from the Holocaust as a serious challenge, even a rift for theists.

* 2.143 *
Eckhardt, Alice L., and A. Roy Eckhardt. *A Long Night's Journey into Day; A Revised Retrospective on the Holocaust*. Rev. ed. Detroit: Wayne State University Press and Oxford and New York: Pergamon, 1988. LC 88-10668. ISBN 0-8143-2085-6.

The Eckhardts write of the singularity of the event, speaking of the Holocaust as uniquely unique. Christians have particular responsibilities to confront the Holocaust because it was perpetrated in Christendom by baptized Christians.

* 2.144 *
Eliach, Yaffa. *Hassidic Tales of the Holocaust*. New York and Oxford: University Press, 1982. LC 82-7928. ISBN 0-19-503199-7.

Eliach presents an extraordinary compilation of Hassidic tales of faith, hope, and miracles recounting the experiences of Hasidim during the Holocaust. These pretisti and mystical Jews were devastated by the Nazis, but they maintained faith and displayed great spiritual courage.

* 2.145 *
Fackenheim, Emil L. *The Jewish Return into History*. New York: Schocken, 1978. LC 77-87861.

A leading Jewish theologian analyzes why the Holocaust and the State of Israel are at the center of contemporary Jewish consciousness and thought. He sees Israel as a moral necessity after the Holocaust.

* 2.146
International Symposium on the Holocaust, Cathedral of St. John the Divine. *Auschwitz: Beginning of a New Era? Reflections on the Holocaust*. Ed. by Eva Fleischner. New York: Ktav, 1977. LC 76-53809. ISBN 0-87068-499-X.

This is an invaluable collection of papers by leading Jewish and Christian scholars from a wide range of disciplines delivered at the historic international symposium on the Holocaust held at the Cathedral of St. John the Divine. There are particularly impressive discussions of the theological implications of the Holocaust and Christian anti-Semitism.

* 2.147 *
Greenberg, Irving. "'Cloud of Smoke, Pillar of Fire': Judaism, Christianity, and Modernity after the Holocaust." In *Auschwitz: Beginning of a New Era?* Ed. by Eva Fleischner. New York: Ktav, 1977. LC 76-53809. ISBN 0-87068-499-X.

In this seminal article, Greenberg outlines a neo-Orthodox theological perspective developing the notion of moment-faith and faith-doubt dialectic. He focuses on Job and Isaiah's suffering servant and suggestive biblical models of arguing with God while still remaining within the tradition. He argues that no theological position can be credible if it does not take into account the challenge of one million burning babies.

* 2.148 *
Huberband, Shimon. *Kiddush Hashem: Jewish Religious and Cultural Life in Poland during the Holocaust*. New York: Yeshiva University Press, 1987. ISBN 0-88125-121-6.

Huberband was a historian who moved to Warsaw in 1940 and plunged into scholarly work, particularly Ringelblum's Oneg Shabbat archives. His major contribution was his chronicling of specific acts of Kiddush Hashem or martyrdom. This is a major contribution to the historiography of Jewish spiritual resistance during the Holocaust.

* 2.149 *
Kirschner, Robert. *Rabbinic Responsa of the Holocaust Era*. New York: Schocken, 1985. LC 84-23509. ISBN 0-8052-3978-2.

The religious life of the Jews during the Holocaust is revealed in the fourteen responses contained in this volume. Both the questions and the answers reflect the struggle of religious Jews to preserve their integrity during the most extreme conditions.

* 2.150 *
Littell, Franklin H. *The Crucifixion of the Jews*. New York: Harper & Row, 1975. LC 74-32288. ISBN 0-06-065250-9.

One of the most influential and productive Christian Holocaust scholars, Littell here briefly traces the history of Christian anti-Semitism and discusses the German church struggle and the Jews (1933-45). He also examines the State of Israel and the crisis its existence causes Christianity. He argues that Christianity must take responsibility for the Holocaust. Some critics point out that Littell's crisis of religious conscience is too simplistic. Nazism, after all, was an anti-Christian ideology, as much the product of modern secularism as of the heritage of Christian anti-Judaism. Religion is only one ideology among many shaping human action.

* 2.151 *
Neher, André. *The Exile of the Word: From the Silence of the Bible to the Silence of Auschwitz*. Philadelphia: Jewish Publication Society, 1981. LC 80-12612. ISBN 0-8276-0176-X.

In a wide-ranging discussion on the major theological questions arising out of the Holocaust, Neher takes up the question of God's silence. He interprets the problem in terms of the tradition of God's silence or concealment that is evident throughout the Biblical literature.

* 2.152 *
Oshry, Ephraim. *Responsa from the Holocaust*. Trans. by Y. Leiman. New York: Judaica Press, 1983. NUC 85-5386.

This is a powerful and poignant collection of rabbinic responsa during the Holocaust that reveals the depth of the religious spirit.

* 2.153 *
Rosenbaum, Irving J. *The Holocaust and Halakha*. New York: Ktav, 1976. LC 76-7407. ISBN 0-87068-296-2.

Most of the rabbinic responsa during the Holocaust were written in Germany, Poland, Hungary, and Lithuania; the topics covered included suicide, abortions, and the justifiability of murder. In this scholarly study, Rosenbaum examines how Jews attempted to conform to Halakhic requirements during the Holocaust.

* 2.154 *
Rubenstein, Richard L. *After Auschwitz: Radical Theology and Contemporary Judaism*. Indianapolis: Bobbs-Merrill, 1966. LC 66-27886.

Rubenstein, a leading Jewish theologian, first articulated his death-of-God position in this series of penetrating essays. He asserted the failure of traditional covenant Judaism to deal with the Holocaust. He concluded that, contrary to Jewish teaching, Auschwitz made it impossible to believe that God rules over history and that Jews are a Chosen People. He opted for a neopagan celebration of nature rather than a covenantal sanctification of time.

* 2.155 *
Ruether, Rosemary Radford. *Faith and Fratricide: Theological Roots of Anti-Semitism*. New York: Seabury Press, 1974. LC 74-11341. ISBN 0-8154-1183-2.

Ruether argues that anti-Semitism is endemic to Christology and lays the foundation for understanding the Christian role in the Holocaust. She urges a kind of relativization of the meaning of Christian scripture. From the perspective that Christian theology is responsible for much of anti-Semitism, she constructs a new foundation for Christian theology to eliminate the promises upon which Christian anti-Semitism have been based.

* 2.156 *
Zimmels, H.J. *The Echo of the Nazi Holocaust in Rabbinic Literature*. New York: Ktav, 1977. LC 76-56778. ISBN 0-87068-427-2.

Zimmels focuses on responsa dealing with such topics as mixed marriages, reburial, adoption, unclaimed property, the sanctity of life, and the desecration of cemetaries and synagogues.

Chapter 3

THE ISSUE OF THE HOLOCAUST AS A UNIQUE EVENT

by **Alan Rosenberg** and **Evelyn Silverman**

If the Holocaust was a truly unique event, then it lies beyond our comprehension. If it was not truly unique, then there is no unique lesson to be learned from it. Viewed solely from the perspective of its uniqueness, the Holocaust must be considered either incomprehensible or trivial. A contexualist analysis, on the other hand, finds that it was neither "extra historical" nor just another atrocity. It is possible to view the Holocaust as unprecedented in many respects and as an event of critical and transformational importance in the history of our world. Using this method, we can determine the ways in which the uniqueness question both helps and hinders our quest for understanding of the Holocaust.

The question of the "uniqueness" of the Holocaust has itself become a unique question. When we approach the Holocaust, we are at once confronted with a dilemma: if the Holocaust is the truly unique and unprecedented historical event that it is often held to be, then it must exceed the possibility of human comprehension, for it lies beyond the reach of our customary historical and sociological means of inquiry and understanding. But if it is not a historically unique event, if it is simply one more incident in the long history of man's inhumanity to man, there is no special point in trying to understand it, no unique lesson to be learned. Yehuda Bauer states the problem from a somewhat different perspective:

> If what happened to the Jews was unique, then it took place outside of history, it becomes a mysterious event, an upside-down miracle, so to speak, an event of religious significance in the sense that it is not man-made as that term is normally understood. On the other hand, if it is not unique at all, then where are the parallels or the precedents?[1]

Of all the enigmas, paradoxes, and dilemmas facing Holocaust scholarship[2] the "uniqueness question" is surely the most vexing and divisive; it is the one question most likely to evoke partisan debate and to generate emotional heat in discussion.[3] This is most recently evident in what has come to be called the "Historian's Debate" or, the *Historikerstreit*, a volatile debate of German origin about which we will say more later.

The prominence of the issue of uniqueness, however, has not often been dealt with systematically in the literature. No previously published bibliography on the "uniqueness question" exists, and although many important writings on the Holocaust implicitly include the issue, relatively few writings in the vast Holocaust literature address the question of uniqueness directly. Thus the reader will find that the bibliography at the end of this introduction contains fewer annotations of articles that deal directly with the issue and many more whose main focus is elsewhere and from which the uniqueness issue has to be inferred.

In our own efforts at analysis of the issues underlying the "uniqueness question," we have been struck by the very oddity of the question itself, for it is strange that there should be argument about it at all. What strikes us as peculiar about it is that the legitimacy of the question as such is so taken for granted, so readily is it assumed that the uniqueness of the Holocaust is not merely a fit subject for analysis but is a problem of the very first rank in importance.

The anomaly here is just that the "uniqueness question" itself is taken to be crucially relevant to an understanding of the Holocaust although it is relevant to few—if any—other landmark events of history. One finds little discussion, for example, of the "uniqueness" of the Protestant Reformation or the Industrial Revolution. The atomic destruction of Hiroshima and Nagasaki—surely qualified as "unique" and "unprecedented" in terms of their implications for the future of humankind—is simply not the subject of debate concerning its "uniqueness;" nor does it involve controversy and serious divisions of opinion. If the "uniqueness" of such events as these, events that have radically altered our world, is not in question, why is it that the "uniqueness question" has assumed such prominence in the context of Holocaust studies? Why is the question itself so hotly contested? Some authorities on the history of the Holocaust go so far as to claim that the stance that one takes with respect to the "uniqueness question" determines the way in which one relates the Holocaust to the rest of human history, influencing every dimension of one's interpretation and evaluation of the event itself.

Comparability or Uniqueness

According to Saul Friedländer, for example, before we can begin to analyze any number of the central issues surrounding the Holocaust we must first deal with "a preliminary issue of crucial importance for every aspect of the Holocaust: are we dealing with a phenomenon comparable with some other historical event or are we facing something unique not only within any traditional and historical context, but even within Nazism itself?"[4] George Kren and Leon Rappoport call the "uniqueness question" very important, for, "depending upon how it is answered, the general orientation of interpretive analysis will obviously vary a great deal."[5] And again, insistence upon its historical uniqueness may, according to Yehuda Bauer, render the Holocaust irrelevant except as a specifically Jewish tragedy. Here is the thrust of Bauer's argument:

> If what happens to the Jews is unique, then by definition it doesn't concern us, beyond our pity and commiseration for the victims. If the Holocaust is not a universal problem, then why should a public school system in Philadelphia, New York or Timbuktu teach it? Well, the answer is that there is no uniqueness, not even of a unique event. Anything that happens once, can happen again: not quite in the same way, perhaps, but in an equivalent form.[6]

In what follows we shall be addressing the problems and issues that are raised by texts like these, texts cited here simply as evidence that—for Holocaust studies—the "uniqueness question" is at once paramount and problematic.

It is clear, moreover, that the "uniqueness question" has become a matter of concern to the Jewish and Christian lay community as well as to professional scholars in the field. One need only think of the public debate over the issues of the inclusion of the Holocaust in the social studies curriculum of the New York City school system or the U.S. Holocaust Memorial Council to see how sensitive the issue has become, especially within the Jewish community itself.[7] We may ask if this special sensitivity is not itself an impediment to more widespread dialogue, thus hampering the very cause of understanding that Jews support. For, as Professor Ismar Schorsch states, the Jews' "obsession" with the uniqueness claim "impedes genuine dialogue, because it introduces an extraneous contentious issue that alienates potential allies from among other victims of organized human depravity. Similarly, our fixation on uniqueness has prevented us from reaching out by universalizing the lessons of the Holocaust."[8]

Three Principal Options

Considerations such as these clearly imply that, if we are to widen and deepen our understanding of the Holocaust, we must deal with the claim of "uniqueness" by developing a strategy that will free us from the conceptual muddles that presently cloud the issue. We must be clear as to the meaning of the claim itself if we are to escape the mystification that frequently has surrounded it.[9] We appear to have three principal options:

1) We can dismiss the whole question of "uniqueness," on one of two grounds. Eberhard Jäckel, for instance, suggests that the uniqueness issue adds little of value to our understanding of the Holocaust. He asserts the event's uniqueness but then states, "incidently, the question of uniqueness is after all not all that decisive. Would it change anything, had the National-Socialist murder not been unique?"[10] On the other hand, Schorsch, as mentioned above, recommends dismissal of the issue on the grounds that it only serves to add a politically divisive element to the discussion.

2) We can attempt to account for why it is that the "uniqueness" claim has become integral to the discussion of the meaning of the Holocaust while it has been treated as merely peripheral to the analysis of other historical events of major consequence.

3) We can concentrate our analysis upon how the "uniqueness question" helps as well as hinders us in our quest to elucidate the meaning and significance of the Holocaust.

Though we are sympathetic with those who confine their strategy to the first option, we shall reject it as unrealistic. For, while it is true—as Schorsch points out—that the claim to uniqueness sometimes does pose a difficulty for those who would gain a better understanding of the Holocaust by comparing it with other cases of mass human destruction, it does not seem to us that we can evade the "uniqueness question" by simply disregarding it. The "uniqueness question" is much too central to the literature of the Holocaust to be ignored. The second option as listed above is of decisive import, for it is always helpful to understand what lies behind any particular perspective on an event, and especially so when the range of perspectives on the event is so much a part of the event itself and gives rise to so much controversy. We shall be exercising the third option, because it builds upon the second—depending as it does upon clarification of the meaning of the claim of "uniqueness" with respect to the Holocaust—although a full account of the matter lies beyond the scope of this chapter.

Explicating the Uniqueness Question

In the end we shall try to show why explicating the "uniqueness question" is the strategy that is most fruitful in understanding the Holocaust itself. However, although we shall be adopting this third option, let us first sketch some of the factors that have tended to make the "uniqueness question" itself a part of the problem in understanding the Holocaust. Before we can see how it can be treated as part of the "solution," so to speak, we must see why it has become "part of the problem."

It seems to be beyond question that the peculiar role that the "uniqueness question" has come to play in relation to the historical accounts and understanding of the Holocaust is largely due to the insistence of a major part of the Jewish community that the Holocaust must be viewed as unique.[11] It was a segment of the Jewish community, in fact, that devised and accepted the very label "Holocaust" in order to express the uniqueness of the event,[12] literally defining it as such by the name that they gave it.[13] The process by means of which a series of historical incidents becomes known as an "event" is well known, for it is only by gathering into meaningful clusters the apparently separate and unrelated facts of historical happenings that we are able to form coherent concepts of what has happened in the past.

The naming of such a cluster is but one step in the process of self-understanding, and so it is easy to see why a segment of the Jewish community has come to view the naming of the Holocaust as an attempt to capture and preserve the uniqueness of meaning that is implicit in the facts so named. As those facts became known in the aftermath of World War II they immediately gave rise to a numbing horror in which the human mind seemed to be incapable of dealing with them, of grasping them in the normal fashion in which we deal with the factual materials of history. The awful depth and scope of these "incidents," of these particular historical facts, were of such horrible dimensions as to seem completely incomprehensible. It is from this response, we believe, that the claim to the "uniqueness" of the Holocaust was generated.[14] And it is in the context of this response that the search for those characteristics and traits that mark the Holocaust as unique must be understood. For it is precisely this search, and the various proposals that have issued from it, that is responsible for making the "uniqueness question" a part of the event which the "Holocaust" names: it has become part of the problem of the understanding and comprehension of what happened. The peculiar question of "uniqueness" may not have been an inevitable component of the problem, but it is clearly, at this point, an inescapable one.

Quite aside from the origins of the "uniqueness question" and its integration into the total problematic of the literature of the Holocaust, at least three other substantive problems concerning the characterization of the Holocaust as "unique" can be readily stated, though they are not so readily solved. We must, first of all, be clear about what we mean when we claim an event to be unique. Second, we must be clear as to what element or elements of the event make it unique. Finally, we must at least try to be clear about the implications of the decision to classify the Holocaust as unique and try to understand how that decision may affect our interpretation of the event itself.

What Constitutes Uniqueness?

Existing Holocaust scholarship, surprisingly, is of little help in determining criteria for what constitutes "uniqueness" with respect to the Holocaust, or any other historical event, for that matter. Often terms other than "unique" are used throughout the literature, words such as "singularity" or "particularity" or "unprecendented" and phrases like "without equal" or "epoch making." Sometimes these are all used interchangeably, synonymously, and other times each term seems to be selected to establish a particular focus or emphasis of meaning for the concept of uniqueness. Should we consult ordinary language, we gain even less help. The *American College Dictionary* gives three possible defnitions of "unique": 1) "of which there is but one"; 2) "having no like or equal"; and 3) "rare and unusual." In such terms, every event can be called unique, for no event of history is ever literally duplicated or "happens" twice, or is exactly "like" any other event, or its "equal." Moreover, from the point of view of those who believe in the uniqueness of the Holocaust it would seem to trivialize the importance of the Holocaust to call it simply "rare" or "unusual."

In order to avoid such trivialization we must look at the actual use of the claim itself; we must analyze the intentions of those who have insisted upon the "uniqueness" of the Holocaust, and we must try to grasp the point of the claim. In this way, it seems to us, we can make sense of the question. It would seem that for many scholars the claim of "uniqueness" is intended to set apart from other historical events just that singular event that has the potential of transforming a culture, or altering the course of history, in some profound and decisive way. If the Industrial Revolution, for example, is said to be a "unique event" in the history of the West, it is because it is viewed in this transformational light; it changed our Western culture, altered its values, and so can be viewed as a cause of a major "turning point in history."[15] Such a way of defining the "uniqueness" claim corresponds closely to the definition offered by Emil Fackenheim, for his "epoch making event"[16] is just what is meant by terming an event as actually or potentially "transformational" of the *status quo ante*, as radically altering the course of history.[17] Given such a definition we can see how it is possible to claim that the Holocaust, as well as other events, such as the atomic bombing of Japan, can be classified as "unique."

Yet we find interpreters of the Holocaust seriously divided over the preliminary question of uniqueness. In the first instance, there are those who view the whole issue of uniqueness as unimportant, for there is, as we have seen, a trivial sense in which all historical events are unique.[18] They see the Holocaust as unique only to the extent that every historical event is necessarily different from every other historical event; because "history never repeats itself," contrary to what has sometimes been popularly believed, it follows that the "uniqueness" of the Holocaust is affirmed. But such an affirmation is clearly a "trivialization" of the "uniqueness question."

There is yet a second group that falls within the camp of the "trivialists." They are quite willing to see the Holocaust as an event of major importance, but they nevertheless agree that the claim of uniqueness cannot be sustained in any non-trivial form. They argue that too much has been made of what have been called the "exceptional" features of the Holocaust. Ernst Nolte, for example, has been interpreted to have reduced the uniqueness of the Holocaust to the "technical process of the gassing."[19] Without denying the existence of unique features this group concentrates on showing that the Holocaust grew from the events that led up to it. In their view the Holocaust may simply be regarded as just one more incident—albeit a flagrant one—of man's inhumanity to man, one more horrible atrocity in a century filled with them. They cite such precedents as the destruction of the Armenians by the Turks[20] and the mass destructions of the Russian Revolution, drawing analogies between the atrocities of the Gulag Archipelago and Auschwitz, and even reaching back to the genocidal near-extermination of the American Indians for parallel cases.

Some of these critics grant that whatever uniqueness the Holocaust may possess can only be seen within the context of Jewish history.[21] But some Jewish intellectuals, Jacob Neusner[22] and Arnold Eisen,[23] for example, go so far as to hold that even within the context of Jewish history the Holocaust cannot be viewed as unique. They contend that the Holocaust should be understood as one event in a succession of events, one link in a long chain of events aimed at the elimination of the Jews as a people commencing with the destruction of the Second Temple in 70 CE.[24]

In sharp contrast to the "trivialists," those whom we have called "absolutists" are certain that no other event in history even remotely resembles the Holocaust or furnishes a precedent for understanding it. Its singularity is such that it exceeds the power of language to express; its meaning is such that it belongs to "another planet." It is incomprehensible, completely outside the normal dimensions of our terrestrial history, beyond all historical explanation and appraisal. It is, they say, not merely unique; it is, to use the Eckhardts' phrase, "uniquely unique."[25]

Menachem Rosensaft sums up this view succinctly: the "Holocaust stands alone in time as an aberration within history."[26] And Elie Wiesel writes that "the universe of concentration camps, by its design, lies outside if not beyond history. Its vocabulary belongs to it alone."[27] In Bauer's striking characterization, the Holocaust is viewed by these writers as an "upside-down miracle."[28] These absolutists see the Holocaust as unique simply because it happened, and concerning their view nothing needs to be added.

Contextualists

Those reluctant to accept either the trivialist or the absolutist position may be termed "contextualists." Contextualists find that, although there may be distinct features of the Holocaust that set it apart and that might remain of more importance than its similarities and resemblances to other events, it is central to their thesis that the Holocaust always be examined within the context of history. Comparison, many state, does not preclude uniqueness. Often it is the very act of comparison, the examination of the Holocaust against the backdrop of history, that serves to highlight those features that render the event unique, but only relatively so. Other turning points in history, other great crises, they suggest, contain elements both comparable with and related to the Holocaust.

With this approach the Holocaust is neither "extra historical," in the sense claimed by the absolutists, nor just another atrocity, as the trivialists maintain. This means that it is possible to view the Holocaust as unprecedented in many respects, that it is an event of critical and transformational importance in the history of our world, and yet it is still an event that must be addressed as a part of that history. It can and should be compared to other genocidal incidents, described and analyzed in language free from the "mystification" that only blocks our understanding, and made as accessible to explanation as possible. It should not be assumed, on *a priori* grounds of its absolute "uniqueness," that what caused the Holocaust is forever beyond the reach of the tools of historical analysis, or that the consequences cannot be explored by means of social theory.

The *Historikerstreit*

Here we must note what has become known as the ***Historikerstreit*** [historians' debate]. In this debate, a group of reknowned German scholars, most of whose essays and books have not yet been translated from the German, consider many important issues of substance and method, including those of the role of the Third Reich in German history, the place of Germany in world politics, as well as issues of German national pride. All of these works deal on some level with just how and to what extent the Third Reich and the Holocaust can be contextualized within German and world history. But from our perspective it is important to note that "of all the issues raised by the controversy, the singularity of Auschwitz is the most central and the most hotly debated."[29]

It was Ernst Nolte's essay of 1986[30] together with Jürgen Habermas'[31] response that first triggered the Historians' Debate. Habermas was responding to some historians,[32] such as Ernst Nolte, Michael Stürmer and Andreas Hillgruber who he believed had used the contextualization of the Holocaust in such a way as either to completely eliminate or to relegate to insignificance any of its unique aspects. Nolte, for example, takes the idea of contextualization to such an extreme and so relativizes the events of the Holocaust that he renders it a rather normal happening of our era, almost to be expected when examined in the context of other historical events of our time, highly analogous in many respects to the Russian Revolution and so not even unique in the sense of being unprecedented. Peter Gay has called Nolte's approach "comparative trivialization"[33] in which the unique qualities of the Holocaust are reduced to features of insignificant implication.

The uniqueness of the Nazi crimes, their comparability to other atrocities, becomes a crucial question for German national identity and Germany's place in world history. As Charles S. Maier has explained it:

> If Auschwitz is admittedly dreadful, but dreadful as only one specimen of genocide...then Germany can still aspire to reclaim a national acceptance that no one denies to perpetrators of other massacres, such as Soviet Russia. But if the Final Solution remains noncomparable...the past may never be "worked through," the future never normalized, and German nationhood may remain forever tainted, like some well forever poisoned.[34]

Habermas and others consider that Nolte and the conservative historians have used extreme historicization or relativization of the Holocaust and presented it with apologist intent to help Germany "regain a sense of the lost national identity."[35]

Other positions regarding the uniqueness issue and the contextualization or comparability of the Holocaust and the Third Reich emerged from Habermas' confrontation with those he called the "conservative historians."[36] For our purposes, the most important position is that contextualization or the comparative method need not eliminate the unique elements of the Holocaust but could highlight both its singularity and its similarity to other events.[37] The scope of this essay precludes further exploration of this important and fascinating debate.[38] What is significant to us here is that once again this debate puts the question of uniqueness into the forefront of our understanding of the Holocaust.

Intention Versus Methodology

It would be misleading to claim that, quite aside from the historians of the *Historikerstreit*, all those scholars we categorize as contextualists speak with a single voice concerning the "uniqueness question." Steven Katz[39] and Saul Friedländer,[40] for instance, take an "intentionalist" approach. They hold the view that it is the "intention" of the Nazis to eliminate Jewry totally that marks the Holocaust as unique among comparable pogroms and genocides. Others, such as Richard L. Rubenstein[41] and Henry Friedlander,[42] take a more "methodological" point of view. They see the uniqueness of the Holocaust more in terms of the distinctive bureaucratic and technological methods of destruction employed. The impact of each position can be seen by comparing the following texts. In "Whose Holocaust?" Yehuda Bauer takes the intentionalist approach:

> The uniqueness of the Holocaust does not...lie in numbers. It does not lie in the method of mass murder....What makes it unique is the existence of two elements: planned total annihilation of a national or ethnic group, and the quasi-religious, apocalyptic ideology that motivated the murder.[43]

By contrast, here is Robert E. Willis representing the approach from the methodologist standpoint:

> For whatever similarities are present between Auschwitz and other cases—and there are many—the former is distinguished by being the first instance of a situation in which the full bureaucratic and technical apparatus of the state was mobilized for the primary purpose of extermination.[44]

Some methodologists make it clear that they fully recognize the important role that the intentionalists ascribe to the "uniqueness" of the Nazis' emphasis on "total extermination," while insisting that the special bureaucratic and technological means employed in that destruction are the more decisively unique feature of the event.[45]

Yet other contextualists unite both the intentionalist and the methodological apprehension of the Holocaust's uniqueness. It is not necessary after all that only one distinct type of feature render an event unique. Jäckel, for example, holds the Holocaust to be unique in both method and intention:

> This is not the first time I argue that the murder of the Jews was unique because never before had a state, with authority of its responsible leader, conceived and announced its intention to liquidate as completely as possible a certain group of people...and to implement its decision by means of all the official instruments of power at its disposal.[46]

These very sharply defined differences of focus on what constitutes the uniqueness of the Holocaust are responsible for serious divergences of interpretation of the event itself. For it is clear that the absolutists, trivialists, and contextualists employ their respective views of the "uniqueness question" as interpretive frameworks for understanding the Holocaust itself. The preliminary question of uniqueness helps to determine, by the way in which it is answered, the conceptual apparatus for exploring the other problems of the Holocaust.

Interpretive Grids

With these very different approaches to the Holocaust locked into the different interpretive grids through which the event itself is to be viewed and interpreted, from the preliminary stage on, it is small wonder that the eventual interpretations that are reached should themselves be widely variant, and we can see how each interpretation of the uniqueness question will have very different implications. The absolutist position, while it forces us to see the uniqueness of the event, renders the Holocaust forever incomprehensible, outside the context of our age, our language, and our capacity for understanding.[47] While many absolutists urge that discussion of the Holocaust be continued, as Bauer asks, if the Holocaust has no universal lessons for all men, why should anyone study it?[48] One might question the value of including an incomprehensible event in a school curricula, for example.

When the trivialist position is taken, attention is drawn away from any unique features the Holocaust might have. Unlike the absolutist view, the Holocaust is placed within the context of history, but the event becomes of no more concern to us than any other historical event. All transformational potential is denied and no particular lessons can be derived from it.

Contextualists, as we have said, place the Holocaust as a historical event, neither necessarily beyond our comprehension nor beyond the reach of our customary tools of social analysis. Their use of contextualization can serve either to highlight or to minimize any possibly unique features with strikingly different consequences. As we have seen the contextualization of the Holocaust can lead either to trivialization or to expansion of our understanding of the causes of events like the Holocaust. Such expanded understanding may give us the knowledge that will enable us prevent any possible recurrence.

Within the contextualist debate two major emphases emerge with differing implications. The methodologists, placing the focus as they do on the technological and bureaucratic means of destruction, tend to downplay the importance of the victims of the Holocaust. On the other hand the intentionalist position places all focus of emphasis on the Jews as victims. This emphasis on the particularity of the Jewish situation tends to obscure relevant analogies with the predicaments of other groups and also obscures the more universal implications for the future of all humankind. When speaking of the Jews' special claim to uniqueness, Geoff Eley has stated: "...to insist on the uniqueness of the event is a short step to insisting on the exclusiveness of interpretation which asserts an empathetic privilege and even Jewish proprietorship in the subject."[49] As we have noted earlier one possible result of this approach is to yield political disharmonies with other groups who have felt themselves to have been similarly victimized in other catastrophes and who might feel that the insistence on Jewish uniqueness serves to underplay their own experiences.[50]

Conclusion

What is important is not that the reader should accept any one approach to the "uniqueness question" as true and the others as false, but that he or she should try to discover which of these approaches yields the most coherent and intelligible results, which framework elucidates the problems of understanding the Holocaust most clearly and is the most promising for understanding its historical and moral significance. It is not a simple matter to decide, and the fact that there are subtle differences within each type of approach does not make the task any easier.

NOTES

1. Yehuda Bauer, *The Holocaust in Historical Perspective* (Seattle: University of Washington, 1978), 31. For different formulations of this problem, see Emil Fackenheim, *To Mend the World: Foundations of Future Jewish Thought* (New York: Schocken Books, 1982), 20; Henry L. Feingold, "How Unique Is the Holocaust?" in *Critical Issues of the Holocaust*, ed. by Alex Grobman and Daniel Landes (Los Angeles: Simon Wiesenthal Center and Rossel Books, 1983), 397; and Robert McAfee Brown, "The Holocaust as a Problem in Moral Choice," in *When God and Man Failed: Non-Jewish Views of the Holocaust*, ed. by Harry James Cargas (New York: Macmillan Publishing Co., Inc., 1981), 99.

2. For a more detailed analysis of the enigmas and paradoxes facing Holocaust scholarship, see Alan Rosenberg, "The Problematic Character of Understanding the Holocaust," *European Judaism* 17:2 (Winter 1983/84): 16-20; and Alan Rosenberg, "The Crisis in Knowing and Understanding the Holocaust," in *Echoes from the Holocaust: Philosophical Reflections on a Dark Time*, ed. by Alan Rosenberg and Gerald Myers (Philadelphia: Temple University Press, 1988), 379-395.

3. See Pierre Papazian, "A 'Unique Uniqueness'?" and the symposium it generated, "Was the Holocaust Unique?: Responses to Pierre Papazian," *Midstream* 30:4 (April 1984): 14-25.

4. Saul Friedländer, "On the Possibility of the Holocaust: An Approach to a Historical Synthesis," in *The Holocaust as Historical Experience*, ed. by Yehuda Bauer and Nathan Rotenstreich (New York: Holmes and Meier, 1981), 1.

5. George Kren and Leon Rappoport, "Failure of Thought in Holocaust Interpretation," in *Towards the Holocaust: The Social and Economic Collapse of the Weimar Republic*, ed. by Michael N. Dobkowski and Isidor Wallimann (Westport, CT: Greenwood Press, 1983), 380.

6. Yehuda Bauer, "Right and Wrong Teaching of the Holocaust," in *The International Conference on Lessons of the Holocaust*, ed. by Josephine Z. Knopp (Philadelphia: National Institute on the Holocaust, 1979), 5.

7. See Ismar Schorsch, "The Holocaust and Jewish Survival," *Midstream* 17:1 (January 1981): 39; and Paula E. Hyman, "New Debates on the Holocaust,"

The New York Times Magazine (14 September 1980): 80-82.

8. Schorsch, 39.

9. For the significances of the issue, see Henry Friedlander, "Toward a Methodology of Teaching about the Holocaust," *Teacher's College Record* 80:3 (February 1979): 524-525 and Rosenberg, "The Crisis in Knowing and Understanding the Holocaust," 389-392.

10. Eberhard Jäckel, "The Miserable Practice of the Insinuators: The Uniqueness of the National-Socialist Crime Cannot Be Denied," *Yad Vashem Studies* 19 (1988): 111.

11. Schorsch, 39.

12. Lucy S. Dawidowicz states, "The Holocaust is the term that Jews themselves have chosen to describe their fate during World War II." *The War Against the Jews: 1933-1945* (New York: Holt, Rinehart and Winston, 1975), xv.

13. For a brilliant historical analysis of how the term "Holocaust" became the name for what happened to the Jews under Hitler, see Gerd Korman, "The Holocaust in American Historical Writing," *Societas* 2:3 (Summer 1972): 259-262.

14. Rosenberg, "The Crisis in Knowing and Understanding the Holocaust," 386.

15. On the question of transformational events, see George M. Kren and Leon Rappoport, *The Holocaust and the Crisis of Human Behavior* (New York: Holmes and Meier, 1980), 12-15; and Alan Rosenberg and Alexander Bardosh's critique of the same in *Modern Judaism* 1:3 (December 1981): 337-346.

16. Emil Fackenheim, *The Jewish Return into History* (New York: Schocken Books, 1978), 279.

17. For an analysis of what has been radically altered in history by the Holocaust, see Kren and Rappoport, 131-143; and Alan Rosenberg, "The Philosophical Implications of the Holocaust," in *Perspectives on the Holocaust*, ed. by Randolph L. Braham (Boston: Kluever-Nijhoff Publishers, 1983), 8-16.

18. For an incisive analysis of the problem, see Carey B. Joynt and Nicholas Rescher, "The Problem of Uniqueness in History," in *Studies in the Philosophy of History*, ed. by George H. Nadel (New York: Harper and Row, 1965), 3-15; and Alice L. Eckhardt and A. Roy Eckhardt, "The Holocaust and the Enigma of Uniqueness: A Philosophical Effort at Practical Clarification," *The Annals of the American Academy of Political and Social Science* 450 (July 1980): 166-167.

19. Ernst Nolte, "A Past That Will Not Pass Away (A Speech It Was Possible to Write, But Not to Present)," *Yad Vashem Studies* 19 (1988): 71.

20. See Papazian, 14.

21. Papazian, 14.

22. Jacob Neusner, *Stranger at Home: "The Holocaust," Zionism and American Judaism* (Chicago: University of Chicago Press, 1981), 6-8.

23. Eisen's remarks appear in "The Meaning and Demeaning of the Holocaust: A Symposium," *Moment* 6:3-4 (March/April 1981): 3.

24. For a good brief critical discussion see *Holocaust: Religious and Philosophical Implications*, ed. by John K. Roth and Michael Berenbaum (New York: Paragon House, 1989), 3-5.

25. A. Roy Eckhardt with Alice L Eckhardt, *Long Night's Journey into Day: Life and Faith after the Holocaust* (Detroit: Wayne State University Press, 1982), 43-50.

26. Menachem Rosensaft, "The Holocaust: History as Aberration," *Midstream* 23:5 (May 1977): 55.

27. Elie Wiesel, "Now We Know," in *Genocide in Paraguay*, ed. by Richard Arens (Philadelphia: Temple University Press, 1976), 165.

28. Yehuda Bauer, *The Holocaust in Historical Perspective* (Seattle: University of Washington Press, 1978), 31.

29. Richard J. Evans, "The New Nationalism and the Old History: Perspectives on the West German Historikerstreit," *Journal of Modern History* (December 1987): 781.

30. Nolte, 65-73.

31. Jürgen Habermas, "A Kind of Indemnification: The Tendencies toward Apologia in German Research on Current History," *Yad Vashem Studies* 19 (1988): 75-92.

32. For an excellent understanding of Habermas' intervention in the German Debate, see John Torpey, "Introduction: Habermas and the Historians," *New German Critique* no. 44 (Spring/Summer 1988): 5-24.

33. Peter Gay, *Freud, Jews and Other Germans* (New York: Oxford University Press, 1978), xi.

34. Charles S. Maier, *The Unmasterable Past: History, Holocaust, and German National Identity* (Cambridge, MA: Harvard University Press, 1988), 1.

35. Otto Dov Kulka, "Singularity and Its Relativization: Changing Views in German Historiography on National Socialism and the 'Final Solution'," *Yad Vashem Studies* 19 (1988): 163.

36. See Martin Broszat and Saul Friedländer, "A Controversy about the Historicization of National Socialism," *Yad Vashem Studies* 19 (1988): 1-47.

37. For an excellent discussion of this position see Jürgen Kocka, "The Weight of the Past in Germany's Future," *German Politics and Society* (February 1988): 22-29.

38. For further reading see Richard J. Evans, *In Hitler's Shadow: West German Historians and the Attempt to Escape from the Nazi Past* (New York: Pantheon Books, 1989); and Ian Kershaw, *The Nazi Dictatorship: Problems and Perspectives of Interpretation*, 2d ed. (London and New York: Edward Arnold, 1989), 150-191.

39. Steven T. Katz, "The 'Unique' Intentionality of the Holocaust," *Modern Judaism* 1:2 (September 1981): 161-183.

40. Friedländer, 1-6.

41. Richard L. Rubenstein, *The Cunning of History* (New York: Harper and Row, 1975), 6-7, 22-35.

42. Henry Friedlander, "Toward a Methodology of Teaching about the Holocaust," 530-531.

43. Yehuda Bauer, "Whose Holocaust?" *Midstream* 26:9 (November 1980): 45.

44. Robert E. Willis, "Confessing God after Auschwitz: A Challenge for Christianity," *Cross Currents* 28:3 (Fall 1978): 272.

45. See Leo Kuper, *Genocide* (New Haven: Yale University Press, 1981), 120-122, 135.

46. Jäckel, 110.

47. For an excellent analysis of the problem of incomprehensibility, see Dan Magurshak, "The Incomprehensibility of the Holocaust: Tightening Up Some Loose Usage," in *Echoes from the Holocaust: Philosophical Reflections on a Dark Time*, ed. by Alan Rosenberg and Gerald Myers (Philadelphia: Temple University Press, 1988), 421-431.

48. Bauer, "Right and Wrong Teaching of the Holocaust," 5.

49. Geoff Eley, "Holocaust History," *London Review of Books* (3-17 March 1982): 6.

50. Papazian, 18.

Chapter 3: Annotated Bibliography

* 3.1 *
Arendt, Hannah. *Eichmann in Jerusalem*. Rev. & enl. ed. New York: Viking Press, 1964. LC 64-25532.

In the epilogue of her well known book, Arendt concludes that the Nazi crimes were unique "politically and legally." She says, "...these 'crimes' were different not only in degree of seriousness but in essence." She sees the key difference to lie in the Nazi intention to murder all Jews worldwide, thus creating a new kind of crime that she calls a "crime against humanity."

* 3.2 *
Bauer, Yehuda. "Against Mystification." In *The Holocaust in Historical Perspective*. Seattle: University of Washington Press, 1978. LC 78-2988. ISBN 0-295-95606-2.

Bauer confronts the dilemma of conceptualizing the Holocaust as unique: if totally unique, it lies outside historical understanding; if not at all unique, then "where are the parallels and precedents?" He places the Holocaust within the context of history as "parallel" to other acts of genocide, but claims that the Nazis' wish to murder all Jews simply by virtue of the fact that they were Jews and not for any secondary gain, whether political or economic, sets the Holocaust apart as a unique event. In this way Bauer establishes what we call the intentionalist approach to the uniqueness issue. He takes issue with using the term genocide to apply to the Holocaust because, according to Bauer, Lemkin, the jurist who first coined the word, never understood the term "genocide" to apply to the complete physical annihilation of an entire group—a fate the Nazis clearly intended for the Jews—but only to the destruction of a group's national or ethnic or religious identity, its "murderous denationalization." Thus the Holocaust can be seen as comparable to other genocidal events—the Armenian massacre, for instance—but unique in and of itself because of the unique intention involved: according to Bauer, the Turks never intended to murder all the Armenians.

* 3.3 *
Bauer, Yehuda. "Essay: On the Place of the Holocaust in History; In Honour of Franklin H. Littell." *Holocaust and Genocide Studies* 20:2 (1987): 209-220.

Bauer reiterates his position that it is the motivation of the Nazis that sets the Holocaust off as a unique event in history and apart from other mass destructions and genocides. Unlike his position in earlier writings, however, Bauer now characterizes the Nazis' motivation, their desire to murder the Jews, as "a global ideology, not just a Germanic one" that involved ridding the entire world of all Jews. According to Bauer, the closest parallel in history to date is the Armenian massacre, which he calls a "Holocaust-related event." In that case, however, the motivation was primarily political; and perhaps just as importantly to Bauer, at no point did the Turks express the desire to murder all Armenians worldwide but only within Turkey's political boundaries. These differences, crucial to Bauer, still set the Holocaust apart as a unique historical event.

* 3.4 *
Bauer, Yehuda. "Is the Holocaust Explicable." In *Remembering for the Future: Working Papers and Addenda*. Vol. 2. Ed. by Yehuda Bauer, et al. Oxford: Pergamon Press, 1989. ISBN 0-08-036754-2.

Bauer, in a paper presented at a world conference entitled "Remembering for the Future," again asserts that the Jewish Holocaust is a unique, unprecedented event in history. Bauer defines "Holocaust" generically as the "planned, total annihilation of a whole people...for ideological reasons." For Bauer, "the cases of the Armenians and the Jews would fit here, with the ideological factor being decisive in the case of the Jews, thus setting this Holocaust apart." Whereas the annihilation of the Armenians was limited to Turkey, the uniqueness of the Jewish destruction stems from the fact that it is the only event in history to date where the annhilation was intended on a global scale.

* 3.5 *
Bauer, Yehuda. "The Place of the Holocaust in Contemporary History." In *Studies in Contemporary Jewry*. Ed. by Jonathan Frankel. Bloomington: Indiana University Press, 1984. ISBN 0-253-39511-9.

In this later article Bauer reinforces his idea that genocide and holocaust are two distinct kinds of events, locatable on a continuum of evil that stretches from "mass murder" to "genocide" to "holocaust." Genocide involves the destruction of a group's national, ethnic, or religious identity and might involve mass murder. A holocaust, Bauer notes, using a lower case "h" to denote a generic class of events and not the Jewish Holocaust, involves the total physical annihilation of a group, the murder of all its members for ideological reasons. To Bauer the Holocaust—the destruction of the European Jews—is a unique form of holocaust because it is the only one that fulfilled the criteria in the extreme form. The Armenian massacre, about which Bauer now states that the Turks did in fact intend to totally annihilate all Armenians in Turkey, offers an analogous but not identical kind of event because there were ideological differences. "On the continuum the two events stand next to each other." Thus Bauer appears to be saying that the Armenian massacre fits into the general category of holocaust.

* 3.6 *
Bauer, Yehuda. "Whose Holocaust?" *Midstream* 26:9 (November 1980): 42-46.

Bauer again deals with the uniqueness issue; this time he sets his discussion in a warning that de-Judaizing the Holocaust by denying its uniqueness can possibly be one of the first steps in allowing the rebirth of a more rampant anti-semition. He argues that the memory of the outrageous horror of the Holocaust has inhibited this potential rebirth. As in previous writings, he again states that the Holocaust is unique in intention in that the Nazis wanted to totally annihilate the Jews. He still distinguishes between genocide and the Holocaust, but now introduces the idea that the "Holocaust is both the name for a specific, unique event in recent history, and also a generic concept: The planned total annihilation of a national or ethnic group on the basis of general ideology." This differs from genocide in that a genocide would not necessarily involve the murder of a people but possibly only the destruction of a people's identity. Bauer has here included in his definition of the Holocaust the concept that a holocaust must not only be a "planned total annihilation" but that it must be powered by "ideological reasons."

* 3.7 *
Berenbaum, Michael. "The Uniqueness and Universality of the Holocaust." *American Journal of Theology and Philosophy* 2:3 (1981): 85-96.

Berenbaum asserts that the Holocaust is analogous, though not equivalent, to other events in history, and that the comparison of the Holocaust to those other historical events does not necessarily detract from its uniqueness, but rather serves to highlight those elements unique to it. The Holocaust remains unprecedented in both world and Jewish history for four reasons: 1) it was biologically based; 2) it was a sustained episode of anti-semition; 3) it was legally sanctioned by the State; and 4) the intention of the Nazis was to annihilate all Jews.

* 3.8 *
Dadrian, Vahakn N. "The Convergent Aspects of the Armenian and Jewish Cases of Genocide: A Reinterpretation of the Concept of Holocaust." *Holocaust and Genocide Studies* 3:2 (1988): 152-169.

Dadrian claims that both the Armenians and the Jews have had similar destructions visited on them. The Armenian massacre and the annihilation of the Jews were both genocides carried out with similar method and intention. But although perhaps not objectively unique, each destruction is subjectively unique as it is experienced by its victims. This subjective experience of uniqueness holds for all groups towards whom genocide has been directed.

* 3.9 *
Dawidowicz, Lucy. "Thinking about the Six Million: Facts, Figures, Perspectives." In *The Holocaust and the Historians*. Cambridge, MA: Harvard University Press, 1981. LC 80-29175. ISBN 0-674-40566-8.

In the context of a review of the total loss of human life during World War II, Dawidowicz argues that the fate of the Jews was essentially different from other mass murders perpetrated by the Nazis. The author states that "never before had the principles and methods of rational organization been employed...for purposes of mass murder," thus implying that this aspect of the Holocaust is unprecedented. But for Dawidowicz, the Holocaust stands as a unique event in two other major respects. First is the Nazi intention to annihilate all Jews, and second is the unique effect on Jewish history of having such a great proportion of its people murdered in so short a time. Although the overall effect of this proportion of victims is yet to be evaluated, the one point about which Dawidowicz is emphatic is that the continuity of Ashkenazic Jewish culture has been destroyed irrevocably. The danger of universalizing the Holocaust, to Dawidowicz, is that it can be seen to mitigate the moral responsibility of Nazi Germany. For a similar presentation with discussion, see Dawidowicz, Lucy." The Holocaust was Unique in Intent, Scope, and Effect." *Center Magazine* 14:4 (July/August 1981): 56-64.

* 3.10 *
Deutscher, Isaac. "The Jewish Tragedy and the Historian." In *The Non-Jewish Jew and Other Essays*. London: Oxford University Press, 1968. LC 68-57295.

In a brief essay, Deutscher, an eminent Marxist historian, discusses the relationship of the historian to the study of the Holocaust. He concludes that the Holocaust, as an event in which every Jewish person was to be murdered, is and will remain absolutely unique and beyond comprehension to the historian.

* 3.11 *
Eckhardt, A. Roy. "Is the Holocaust Unique?" *Worldview* 17:9 (September 1974): 31-35.

Eckhardt postulates a continuum of universality and particularity of events. All historical events are unique and to deny this is to gloss over real differences. Some events, however, are so unique as to be on a "level of incomparability (e.g., God, the Jewish people, the Devil....)" It is in this classification that Eckhardt places the Holocaust. He believes it is so different from other historical events that it is discontinuous with them, or "uniquely unique."

* 3.12 *
Eckhardt, A. Roy, and Alice L. Eckhardt. "The Holocaust and the Enigma of Uniqueness: A Philosophical Effort at Practical Clarification." *Annals of the American Academy of Political and Social Science* 450 (July 1980): 165-178.

The Eckhardts seek to analyze the Holocaust in such a way as to avoid mystifying the event—making it incomprehensible—and yet to preserve its singularity. To accomplish this, they set out three major categories of uniqueness. The first is the category of "ordinary uniqueness," a category into which all events fall, for all historical events are qualitatively different from one another. The second is the category of "unique uniqueness," a category into which "epoch making events" can be placed, events of such "singular importance" that they transform history. The third category, that of "transcending uniqueness," includes "events that are held to be essentially different from not only ordinary uniqueness but even unique uniqueness." Events in this category have the quality of absolute incomparability. The fields of science and history approach events from the stances of the first two categories, whereas the third category can only be understood by the experience of the beholder, involving a "radical leap from objectness to subjectness." The Eckhardts advise us that the

Holocaust must be approached from all three stances in order to avoid falsification of the event.

* 3.13 *
Eckhardt, A. Roy, with Alice L. Eckhardt. *Long Night's Journey into Day*. Detroit: Wayne State University Press, 1982. LC 81-14788. ISBN 0-8143-1692-1.

In a book that deals with the effect of the Holocaust on contemporary Jews and Christians, the Eckhardts devote a chapter to the central issue of the event's uniqueness. Again they maintain that a satisfactory analysis of the Holocaust must dialectically include both the singularity and the universality of the event. Once again calling the Holocaust "uniquely unique," referring to it as "metanoia, a climactic turning around of the world," they explain how it is also useful to both examine those elements that imbue the Holocaust with this quality of uniqueness as well as to see the ways in which it fits into historical context, that is, to see how "the Holocaust manifests discontinuity as well as continuity with the past."

* 3.14 *
Fackenheim, Emil. "Concerning Authentic and Unauthentic Responses to the Holocaust." *Holocaust and Genocide Studies* 1:1 (1986): 101-120.

In this article, Fackenheim states that it is not useful to define the Holocaust in terms of the unique and the universal, but rather in terms of authentic and unauthentic responses. Unauthenticity must follow if the Holocaust is seen as either solely unique or universal, for calling the Holocaust unique cuts it off from other historical events, and treating it universally unduly dilutes its significance. According to Fackenheim, the unique and the universal can be united through the medium of history if the Holocaust is considered as a historical event that is a "transmutation of history."

* 3.15 *
Fackenheim, Emil. *From Bergen-Belsen to Jerusalem: Contemporary Implications of the Holocaust*. Jerusalem: Cultural Department, World Jewish Congress, and Institute of Contemporary Jewry, Hebrew University, 1975. LC 78-311780.

In this earlier discussion of the Holocaust, Fackenheim strongly stresses the need to recognize the uniqueness of the Holocaust. Although he asserts that we must see the Holocaust as an event that occurred within the context of history and that we must try to explain the conditions that existed that could allow the Holocaust to happen, scholars must acknowledge that "each and every explanation is false, if not downright obscene, unless it is accompanied by a sense of utter inadequacy." He also asserts that comparisons to other somewhat similar events that have occurred, such as Hiroshima, not only serve to trivialize the Holocaust but also evade its essential uniqueness.

* 3.16 *
Fackenheim, Emil. "The Holocaust and Philosophy." *The Journal of Philosophy* 82:10 (October 1985): 505-514.

Fackenheim categorizes the Holocaust as a unique event, a "novum in the history of evil," and still asserts the importance of recognizing its uniqueness. The Armenian massacre, Fackenheim states, was a case of genocide, an attempt to murder a whole people. But Fackenheim finds important differences between that genocide and the Holocaust and concludes that "the Holocaust, then, is but one case of the class 'genocide.' As a case of the class: 'intended, planned, and largely successful extermination,' it is without precedent and, thus far at least, without sequel." For a response to Fackenheim's position taken in this article see Berel Lang, "Uniqueness and Explanation" *Journal of Philosophy* 82:10 (October 1985): 514-515.

* 3.17 *
Fackenheim, Emil. *To Mend the World: Foundations of Future Jewish Thought*. New York: Schocken Books, 1982. LC 81-16614. ISBN 0-8052-3795-X.

Fackenheim here says that the Holocaust is a unique event for both Jewish and world history because it presents a constellation of features not applicable to any other historical event. These features involve the fact that a large percentage of the total Jewish population was murdered; that the Nazis intended that no Jews survive; that being of Jewish birth constituted sufficient reason to be put to death; that although the Holocaust involved extensive physical brutality and murder the majority of the perpetrators were not sadists but "ordinary job holders with an extraordinary job"; and that the extermination of the Jewish people was an end in itself—no other "pragmatic" purpose for their death presented itself. Fackenheim recognizes that other catastrophic events have their own unique characteristics and must be understood in their own uniqueness.

* 3.18 *
Feingold, Henry L. "Determining the Uniqueness of the Holocaust: The Factor of Historical Valence." *Shoah* 2:2 (Spring 1981): 3-11.

Feingold reviews the positions of the universalists who place the Holocaust within the context of history on a continuum with other genocidal acts, and the particularists who insist on the Holocaust's essential uniqueness. With careful consideration of the events, Feingold arrives at the idea that the meaning of the

Holocaust, a meaning with which we are still struggling, lies more in the ways in which it differs from other genocides and not in the ways it is similar. Those key differences lie in the methodology employed in the execution of the Nazis' plan to exterminate the Jews and, novel to Feingold, in the fact that in destroying such a large portion of the Jewish population it destroyed a people whose contributions had a major impact on Western culture, thus transforming the future development of Western civilization. This impact, according to Feingold, will not be equally felt with the destruction of those other groups, such as the Armenians or the Gypsies, whose thinkers did not play as significant a role in the development of European culture.

* 3.19 *
Feingold, Henry L. "How Unique Is the Holocaust?" In *Genocide: Critical Issues of the Holocaust*. Ed. by Alex Grobman and Daniel Landes. Los Angeles: Simon Wiesenthal Center and Chappaqua, NY: Rossell Books, 1983. LC 83-3052. ISBN 0-940646-04-8.

Feingold asserts the uniqueness of the Holocaust and warns against trivializing the event by using it as a metaphor for all cases of oppression. He again stresses the idea that the Holocaust was unique in that it destroyed the Jews, a unique people, who produced a great many significant thinkers without whom European society would not be the same. He also characterizes the Holocaust's uniqueness as resting on a few essential characteristics: in its radical evil, in its scale, and more importantly in that it was the first time that the modern Western industrial system—a system intended to improve the quality of human life—was systematically used for the destruction of life.

* 3.20 *
Feuer, Lewis S. "The Reasoning of Holocaust Theology." *This World* no.14 (Spring/Summer 1986): 70-82.

Feuer, a well known philosopher, rejects the idea that it is useful to call the Holocaust unique. A unique event, he reasons, is one that can never happen again, "that is of necessity a class with one member." And yet a major, and to Feuer appropriate, concern about the Holocaust is that we understand it in such a way that we can ensure that a similar event will not happen again. If it were truly unique, as uniqueness is defined above, then our efforts to prevent recurrence are pointless: by definition this could not happen. Therefore Feuer suggests that it is more useful to understand the Holocaust as being unprecedented and not unique.

* 3.21 *
Fox, John P. "The Holocaust: A 'Non-Unique' Event for All Humanity?" In *Remembering for the Future:* *Working Papers and Addenda*. Vol. 2. Ed. by Yehuda Bauer, et al. Oxford: Pergamon Press, 1989. ISBN 0-08-036754-2.

Fox states that to gain insight into the significance of the Holocaust for humankind, we must abandon "the bitter and often pointless debate about whether, for a number of reasons, the Holocaust should be considered a totally 'unique' or 'mystical' event in the whole of human history." He feels a more correct approach must include the study of those constant conditions of humankind and society that facilitated an event like the Holocaust. It is within this context that Fox claims that "what made the Holocaust 'unique'" was the conjunction of both the presence and leadership of Adolf Hitler with "all the psychological and social features of 'man in society'...."

* 3.22 *
Freeman, Michael. "Genocide and Social Science." *Patterns of Prejudice* 20:4 (1986): 3-15.

From the point of view of the social sciences, Freeman finds that "the debate between uniqueness and comparison [of the Holocaust] may be misleading by presenting us with a false choice." Some argue that emphasizing the differences between the Holocaust and other genocidal events betters further understanding; others consider that a comparative emphasis better achieves this same end. Freeman believes that both approaches may be useful in understanding any case of genocide, including the Holocaust.

* 3.23 *
Friedlander, Henry. "Toward a Methodology of Teaching about the Holocaust." *Teachers College Record* 80:3 (February 1979): 519-542.

Recognizing that the Holocaust is increasingly being taught in American schools and colleges, Friedlander offers a rationale with which to approach the topic. In the course of his discussion he highlights the obvious importance of the issue of uniqueness in teaching about the Holocaust. Only if comparisons to other historical events can be made can we rightly and productively integrate the subject into a school curriculum. Friedlander warns that those who would make the uniqueness of the Holocaust into "sacred history" stifle serious historical discussion. Friedlander also discounts the concept that a unique aspect of the Holocaust includes the intention of the Nazis to annihilate the Jews and instead focuses on the methodology employed as its outstandingly unique feature, saying that "...in technological efficiency it was *sui generis*...."

* 3.24 *
Friedländer, Saul. "On the Possibility of the Holocaust: An Approach to a Historical Synthesis." In *The Holocaust as Historical Experience*. Ed. by Yehuda Bauer and Nathan Rotenstreich. New York: Holmes & Meier, 1981. LC 80-23136. ISBN 0-8419-0635-1.

Friedländer attempts to determine why, although three decades have passed, our historical understanding of the Holocaust is no better now than just following the war. One of the first topics he discusses is the issue of the Holocaust's uniqueness. He claims that the Holocaust was unique both inside Nazism and without. Inside Nazism it was unique because the Jews were the only group the Nazis intended to annihilate totally and they were the only group identified with absolute evil. In world history, Friedländer finds that "although there are precedents for an attempt at total physical eradication, the Nazi exterminatory drive was made unmistakably unique by its motivation." Although the uniqueness of the Holocaust denies our ability to use "explanatory categories of a generalizing kind," it should not prevent us from trying to identify and explain the historical trends that led up to the Holocaust.

* 3.25 *
Frey, Robert S. "Issues in Post-Holocaust Christian Theology." *Dialog: A Journal of Theology* (Summer 1983): 227-235.

Frey asserts that the Holocaust is a significant event for Christian theology and as such must be the concern of all denominations. In introducing his discussion, he tries to establish a rationale for determining the Holocaust's significance and in this context confronts the uniqueness issue. To him the Holocaust's uniqueness lies in the methodology of the event—the fact of a mass murder being carried out by a "state sponsored, technologically sophisticated system," in a thoroughly rational manner—as well as being reflected in a more intentionalist position that recognizes the Nazi attempt to murder all Jews by virtue of their being Jewish.

* 3.26 *
Friedman, Philip. "'Righteous Gentiles' in the Nazi Era." In *Roads to Extinction: Essays on the Holocaust*. Ed. by Ada June Friedman. New York: Jewish Publication Society and the Conference on Jewish Social Studies, 1980. LC 79-89818. ISBN 0-8276-0170-0.

Friedman, a prominent Jewish historian, concludes his essay with a statement that recognizes that the methodology employed in the Holocaust—a mass murder conducted under the auspices of a full state bureaucracy—was historically unprecedented.

* 3.27 *
Goldberg, Hillel. "Holocaust Theology: The Survivors Statement—Part I." *Tradition* 20:2 (Summer 1982): 141-154.

Goldberg, Hillel. "Holocaust Theology: The Survivors Statement—Part II." *Tradition* 20:4 (Winter 1982): 341-357.

Goldberg, who approaches the Holocaust from the Orthodox Jewish point of view, asserts that the Holocaust only seems unique, for every major Jewish catastrophe appears so for the people who live through the experience. "The Holocaust survivors remind us of the Jewish ability to respond to watershed disasters, each seen as unique in its own time." But this uniqueness should not be seen as a reason to assume its incomprehensibility for all time with regards to Jewish theology. A new theology not yet developed, Goldberg claims, is as necessary for an adequate response to the Holocaust as it was for other previous Jewish catastrophes, but those who choose to present the Holocaust as an event qualitatively different from other catastrophic events in Jewish history encourage silence and not speech on the issue and would prevent a new theology from developing.

* 3.28 *
Habermas, Jürgen. *The New Conservatism: Cultural Criticism and the Historians' Debate*. Ed. and trans. by Shierry Weber Nicholsen. Cambridge, MA: MIT Press, 1989. ISBN 0-262-08188-1.

Throughout two sections of his book Habermas, whose response to Nolte first triggered the German Debate, repeatedly criticizes those historians who would use the relativization of the Holocaust to deny its uniqueness. Their denial, he states, is put forth for apologetic reasons, in order to relieve Germans of the moral responsibility of the Nazi crimes of the past. Habermas believes that Auschwitz was an epoch-making event in that it "altered the conditions for the continuation of historical life contexts—and not only in Germany."

* 3.29 *
Hancock, Ian. "Uniqueness, Gypsies and Jews." In *Remembering for the Future: Working Papers and Addenda*. Vol. 2. Ed. by Yehuda Bauer, et al. Oxford: Pergamon Press, 1989. ISBN 0-08-036754-2.

Hancock, who was a special advisor to the U.S. Holocaust Memorial Council, denies the Jewish uniqueness of the Holocaust by extending it to encompass the Gypsies as well. He asserts that both the Jews and the Gypsies suffered the same fate during the Nazi Holocaust for exactly the same reasons thereby disclaiming that the Jews were the exclusive victims of the Nazi exterminating drive, a position frequently taken in the literature. Hancock cautions against generalizing the event beyond the Jews and Gypsies, however, emphasizing that no other groups were targeted for destruction with the same manner and intention as they were.

* 3.30 *

Heuser, Beatrice. "The *Historikerstreit*: Uniqueness and Comparability of the Holocaust." *German History* 6:1 (1988): 69-78.

Heuser reviews those writers important to the *Historikerstreit* with respect to their positions on the uniqueness and comparability of the Holocaust. She groups them into three categories. Some believe the event to be singularly unique and incomparable. The majority hold that a comparative approach can be used to show both its singularity and its similarity to other such events, accepting that comparison does not deny uniqueness. Lastly, there are some like Ernst Nolte who seem to use the event's comparability in an apologist manner, minimizing the unique elements of the Holocaust and thus trying to mitigate the moral responsibility of the German people for this crime.

* 3.31 *

Hilberg, Raul. "German Motivations for the Destruction of the Jews." *Midstream* (June 1965): 23-40.

Hilberg, noted historian and author of *The Destruction of the European Jews,* a work often referred to as a foundation for those who take a methodologist's position on the uniqueness of the Holocaust, here explores the possible motivations of the Germans in their attempt to destroy all Jews during the Holocaust. He introduces his article with a statement declaring the Holocaust's uniqueness: "in conception and execution, it was a unique occurance. When Adolf Hitler came to power in 1933, a modern bureaucracy set out for the first time to destroy an entire people."

* 3.32 *

Hilberg, Raul. "The Significance of the Holocaust." In *The Holocaust: Ideology, Bureaucracy and Genocide*. Ed. by Henry Friedlander and Sybil Milton. Millwood, NY: Kraus International Publications, 1980. LC 80-16913. ISBN 0-527-63807-2.

Hilberg attempts to arrive at the significance of the Holocaust for Western civilization. He asserts his position that the Holocaust is unique by terming it "*sui generis*" and "irreducibly distinct" from all other historical events. The implication of this uniqueness, Hilberg says, is that "one cannot explain it in terms of anything else....It demands its own literature and its own sources."

* 3.33 *

Jäckel, Eberhard. "The Miserable Practice of the Insinuators: The Uniqueness of the National-Socialist Crimes Cannot Be Denied." *Yad Vashem Studies* 19 (1988): 107-113.

Jäckel strongly criticizes those historians in the *Historikerstreit* who would seem to deny the uniqueness of the Holocaust. In an often quoted statement, he articulates a fact he considers "obvious" and "well known," that "the murder of the Jews was unique because never before had a state, with the authority of its responsible leader, decided and announced its intention to liquidate as completely as possible a certain group of people, including the aged, women, children and babies, and to implement the decision by means of all the official instruments of power at its disposal." Jäckel, however, does not consider the "question of uniqueness" to be decisive and provocatively asks, "Would it change anything had the National-Socialist murder not been unique?"

* 3.34 *

Jakobovits, Immanuel. "'Faith Ethics and the Holocaust': Some Personal, Theological, and Religious Responses to the Holocaust." *Holocaust and Genocide Studies* 3:4 (1988): 371-381.

Jakobovits succinctly summarizes the response of the Orthodox Jewish community to the claim that the Holocaust is unique. They deny "the uniqueness of the Holocaust as an event different in kind, and not merely in extent and barbarity, from any previous national catastrophe." They arrive at this position by seeing the destruction of European Jews as just another event within the pre-ordained realm of God's providence. Therefore they reject any term, such as Holocaust or Shoah, that sets it apart from previous Jewish catastrophes.

* 3.35 *

"Jewish Values in the Post-Holocaust Future: A Symposium." *Judaism* 16:3 (Summer 1967): 266-299.

This symposium on Jewish values after the Holocaust contains within it one of the earliest discussions of the uniqueness-universalist debate. Some of the major thinkers who express their ideas here are George Steiner, Elie Wiesel, and Emil Fackenheim. Both Weisel and Fackenheim emphasize the Holocaust's uniqueness, whereas Steiner urges a more universalist approach.

* 3.36 *

Katz, Steven T. "The 'Unique' Intentionality of the Holocaust." *Modern Judaism* 1:2 (September 1981): 161-183.

Katz tries to determine if the Holocaust is unique as an act of genocide, distinguishing first between genocide as an attempt to destroy totally the identity of a group and genocide as an attempt to murder a group as a whole. He then examines the Holocaust as an act of genocide in terms of both Jewish and world history, including in his examination such events as the Armenian massacre and the destruction of American Indians, and concludes that the Holocaust is unique in terms of the intention of the Nazis to murder all Jews, thus falling into the second category of genocide.

* 3.37 *
Kren, George M. "The Holocaust: Some Unresolved Issues." *Annals of Scholarship* 3:2 (1985): 39-61.

Kren takes issue with various scholars' positions on the uniqueness issue, including those of Lucy Dawidowicz, Emil Fackenheim, Henry Feingold, and A. Roy Eckhardt, among others. He concludes that "what differentiates the Holocaust from previous forms of mass killings is that it entailed a long range, systematically planned, bureaucratically administered decision...to eliminate population groups possessing certain characteristics defined by arbitrary, although formally rational criteria."

* 3.38 *
Kren, George M., and Leon Rappoport. *The Holocaust and the Crisis of Human Behavior*. New York: Holmes & Meier, 1980. LC 79-2381. ISBN 0-8419-0544-4.

Kren and Rappoport approach the Holocaust as a transformational event that they conceptualize as a "new level of mass destruction." Surveying the key categories of motives, methods, and emotions, they conclude that the Holocaust was qualitatively different from all previous acts of mass destruction. The motives of the Nazis were unique. In no other case was a people slated for total destruction as state policy. The methods employed, the fact that the killing process was "conducted more like a large scale industrial enterprise," was also different from other mass destructions. Furthermore, they state that the uniqueness of the Holocaust is evident when "the focus of inquiry is shifted from historical trends to the level of personal experience." The emotions that "accompanied or followed it" are qualitatively different from those experienced in other mass destructions.

* 3.39 *
Kulka, Otto Dov. "Singularity and Its Relativization: Changing Views in German Historiography on National Socialism and the 'Final Solution'." *Yad Vashem Studies* 19 (1988): 151-86.

Kulka, in response to the *Historikerstreit*, analyzes the shift some major German historians have exhibited in their tendency to relativize or historicize the uniqueness of the Third Reich and the Holocaust. Earlier writings by these same authors, Kulka shows, stressed the Holocaust's singularity, especially with respect to the importance anti-Semitism played in National Socialist ideology. He contrasts these writers with historians who have consistently considered the Holocaust to be a unique event in world history.

* 3.40 *
Kuper, Leo. "Genocidal Process: The German Genocide Against Jews." In *Genocide: Its Political Use in the Twentieth Century*. New Haven: Yale University Press, 1981. LC 81-16151. ISBN 0-300-02795-8.

Kuper states that the Holocaust had many unique elements. He includes among them the global scope of the Nazi intention to annihilate all Jews. Kuper emphasizes the bureaucratic organization and systematic nature of the killing process that yielded death camps organized in much the same way as a modern industrial plant.

* 3.41 *
Lanzmann, Claude. "From the Holocaust to the Holocaust." *Telos: A Quarterly Journal of Radical Thought* 42 (Winter 1979-80): 137-143.

Lanzmann states emphatically that the Holocaust was indeed unique, an incomparable crime, that calls forth an "entirely new metaphysical-juridical concept of 'crime against humanity.'" Although unique, one must not consider it a historical aberration, but rather as an event within historical context, where history has provided the necessary but not sufficient conditions for its occurrence. To Lanzmann the Holocaust is "a product of the entire Western World." To submerge the specificity of the event, however unique in its methodology and in the degree of its antisemitism, is to gloss over the moral responsibility of the Nazis and the fact that the "Holocaust was the enactment of Nazism."

* 3.42 *
Marrus, Michael Robert. "The Holocaust in Perspective." In *The Holocaust in History*. Hanover, NH: University Press of New England, 1987. LC 87-6291. ISBN 0-874-51-0.

Marrus affirms how careful we must be in using the concept of uniqueness in relation to the Holocaust. Historians, unlike social scientists, he explains, always study unique events and not general concepts such as "a war, rather than warfare and the Holocaust, rather than genocide." To apply the concept of uniqueness to the Holocaust in such a way as to make it a "political or theological affirmation" places the Holocaust in a category that limits historical study. Within this framework, Marrus accepts the Holocaust as unique in the sense of being unprecedented. He agrees with Bauer's position that one of the unique elements of the Holocaust was the intention of the Nazis to murder all Jews, but he also believes that the "killing process" utilized was unprecedented.

* 3.43 *
Neusner, Jacob. *Stranger at Home: "The Holocaust," Zionism, and American Judaism*. Chicago and London: University of Chicago Press, 1981. LC 80-19455. ISBN 0-226-57628-0.

In the preface to his book about American Judaism, Neusner, a prominent Jewish thinker, offers an interesting concept of the uniqueness of the Holocaust. Accepting the Holocaust as "self evidently unique" to the Jewish community, Neusner focuses on the function its uniqueness plays in American Judaism. Coupled with the establishment of the state of Israel, the uniqueness of the Holocaust makes up a part of a new myth about which American Jews, a religiously and culturally fragmented group, can organize their experience about themselves—a myth of "Holocaust and redemption." Neusner questions the value of this myth as a way for Jews to understand themselves in the American context, stating that the Holocaust is simply history and not "mythic theology."

* 3.44 *
Nolte, Ernst. "Between Historical Myth and Revisionism?: The Third Reich from the Perspective of 1980." *Yad Vashem Studies* 19 (1988): 49-63.

Nolte, in an essay on the place of Nazism within German history, examines the uniqueness of the Holocaust. While he admits to the fact that the Holocaust was both "singular and unique" and "without precedent in its motivation and execution," the thrust of his argument advances the idea that the Nazi Holocaust was in its essence both a reaction to and a "distorted copy" of the earlier annihilations of the Russian Revolution, making it "not a first act, not the original." Many historians have interpreted these remarks of Nolte's as being apologist in nature for the crimes of the Third Reich.

* 3.45 *
Nolte, Ernst. "A Past That Will Not Pass Away—A Speech It Was Possible to Write, But Not to Present." *Yad Vashem Studies* 19 (1988): 65-73.

In the article that triggered the *Historikerstreit*, Nolte claims that "with the sole exception of the technical process of gassing" Auschwitz was not unique. Nolte raises a series of questions, the most important of which are "wasn't the 'Gulag Archipelago' more original than Auschwitz? Wasn't the 'class murder' of the Bolsheviks the logical and factual precursor of 'racial murder' perpetrated by the National Socialists?...In its ultimate orgins, didn't Auschwitz perhaps spring from a past which indeed would not wish to pass away?" With these questions Nolte seems to imply that the atrocities of Auschwitz were not unique but merely a copy of the Gulag.

* 3.46 *
Papazian, Pierre. "A 'Unique Uniqueness?'" *Midstream* 30:4 (April 1984): 14-18.

Papazian takes issue with scholars who claim categorical uniqueness for the Holocaust, where uniqueness means that an event had no precedent and can have no antecedent. The Holocaust may have unique elements, and be unique to the Jewish people, who "never before were the victims of a premeditated state policy of total elimination of a national minority," but as genocide it was not unique in history but analogous to other genocidal events such as the Armenian massacre. Insisting on the Holocaust's uniqueness, Papazian believes, has the effect of "diminishing the gravity and moral implication of any genocide anywhere, anytime." He reviews the positions of many prominent writers whose works touch on the concept of the Holocaust's uniqueness, including those of Lucy Dawidowicz, Elie Wiesel, A. Roy and Alice L. Eckhardt, and George M. Kren and Leon Rappoport, among others, and criticizes each. See "Was the Holocaust Unique?..." below (3.56) for responses.

* 3.47 *
United States. President's Commission on the Holocaust. *Report to the President*. Washington, DC: Government Printing Office, 1979. LC 80-600962.

President Carter appointed this commission on November 1, 1978 in order to establish appropriate ways to commemorate the Holocaust. As a preface to the commission's report, Elie Wiesel wrote a letter to the President in which he made an important statement regarding the uniqueness of the Holocaust. "The universality of the Holocaust lies in its uniqueness; the Event is essentially Jewish, yet its interpretation is universal." The Commission considered the uniqueness of the Holocaust to be one of the two most important elements in the philosophical rationale that underlay its work. They found the Holocaust's uniqueness to lie in the fact that it was a "systematic, bureaucratic extermination" different in its "manner and purpose." With regards to the Nazis' purpose, what was novel in their approach was that they claimed that "There is evidence indicating that the Nazis intended to ultimately wipe out the Slavs and other people; had the war continued...Jews might not have remained the final victims of Nazi genocide, but they were certainly its first." And what was unprecedented was the intention to physically annihilate an entire people.

* 3.48 *
Rosenberg, Alan. "Was the Holocaust Unique? A Peculiar Question?" In *Genocide and the Modern Age: Etiology and Case Studies of Mass Death*. Ed. by Isidor Walliman and Michael N. Dobkowski. Westport, CT: Greenwood Press, 1987. LC 86-9978. ISBN 0-313-24198-8.

Rosenberg raises the complex issues surrounding the uniqueness question and creates a topology for the classification of the various ways this issue has been approached in Holocaust literature. He generates a critique of some of the central approaches taken about the uniqueness of the Holocaust.

* 3.49 *
Rosensaft, Menachem. "The Holocaust: History as Aberration." *Midstream* 23:5 (May 1977): 53-55.

Rosensaft, representing the absolutist position on the uniqueness issue, sees the Holocaust as a totally unprecedented, incomprehensible historical aberration, beyond the methods of historiography, beyond normal language, and incomparable to other historical events.

* 3.50 *
Rotenstreich, Nathan. "The Holocaust as a Unique Historical Event." *Patterns of Prejudice* 22:1 (Spring 1988): 14-20.

Rotenstreich attacks those historians in the *Historikerstreit* who try to show that the Holocaust was not unique. They claim that the Holocaust was either preconditioned by or a copy of Soviet atrocities. He argues that they have a confused notion of what it means for an event to be unique and that they generate a false analogy between race and class murder, postulating cause and effect relationships that did not exist. Rotenstreich also claims that the intent of these historians was apologetic, that their goal was to discredit the singularity of Nazism and the Holocaust for the purpose of diminishing German moral responsibility.

* 3.51 *
Rubenstein, Richard L. *The Cunning of History: The Holocaust and the American Future*. New York: Harper and Row, 1975. LC 75-9334. ISBN 0-06-067013-4.

Rubenstein states that there were unique elements to the Holocaust, namely, that it was an unprecedented attempt at genocide carried out by a legally sanctioned state bureaucracy. This uniqueness, however, must be seen in the context of the Holocaust as "an expression of some of the most significant political, moral, religious and demographic tendencies of Western civilization in the twentith century," as well as against the background of the extreme violence of our era.

* 3.52 *
Schorsch, Ismar. "The Holocaust and Jewish Survival." *Midstream* 27:1 (January 1981): 38-42.

According to Schorsch, an awareness of the Holocaust is steadily increasing among both the Jewish community and the general public. Its recollection serves the function of helping to unify the potentially divisive factions of American Jewry and has become, even more than Israel, a major part of American Jewish identity. Schorsch finds that the persistent claim of the Holocaust's uniqueness, however, adds nothing to the horrors of the Jewish genocide. He finds it to be both historically and politically counter-productive, and advises that it be rejected. The "fixation on uniqueness has prevented us from reaching out by universalizing the lessons of the Holocaust," Schorsch states, and it only "alienates potential allies from among other victims of organized human depravity."

* 3.53 *
Stein, Richard A. "Against Relativism: A Comment on the Debate on the Uniqueness of the Shoah." *Patterns of Prejudice* 21:2 (1987): 27-33.

Stein criticizes the many writers and historians who have reassessed the uniqueness of the Holocaust. He concludes that the Holocaust is in fact unique "in absolute, not relative terms" because of differences in its "motivation, method, scope, and impact." He also adds that its uniqueness stems from the uniqueness of the Jewish people.

* 3.54 *
Steiner, George. "The Long Life of Metaphor—a Theological-Metaphysical Approach to the Shoah." In *Comprehending the Holocaust: Historical and Literary Research*. Ed. by Asher Cohen, et al. Frankfurt am Main: Peter Lang, 1988. LC 88-8235. ISBN 3-631-40428-X.

George Steiner, the reknowned literary critic, discusses the uniqueness issue within the context of the hermeneutic dilemma that the Holocaust presents to Judaism. The dilemma becomes manifest in the questions of whether there is language adequate enough in which to speak about Auschwitz, and, on a theological level, whether after the Holocaust there is any longer language adequate enough to speak to, or about, God. He denies the uniqueness of the Holocaust on quantitative and qualitative grounds, rejecting both the intentionalist and the methodologist arguments for uniqueness. Steiner, however, recognizes that the centrality of the Holocaust's "presumed uniqueness" functions as "the cement of Jewish identity," uniting Jews of all cultures and religious leanings.

* 3.55 *
Talmon, J.L. "European History—Seedbed of the Holocaust." *Midstream* (May 1973): 3-25.

Talmon, an important Jewish historian, asserts that the Holocaust was in fact unique, different from all other earlier massacres. Its key differences lie in the intention of the Nazis to annihilate completely all Jews as well as in the systematic methods utilized for their killing. He analyzes those events and ideas that may have made the Holocaust possible.

* 3.56 *
"Was the Holocaust Unique?: Responses to Pierre Papazian." *Midstream* 30:4 (April 1984): 19-25.

The major writers whom Papazian criticized in his above cited article defend their positions and show where they agree and disagree with Papazian's comments on the uniqueness issue. Included are responses from Yehuda Bauer, Lucy S. Dawidowicz, A. Roy and Alice L. Eckhardt, George M. Kren and Leon Rappoport, and Nora Levin, among others.

* 3.57 *
Wertham, Frederic. "Looking at Potatoes from Below." In *A Sign for Cain: An Exploration of Human Violence*. London: Robert Hale, 1966. LC 66-20825.

Wertham strongly asserts that in process and methodology the Holocaust was completely unprecedented. He adds, however, that, although unprecedented, it was not a unique occurrence in the sense that it cannot happen again under similar circumstances.

* 3.58 *
Willis, Robert E. "Confessing God after Auschwitz: A Challenge for Christianity." *Cross Currents* 28 (Fall 1978): 269-287.

In examining the significance of the Holocaust for Christian theology, Willis analyzes the uniqueness of the Holocaust in terms of the uniqueness of Auschwitz. He concludes that the Holocaust was qualitatively unique and discontinuous with other evil events. The key to its uniqueness lies in the methodology employed—the "bureaucratic and technological apparatus of state" that was put into effect.

Chapter 4

THE VICTIMS WHO SURVIVED

by Sidney M. Bolkosky

I'm tired of being "a survivor." I want to be a person again.

A survivor of Auschwitz

Between 1933 and 1945, one-third of the Jews of the world lost their lives in the Holocaust.[1] Approximately four million Jews remained in Europe after World War II. Estimates of the number who survived the Nazi death, labor, and concentration camps, and the infamous death marches with their aftermath of more disease, starvation, and violent death, range from 250,000 to 300,000 people, the "saving remnant." Other Jews managed to stay alive in hiding or with partisan groups.[2] Still others endured the hardships of survival in the Soviet Union. From these numbers, approximately 250,000 Jewish refugees, "displaced persons," relocated from their former homes. Of these, 142,000 went to Israel, 72,000 to the United States, and 16,000 to Canada. From 1945-1951, approximately 550,000 more Jews left Eastern Europe.[3]

A "conspiracy of silence" seemed to follow the war: liberators who witnessed the camps were stunned into silence, struggling to cope with what they had seen; survivors were desolately silent, knowing they were already perceived as reminders of death; the perpetrators were indifferently silent, eager to continue their normal lives; the historians were baffled and silent; governments were ignorantly and defensively silent.

Victims who spoke of their experiences found themselves confronted by quizzical, unsympathetic listeners. One survivor recalled that "the message was

---

Studies of survivors' testimonies that concentrate on the ability of the afflicted to find meaning in suffering are at best problematic in the face of the overwhelming force of Holocaust testimonies. To many of those who survived, survival was not a triumph but an unbearable burden. "Nothing can ever be good again" and "All my happiness is gone for ever" are recurring motifs in their testimonies. The lives of survivors are forever haunted by images, sounds, and smells that contain ominous questions about survival and about guilt for having survived. "Why me?" and "Why was I saved?" appear in the testimonies over and over again. As Elie Wiesel phrased it, the question is not "to be *or* not to be" but rather "to be *and* not to be." One woman, a survivor of Auschwitz, compared herself to a hollow tree: "still alive but empty inside." The appended diary by Agi Rubin embodies these themes of despair, guilt, and inner emptiness.

'cry and you cry alone.' So we kept quiet."[4] Since around 1980, however, significant numbers of victims began to modify their attitudes of silence and survivor testimonies have supplemented historical examinations of the Holocaust with moving, personal evidence. Like all sources, these "life records" ought to be considered carefully and critically. As some historians have pointed out, oral histories, especially ones so laden with emotional trauma, cannot substitute for more traditional, written documents.[5]

While victims of the Holocaust directly experienced the consequences of the actions of the perpetrators, they could not know the character of the vast apparatus with its networks of bureaucracies and the professional involvements of every socio-economic stratum—the businessmen or the administrators, the physicians or the plumbers, the ideologues or the technicians. Nor could they know about the enormity of the camp system, its dependent relationships with the railroads and the military-industrial complex of Germany. Indeed, most could not know much about what occurred in the next barracks, much less the next camp. Should a student of the Holocaust wish to know how it came about and how it progressed, or raise questions about why it overwhelmed the Jews of Europe, he or she would be better served by turning to documents, records, and historical texts.

A survivor's testimony, then, constitutes only a small contribution to the subject of the history of the Holocaust and ought not supplant more traditional and professional approaches to history. Those testimonies, however, provide a deeper insight into the nature of the Holocaust. Even if a testifier incorrectly identifies an individual, offers misinformation about statistics, or misrepresents the chronology of events,[6] the value of the testimony still remains: the victim's experience, personalized, direct, and concrete, draws the listener into an intimate knowledge of the Holocaust; penetrates the very heart of the darkness in ways that not even diaries or other written accounts can approximate.

From these fragments of fragments, the centrality of loss for survivors emerges: the loss of a culture, brutally erased from the world physically and spiritually. Their testimonies give specific names of family members and friends, villages, and towns to this abstract loss. Even a historian who focuses primarily on the perpetrators ought to retain this central point. Whatever aspect of the Holocaust one addresses, the anguish of one person recounting his or her specific loss complements the broader historical information, confronts a listener directly and explicitly.

After years of silence, for those who decided to bear witness, the poverty of language presented an immediate barrier to communication. Few words that deal with the Holocaust are without controversy or qualification, in part because of the apparent inadequacy of conventional language: not the differences in tongues, but the utter lack of common usage for words like "bunk" or "cold," "roll call" or "train" hinder full appreciation of the narratives. "How can I tell you this?" recurs almost as a refrain; and the meaning is quite literal. What words will convey this extraordinary, other-worldly, unbelievable ordeal? The Czech writer, Helena Malirova, wrote as early as 1937 that "there is no human tongue capable of conveying the crimes perpetrated by the Nazis."[7] A failure to find common meanings for words in part explicates the fear that many victims retained, expressed eloquently by Primo Levi in his final work, that no matter how articulately or how much they spoke, survivors would be disbelieved.[8] "I don't believe this myself," exclaimed one man. "How can I expect you [the interviewer] or my children or anyone who wasn't there to believe it?"

Weighted words, full of recollections, heavy with associations that encase the meanings, become locked in a specific context. Elie Wiesel, among others, has written of the multiple meanings of each word: "Every word carries a hundred meanings."[9] Some survivors cannot see or speak about chimneys without recalling the chimneys at Auschwitz; some cannot hear a train without reliving the horrifying, box car deportation which caused the deaths of their families and divided their own lives into before and after; some cannot think of a word like "bunk" without envisioning the boards that served as beds in the camps.

This past and its lexicon remain inescapable and permeate the present for survivors. "The two worlds haunt each other," Lawrence Langer has noted, the one polluting the other.[10] Not only do these recollections infect the present, they settle like some miasma upon the warmer glow of the pre-war past. Memories, then, become "unspeakable" in over-determined ways. To many survivors, the events of the past may be unnerving to recall and thus to retell. But the more immediate problem of how to tell, what words to use, compounds the phenomenon, complicated again by the conviction that no listener can share the meanings of specific words.

Even the epithet, "survivor," creates controversy. A popular view of the victims revolves around Auschwitz, the place that has come to symbolize the six death camps and the quintessence of the Holocaust. Survivor, in that appraisal, means a person who suffered the vicissitudes, the atrocities, tortures, and attendant miseries of those hellish places. Some victims of those camps also believe that only those who lived through such horrors may be classified "true" survivors. A working definition adopted by some psychologists reenforces this stark and reduced one: "a survivor is someone who has survived an immediate and traumatic life-threatening experience."[11]

Given the program of the "Final Solution," however, the annihilation of the Jews of Europe, any European Jew who stayed alive from 1933-1945 might be termed a survivor. This would include those who managed to flee from Europe, those who were hidden, who made their ways to the Soviet Union, who joined partisan groups, who managed to evade the Germans by hiding in forests or barns or bunkers.

Jews who managed to survive endured the hardships of the destruction process with its ongoing, cumulative, efficient, and systematic procedures. In Germany, the process began with discriminatory laws, reaching a significant plateau in 1935 when the Nuremberg Laws removed civil and human rights from German Jews. Upon occupying Poland, the German military government passed similar laws, removing citizenship and all civil rights from Polish Jews.[12] Thus, the first stage of survival entailed intensified separation and isolation from non-Jews, removing them from what sociologist Helen Fein called their "universe of obligation."[13] The laws escalated degradation and humiliation and prepared the way for forced deportation. When Germany invaded Poland, over two million more Jews fell under their jurisdiction—which now included Czechoslovakia and Austria—and the numbers increased until, by 1942, German authority had almost all of Europe's Jews in its grasp.

Along with the non-Jewish victims of the war, Jews became subject to occupation, martial law, rationing, and curfews. But for Jews, just as the military government removed their citizenship, the other legislation took devastatingly harsher forms. Food rationing for Polish Jews was approximately one-third what it was for non-Jews.[14] By the end of September 1939, Reinhard Heydrich, one of the principal architects of the "Final Solution," had ordered ghettos established in major cities and towns on railroad lines.[15] By 1941, typhus had overtaken almost every ghetto; diseases, lice, malnutrition, overcrowding, and starvation began to take their tolls almost immediately. By mid-1944, when the Lodz Ghetto, the last major ghetto in Poland, was liquidated, between 500,000 and 700,000 Jews had died in ghettos.[16]

Those who survived recall watching their families wither away; enduring severe, forced labor conditions; living daily with uncertainty, confusion, and terror. They recall fathers and grandfathers suddenly appearing without their traditional beards, shaved or cut off by vindictive soldiers or SS men in the streets, a symbolic gesture which underscored the loss of their traditional authority. Such actions reduced those authority figures to helplessness as their families suffered the abuses of German policies. Traditional family roles and cohesion began to disintegrate: "I saw my father without his beard," said one woman who was thirteen at the inception of the Lodz Ghetto, "and he sat on a chair in the middle of the room and wept. All of us began to cry, the children, the baby, my mother and grandmother. It was like everything that held my life together suddenly fell apart."

Survival, then, entailed overcoming the loss of order and traditional authority; coping with the breakdown of family and community. In the testimony cited above, the beard and its senseless removal encapsulated all this. And the woman's conclusion to her story must be heard in the context of Jewish history and tradition to fathom its layered meanings: "I think my father gave up then—I knew he would not live much longer."

Jews in Eastern Poland and the Soviet Union, invaded by Germany in June 1941, immediately confronted violent deaths at the hands of the Einsatzgruppen or SS mobile killing units. Survival in those regions, before the Nazis implemented mass deportations to killing centers, involved combinations of fortuitous circumstances and blind luck. Escaping a ghetto meant abandoning family. Such an escape, already burdened with guilt, rarely included a definite destination and carried little prospect of help from non-Jews. Joining partisan groups in the vast forests of Eastern Europe forced the same abandonment and uncertainty.

Einsatzgruppen operations or *Aktionen* utilized native anti-Jewish elements and Jews lived in terror of daily raids which arbitrarily targeted particular groups—old people one time, children another—and drove them into makeshift hiding places like cellars, bunkers, or false rooms. Children learned not to cry; their parents learned to be prepared to smother them in order to save the lives of those hidden together. Between June 1941 and December 1942, when their operations ceased, the Einsatzgruppen murdered 1.4 to 1.5 million Jews in Eastern Europe.

For those fortunate enough to have non-Jewish people willing to offer assistance—at the risk of their own lives—a child might be saved, a family hidden for a while or smuggled through the countryside to some sort of hiding place. As one survivor observed, it was only after he had lost everyone in his family that escape for him became possible: there was nothing more to lose. Yet another, at age seven, was hidden by a Ukrainian peasant in a loft in his barn for more than two years. She and her parents and sister remained in almost complete silence for those years; lice-ridden, diseased, with muscles atrophied and in the most unsanitary of conditions. They crawled out from the barn, unable to walk, as the Russian armies advanced.

Such stories demonstrate that survival, in Langer's words, was "less a triumph of the will than an accident of the body, combined with so many gratuitous and fortuitous circumstances that we will probably never be able to disentangle chance from choice, or relate effect to cause."[17] Terrence Des Pres, in his pathbreaking work, *The Survivor: An Anatomy of Life in the Death Camps*, has suggested that determination and survival went hand in hand, that "it depended...on social bonding and interchange...on keeping dignity and moral sense active."[18] But in a book that describes methods of degradation and humiliation that stretch the human imagination, a book which includes a chapter entitled "The Excremental Assault," breaking the silence on this hitherto unspeakable subject, this type of traditional, idealistic language seems inappropriate and inadequate as it tries to salvage some shred of human dignity from the death camps.

A survivor of the Holocaust lives first with the identity of a victim—a victim who survived. As earnestly as he or she may yearn to throw off that status, to "be a person again," it remains irreducible and inescapable. Few survivors contend that they have freed themselves from the unique burdens of their pasts. Most recognize that "no matter how hard we try, no matter what someone tells you, we are all psychologically scarred forever."

Psychologists of all sorts have produced theories of "survivor syndromes" to explain and delineate the psychological, social, and political consequences of the Holocaust.[19] The suggested symptoms include anxiety, disturbances of cognition and memory, chronic depression, guilt, tendencies toward seclusion and isolation, and a heightened sense of vulnerability to danger. Post-Holocaust difficulties among survivors also often prove traumatic, according to some theorists, and are accompanied by drastic personality changes.[20]

Many survivors attest to the aftermath of such traumatic events; they openly discuss nightmares, "unreasonable" fears, and anxieties directly and palpably related to their Holocaust experiences and to the loss of families, communities, perhaps religion and dignity. For all the attempts at categorizing and formulating a "survivor syndrome," however, and despite the recurrent presence of obvious elements of the symptoms, generalizing and abstracting seems insensitive and unwise. While some seem to exemplify the syndrome with textbook exactness, others appear to have escaped several of the symptoms: those who speak of clinging to the slightest of human conventions under the most inhuman circumstances contrast those who speak from apparent deep depression of the loss of feeling and social awareness. Paradoxically, interviews with survivors regularly reveal both types of sentiment in the same person, again defying simple categorization.

To attribute survival to a strong "will to live" or, as one survivor put it, "the power of positive thinking," seems rather foolish under such circumstances. Viktor Frankl, survivor and psychiatrist, has proffered a "will-to-meaning" which suggests that victims had the choice, the "ultimate freedom," to determine their attitude toward their plight. He argued that the ability to rise above the circumstances of the camp, finding meaning in the suffering, made some victims "worthy of their suffering."[21] Yet, positive attitudes of this sort, revelation of meaning to their suffering, rarely emerge from survivor narratives. Indeed, the unresolved quest for meaning betrays a possible source for survivor depression and discontent.

While many survivors, striving to find meaning in their experience, speak of the will to live, many others openly confess their deep depression during the war, the wish to die after losing families or witnessing some horrible tortures. Still others openly admit to an utter lack of concern, an apathy and indifference especially in the camps. Yet others suggest they acquired "survival skills," ways of "floating above the reality," or "pulling down the shade," or "becoming small and even invisible as if no SS man could see me in Auschwitz." The search for "survivor prototypes," given this wide range of attitudes, seems futile and artificial; and such optimistic conclusions as Frankl's, when applied to survivor experiences, appear at best problematic in the face of the overwhelming force of Holocaust testimonies.

Rather than a triumph, survival, to many victims who survived, oppressed them like some unbearable weight. "Nothing can ever be good again," one child survivor told psychoanalyst Edith Sterba, "and even if it is good, what good is it to me if my family is not here to enjoy it....I cannot forget my family. It will never be possible to replace the loss of my family....All my happiness is gone forever."[22] Charlotte Delbo, in a poignant yet shocking admission, revealed that as she gave birth to a child in 1952 she "didn't think of the joy that a child would bring me; I was thinking...of the women my age [32] who had died in degradation without knowing that joy."[23] And a survivor of Lvov, upon the birth of his grandchild, immediately commented upon the specific ways infants were murdered by the Einsatzgruppen. A sense of having survived at the expense of others lingers in these thoughts, as it permeates such frank works as Borowski's: "It is true, others may be dying, but one is somehow still alive, one has enough food, enough strength to work...."[24]

Once again, memories intersect, haunt the present and impede what might be considered a "normal, happy existence." Images, sounds, smells linger arduously, bearing ominous questions about survival and guilt. "How come me? Again and again I have asked myself

'Why was I saved?'" burst out one survivor. And another: "Why me? Okay, I can see my [old] parents or the child, but why not my brother or my sister?" In this demanding entreaty, the survivor seems to acknowledge the standards of Auschwitz: yes, the parents and children were too old to work, but why not the healthy young man and woman, his brother and sister? To whom is the question addressed? Does he question himself, or the interviewer, or God? Behind the questions lurks awareness of arbitrary, indiscriminate luck.

A bizarre sort of guilt lurks, too. Like much about the Holocaust, the guilt remains paradoxical: irrational and logical. Irrational for obvious reasons—no victim had choices; the selections may have been random in their perception, but Dr. Mengele and his ilk had their own insanely logical criteria. At the base of some "survivor guilt"—another inadequate term—lies Borowski's brooding recognition that life depended on death. The monumental uncertainties, deeply irrational guilt, and the recollection of impotence in the face of overwhelming forces remain irreducible and immovable.

Intimations of the inadequacies of language, the prospect of exacerbating anguished memories, the disquieting implications of guilt which do not consider the realities of the Nazi system, along with myriad other factors coalesce to constrain speaking. Survivors' silence about their experiences ought not mystify us. Yet, after years of relative silence, some survivors have taken their cues from Elie Wiesel who admonished them to be witnesses. He echoed the Jewish historian Emmanuel Ringelblum's call from the Warsaw Ghetto that Jews witness the catastrophe and "write and record" it.

A witness transforms memory into history, and some survivors intuited the prospect of sharing their memories in order to preserve the historical record. For others, witnessing brought the prospect of retelling in order to regain dignity and meaning, or to discover a reason for their turmoil and their survival. If speaking has not freed them from their nightmares or unburdened them of their memories, if it has not uncovered the mystery of the meaning of Jewish suffering during the Holocaust, if it has not conferred a lost dignity, it has revealed new, deeper levels of Holocaust history.

With or without testifying, survivors have created new lives for themselves. They have not, because they cannot, completely freed themselves from their pasts. Nevertheless, for all that they carry with them, they endured, bore children, in some cases overcame postwar urges for suicide, and became vital parts of their communities. Their stories and their voices present the rest of the world with profound questions about the human spirit, endurance, and survival. They rarely provide affirmative answers, hope, or inspiration simply because of the nature of the Holocaust, a process which disallowed avenues for martyrdom and heroism, for triumphant joy at final victory.

For survivors, Elie Wiesel has said, the question is not "to be *or* not to be," but "to be *and* not to be." One woman, a survivor of Auschwitz, compared herself to a hollow tree that still lived, "still alive, but empty inside." They adumbrate our present and future and tacitly challenge us to examine what their heritage of pointless murder means for our own lives and the lives of our children.

NOTES

1. Raul Hilberg, "The Statistic," in *Unanswered Questions: Nazi Germany and the Genocide of the Jews*, ed. by Francois Furet (New York: Schocken Books, 1989), 155-171.

2. Martin Gilbert, *The Macmillan Atlas of the Holocaust* (New York: Macmillan, 1982), 236.

3. Raul Hilberg, *The Destruction of the European Jews* (New York: Quadrangle Books, 1961), 729-737.

4. All quotations from survivor testimonies come from interviews on audio and/or videotape housed in the University of Michigan-Dearborn Holocaust Survivor Collection of the Mardigian Library.

5. See, for example, Lucy S. Dawidowicz, "How They Teach the Holocaust," *Commentary* (December 1990): 25-32 and "Interview with Lucy S. Dawidowicz," *Booklist* (15 June 1989): 1753-1754.

6. Benzion Dinur, commenting on the value and uncertainty of survivor memoirs and testimonies, argued that the reason behind such misinformation "need not be any desire to 'amend' or to 'improve' upon actual events for any ulterior purpose." Dinur continued that such errors grow naturally from the nature of such reminiscences. Benzion Dinur, "Problems Confronting 'Yad Vashem' in Its Work of Research," *Yad Vashem Studies* 1 (1957): 7-30.

7. Nachem Blumenthal, "On the Nazi Vocabulary," *Yad Vashem Studies* 1 (1957): 49-66.

8. Primo Levi, *The Drowned and the Saved*, trans. by Raymond Rosenthal (New York and London: Summit Books, 1988), 11-12.

9. Elie Wiesel, "A Plea for Survivors," in *A Jew Today* (New York: Vintage Books, 1978), 218-247.

10. Lawrence Langer, *Versions of Survival: The Holocaust and the Human Spirit* (Albany: State University of New York Press, 1982), 88.

11. Jack Nusan Porter, "Is There a Survivors' Syndrome?" *Journal of Psychology and Judaism* 6:1 (Fall/Winter 1981).

12. See, for example, Nuremberg documents that treat the legal status of Jews in Eastern Europe in *The Holocaust: Selected Documents in Eighteen Volumes*, ed. by John Mendelsohn (New York: Garland Publishers, 1982), 199-223.

13. Helen Fein, *Accounting for Genocide* (New York: Free Press, 1979), 92.

14. International Military Tribunal, Document 864-PS, *Crimes of War and Aggression*, XXVI, 377-383.

15. "Heydrich's Instructions to Chiefs of Einsatzgruppen, September 21, 1939," *A Holocaust Reader*, ed. by Lucy S. Dawidowicz (New York: Behrman House, 1976), 59-64.

16. Hilberg, "The Statistic" and *Destruction*, 173.

17. Langer, 28.

18. Terence Des Pres, *The Survivor: An Anatomy of Life in the Death Camps* (New York: Oxford University Press, 1976), vii.

19. Porter, 33-52; Henry Krystal, ed., *Massive Psychic Trauma* (New York: International Universities Press, 1968); for an excellent review of the psychological literature, see Arlene Steinberg, "Holocaust Survivors and Their Children: A Review of the Clinical Literature," *Healing Their Wounds: Psychotherapy with Holocaust Survivors and Their Families* (New York: Praeger, 1989).

20. William Niederland, "Clinical Observations on the 'Survivor Syndrome'," *International Journal of Psychoanalysis* 49 (1968): 313-315.

21. Viktor E. Frankl, *Man's Search for Meaning* (Boston: Beacon Press, 1959).

22. Edith Sterba, "The Effect of Persecutions on Adolescents," in *Massive Psychic Trauma*, ed. by Henry Krystal (New York: International Universities Press, 1968), 51-60.

23. Charlotte Delbo, quoted in Langer, 88.

24. Tadeus Borowski, *This Way for the Gas, Ladies and Gentlemen*, trans. by Barbara Vedder (New York: Penguin Books, 1976), 48.

CHAPTER 4: ANNOTATED BIBLIOGRAPHY

Major Titles

* 4.1 *
Brenner, Robert Reeve. *The Faith and Doubt of Holocaust Survivors*. New York: The Free Press, 1980. LC 79-006764. ISBN 0-029-044-200.

Brenner examines the ways in which the Holocaust affected the religious beliefs of those who survived. Drawing on the responses of almost one thousand survivors, Brenner attempted to discover what survivors thought then, and think now, about God, the Jewish people, and the religious doctrines they had once been brought up to believe in. Fifty-two percent responded that the Holocaust had little or no effect on their religious behavior. Others found their faith challenged in that they questioned the existence of a god that would permit such atrocities.

* 4.2 *
Dimsdale, Joel E., ed. *Survivors, Victims, and Perpetrators: Essays on the Nazi Holocaust*. Washington, New York, and London: Hemisphere, 1980. LC 79-24834. ISBN 0-89116-145-7.

Dimsdale's collection of essays is of varying quality; it contains some important articles by Leo Eitinger, Robert Jay Lifton, and others on psychological effects of survivors' experiences, the impact on children of survivors, coping mechanisms and psychotherapy. The book is divided into three parts—"The Setting," "The Victim," and "The Perpetrator"—and contains an excellent historical article by Raul Hilberg on "The Nature of the Process," excerpts from the diaries of Goebbels and Hoess (commandant of Auschwitz), and essays by George Mosse on Weimar intellectuals and the rise of Nazism and by John Steiner on "The SS Yesterday and Today: A Sociopsychological View."

* 4.3 *
Epstein, Helen. *Children of the Holocaust: Conversations with Sons and Daughters of Survivors*. New York: G.P. Putnam & Sons, 1979. LC 78-023429. ISBN 0-14-011284-7.

Epstein's was the first book to deal with the situation and phenomenon of the second generation. Much of her book is autobiographical, moving back and forth between her own story and those of others she interviewed in Canada, Israel, and the United States. She found consistent patterns of behavior including guilt, anxiety, and the need to protect parents. Her examples demonstrate that some survivors placed extraordinary burdens of guilt on their children, often shrouded in silence, because of their experiences; that some children of survivors experienced deep-rooted anxieties and fears that derived from their unique status; and that in most cases the guilt and anxiety were accompanied by exaggerated needs to protect or shield their parents.

* 4.4 *
Hass, Aaron. *In the Shadow of the Holocaust: The Second Generation*. Ithaca, NY: Cornell University Press, 1990. LC 90-55124. ISBN 0-8014-2477-1.

Drawing on interviews and survey materials, Hass provides an informed account of the experiences of the second generation in terms of depression, guilt, anger, feelings of being different, and difficulty in separating from parents. Hass devotes particular attention to how much survivors talked about their experiences to their children and how this affected the children. He also examines the attitude of the second generation to such issues as anti-Semitism, Jewish identity, Israel, God, and intermarriage.

* 4.5 *
Krystal, Henry, ed. *Massive Psychic Trauma*. New York: International Universities Press, 1968. LC 68-29657. ISBN 0-8236-8146-7.

Although it has received criticism in the last ten years, Krystal's psychoanalytic work on massive psychic trauma continues to offer a starting point for the study of the effects of the Holocaust on victims who survived. He has identified, along with William Niederland, a "survivor syndrome" which includes varying degrees of avoidance, depression, intrusion of memories, and other symptoms.

* 4.6 *
Langer, Lawrence. *Holocaust Testimonies: The Ruins of Memory*. New Haven: Yale University Press, 1991. LC 90-044768. ISBN 0-300-04966-8.

Langer continues his earlier thesis (see 4.7) now supported by his extensive viewing of the videotapes in the Fortunoff Video Archives for Holocaust Testimonies at Yale. Langer here posits five types of memory: "deep memory," "anguished memory," "humiliated memory," "tainted memory," and "unheroic memory." "Deep memory" refers to the coexistence of "two adjacent worlds that occasionally intrude on each other"; "anguished memory" disallows any closure or resolution of painful recollections as it "imprisons the consciousness it should be liberating"; each of the other three deals with various aspects of humiliating experiences or recollections which survivors find shameful or "tainted." For another interpretation, see 2.134.

* 4.7 *
Langer, Lawrence. *Versions of Survival: The Holocaust and the Human Spirit*. Albany: State University of New York Press, 1982. LC 81-14560. ISBN 0-87395-583-8.

Langer has relentlessly pursued the strands of Holocaust narratives and memoirs to rebut any sanguine theories of inspiration or tutelary conclusions—particularly those of Frankl and Des Pres. Langer argues that any value judgments based on the morality of civilized life are spurious when applied to life as it was lived in the concentration and death camps. He argues that victims of the Holocaust daily were presented with "choiceless choices," alternative courses of action in which equally horrible ends resulted. Langer's is perhaps the most important work on survivor testimonies. It is a seminal and uncompromisingly honest interpretation of survivors' accounts.

* 4.8 *
Levi, Primo. *The Drowned and the Saved*. Trans. by Raymond Rosenthal. New York and London: Summit Books, 1988. LC 87-018052. ISBN 0-671-63280-9.

In his last book before his death, Primo Levi offers his final penetrating, searing reflections on the nature of the survivor's experience. Particularly powerful and suggestive are his concept of "the gray zone," the area between moral judgments in which the experiences of the victims become blurred with the behavior of the perpetrators, experiences for which there can be no mediation and no relief, and his discussions of the tainted lives full of paradoxical shame. His is perhaps the most disturbing and necessary of survivor essays.

* 4.9 *
Moskovitz, Sarah. *Love Despite Hate: Child Survivors of the Holocaust and Their Adult Lives*. New York: Schocken, 1983. LC 81-084112. ISBN 0-805-238-018.

At the end of the war, the British government allowed one thousand child survivors to enter England. The German refugee Alice Goldberger established and ran a home for some of these children in Surrey. Moskovitz interviewed twenty-four of these survivors, most of them citizens of the U.S. or Israel. They still suffer continuing feelings of loss and outsiderhood but they are reasonably well-adjusted and actively involved in communal affairs.

* 4.10 *
Sichrovsky, Peter. *Born Guilty: Children of Nazi Families*. New York: Basic Books, 1988. LC 87-47773. ISBN 0-465-00741-4.

Sichrovsky, an Austrian-born journalist, investigated how children and grandchildren of former Nazi war criminals deal with their heritage. He found that, initially, they knew very little of their parents' or grandparents' activities. The ways in which the children discovered their ancestors' crimes varied widely, as did their reactions to what they learned. Reactions ranged from severe guilt to outright denial.

* 4.11 *
Sigal, John J., and Morton Weinfeld. *Trauma and Rebirth: Intergenerational Effects of the Holocaust*. Westport, CT: Praeger Publisher, 1989. ISBN 0-275-92906-X.

In an empirical study, the authors examine the psychological consequences of the Holocaust across three generations of a sample group in Montreal. They challenge the dominant thrust of previous studies which emphasized dysfunction in the family life of survivors and psychological impairment in their children.

* 4.12 *
Wiesel, Elie. *Night*. Trans. from the French by Stella Rodeway. New York: Avon, 1969. LC 72-33106. First published in Yiddish in 1958.

Perhaps the first and still one of the most powerfully moving survivor accounts, Wiesel's autobiographical novel has become the classic survivor testimony. Tracing the experience of his family from Sighet, Transylvania, into the ghetto, then to Auschwitz, and finally the death march and Bergen Belsen, Wiesel expresses the disillusionment, anguish, and utter disorientation wrought by the Holocaust on children and families. The opening pages brilliantly describe pre-Holocaust Jewish life and the final passages stand in stark contrast to that opening. For another interpretation, see 2.121.

Briefly Annotated Titles

* 4.13 *
Bar-On, Dan. *Legacy of Silence: Encounters with Children of the Third Reich*. Cambridge, MA: Harvard University Press, 1989. LC 89-7484. ISBN 0-674-52185-4.

Israeli psychologist Bar-On interviewed middle-aged Germans concerning their feelings about their knowledge that relatives and parents had committed crimes during the Holocaust. Bar-On found that between parents and children there were "double walls" of denial. For another interpretation, see 8.1.

* 4.14 *
Bergmann, Martin S., and Milton Jucovy, eds. *Generations of the Holocaust*. New York: Columbia University Press, 1990. LC 81-068405. ISBN 0-231-07423-9.

Generations of the Holocaust is the work of the Group for Psychoanalytic Study of the Effect of the Holocaust on the Second Generation. Contributors stress the complexity of survivors' influences on children. The editors also include a section on the children of Nazis.

* 4.15 *
Frankl, Viktor E. *Man's Search for Meaning: An Introduction to Logotherapy*. New York: Simon & Schuster, 1984. LC 84-10520. ISBN 0-671-24422-1 pa.

A psychiatrist survivor attributed his survival to the development of a philosophy which focuses on the meaning of life. Logotherapy is based on finding meaning in and through suffering. Frankl challenges the Bettelheim thesis that those who became more like their tormentors had the best chance of living. For another interpretation, see 2.23.

* 4.16 *
Friedlander, Saul. *When Memory Comes*. New York: Farrar, Straus and Giroux, 1979. LC 74-857796. ISBN 0-374-52272-3.

When Memory Comes is a powerful and suggestive memoir of a Jewish orphan's Holocaust experience dealing with the issue of memory and history. Friedlander was left by his parents, at age seven, in a Catholic seminary in France. He was baptized and trained for the priesthood. When the war ended, he discovered his actual identity and made his way to Israel in 1948.

* 4.17 *
Gill, Anton. *The Journey Back from Hell*. New York: William Morrow, 1989. LC 88-038663. ISBN 0-380-70777-2.

Gill explores the variety of adjustments made by 120 survivors to the concentration camp experience. He also examines how they adjusted after liberation. His book is based on interviews with survivors of varying social and political backgrounds and from many countries.

* 4.18 *
Levi, Primo. *Survival in Auschwitz: The Nazi Assault on Humanity*. New York: Collier Books, 1961. First published as *If This Is a Man*. Trans. from the Italian by Stuart Woolf. New York: Orion Press, 1959. LC 59-13327.

This was Levi's first book. It is a brilliant, frank, and moving account of life and death in Auschwitz in which he offered remarkable perceptions into the nature and meaning of survival. It remains a classic along with Wiesel's *Night*. For another interpretation, see 2.66.

* 4.19 *
Luel, Steven A., and Paul Marcus, eds. *Psychoanalytic Reflections on the Holocaust*. New York: Ktav, 1984. ISBN 0-088125-041-4.

The ongoing impact of the Holocaust on survivors and especially on society in general is the subject of this collection of essays. Most essays focus on the psychological and moral implications of the Holocaust.

* 4.20 *
Porter, Jack Nusan. "Is There a Survivors' Syndrome?" *Journal of Psychology and Judaism* 6:1 (Fall/Winter 1981).

In a review of the psychological literature on survivors and children of survivors up to 1981, Porter concludes that there are survivor syndromes. He draws upon the work of Niederland and Krystal in particular.

* 4.21 *
Rabinowitz, Dorothy. *New Lives: Survivors of the Holocaust Living in America*. New York: Avon Books, 1976. LC 76-13709. ISBN 0-380-01790-3.

Rabinowitz has compiled a sensitive and thoughtful collection of interviews with 108 survivors living in America. The interviewees discuss the Holocaust, the difficulties of beginning again, acclimating to America, and reconstructing their lives.

* 4.22 *
Sichrovsky, Peter. *Strangers in Their Own Land*. New York: Basic Books, 1986. ISBN 0-14-009965-4.

Sichrovsky here investigates how children and grandchildren of Holocaust survivors now living in Austria and Germany deal with their situations.

* 4.23 *
Steinberg, Arlene. "Holocaust Survivors and Their Children: A Review of the Clinical Literature." In *Healing Their Wounds: Psychotherapy with Holocaust Survivors and Their Families*. Ed. by Paul Marcys and Alan Rosenberg. New York: Praeger, 1989. LC 89-8638. ISBN 0-275-92948-5.

Steinberg reviews the clinical literature on survivors and their families up to 1989. Her work is thorough and objective.

* 4.24 *
Steinitz, Lucy Y., and David M. Szonyi. *Living after the Holocaust: Reflections by Children of Survivors Living in America*. New York: Bloch Publishing, 1979. LC 76-8322. ISBN 0-686-77156-7.

The editors, themselves children of survivors, collected a series of essays, poems, and reflections on what it means to be part of the second generation. They emphasize the privilege and responsibilities of their status.

* 4.25 *
Wiesel, Elie. *A Jew Today*. Trans. from the French by Marion Wiesel. New York: Vintage Books, 1978. LC 77-00261. ISBN 0-394-42054-3.

A Jew Today contains some of Wiesel's most profound essays, including two on survivors. His "A Plea for Survivors" raises the question of silence, remembering, and the treatment of survivors in the post-Holocaust world.

* 4.26 *
Young, James E. *Writing and Rewriting the Holocaust: Narrative and the Consequences of Interpretation*. Bloomington: Indiana University Press, 1988. LC 87-35791. ISBN 0-253-36716-6.

Young's book is a provocative and scholarly work on historical and literary interpretation of oral, visual, and written texts on the Holocaust. Young is somewhat over-theoretical in places but his insights into the problems that surround narrative accounts of the Holocaust are extraordinary. For another interpretation, see 2.138.

Appendix: The Diary

by **Agi Rubin**
with commentary by **Sidney Bolkosky**

Part I: Description

April 20, 1945. 10:00 p.m.

We are surrounded by flames. Our liberators are coming. And our enemies are also approaching. So we, forsaken, tired and hungry, are walking toward liberation. The marching mass, the long line of the transport, drags itself along. It moves slowly and painfully, on and on.

I see only four people. A dying woman who still wants to live, her two daughters, and myself. We surround the dying one, and we are begging her to look at us. She must go on. She wants to continue, but she falls back. Her strength is gone. She cannot move. There is nothing to do. We are not going either. Let them shoot us. That is all we can expect from the German overlords.

I look around: flames, terrible screams coming from the line. I look up at the sky. I call for my father who is suffering somewhere in Russia. "Help me, Father. You are the only one. Only you are waiting for me. I still have to live for your sake." I receive no answer. Only dying words.

[Mr. Bolkosky's commentaries are set off by indentation.]

> One day after her official liberation, on April 23, 1945, Agi Rubin began her journal to retell the final days of her personal experience of the Holocaust. Part I, a descriptive account, begins near the end, on a road from Ravensbruck concentration camp. It concludes in a barn in a prisoner of war camp near the small town of Mulberg. Before the death march from Ravensbruck, there was Auschwitz, and the death march in January. And before that, Agi faced the flames of the crematorium at Auschwitz every day from May 1944 until November. She and her family, along with more than 25,000 other Jews, had been torn from their home in Munkacs, an Orthodox and Hasidic center in Carpatho-Ruthenia. In 1939, Hungary had occupied the region, and in 1944 the Germans came. Shortly after that, Agi's father was taken to forced labor in Russia.
>
> Sometime after May 15, 1944, members of the Hungarian fascist Arrow Cross Party forced the Jews of Munkacz into a brick yard where they kept them for four weeks. Then came the deportation—the dividing line in so many lives: the stench, the darkness, starvation and thirst and dying of the cattle car. Auschwitz, she recalled in an interview, made her "divided, forlorn" forever as her mother, aunt, and little brother went to one side and she, reluctantly, to the other. In Auschwitz, Agi clung to her two girlfriends from home and their mother. They adopted each other and she became the "lager-sister" [camp sister] and daughter to "My Lady," her "lager-mother." Their Auschwitz family survived even the first death march from Auschwitz to Gleiwitz and then to Ravensbruck.
>
> By April 1945, the western Allies had reached Bergen-Belsen and drawn within sixty miles of Ravensbruck; the Russians approached from the east and had reached a point some thirty miles from the camp. In a host of evacuations that served no purpose other than the agonizing murder of thousands of prisoners, the Germans evacuated Ravensbruck on April 15. Seventeen thousand women and 40,000 men struggled westward amidst flames and shooting. Martin Gilbert has quoted one Red Cross observer of this march: "As I approached them, I could see that they had sunken cheeks, distended bellies and swollen ankles...All of a sudden, a whole column of those starving wretches appeared. In each row a sick woman was supported or dragged along by her fellow-detainees. A young SS woman supervisor with a police dog on a leash led the column, followed by two girls who incessantly hurled abuse at the poor women." Hundreds died of exhaustion and hundreds more were shot.[1] For Agi, yet another dividing point in her life came as the march arrived at a wooded area outside the town of Malchow—another of what she later called her "foundations," an event

76 GENOCIDE

which has haunted her incessantly, inescapably, the death of "My Lady." Somehow, she and her two "sisters" continued, dazed, broken, almost automatons, until the end, the place where liberation finally stopped the march, in a barn, in a makeshift prisoner of war camp at Mulberg.

Delirious, I even turn to the guards: "Herr Posten! Herr Posten! Sir, if you know God a little bit, bring me a little wagon for the dying one. With this maybe I can save a life." No answer. The gentlemen are passing by. A wagon does not arrive.

Suddenly, I have a thought. I grab my lady and start pulling her along. "Let's run. Let's take her. Let's save her. The liberators are here. She has to live." We don't carry her too far.

We stop, and she falls down. And the three of us, two sisters and I, the lager-sister, remain standing. Now we wait for the end. I don't want to leave them. And the countless rows, the dark rows, pass us by.

Someone among them calls out. "Agi, Agi, come with us. You can see they are barely alive. You are strong. You can still work. You cannot stay with them. Come with us."

They are enticing me. Suddenly, I turn around and look at my threesome. Maybe I could go to my father, to my liberators. But still no. Something is telling me that I should stay. No, no, I'm not going to leave them. I grab my girlfriends. We hug each other and cry bitterly under the sky. This is how we remain together and wait for the truck that will eventually come for us.

A lifesaver. A truck arrives, and they throw us in it. The truck takes us further and further, and we leave the transport behind. God Almighty, a miracle has happened. We are sitting together. And, sitting up, we soon fall asleep.

Half delirious, Agi dragged her lagermother to some imagined liberation—a vision, a fantasy of her heroic father rescuing them all. Illusions compounded illusions as other marchers called to her to save herself because she "can still work." This march, unlike earlier ones, would serve absolutely no purpose. The Germans had run out of work tasks for slave laborers. Yet the illusion lingered. As if to demonstrate the chaos, the pointless confusion, a German truck stops and assists the four companions. Sleep comes—a relief about which Agi later said: "And I hate myself for it. We slept." All sleep, for Agi, contains that one.

As in a half-dream, I hear that the mother doesn't live anymore. I wake up. But then we say, "Let's not disturb her." After all, we know that this is the end.

We fall into a very deep sleep. Neither the flames around us nor the liberation interests us because that's impossible. We don't care about anything. We don't even see who else is on the truck and how we are escaping from the Germans. I'm sleeping because I haven't slept for two weeks. And because I'm out of my senses. And because I don't want to be aware of anything.

We come to a sudden stop, and they throw us out of the truck. The truck [driver] has accomplished his task, and he turns around and disappears.

An elderly German man receives us. He listens to our sufferings, about the starvation and the misery. We three introduce ourselves as the dead mother's daughters, and the German is almost fatherly toward us. We surround our dead one who lies on the ground.

We want to speak with her, but no words come out. We stare at the ground until we are shoved in the back by a German guard. "Remove that corpse immediately!" I look at him in bewilderment. I don't move. Then he hits me hard across the face.

Dizzy and hysterical, I fall to the ground. I get up still crying and disoriented. Then the old German consoles me. He says to the guard that he shouldn't hurt me.

We removed the coat from the corpse. And we ate a piece of potato that had been in her pocket. Don't be surprised. We were hungry.

Later, they brought a few stretchers for the very sick ones. We have to move on again. I bent down to the dead one, very close to her, and I asked for her forgiveness. I wanted to pray but I couldn't. I had only the tears in my eyes.

We kissed her and left her in the end of a ditch. We went on with the heavy stretchers. We went and we went. We wanted to get to some place warm, wherever that could be.

Surprise. We arrive at a barn that is filled with hay. Without thinking, we throw ourselves into that linen. There is no word nor thought within us. One moment and we are all in a deep sleep. Let's dream, let's forget. This day has brought enough.

April 21, 1945.

We get up and look around the room. Soon we are meeting our companions in the barn. They are Hungarians, Poles, Russians, French, Mischlingen. None make a very good impression on me.

The sun comes in. Food is arriving. Bread, margarine, and black coffee that we haven't seen in many weeks. To us, this is like a fairy tale, a Cinderella story. We could have eaten all the bread, and there was enough to fill us. But we don't dare. "What will happen tomorrow?" We look at it and put it aside.

As the healthiest among us three, I start to work. I bring water and wash the sick ones. The morning goes by quickly. Sleeping, eating, drinking coffee, washing ourselves for the first time in two weeks. Noon comes and dinner arrives—a two-course meal! Soup and a potato. So we are kept busy. We are under shelter and getting food, but are afraid of having to go on. So we don't eat everything.

In the afternoon, we were surprised by a policeman at the window who speaks Hungarian. He had served in Germany. We spoke with him and he promised to bring canned milk in the evening. We look forward to that reunion. But he disappeared, and we never saw him again.

There is dead silence in the room. Suddenly the door opens, and the opening of this door brings back our lives. A clean-cut officer enters whom I immediately like. And others, too. Unusual feeling—they are not Germans yet they wear military uniforms. But these are our friends. They come in and bring smiles and contentment. Who they are we don't know. We only know that they are good.

One bends down, but before he does, he looks like he is afraid of something. He says to us, "Juden?" Then he looks to the side, and he tries to hold back his tears. He leaves the room, wipes his eyes, and comes back.

Using his kindest words, he tries to comfort us. He tells us that he is a prisoner of war, a Jew. They are going to take us to the hospital which is a very good place. Suddenly, we are unsure. "A hospital? What is this?" All three of us answer in horror that we are healthy. We are afraid to go to this hospital. But the Jewish friend whose name we don't yet know stops the words in our mouths. "Don't be afraid. We are taking you to a good place. A place where we will take care of you."

Soon we gather ourselves and our belongings—a quarter of a bread and a potato. The wind is biting and we walk alongside this Jewish man. The raindrops that hit our faces almost raise our spirits. But they are still faces of tired, broken prisoners, completely in a daze.

As we walk, I think of those from our transport still on the march—still being harassed, kicked, herded along. Suddenly a police car approaches us and stops. We are lucky. It goes on, and we are able to continue our journey. Eventually, we come to the hospital.

In the courtyard, new faces greet us. These men look at us with astonishment. We are still in our dirty camp clothes, so it is not surprising that they are shocked by our appearance. We go down a hallway, into one of the rooms, where we are met by Frenchmen. We don't understand each other's languages, but we do understand their kindness and compassion. Soon we are able to take warm showers and then to sink into bed. How good it feels!

The room fills with inquiring Frenchmen, Yugoslavs, Britishers, and others of many nationalities. These are soldiers who had not seen anyone like us before. They are very interested in our fate. And when they leave, they bid good-bye with sadness and sensitivity in their eyes. They don't want to overly disturb us.

Now a bucketful of sweet milk arrives, and everyone can have as much as they want. And we don't have to stand in line for it! This didn't happen to us in the German camps. But now this has happened too!

Next, a very kind-looking French doctor comes in. He goes around and writes down everybody's ailment on his chart. Yes, we have come to live this, too!

I am here in a prisoner of war camp—me as a woman, as a child. The American and English care [CARE] packages come, and they provide what we need in the camp. After dinner, the doctor says goodnight. He wishes us rest and peace. "By tomorrow, not one German will remain here at the hospital. They will no longer rule over us." We take his word and sink toward sleep. For the first time since I can remember, we can stretch out on white sheets. We can rest. They are not going to wake us in the morning for the *Appel* [roll-call].

From out of deep sleep we wake for breakfast. Hot tea is awaiting us. From the potatoes that remain, I fix a good puree that we spread over the bread. We still restrict ourselves to one slice of bread only. We may need the rest for tomorrow. But the biggest specialty at home wouldn't have tasted as good as this English tea and pureed potato. Hungry people appreciate anything that means food.

After breakfast, we get a very profitable visitor who brings us men's shirts and men's underwear. It doesn't matter, it's clean. We are not scratching and always imagining the lice.

Many of the visitors' names we don't know. We can't even write down their names because there are so many. Among them is the Jewish man who brought us to the hospital. He takes the three of us as sisters. His name is Marco Rubinich Belgrade.

All the men are very courteous and kind, but this one is different. His name we must mark down, and even if we didn't, we would remember. From his story, I learn that he went through some of the same suffering that we did. He lost his family. But he himself didn't suffer as much because he was a prisoner of war and treated as a soldier through political arrangements. Thus, he didn't see the Auschwitz crematorium but only heard about it. Only through our stories did he learn what was done.

It's enough to listen to these horrors. The gas, the crematorium, the forced marches. It's enough to hear about it, let alone to see it. But enough about this.

Marco comes in very often and always arrives with fresh news. "Be happy. Tomorrow, or the day after tomorrow at the latest, we will be free. All the German dogs have left the hospital already. Now we are done with them. Brothers, sisters, be happy!"

The poor man was wasting his breath trying to make us feel good. We still don't believe anything. Up until the last moment, the crematorium is our nightmare. We are telling everybody about it, whether we want to or not. Our stories are only about the crematorium, whether we want to or not. Either in my dream or if I am awake, I can only see the flames in front of me. And the vision never fades.

> With her economy of words, this repeated passage appears arresting and may lie at the heart of Agi's—and most survivors'—consciousness. Their thoughts, if not their words, "whether we want to or not" remain with the flames, with the crematorium. Agi's experience in Auschwitz may symbolize that more than most. As her daily task, the Germans assigned her to sort the clothes of dead Jews. She worked each day directly across from one of the crematoria; watched the flames and the smoke and refused to believe—both believed and did not believe. And so, whether she wants to or not, she speaks of simultaneously expressing another feeling: "but enough about this."

Too much talk tires us, so it's better for us to rest. The visitors are courteous. They would like to sit longer, but the doctor makes them leave.

This is our new life. The day goes fast and it is good. But now it's quiet. It's night. Let's sleep. Let's dream that we shall be happy.

> Behind the diary is her story, her recollections of how "everything always happened at night...the screaming and the crying" and her "no sleep without nightmares" without "the sounds...in the night." To speak of happiness under such circumstances and with such memories demands a double definition, a historically specific context. The camp at Mulberg, among the POWs, defined a new happiness: free from torture, from starvation, from the fear that there would be no bread or potato tomorrow; and haunted by the memories and the reality of lost family, childhood, community.

April 22, 1945. The Liberation Day.

There is a lot of commotion in the hallway. We wake up wondering—maybe it's our liberators. We don't wait very long because the men rush in with great joy. "The Russians are here! Be happy! We are free! In a week or two Germany will be completely *kaput*!"

Later on, a very high-ranking Russian officer and his retinue come in. Our friend Marco is with them as their translator. His face glows with happiness. He introduces us to the officer. We show him the numbers on our arms that we received in Auschwitz. The officer shakes his head. "This is rare."

This is not the way I pictured the liberation. It's not true. I don't believe it. "They can still take us back," I think to myself with fear. But I don't say anything out loud. The high-ranking officer kindly says good-bye.

In the room, we just look at each other. We can't speak. Everybody's eyes are filled with tears. But nobody dares to show it.

Everybody can go wherever they want when they are healthy. Now we are free. We are no longer under the Germans.

Later, Marco comes back and asks if we want to go to Palestine. He can register the three of us as Palestinian or as British citizens. He tells us that Munkacz will be under the Russians. And once that happens, we would not be able to leave.

We asked for time to think about it. After a few hours, we decided to stay with our first thought: we are going home. We are going home to look around our town. And after that, we will emigrate somewhere. Marco agrees with our plan although he fears it might then be too late to get out. But he doesn't want to confuse us. In a case like this, you can't tell someone what to do. So we will be registered as Munkaczi and as Hungarians.

We talked about the past and the future. And about the future and the past. We have suffered enough. Now good will come. Let the sunshine brighten our life.

As concerns the food, it's not even news anymore. I think we could get back very fast to a regular life—a normal, human way of life as we were used to years before.

I was liberated in a prisoner of war camp among very fine people. They took care of us with good will and compassion. Life is unusual, and so is this liberation. Who knows where my poor father is suffering? Who knows what he is thinking about his family from which hardly anybody remains? Who knows where he is liberated? Who knows where and when I will see him again?

Father, you are alone and you are my only thought. I am liberated, but I am afraid to go home. I am afraid for myself. But let's wait now. We shall see what will happen. Now let there be peace, peace of mind.

Part II: Reflections

April 1946 (?)—Auschwitz: An Endless Haunting.

> **One of the countless, inexplicable reunions, Agi discovered that her father had survived in Russia and had returned to Munkacz shortly after its liberation by the Red Army in October 1944. After three months in Mulberg, she had heard rumors that her father lived and managed to find her way back to Munkacz amidst the postwar chaos. Her father had rented a large house which served as a haven for those few who returned—an "open house" for those in transit. She convinced her father, two aunts, and cousin that they should follow Marco's advice and emigrate. One aunt had discovered the address of a third aunt who had married and emigrated to America before the war. With the American aunt's assistance, Agi and her family, ten people in all, attained passports and visas to leave Czechoslovakia in 1948. But what follows in her diary marked the first anniversary of Agi's liberation, an anniversary which stimulated reflections that have never left her.**

The sound on the radio tells me it's twelve o'clock. I'm sitting and thinking back. The sound of the music tears at my heart because it always takes me back and makes me remember. Remember what? Don't ask. I shouldn't even write it. It's Auschwitz. Auschwitz and its flames and its electrified barbed wire.

I'm standing all alone in a large crowd. My face is close to the wires. I'm looking into the distance. I want to muffle the sounds that I hear, but they are too close. Just a little quiet, a little peace, a few people—that's all I want around me. Not even other people, but just myself alone. I'd like to be able to think, but thinking is impossible.

Beyond the wire fence there is another crowd of people. But these are different from ourselves. These people are free. They are the ones who rule over us.

They are the German dogs. God, suddenly I can't even find words to describe them properly.

God, You took my mother away, and my little brother. Where did You take them? To the fire?

I'm looking into the fire. And I think I would go completely crazy if I thought that You, God in Heaven, You are also looking upon all of this. And You have not gone crazy.

You looked upon us while the innocent children, and my dear ones, were taken there. To *us* You granted the gift of having to suffer, of having to see all this, and of having to continue to exist. To *them* You gave Your mercy. They listened to the music in freedom. We were there to play the music for them. We played and we listened through our broken hearts. We were their prisoners. We were the ones whose minds You took away completely.

> **Here are sounded several motifs of Agi's life that reflect the "haunting" of survivors: the ineffable name, not of God, but of Auschwitz ("I shouldn't even write it"); the questions, from a Munkacever who remembers the famous Munkaczi rebbe and the quality of religious life in the Carpatho-Ruthenian region where Jews breathed religious piety as naturally as air,[2] about God and mercy, insanity and survival. Fire, the phenomenon and the word, have assumed different meanings and significance in Agi's mind and life. Every fire bears the one she faced each day across from the crematorium, as every sleep partakes of that sleep for which "I hate myself" because her lager-mother slipped away while it enveloped her. Now, one year after, she ponders and agonizes over the possible meanings of these motifs, over the unholy or even absurd conclusions that lurk beneath the surface.**

So I'm standing and I'm gazing. And the music plays unceasingly in my ears. It takes me home, sometimes all the way back home.

Can anyone comprehend what is going on? Broken-hearted Jewish prisoners are playing the music of broken hearts. They play "In Havana" and other sentimental pieces. They play "The Angels are Singing When You Talk to Me, My Sweetheart." But that is still nothing: They are playing "Mama."

The others, the killers, the ruthless German dogs with their wine bottles and their cigarettes, they are enjoying themselves. They are having a party. If we are lucky, they'll throw down a cigarette butt. One of us will pick it up.

We are the prisoners doomed to death. And I can only call ourselves stupid, ignorant, crazy. Because to live like this—denied everyone and everything, kicked and shoved underfoot, degraded and humiliated, doped and numb—only people who would just as soon be dead could live through this. Having lived it, we are no longer among the living. The living could not survive it.

Now, suddenly, I realize I have tears in my eyes. They are streaming down my face. Suddenly, I feel like I am home again and with my family. I am with those who were everything to me. It feels like a very long time ago that we were all together. But the fire, the cursed flames, still don't let me think. They wake me up from my dreams, and my dreams hold the only hope for going on. The flames have awakened me again. Their hissing and crackling have awakened me again.

God, Oh God, give me a little strength. Give me a little sense and take away the daze. I can't even think from the dope. I would like to be able to think that it still might be true that somebody, somewhere, waits for me.

This cannot be true: That I am here, on this earth, all by myself. That there is fire. That there are people. That there are bones. That there are the suffocated innocents. This is impossible: That ours, that mine, are there.

"Time had no meaning," Agi said during an interview. It has become a permeable boundary again. Where is she as she writes these words? In her father's house in Munkacz in 1946? In the barracks, at the crematorium, listening to the prisoners entertain the SS in 1944? Is she alive or dead? Or is she "alive *and* dead"?[3] The diary now includes an attempt to confront the past, to analyze or reflect upon the events that altered and marked Agi's life and continue to assert a multivalent power over every thought, act, and word.

So perhaps it is good that I can only think rarely and rarely do I come to my senses. For it seems like now, at these moments, I am out of the daze. I can think clearly. I can see the whole truth.

You can do without mind and thought and still exist. But a living human being has to think. Therefore, we are not people anymore. We can't call ourselves human beings because we can no longer think. And without this, life ceases to be life. It is gone completely.

I feel like a dead, degraded, cowardly Jew. And tomorrow, maybe tonight, I will have to get up to work and put on a living face. I will have to sew up the clothes and cut up the materials left by those who have gone to the flames. I will have to listen to the humiliating curses and feel completely numb and ignorant. All of this is true. All of this is real.

My thoughts have started to wander again. They are wandering to Auschwitz. They are visiting the flames. They are in Heaven and talking with God. And who knows where else they are wandering?

My pen wants to go on and on by itself. It is sliding from my hand. At times like this my strength leaves me. It leaves me each time I see it all again. When I see the truth once more.

Music is supposed to be a good tonic. It's supposed to quiet your nerves. And so it quiets mine. But now I am turning off the radio. I don't want music. I don't want Auschwitz music. I don't want flame music. I don't want to see it all again. I don't want the haunting.

Now I ask You, God, again:

Give me a little peaceful dream. Or no dream at all. Because yesterday and always I only dream about my dead ones. This is not true, God! Tell me it's not true! And tell me I'm not questioning You in such an ugly way.

Now, as a cowardly soul, I beg Your forgiveness. I thank You for at least giving my father back to me. Please give him peace of mind in his life. Give peace and well-being to all my loved ones. Give me no more dreams that will make me think back and remember again. Give me quietness.

God in Heaven, Amen.

May 6, 1946.

God, what's wrong with me? I'm choked with my own cry. I would like to cry, but I can't. Today, too, I came home full of anger. For no reason. I went to the theater and to a coffee house. And my poor companion couldn't figure out what happened to me, with this unfortunate crazy soul. He couldn't understand my behavior. He questioned, but unsuccessfully. I couldn't answer. I could find no reason myself. How could I answer it? One thing I can say: That to think back is very painful. And I'm longing after a mother.

What is a family? Only a word. A home and food. Some passengers who by chance find a resting place. But when the comedy is over, the stage is taken apart. And soon it disappears.

"It's hard to be smart. But it's harder yet, with a smart head, to live as though ignorant."

People who dream of happiness, they wake up to sorrow. People who dream of sorrow, they wake up joyfully and meet their surroundings with happiness. This is an unsolved mystery, but tomorrow we might find a wise one who will solve it. Maybe tomorrow, maybe in ten thousand years. Or maybe the wise one is already among us.

Nobody is right, and nobody is mistaken. What is true is the truth: Justice.

April 1950, Philadelphia.

Five years is like half a century when you live your life with bitterness and reminiscing. Even when you are at a party, and you are in a good mood, later you realize your guilt. Is this anger? Is this conscience? Is this self-consciousness or self-criticism?

But why? This is a mystery deep within the soul. But what do you want, my soul, if I can call you that? Five years. it's not long to write it down, and it's very easy to pronounce it. But, when I remember, I am carried back even more clearly than any time before.

It's five years today that I was liberated from the Germans' chain. In my egotistic human way, I was happy then that I existed. That I remained alive. I was happy for every given day. For every bite that I received. But then I didn't live yet. I just thought I lived. My head was full of haze. I didn't plan because I thought everything came naturally, by itself. To like and be liked I took for granted. And I didn't know that I would always and always be carried back.

And yet I'd just stepped into life's school. I was only a child then, but the dolls I used to play with were so far from me. I had to mature very quickly. But it was too fast, and it didn't bring any fruit. Because at this stage of my life I still can't give myself any clear ideas.

I don't know what I am. I don't know when I'm doing right or wrong. Am I right when I am thinking? And *for what* I am thinking? Many times, I think I was just born for trouble. To be a burden and sorrow to everybody, because I cannot laugh. They say, "If you laugh, everybody laughs with you. And if you cry, you are alone."

Yes, my diary, I am here in America, Amerika! After many fights, I consented to come here rather than to Palestine. I consented to come here because of my family. I didn't take anything too seriously. And that's why I'm fighting now with everybody. Every day is a fight. Because I'm trying to make myself understood. My rights, my principles, and somebody else's—with my own double standards! But nobody's right and nobody's wrong. Only the truth is right. But that is so rare. Now I'm pushing the years back. For me, that's like putting the clock back a few minutes. Time elapses, but the impossible does not fade from my eyes.

Five years ago I finished my diary with a sentence that was full of hope that I will see my father again. Yes, God helped me. My dream became a reality. We met in my home town and with unbelievable happiness we were reunited. But my father left our home when I was a child, when he was taken away to the forced labor camp. And now he's realizing his daughter has her own thoughts about life's problems.

I knew we should get out of my home town because it would be Russian. And I also knew that in my home town, where I lived my sweetest, happiest life, it would never return. I wanted to escape from the memories because I didn't want to live through first the good, then the miserable destroying of life. Either way, for us to pack and leave meant little. We'd already tasted wandering, and it seems like this is the pattern of our lives—pack and go, pack and go.

1965: In Hospital.

After being established in the States as a citizen, wife, and finally a mother of three young children, I was told that I was sick and would have to part from my family for an indefinite time of hospitalization. This agony evoked all the dormant horrors of being a camp inmate. As I entered the hospital corridor, it looked like a typical jail. I was becoming a prisoner all over again. Entering the room and meeting my roommate only added to my sense of a nightmare returned. The lady was German.

As a fourteen-year-old carefree child whose interests were school, family, and friends, I watched our little city of Munkacz become a strange place. It filled with Hungarian and German occupying soldiers. Our neighbors whom we'd known all our lives suddenly became alien to us. We had to wear the yellow star. Still we walked our streets not realizing the seriousness of the situation.

One sunny, spring day, two German soldiers took up residence in our home. After two weeks, the order came to pack up five kilos of belongings and leave our house. We marched with our fellow Jews to a brick factory on the outskirts of the city. We made our new home under the skies. My mother and my young, newly-wed aunt, my beautiful six-year-old brother, and I. We had no father at our side to protect us because he had been taken to a forced labor camp well before. My aunt became the head of our household. She found a sleigh and out of it improvised a bedroom. We felt lucky to have such privileges.

The young people formed a working unit, throwing bricks to each other and making a kind of fence for privacy. And so we lived. Four weeks after this, we were wakened by a harsh command: "Pack! We are taking you to a place where you will work."

It was dark and gloomy when we were loaded on a caravan of closed cattlewagons, filled to capacity without even standing room. My mother made up a corner in her lap, and we all huddled together very quietly.

I remember my mother's thoughts were with my father's safety. And to me she kept saying, "I hope God will watch over you not to starve. I know you have a headache, my child." She must have had a premonition that I would be the only one to be spared from the gas chambers.

Yes, the train came to a halt after four or five days of travel. Suddenly, the gate of the wagon was opened up, and the carload was ordered to form lines. "Push! Push! Fast! Fast!"—mothers holding onto their babies and older ones. My first thought of the striped clothes and shaven heads: "This is the crazy unit."

Soon I found myself in front of an extremely tall German officer who ordered me to the left. I ran back to my mother. I wanted to be with my family [who were sent to the right]. How lucky they are to be together. And I shouldn't be with them?

But Mengele, the Angel of Death, would not grant me the other side. After three attempts to run back to the moving line, I was thrown to the sandy gravel, pleading to my mother. With a concerned ache in her eyes, she saw her child being thrown and pushed.

With a wave of her gentle hand, she accomplished what could not be done by bayonet force. "Go, my child, go. We will see each other tomorrow."

And I've been going ever since then.

NOTES

1. Martin Gilbert, *The Macmillan Atlas of the Holocaust* (New York: Macmillan, 1982), 227.

2. See Herman Dicker, *Piety and Perseverance: Jews from the Carpathian Mountains* (New York: Sepher-Herman Press, Inc., 1981) and *The Marmaros Book* (Tel Aviv: Beit Marmaros, 1983).

3. Hank Greenspan, "Lives as Texts: Symptoms as Modes of Recounting in the Life Histories of Holocaust Survivors," to appear in *Storied Lives*, ed. by R. Ochberg and G. Rosenfeld (New Haven: Yale University Press).

Chapter 5

THE ARMENIAN GENOCIDE: REVISIONISM AND DENIAL

by **Rouben Adalian**

The Turkish government has adopted three lines of argument to convince the world that nothing out of the ordinary happened to the Armenians during the years 1915-1923. Three theses have been advanced: the denial thesis; the revisionist thesis; and the justification thesis. The three theses can in turn be divided among six categories of authors as follows: participants, apologists, rationalizers, revisionists, disinformers, and distorters. In the years since 1923 several factors have contributed to the world's acquiescence in the Turkish program of denial and revisionism. First, Turkey became respectable as the Turkish Republic under Kemal Attaturk; second, Turkey joined the United Nations as a charter member in 1945; and third, Turkey joined the North Atlantic Treaty Organization in 1952.

In the unfolding process of genocide, denial is the final stage. There was little doubt at the end of World War I that the Young Turk government had implemented measures which resulted in the decimation of the Armenian population in the Ottoman Empire. Yet two years later, the effort to rehabilitate the survivors was abandoned. Three years after that, the question of responsibility was entirely forgotten. Since then, the government of Turkey has found it convenient to deny that anything out of the ordinary happened to the Armenians.

The coverup of the Armenian genocide was not the work of the Turkish government alone. The course of political developments in the decades following World War I furnished a favorable environment for ignoring the consequences of genocide. The silence of the international community emboldened the Turkish government to make the denial of the Armenian genocide a state policy. Only the matter of legitimizing the official view on the non-occurrence of the event remained.

Post-War Unsettlement

The rapid changes in government that took place after World War I, including the shift of power from Istanbul to Ankara and the emergence of new leaders, hopelessly complicated the effort for a serious deliberation on the Armenian genocide. Defeated in war, the Young Turk cabinet resigned in 1918. The Committee of Union and Progress (CUP), which led the Young Turk movement, disbanded. The administration of what

THE ARMENIAN GENOCIDE: 1915-1923
AN INTRODUCTION

by Rouben Adalian

When in the Spring of 1915 the Young Turk government issued orders for the mass deportation of the Armenians from Armenia and Anatolia to Syria and Mesopotamia, the U.S. ambassador to Turkey, Henry Morgenthau, realized that the edicts were only part of a larger scheme to destroy the Armenian people. In prior decades Armenians in the Ottoman Empire had endured large-scale atrocities and tens of thousands had fallen victim to the brutal repression practiced by the Ottoman sultans. Yet, the sultans had had no policy that affected the totality of the Armenian population throughout the empire. By 1923 when the modern-day Turkish Republic was founded, close to two million Armenians had vanished from a part of the world which they had inhabited for thousands of years. The only exception to this annihilation was a community that survived in Constantinople.

"The Murder of a Nation"

Morgenthau and Arnold Toynbee, then a young scholar entrusted with the task of documenting the events of 1915 and 1916, described the forcible removal of the Armenians from their homes and their expulsion to the desert as "the murder of a nation." The Young Turk government carried out the deportations under conditions of extreme deprivation and at a pace that induced death by starvation, dehydration, and exhaustion. It also organized special units which conducted a thoroughgoing slaughter of civilians—men, women, and children. Called a resettlement plan, the deportations and massacres were nothing less than a gigantic scheme to deprive the Armenians of their property, lives, and right to continued habitation in their ancestral homeland.

In the final analysis the genocide resulted in the theft of the contested homeland of the Armenians, for without Armenians there could be no Armenia. The possibility that the aspirations of this people might lead to a claim to a separate national existence had become anathema to the Young Turk party that governed the Ottoman Empire during World War I. Their solution was to destroy both the people and their nationalist aspirations.

Armenians as a Subject Minority

The Armenians had lived as a subject minority in the Ottoman Empire for some 400 years. Influenced by Western political thought in the nineteenth century, they began to organize and to petition the government to improve their living conditions, which were characterized by maladministration and the absence of security. In some parts of the Ottoman state Armenians fared well; they were dominant in certain sectors of the economy such as commerce and the specialized crafts. The combination of their financial success and their political activism became the source of an autocratic regime's obstinante refusal to consider reform, for reform and improvement might have led to a measure of self-government.

The Young Turks

No less opposed to the regime were the reform-minded Ottomans who organized the Committee for Union and Progress. This group, known as the Young Turks, overthrew the Sultan. Their own nationalist plank, however, tended to emphasize once again racial privilege for Turks and exclusion of the Armenians who clearly gained nothing in the change of government. On the contrary, as Germany encouraged the war party to join in the impending conflict in 1914, the Armenians were caught in a vise. To the east where the Ottomans intended to advance lay the vast stretches of the Russian Empire. Because most of the Armenians lived on either side of the border, inevitably their homes would be engulfed in a battle area. Although loyal to their government, with thousands responding to the draft, the Armenian population was not sympathetic to the cause of the war.

A Homogenous Turkish State

Determined to use the opportunity of war and the alliance with Germany to restore the prestige of the declining Ottoman state, the Young Turks moved mercilessly against the Armenians whom they accused of treason and sedition once the war began to go badly for them. Unable to create the envisioned empire that would include all of the Turkic peoples to the East, the Ottoman government devised a method of purging the state of an ethno-religious minority whose existence stood at odds with the ideology of the extremist Young Turks. The decision to wage war against an unsuspecting civilian population was but an incremental escalation of a succession of decisions taken illegally and secretly to bring about the entry of the Ottomans into World War I.

(continued on page 87)

The genocide was the culmination of the policy to create a homogenous Turkish state. By the time all the fighting in the Middle East had ended and the Ottoman Empire had fallen, the Armenian presence had been erased from those areas that would constitute Kemal Ataturk's Republic of Turkey.

ANNOTATED BIBLIOGRAPHY

* 5.A *
Adalian, Rouben, ed. *The Armenian Genocide in the U.S. Archives, 1915-1918*. Alexandria, VA: Chadwyck-Healey Inc., 1991-92. Microfiche.

U.S. archival holdings documenting the Armenian genocide are comprehensively reproduced on microfiche in this microform production. Included are 30,000 pages of evidence from the records of the Department of State, the Commission to Negotiate Peace, the Office of National Intelligence, from the papers of Ambassador Morgenthau and President Wilson, as well as from other agencies of the U.S. government which were involved in gathering evidence on the Ottoman Empire during and after World War I. The documents also show the extent to which the U.S. government attempted to rescue the survivors through relief efforts.

* 5.B *
Dadrian, Vahakn N. "Documentation of the Armenian Genocide in Turkish Sources," In: Israel W. Charny, ed. *Genocide: A Critical Bibliographic Review*. V.2. New York: Facts on File, 1991. ISBN 0-8160-1903-7.

Despite their longstanding denial of the genocide, various authors, scholars, memoirists, and government officials of the late Ottoman era have obliquely or inadvertently revealed the Young Turks' violent handling of the mass of the Armenian population in the Ottoman state.

* 5.C *
Dadrian, Vahakn N. "Genocide as a Problem of National and International Law: The World War I Armenian Case and its Contemporary Legal Ramifications." *Yale Journal of International Law* 14, no. 2 (1989), 221-334.

In this detailed examination of the courts-martial convened in Constantinople after World War I to try the principal conspirators in the deportation of the Armenian population and the expropriation of their propery, Dadrian shows that the judicial record clearly established the criminal behavior of the Young Turk government in its policies against the Armenians. Yet despite depositions taken from high ranking military officers, the incriminating evidence authenticated by Turkish legal experts, and the verdicts handed down by Ottoman courts, political changes and public pressure ultimately voided the convictions of the perpetrators of the genocide.

* 5.D *
Hovannisian, Richard G. *The Armenian Holocaust: a Bibliography Relating to the Deportations, Massacres, and Dispersion of the Armenian People, 1915-1923*. Rev. 3d ed. Cambridge, MA: Armenian Heritage Press, 1980. ISBN 0-935411-05-4.

The first part of this work is an inventory of the major archival holdings documenting the condition of the Armenians in the Middle East during World War I. The countries with important repositories include Great Britain, France, Austria-Hungary, Germany, the United States, and Armenia. The second part lists published works on Armenian genocide written by eyewitnesses, survivors, relief workers, diplomats, and scholars. Hovannisian identifies some 400 works, mostly in English, French, and German.

* 5.E *
Kloian, Richard D., ed. *The Armenian Genocide: News Accounts From the American Press, 1915-1922*. 3d ed. Berkeley: ACC Books, 1985. LC 85-217742.

Despite the Ottoman government's efforts to censor the news, reports about the condition of the Armenian population reached the Western media. Kloian's collection includes a representative sample of articles that appeared in the American periodical press, such as *The New York Times*, *The Literary Digest*, *The Outlook*, *Missionary Review*, and *The Independent*. The 124 articles in *The New York Times*—with typical headlines reading "Wholesale Massacres of Armenians by Turks" (29 July), and "Turks Depopulate Towns of Armenia" (27 August)—which appeared in 1915 alone meant that the American public was fully aware of the scale of the atrocities committed against the Armenians in the Ottoman Empire.

* 5.F *
Morgenthau, Henry. *Ambassador Morgenthau's Story*. Garden City, NY: Doubleday, Page & Co., 1918. LC 38-14073.

By virtue of his office, Morgenthau, the U.S. ambassador to the Ottoman Empire from 1913 to 1916, was acquainted with the Young Turk cabinet. In this account of his conversations and written communications with cabinet members, he leaves little doubt that Talaat, the Minister of the Interior, was the central figure in the implementation of the Armenian genocide.

(continued on page 88)

(continued from page 87)

* 5.G *
[Toynbee, Arnold Joseph]. *The Treatment of Armenians in the Ottoman Empire, 1915-1916: Documents Presented to Viscount Grey of Fallodan, Secretary of State for Foreign Affairs, by Viscount Bryce.* Preface by Viscount Bryce. Presented to both Houses of Parliament by Command of His Majesty. London: His Majesty's Stationery Office, 1916. LC 17-2893.

The first official report of the destruction of the Armenian population, the collection consists of 149 documents compiled by Arnold Toynbee. They include numerous eyewitness accounts of the deportations and their consequences by European residents, travelers, missionaries, and diplomatic personnel. The documents are organized according to provinces stretching from the war zone in the east through towns and districts removed from the conflict in the west of Anatolia all the way to the capital and then southward in the direction of the deportations. There are also sections on "The Anatolian Railway" and its use in the transport of deportees, "The Refugees in the Caucasus" who had fled the Ottoman Empire, and "Azerbaijan and Hakkiari" in northern Iran where the Ottoman forces advanced in the beginning of the war and where some of the earliest mass killings of the Christian population, including Armenians and Syrian Nestorians, occurred. For reasons of security many names were withheld and one section in the collection appears under the heading of "The Town of X." "The Key" to these names and places was published in the second edition of the book (Beirut: G. Doniguian and Sons, 1972). In the final section, Toynbee analyzed the data gathered by mid-1916 and estimated that 1,200,000 were deported in 1915 and that half of them perished that year.

remained of the Ottoman Empire was assumed by a new circle of ministers. The central government in Istanbul, however, was weak. It appeared compromised because it accommodated the Allied-imposed settlement.

Upon the insistence of the British, and to a lesser degree the French, some of the Young Turk leaders were court-martialed in 1919-1920. Indicted also were members of the two wartime CUP cabinets. The tribunal handed down a series of verdicts finding the accused guilty of "the organization and execution" of the crime of massacre.[1] Indicative of its moral indecision and evasion of domestic responsibility for dealing with the CUP officials, the Ottoman government was reluctant to carry out most of the sentences. In the case of the top CUP officials, however, the sentences were only a formality. The officials had eluded the law by taking refuge in Germany immediately after the war and were tried only in absentia. The final evasion of any personal culpability occurred with the refusal of Germany to extradite the accused war criminals.[2] The failure to assign criminality to the policies of the Young Turks set the stage for translating the responsibility for exterminating a population into the subject of a debate.

Eastern Armenia Under Communism

Eastern Armenia had been part of the Russian Empire since the early nineteenth century. When, the Russian state disintegrated, as a result of the October Revolution the government of this province was assumed by the local people. In May 1918 they formed an independent republic which lasted only two and a half years. The Red Army put an end to Armenian independence in 1920. Almost immediately the Communist government internally imposed a complete silence on the Armenian genocide.

The lack of Allied resolve to adhere to the objectives of defining the concept of "crimes against humanity" and applying it to the case of the mistreatment of the Armenians was thus matched by the Russian Communists' rejection of all Western notions of appropriate and acceptable political conduct. The Soviet regime introduced new norms of political behavior. The ideological underpinnings of Communism which elevated mass terror into state policy only contributed to the environment in which it could be denied that the fate of the Armenians had been in any way exceptional. These were the years in which the totalitarian state was taking shape and the Communists had reached their own reconciliation with this kind of brutalization.[3]

After six years of warfare and incalculable loss and suffering, Armenian identity became hostage to a redefinition at the hands of ideologues whose manipulation of the historical record only served to further alienate and isolate the Armenian people. Even a minimal effort to document the Armenian genocide was not contemplated. The single greatest catastrophe in Armenian history, virtually all-encompassing in its dimensions and implications, was dismissed as a nonevent. With no effort made to preserve a record of the past, the Communists left the field all the more open to revisionism and denial. They added a powerful incentive, and in many respects accorded virtual encouragement, for Turkey to deny everything to the Armenians.

Abdications and Retributions

The Sovietization of the Republic of Armenia had another effect. The only vehicle available to the Armenian people for pressing their case against the Young Turks for adjudication in any kind of forum was denied to them. All legal options were closed. The Allies had given up on their intention to prosecute. The Ottoman domestic courts had discontinued the trials of the accused. The British had reached a settlement in 1921 with the Turkish Nationalist government for the return of Ottoman officials arrested and incarcerated in Malta on charges of war crimes. The message was clear that, as far as the Allies were concerned, no sanctions would be imposed on Turkey for having a short time before deported, murdered, robbed, and exiled its Armenian population.

The situation posed an excruciating dilemma to Armenians. An underground organization already had been formed for the purpose of meting out punishment to key organizers of the Armenian genocide.[4] Between March 1921 and July 1922, several of the Young Turk party leaders directly responsible for the agencies which implemented the deportations and massacres were assassinated.[5] Each of the slayings occurred outside Turkey. None of the slain were at the time officials of either the Constantinople imperial government or the Nationalist regime in Ankara.

Despite the fact that the hunting down of these men were acts of retribution against individuals, this episode added further ambiguity to the lessons of the genocide. The assassinations plainly were carried out as acts of vengeance by Armenians. It is difficult to say what should have been done with Talaat and the others since no government considered even imprisoning them, but their slayings left the cloudy legacy that surrounds the notion of settling scores.

When the Treaty of Lausanne established Turkey's international boundaries in 1923, the implications for the Armenians were all too apparent. The deported Armenians stranded in Syria were sealed off from their former homes and reduced at last and irreversibly to a people without a country. That the Turks and the Allies at Lausanne ignored the Armenians only codified Communist Russia's dismissal of the Armenian case against Turkey. The Allies in the West for a short while had felt some obligation to the Armenians in view of the genocide. However, they were physically remote from the scene, and the exclusion of the Armenians from the world political arena relieved them of any further connection.[6] Their pledges to settle the Armenians in a "national home" went unfulfilled.

Turkey Reformed

The circle of deniability was complete with the transformation of Turkish society under the leadership of Mustafa Kemal. His determination to secure uncontested sovereignty for Turkey would not countenance the charge of criminality for the Young Turk policies. Many of the CUP rank and file joined his movement. To the extent that they served his purposes, Kemal extended his protection to these men, and thereby signalled his tolerance of the racial policies of the Young Turks. These steps were taken within the framework of the Kemalist program to transform Turkey into a modern nation.

Kemal re-integrated Turkey into the world system of states by discarding the vestiges of the Ottoman past. The changes introduced through a series of reform measures were intended to fundamentally alter Turkish society. The most visible aspects of Kemal's modernization program included, for instance, the adoption of the Latin alphabet for the Turkish language. The legislation of new dress codes doing away with traditional garb for both men and women virtually imposed injunctions against Islamic practices. These tangible alterations of the appearance of Turkish society contributed measurably to a re-evaluation of the unflattering image of the Turk which the media had created in depicting, for a time, an unending series of atrocities against Christian minorities.

More significant in making Turkey acceptable as a modern nation was the political reorganization that took place under Kemal's guidance. The reforms proceeded on so many levels that within a comparatively short time Turkey was able to establish reciprocal relations with a host of countries, many formerly its enemies. This process also finally shut the doors on the Armenian people everywhere. Within a decade after the end of World War I Armenians could not find even a lone voice in the entire arena of global politics to express support for their cause or sympathy for their calamity.

Turkey's neutrality during most of World War II was evidence of Kemal's and his successor's ability to steer through troubled waters. Turkey declared hostilities against Germany near the end of the war in order to join the United Nations as a charter member. Turkey's entry into the North Atlantic Treaty Organization formalized its role in the Western alliance system. From 1952 onward Turkey shared in the responsibility of protecting the free world against expansionist Communism. In return, its own security was guaranteed by the might of the United States as projected through NATO.[7] In thirty years time Turkey traveled so far from the genocidal episode of the early part of the twentieth century that no question remained about any obligations toward the Armenian people.

As the Armenians disappeared from public view, so too did interest in them and their fate slowly fade. In contrast, a vast body of literature began to appear on Turkey. Its modernization process was regarded as a model for underdeveloped countries and became the subject of innumerable studies. Every aspect of the modern Turkish state found its devotees. Many were fascinated by the attempt at secularizing a traditional society. Others measured the progress in industrialization and commercialization. Still others observed the effects of educational policies and the advances made in literacy. Turkish political developments and the deft diplomacy of the Ankara government became the subject of considerable inquiry.

More fascinating to Western observers was the towering figure of Kemal himself upon whom the Turkish people bestowed the ultimate honor of naming him the father of his country, Ataturk. His personality, his style of leadership, his ideas and words, his deeds, his military valor and ability, his political acumen, his mannerisms of dress and behavior, all became topics of continuous study.[8] The more impressive his list of accomplishments grew, the less cause his detractors had to be critical. Under the circumstances, the Armenian genocide lost its relevance.

Armenians in Diaspora

For the Armenians all this meant that the effects of the genocide would be regarded as inconsequential. During those same decades they were absorbed with the sheer struggle for survival as a homeless, stateless, and dispersed people. The shape of their new diaspora began to emerge as they desperately scrambled to reach any country that gave refuge. Within a short time a handful of impoverished Armenian immigrants spread out in all directions away from their ancestral home and reached all the continents of the globe. A quietude eventually descended upon their existence as their cause was forgotten and the challenge of keeping their offspring from completely assimilating into their host societies absorbed all their energies.[9]

Cut off from Soviet Armenia, filled with bitterness toward the Turks, making up such small numbers as to be easily overlooked by society at large, and living among scattered communities, the Armenians exiled from Turkey possessed no resources to dedicate toward preserving the record of the Armenian genocide.[10] Publishing the memoirs of individual survivors and gathering the history and folklore of the towns, cities, and regions once inhabited by Armenians was the most that was accomplished.[11] A methodical study and documentation of the Armenian genocide was beyond the abilities of the Armenian people at the time. Further impeding any scientific effort to understand the genocide was the absence of Armenians trained in the disciplines necessary to begin such a project. The very first segment of Armenian society selected for extermination at the earliest stages of the genocide had been the intellectual elite: the teachers, journalists, lawyers, clergy, and politicians. Therefore those who ended up holding whatever valuable documentation passed into their hands were not equipped to treat them with the scientific and legal precautions necessary to authenticate that evidence beyond a shadow of a doubt. Lastly, most works written by Armenians on the genocide were written in the Armenian language, making them inaccessible to non-Armenians, and even to their own children.

Turning Points

The year 1965 proved a watershed year in the life of the Armenian people. Confronted with the realization that fifty years had passed since the genocide, Armenians across the world organized commemorative events, inaugurated the publication of works on the genocide, and presented petitions to their governments requesting formal recognition of their tragedy. Since that time somber ritual has come to surround 24 April, the date commemorated as the beginning of the genocide. Prior to 1965, April 24 had been regarded more as a day of mourning and memorialized by requiem services in Armenian churches. By 1965, the eschatological interpretation first given the Armenian genocide had proved unconvincing. New generations of Armenians had grown up and taken charge of their communities.

Diaspora-born, more secular in outlook, with a Western education, and not directly bearing the scars of persecution, they defined the Armenian genocide as the central event of the modern Armenian experience. They became gripped by an awareness of their necrologized national history. The question of justice denied, and for how long, rapidly politicized a stratum of Armenian society. But the old realization of powerlessness in the face of indifference became the cause of increasing frustration. The political impotence of the Armenians in the diaspora, the isolation of the Armenian state inside the Soviet Union with its inability to connect meaningfully with the diaspora, and the silence of the world contributed to a process of radicalization. Just as increasing numbers of Armenians were learning to cope with these dimensions of their heritage, a wave of political violence shook the Armenian communities.

Intent on forcing the issue on the nations of the world, and especially upon the Turkish government, small groups of Armenian terrorists appeared on the scene. They primarily targeted the Turkish diplomatic corps. During a ten-year spree lasting from 1975 to 1985, Turkish ambassadors, consuls, attaches, and guards were shot and killed by these gunmen, whose demands were always the same: international recognition of the Armenian genocide and Turkish restitution of Armenian lands.[12] After decades of being ignored, the methods of the militants at first seemed to be paying off as they captured headlines and succeeded in getting their story told.[13] The campaign of violence, however, could not sustain itself. The costs to Armenian society began to mount as the repeated acts repelled more and more Armenians and raised their own set of questions. Countries on whose ground most of the operations were carried out responded with their own security measures to prevent the radicals from gaining access to publicity. Finally, Turkey also formulated its own response policies in order to bring the problem under control and stop the killings.

The long-term effects of the decade of political violence are yet to be analyzed. One short-term result was the intensification of the denial campaign by the Turkish government. Turkey repudiated not just the violence, but also the historic reason and fundamental injustice which propelled the terrorism in the minds of its practitioners.[14] The Armenian genocide became contestable ground. Most of the revisionist and denial literature to appear on the Armenian genocide was produced against this backdrop.

The terrorism subsided, but the denial campaign remained in high gear. The production of denial literature took on a life of its own. With the resources of the Turkish government committed to obstructing, obscuring, confusing, distorting, and in any and every manner denigrating the Armenian genocide and its memory, the denial campaign became an industry. With increasing frequency the literature challenging every aspect and recorded fact of the genocide now reached libraries around the world. Revisionists, deniers, and spokesperson of the Turkish government, masquerading as scholars, historians, and specialists of one sort or another, made a living pounding away at the body of evidence documenting the Armenian genocide.

The stated purpose of the newest phase of the denial program was to control the damage to Turkey's image. The depiction of Turkey as heir to a genocidal state was not a small problem for the Turkish government. That, however, was the lesser of its concerns since Turkey was far too deeply integrated into the world economy and the Western alliance systems to feel seriously challenged. Armenian terrorism provided Turkey the opportunity, once and for all, to confuse the record on the Armenian genocide by claiming it as nothing more than an unfounded charge made by irrational individuals. The violent insistence that there would be consequences to Turkey for failing to acknowledge the Armenian genocide only netted a powerful and elaborate program to deny everything to the Armenians once again, not just irredentist claims to lands inhabited by their ancestors some seventy or more years earlier, and not just the genocide either. The Turkish policy of denial established that everything was deniable; whether there ever was an Armenia, whether the Armenians were actually a people, whether they had a history.[15] It mapped out an extensive program of mockery. Hence in the last two decades the Armenian genocide has been compromised twice over, once by violence staged by Armenian extremists, and again by a growing body of denial literature. For the rest of Armenians there was a penalty to be paid for their inability to establish the record of the genocide.

Defining the Armenian Experience

Opposed to, and apart from, these trends were other developments shaping the understanding of the Armenian genocide. First among these was the continuing progress made by the international community, through the United Nations and other bodies, to agree to covenants respecting the rights of all human beings, codifying conventions on warfare and war crimes, and defining provisions for punishing the commission of genocide. Basic documents giving expression to the concept of human rights were formulated. These achievements were registered with the widespread destruction of World War II in mind. The hope of preventing global conflict, nuclear exchange, or the gross abuse of human rights made a dent in the cold pragmatism of states which once left the victims of the Armenian genocide in the dust.[16]

The second and critical development of the post-World War II period which brought the subject of genocide into focus was awareness of the Holocaust. The imperative to explain how educated men seemingly exercising their rational faculties sent an unimaginable number of people to gas chambers posed a challenge to the moral and intellectual premises of Western civilization. How nations fell prey to racial ideologies of their own choosing, and how they fueled anti-Semitism to the point of reducing Jews to victims of extermination, were questions demanding an answer. Drawing on the lessons of the Holocaust, the examination of past or present violations of the fundamental human right to life now takes a basic body of knowledge on political behavior, social psychology, mass culture, and the ideology of rationalized evil as common principles and tools. The Nuremberg trials set the stage for studying these and many other related issues as serious subjects of inquiry and they have had an inescapable effect on a number of disciplines.[17] Even the precedence of the Young Turk policy of extermination has become a subject of inquiry.[18]

Lastly, the assimilation of the Armenians worked its own influence. Whereas most survivors wrote about their experiences in Armenian, second- and third-generation descendants did so mainly in English and French. As the Armenian genocide became the subject of serious inquiry, scholars, Armenian and non-Armenian, could only be studying it with the post-World War II reassessment and reconsideration of the human experience in view. The vocabulary itself changed as those examining the evidence began to label the destruction of the Armenians a genocide also. It had been described by contemporaries as massacres, atrocities, and race extermination. The word "genocide," however, had an established legal definition to it, which, retrospectively, made the Armenian massacres a more comprehensible unit of history in the context of the twentieth century.[19]

From the point of view of the Turkish government and its apologists, the study of the Armenian genocide posed a serious challenge. The more the record of the Armenian genocide was established, analyzed, and compared, the more the denial position would be exposed as a contrived and sponsored program. Therefore one of the principal strategies of the denial policy has been to create confusion between Armenian political positions and academic research on the Armenian genocide by insisting that one is in the service of the other.

The Arguments

Three lines of argument have been advanced by those disputing the occurrence of the Armenian genocide. The *denial thesis* makes the following points: 1) the high casualty toll among civilian Armenians is explained by the fact that the Armenian-inhabited areas of Anatolia were a theater of war; 2) the Armenians also engaged in civil war against the Turkish populace and suffered additional casualties as a result; 3) the Armenians resorted to massacre and the Turks responded in "counter-massacres;" 4) some subscribers to this theory have extrapolated the argument and posited the case of a "counter-extermination" since the Armenian objective, they maintain, was to annihilate the Turks; 5) the deportations are depicted as an "emigration" or "resettlement" policy designed to remove rebellious Armenians from the war zone where they endangered the Ottoman armies; 6) the Armenian nationalists are accused of provocation by being "extremist" in their demands; 7) they are also accused of resorting to wide-scale terrorism; and 8) the nationalist Armenians are described as persons promoting race hatred.

The denial thesis basically reverses the course of history and depicts the victims as the victimizers. The *revisionist thesis*, on the other hand, builds on presumably reasonable arguments. It frequently draws on the comparative approach. The revisionists do not primarily deny the facts as much as they seek to explain them in a manner that disputes the case for genocide. They rely on these methods: 1) the casualty figure is always minimized by first questioning the size of the original Armenian population in the Ottoman Empire; 2) the spread of epidemics which is common in war is said to have caused most of the deaths; 3) starvation is attributed to "war-time shortages" which occur in every country; 4) the deportations are always regarded as a relocation policy designed for the safety of the Armenians; 5) or as a defensive policy intended to avoid the outbreak of communal hostility; 6) all of the above cumulatively are presumed to demonstrate that there was no policy of genocide. The deaths were incidental to the events.

The most disturbing of all the arguments is the *justification thesis*. The basic thrust of the justification thesis is to defend the policy of genocide by regarding the policy as an acceptable solution to a political problem. The partisans of justification draw heavily on what is called the provocation theory. The logic of this argument says that Armenians engaged in behavior so threatening to Turkish society that the Ottoman government was compelled to take the comprehensive measures implemented during World War I. The justification and provocation theories are built on a contrastive juxtaposition of the Armenians and the Turks: 1) the Armenians constituted enemies within the state; 2) they collaborated with foreign invaders; 3) they sabotaged Ottoman military campaigns; 4) they were revolutionaries preparing for the moment to revolt; 5) the Armenians believed that World War I offered the opportunity to implement their separatist national program; 6) therefore, they activated a campaign of terrorism meant to drive the Turks out of the areas the Armenians hoped to carve out as their national territory; 7) the Turks were caught in a life and death struggle and had no recourse but to eradicate the Armenians in order to save their nation. The justification thesis, therefore, is constructed on the twin pillars of provocation and salvation. Curiously, it admits that the modern state of Turkey was created by liquidating the Armenian population.[20]

The Authors

The revisionist and denial literature can be divided among six categories of authors. Two key *participants* in the genocide wrote their biographies. Neither failed to defend his actions. Their denials soon were grist for

Turkish and non-Turkish *apologists* who were interested in creating public confidence in the new Turkey by covering up for the Young Turks. When the field of Middle East studies was professionalized in the fifties and sixties, academic *rationalizers* appeared. Consonant with the Cold War mentality, they described nineteenth and early twentieth century Armenian nationalism as an instrument of Russian expansionism. Eliminating the special and separate identity of the Armenian national movement and obscuring the oppressive aspect of Ottoman imperialism were their main contributions. The *revisionists* then built on this groundwork by explaining the Armenian massacres as the consequence of inter-ethnic warfare within the larger context of an international conflict where Russians were fighting Turks and the Turks were defending their country. They fashioned a war between two communities, Armenians versus Turks, and absented the hand of the Ottoman government as the real deciding factor. The revisionist arguments soon were approximating the standard Turkish government denials. Under the pressure of Armenian terrorism, which extended its intimidation to the university campus, an alliance was forged between academic revisionism and official Turkish nationalism. With their anti-Communist credentials, Turkish *disinformers* then were able to depict the question of genocide as part of an anti-Western agenda. Finally, the ***distorters*** went on the offensive to rewrite history totally.

Conclusion

The denial of the Armenian genocide demonstrates a number of points about human behavior in a post-traumatic situation: 1) survivors on their own are ill-equipped at first to document their case and have it adjudicated; 2) without intervention by a power stronger than the state engaged in genocide, the case cannot, under any circumstances, be resolved; 3) political pragmatism in the face of a crime of such proportions sets an uncontrollable precedent and exposes the surviving body of the targeted group to further abuse; 4) at the very least, that abuse takes the form of denying criminality and responsibility; 5) thereby, a circumstance is created where victims and victimizers are locked into irreconcilable positions; 6) worse yet, a member of the human family is delegitimized and excluded from fair hearing in any court of law or politics; 7) lastly, unrequitted genocide places its victims and their descendants outside the norms of historical development by alienating them and isolating them from the rest of humanity.

NOTES

1. Vahakn N. Dadrian, "Genocide as a Problem of National and International Law: The World War I Armenian Case and Its Contemporary Legal Ramifications," *Yale Journal of International Law* 14:2 (1989): 306-308.

2. Colin Heywood, "'Boundless Dreams of the Levant': Paul Wittek, the George-Kreis, and the Writing of Ottoman History," *Journal of the Royal Asiatic Society* (1989): 38. On the post-war activities of the CUP see Erick Jan Zurcher, *The Unionist Factor: The Role of the Committee of Union and Progress in the Turkish National Movement 1905-1926* (Leiden: E.J. Brill, 1984).

3. Nikolai K. Deker and Andrei Lebed, *Genocide in the USSR: Studies in Group Destruction* (New York: The Scarecrow Press, Inc., 1958); Aleksandr I. Solzhenitsyn, *The Gulag Archipelago 1918-1956: An Experiment in Literary Investigation*, 3 vols., trans. by Thomas P. Whitney and Harry Willetts (New York, Hagerstown, San Francisco, and London: Harper & Row, 1973, 1975, 1978); U.S. Commission on the Ukraine Famine, *Investigation of the Ukraine Famine 1932-1933, Report to Congress* (Washington, DC: United States Government Printing Office, 1988).

4. Arshavir Shiragian, *The Legacy: Memoirs of an Armenian Patriot* (Boston: Hairenik Press, 1976), 37. Also, Jacques Derogy, *Resistance and Revenge: The Armenian Assassination of the Turkish Leaders Responsible for the 1915 Massacres and Deportations*, trans. by A.M. Berrett (New Brunswick and London: Transaction Publishers, 1990).

5. 15 March 1921, Talaat Bey, former Minister of the Interior and Prime Minister, in Berlin; 6 December 1921, Said Halim, former Foreign Minister, in Rome; 17 April 1922, Dr. Behaeddin Shakir, a Paris-trained physician and party ideologue who served on the Supreme Directorate of the Central Committee of the CUP and headed the Special Organization in charge of carrying out the massacres, and Djemal Azmi, responsible for the massacres in Trebizond, in Berlin; 25 July 1922, Djemal Pasha, former Minister of the Marine and wartime governor of Syria, in Tiflis. For the trial of Talaat's assassin see, *The Case of Soghomon Tehlirian* (Los Angeles: A.R.F. Varantian Gomideh, 1985).

6. Stephen Bonsal, *Suitors and Suppliants: The Little Nations at Versailles* (New York: Prentice-Hall, Inc., 1946), specifically chapter XII, "Armenian Disaster,"

186-201; Yves Ternon, *The Armenian Cause*, trans. by Anahid Apelian Mangouni (Delmar, New York: Caravan Books, 1985); Alan J. Ward, "World War I and the Tragedy of Armenian Self-Determination," *Armenian Review* 31:4 (1979): 339-361; and Yosef Gotlieb, *Self-Determination in the Middle East* (New York: Praeger Publishers, 1982), chapter 7, "Armenia: Eluding National Extinguishment," 118-133.

7. Julian W. Witherall, *The Republic of Turkey, an American Perspective: A Guide to U.S. Official Documents and Government-Sponsored Publications* (Washington, DC: Library of Congress, 1988); Roger R. Trask, *The United States Response to Turkish Nationalism and Reform, 1914-1939* (Minneapolis: The University of Minnesota Press, 1971); Joseph L. Grabill, *Protestant Diplomacy and the Near East: Missionary Influence on American Policy 1918-1927* (Minneapolis: The University of Minnesota Press, 1971); Dankwart A. Rustow, *Turkey: America's Forgotten Ally* (New York: Council on Foreign Relations, 1987); David Barchard, *Turkey and the West* (London, Boston, and Henley: Routledge & Kegan Paul, 1985).

8. Abraham Bodurgil, *Kemal Ataturk: A Centennial Bibliography (1881-1981)* (Washington, DC: Library of Congress, 1984); Lord Kinross, *Ataturk: The Birth of a Nation* (London: Weidenfeld and Nicolson, 1964); Jacob M. Landau, ed., *Ataturk and the Modernization of Turkey* 3 (Boulder, CO: Westview Press, 1984).

9. Rouben Adalian, "The Historical Evolution of the Armenian Diasporas," *Journal of Modern Hellenism* 6 (1989): 81-114.

10. Richard G. Hovannisian, "Genocide and Denial: The Armenian Case," in *Toward the Understanding and Prevention of Genocide: Proceedings of the International Conference on the Holocaust and Genocide*, ed. by Israel W. Charny (Boulder, CO, and London: Westview Press, 1984), 84-99; and "The Armenian Genocide and Patterns of Denial," in *The Armenian Genocide in Perspective*, ed. by Hovannisian (New Brunswick and Oxford: Transaction Books, 1986), 111-133.

11. Sarkis Karayan, "Histories of Armenian Communities in Turkey," *Armenian Review* 33:1 (1980): 89-96.

12. About two dozen Turkish officials were assassinated by the terrorists. Many civilians and others, such as security guards, were also killed. See Anat Kurz and Ariel Merari, *ASALA: Irrational Terror or Political Tool* (Boulder, CO: Westview Press, 1985); Michael M. Gunter, *Pursuing the Just Cause of Their People* (New York, Westport, CT, and London: Greenwood Press, 1986); for a review of both works by Khachig Tololyan, see *Conflict Quarterly* (Summer 1988): 101-105; and Walter Laqueur, *The Age of Terrorism* (Boston and Toronto: Little, Brown and Company, 1987), 227-229.

13. Mark Armen Ayanian and John Z. Ayanian, "Armenian Political Violence on American Network News: An Analysis of Content," *Armenian Review* 40:1 (1987): 13-29; Zaven V. Sinanian, "Coverage of Armenian Issues in *The New York Times*, 1965-1983," *Armenian Review* 40:1 (1987): 31-49; and Garen Yegparian, "Armenian Issues in the *Congressional Record*," *Armenian Review* 40:1 (1987): 51-68.

14. Gerard Chaliand and Yves Ternon, *The Armenians: From Genocide to Resistance*, trans. by Tony Berrett (London: Zed Press, 1983); Pierre Papazian, "The Armenian Nation and the Ottoman Empire: Roots of Terrorism," *The Midwest Quarterly* 27:2 (1986): 215-229; and Khachig Tololyan, "Cultural Narrative and the Motivation of the Terrorist," *Journal of Strategic Studies* 10:4 (1987): 217-233, and "Terrorism in a Textual Community," *Critical Exchange* no. 22 (1987): 23-36.

15. Terrence Des Pres, "On Governing Narratives: The Turkish-Armenian Case," *The Yale Review* 75:4 (1986): 517-531; Roger Smith, "Genocide and Denial: The Armenian Case and Its Implications," *Armenian Review* 42:1 (1989): 1-38; Dennis R. Papazian, "The Changing American View of the Armenian Question: An Interpretation," *Armenian Review* 39:4 (1986): 47-72; and Ronald Grigor Suny, "Background to Genocide: Western Historiography and the Armenian Massacre," in *The Impact of the Genocide on Armenian Culture* (New York: St. Vartan Press, 1983).

16. Leo Kuper, *Genocide: Its Political Use in the Twentieth Century* (New York: Penguin Paperbacks, 1981), chapter 7, "Genocidal Process: The Turkish Genocide Against the Armenians," 101-119.

17. Helen Fein, *Accounting for Genocide: National Responses and Jewish Victimization during the Holocaust* (Chicago and London: The University of Chicago Press, 1979), 10-18; Irving Louis Horowitz, *Taking Lives: Genocide and State Power*, 3d ed. (New Brunswick and London: Transaction Books, 1982), 46-51; Richard L. Rubenstein, *The Age of Triage: A Chilling History of Genocide from the Irish Famine to Vietnam's Boat People* (Boston: Beacon Press, 1983), 12-19; and Michael R. Marrus, *The Holocaust in History* (Hanover

and London: University Press of New England, 1987), 20-23.

18. Vigen Guroian, "A Comparison of the Armenian and Jewish Genocides: Some Common Features," *Thought* 58, no. 229 (1983): 207-223; Robert Melson, "Revolutionary Genocide: On the Causes of the Armenian Genocide of 1915 and the Holocaust," *Holocaust and Genocide Studies* 4:2 (1989): 161-174; R. Hrair Dekmejian, "Determinants of Genocide: Armenians and Jews as Case Studies," in *The Armenian Genocide in Perspective*, ed. by Hovannisian (New Brunswick and Oxford: Transaction Books, 1986), 85-96; Vahakn N. Dadrian, "The Common Features of the Armenian and Jewish Cases of Genocide: A Comparative Victimological Perspective," in *Victimology*, vol. 4, ed. by Israel Drapkin and Emilio Viano (Lexington, MA: Lexington Books, D.C. Heath and Co., 1975), 99-120; "Some Determinants of Genocidal Violence in Intergroup Conflicts--with Particular Reference to the Armenian and Jewish Cases," *Sociologus* 12:2 (1976): 129-149; and "The Convergent Aspects of the Armenian and Jewish Cases of Genocide. A Reinterpretation of the Concept of Holocaust," *Holocaust and Genocide Studies* 3:2 (1988): 151-169.

19. Dickran H. Boyajian, *Armenia - the Case for a Forgotten Genocide* (Westwood, NJ: Educational Book Crafters, 1972); Shavarsh Toriguian, *The Armenian Question and International Law*, 2d. ed. (La Verne, CA: University of La Verne Press, 1988); Michael J. Arlen, *Passage to Ararat* (New York: Farrar, Straus & Giroux, 1975); Rouben Adalian, "How and Why to Teach the Armenian Genocide: Seeking a Humanist Perspective," *Armenian Review* 40:1 (1987): 69-77, and "The Armenian Genocide: Context and Legacy," *Social Education* 55:2 (1991): 99-104.

20. For critiques of revisionist and denial literature see Speros Vryonis, Jr., "Stanford J. Shaw's History of the Ottoman Empire and Modern Turkey. Volume I. A Critical Analysis," *Balkan Studies* 24:1 (1983), also in offprint; for the second Shaw volume, Richard G. Hovannisian, "The Critics View: Beyond Revisionism," *International Journal of Middle East Studies* 9 (1978): 379-388, and "Rewriting History: Revisionism and Beyond in the Study of Armenian-Turkish Relations," *Ararat: A Quarterly* (Summer 1978): 2-10; also Norman Ravitch, "The Armenian Catastrophe: Of History, Murder & Sin," *Encounter* (December 1981): 69-84; Levon Marashlian, "Population Statistics on Ottoman Armenians in the Context of Turkish Historiography," *Armenian Review* 40:4 (1987): 1-59; K. B. Bardakjian, *Hitler and the Armenian Genocide* (Cambridge, MA: Zoryan Institute, 1985); Edward V. Gulbenkian, "The Poles and Armenians in Hitler's Political Thinking," *Armenian Review* 41:3 (1988): 1-14; Vahakn N. Dadrian, "The Naim-Andonian Documents on the World War I Destruction of Ottoman Armenians: The Anatomy of a Genocide," *International Journal of Middle East Studies* 18:3 (1986): 311-360.

Chapter 5: Annotated Bibliography

The Participants

* 5.1 *
Talaat Pasha. "Posthumous Memoirs of Talaat Pasha." *Current History, a Monthly Magazine of The New York Times* 15 (November 1921): 287-295.

Because he was Minister of the Interior at the time of the deportation of the Armenians and on the basis of other incriminating evidence underscoring the primacy of his role in carrying out the decision to exterminate the Armenians, Talaat has been regarded as the key architect of the Armenian genocide. His memoirs, therefore, constitute a unique document. No other state official accused of genocide is known to have written a similar apologia. According to Talaat the deportations were measures taken in response "to the treacherous acts of the Armenians," whom he characterized as a disloyal population. These acts included sabotage, banditry, and collaboration with the enemy during a time of war. Suggesting that the reports about massacres were exaggerated, he maintained that the "atrocities" were committed by outlaws. Talaat argued that the Armenians were in a state of revolt and that the Muslim populace reacted violently to this emergency. He also claimed that the authorities might have prevented the abuses, but held the government blameless for any plans to destroy the Armenians. Talaat was the first articulator of the provocation thesis.

* 5.2 *
Djemal Pasha. *Memories of a Turkish Statesman, 1913-1919*. New York: George H. Doran Co., 1922. Reprint. New York: Arno Press, 1973. LC 73-6295. ISBN 0-405-05328-2.

As Minister of the Marine and Commander-in-Chief of the Fourth Army in Syria, Djemal was another of the Young Turk triumvirs governing the Ottoman Empire during World War I. Like Talaat's, his memoirs also constitute a primary source on the Armenian genocide. They shed considerable light on the ideological predispositions of Young Turk nationalism and on the Ottoman political calculations which sanctioned the deportations and massacres. The unusual aspect of his work is its mixture of admission of the substantive facts of the genocide with elaborate rationalizations framing the events. For instance, Djemal reported that the Ottoman government deported one and a half million Armenians and that 600,000 of them "died." Djemal developed a thesis arguing that the treatment of the Armenians, despite its summary nature, was both episodic and inevitable in the course of developments in Ottoman-Armenian relations. Armenians favored Russian protection and Russia threatened to overrun the Ottoman Empire.

The Apologists

* 5.3 *

Kemal, Mustafa Ataturk. *A Speech Delivered by Ghazi Mustapha Kemal*, October 1927. Leipzig: H.F. Koehler, Publisher, 1929. LC 26-14306. See pp. 409-418, 496-7, 620-630.

Mustafa Kemal led the Turkish Nationalist forces in the War for Independence. In 1923 he founded the Republic of Turkey. He remained its president until his death in 1938. This long speech, delivered to the congress of the Republican People's Party, reviewed the Kemalist struggle for Turkish independence in the aftermath of World War I and the ensuing disintegration of the Ottoman Empire. Beyond the facts and documents assembled by Kemal for this presentation, the speech also had the effect of establishing the outlines of an official history. For Kemal the Armenian genocide was an accomplished fact that did not need dwelling upon. This form of denial simply dismissed a segment of history. Kemal saw the matter in purely political terms and treated the expulsion of the Armenians as a necessary step in the reassertion of complete Turkish sovereignty.

* 5.4 *

Edib, Halide (Adivar). *Memoirs of Halide Edib*. New York and London: The Century Co., 1926. LC 26-14306. See pp. 386-388, 428-430.

Halide Edib was a major literary figure in Turkey in the first part of the century. She was a proponent of westernization and an advocate of women's rights. She also became an ardent supporter of Kemal's reform program. Edib shifted the focus of discussion on the matter of the massacres by obliquely alluding to the genocide as a consequence of "destructive nationalism." She too repeated the charge of treason by Armenian revolutionaries and raised the specter of the extermination of the Turks as a consequence. She avoided the question of responsibility by developing what might be called a deflection thesis which implied that the Germans, in their desire for economic supremacy, hoped to see the Armenians eliminated. The circle of deflection was completed with the suggestion that Armenians and Turks shared equal guilt since both sides engaged in behavior characterized by mutual excesses.

* 5.5 *

Emin, Ahmed. *Turkey in the World War*. New Haven: Yale University Press, 1930. LC 30-9837. Rev. See pp. 217-223.

Ahmed Emin Yalman was an American-trained sociologist and journalist who worked as news editor of the Young Turk party organ during World War I. His close acquaintance with the party organization, and his Western education--he attended Columbia University—made him a particularly perspicacious observer of the Armenian genocide. He developed a number of theses which, in contradistinction to the outright denials or falsifications, are more commonly repeated by equilibrating rationalizers. They include the following: a) the dispute over the exact, or approximate, figure for the Armenian population in the Ottoman Empire, the general purpose being to demonstrate that they were "a scattered minority," and therefore lacking demographic concentration in any part of the state; b) because of their aspirations and sympathies the Armenians constituted "Enemies Within," who were involved in "provocations"; c) that the deportations "actually applied only to the Gregorian Armenians," (p.217) and spared Catholics and Protestants, and thus were not necessarily racially motivated; d) that the Armenian volunteer divisions in the Russian army were first to engage in massacre and consequently "created an unofficial state of war between the Armenians and the Turks" (p.219); e) attacks against the Armenians were only "Counter-massacres." Despite these arguments, Emin has been regarded "the most candid" of Turkish authors on the subject because he is the only one to have admitted the ultimate purpose of the Armenian genocide.

* 5.6 *

Council on Turkish-American Relations. *The Treaty with Turkey: Why It Should Be Ratified*. New York: Council on Turkish-American Relations, 1926. LC 26-13881.

A compilation of articles and statements supporting the American ratification of the Treaty of Lausanne and the establishment of formal relations between the United States and Turkey, this work is a virtual encyclopedia of the apologist literature written by Americans in the early 1920s. Some of the authors had actively raised funds to aid Armenian refugees and were one-time supporters of Armenian independence. Almost all the arguments that subsequent rationalizers, relativists, revisionists, and deniers would rely on appear in this collection.

This work provides the best documentation on the rapidly changed view of American opinion makers for whom political pragmatism and commerical interest were sufficient reasons to abandon any further consideration of the Armenian condition. James Barton, the Secretary of the Foreign Department of the American Board of Commissioners for Foreign Missions, the main arm of the American missionary movement in Turkey, wrote: "an Armenian national home within the boundary of the Turkish Empire is a closed incident...however much we may regret it...that the battle was fought at Lausanne and it was lost." (p.23) In the "Report of the Committee on the Lausanne Treaty to the Executive Committee of the Foreign Policy Association (May 1924)," the organized murder of Armenians and the deaths caused by the war were already treated as an equivalence. "No right minded American will condone the massacre, literally by the hundreds of thousands, of Christian minorities by the Turks. No intellectually honest American, however, will close his mind to the fact that the Turks themselves have suffered cruel hardships as a result of war, famine, and disease." (p.82)

The re-interpretations of Armenian history had also begun. Rayford W. Alley, the president of the Council on Turkish-American Relations, wrote: "In referring to Armenia, we assume...the Armenian race because...Armenia is not now and never has been, except for a few isolated periods in the twelfth and thirteenth centuries, more than a geographical expression." (p.103) Alexander E. Powell was already making excuses for Ottoman policies. In his opinion, "the Armenians have been the unwitting victims of European imperialism." (p.109) As for the "two million Armenian Christians," they were "discontented, disloyal, and longing for independence." The justification theory is observed here creeping into Western literature.

Others invoked the impressive figure of Kemal Ataturk for changing American opinion about the Turks. Lothrop Stoddard described Mustafa Kemal as "the living embodiement of that New Turkey which, like the fabled phoenix, has risen suddenly and dramatically from the ashes of what seemed to be hopeless ruin." George A. Plimpton argued for political support for certain types of racial policies and the suspension of moral judgment for their consequences. Turkey "is now a homogeneous nation, but to achieve this homogeneity it was necessary for her to drive out the Armenians and the Greeks. These alien people were largely merchants, business men and heavy taxpayers, but their presence in Turkey meant constant wars. Their expulsion cost great suffering to them and involved financial sacrifice to Turkey herself. Whether it was right or wrong for Turkey to drive out the Armenians and Greeks is not for us to decide, but it is a fact that it has been done and that peace now reigns within her borders." (p.7) In another type of equivalence, the treatment of the Armenians and of the Greeks is described as a forced exodus. The specific policy of exterminating the Armenians is ignored.

* 5.7 *
Stewart, Desmond, and The Editors of *LIFE*. *Turkey*. Life World Library. New York: Time Incorporated, 1965. LC 65-24361.

Popular literature on Turkey published in the United States often whitewashed the Armenian genocide, as does this example. This beautifully designed and illustrated book, which emphasizes the modernization and westernization of Turkey, also contains a considerable amount of historical narrative. In its organization the work reflects the perceptual change in the West since 1923. Anatolia is described as the homeland of the Turks, whereas other once native peoples are characterized "Previous Tenants." The disappearance of the Armenians from Anatolia is related in capsule form under "The Trials of the Armenians." It explains: "Few peoples have known as many changes of fortune as the Armenians...Under the Ottoman Empire, Armenian merchants and financiers thrived. As the borders of the empire contracted in the 19th Century, however, struggles broke out between Turks and Armenians for possession of Anatolian lands. Many Armenians died; others fled abroad." (p.29)

The Rationalizers

* 5.8 *
Kedourie, Elie. "Minorities." In *The Chatham House Version and Other Middle-Eastern Studies*. New York and Washington: Praeger, 1970. LC 72-97184. See pp. 286-316.

An authority on the Middle East, Kedourie posits the theory that the intellectual and political development of Armenian society in the last decades of the Ottoman era ineluctably led the Armenians down the path to suicide. In other words the genocide was self-inflicted. Kedourie determines that the exposure of the Armenians to modern concepts of government was self-destructive. He describes Armenian nationalism, imbibed from Protestant missionaries acccording to Kedourie, as a toxin. By leaping to these kinds of generalizations and abstractions, Kedourie sidesteps the issue of the decision made by the Young Turks to proceed with a plan of destruction. His basic argument maintains that there is no conscious element in history, only processes, a sort of natural evolution of conflicts. The genocide of the Armenians was the result of a cycle of escalation between a destabilizing nationalism and the defense concerns of the state.

* 5.9 *
Shaw, Stanford J., and Ezel Kural Shaw. *History of the Ottoman Empire and Modern Turkey, vol. 1, Empire of the Gazis: The Rise and Decline of the Ottoman Empire 1280-1808, vol. 2, Reform, Revolution, and Republic: The Rise of Modern Turkey 1808-1975*. Cambridge, New York, London and Melbourne: Cambridge University Press 1976, 1977. LC 76-9179. See vol. 2, pp. 314-317.

The Shaw volumes were the first works published by otherwise legitimate scholars, employed at the university level, to engage in the most brazen form of denial. In earlier works on Turkey, American academics had preferred to overlook the subject of the Armenian genocide. The Shaws chose to accept the available denial theses without any attempt to examine contravening evidence. The Shaws couched the entire episode of genocide through the use of euphemisms such as "evacuation" and "transportation." They also minimized the casualties by estimating that about 400,000 Armenians were moved, of whom about half perished. They also claimed to have examined "the secret records of the Ottoman cabinet" and found no evidence that the central government had issued any orders to massacre Armenians. The Shaws elaborated the provocation thesis by characterizing the Armenians as murderous revolutionaries, saboteurs, and collaborators with the enemy. To make them appear a consequence of war, the events of 1915 were described within the story of the Ottoman campaigns on the eastern front.

* 5.10 *
McCarthy, Justin. *Muslims and Minorities: The Population of Ottoman Anatolia and the End of the Empire*. New York and London: New York University Press, 1983. LC 83-13165. ISBN 0-8147-5390-6. See pp. 47-81, 117-130.

Basing his work on the various types of census registers kept by the Ottomans, McCarthy reconstructs the ethnic composition of Anatolia in the first part of the twentieth century. Entirely dismissing the deportations as a deliberate and comprehensive state policy to alter the demography of the region, McCarthy resorts to the civil war thesis where for "both sides, the war became one of extermination in which the villages of the other side were annihilated." (p.119) The disappearance of the Armenians is explained by the fact that they constituted no more than forty percent of the total population in any one province. The argument also posits the theory of Armenian self-induced or self-inflicted genocide. The question of the organized killings of Armenians is entirely bypassed. Epidemics were the cause of a large number of deaths.

* 5.11 *
Sonyel, Salahi R. "Armenian Deportations: A Reappraisal in the Light of New Documents." *Belleten* 36, no.141 (1972): 51-69.

A claim regularly made by rationalizers has been their continuing discovery of archival documents which belie the genocide. Relying on British documents, Sonyel advances the disingenuous idea that, despite the documents demonstrating a willful plan of deportation, the Ottoman government cannot be "implicated in the massacres." Sonyel concocts one of the strangest combinations of argument: the partial admission of facts (i.e., the deportations) and the absolution of the Ottoman goverment for the consequences of their methods of implementing this policy. "Owing to the shortage of men, most of whom were fighting on the various fronts against the external enemies, the Ottoman government entrusted the guarding of the convoys of Armenians, who were being deported, to non-combatants, usually to convicts released from prisons for the purpose, and to local Kurds, who had old scores to settle with the Armenians. The deportations gave the Kurds the opportunity to deal severely with the Armenians who had already lost the favour of the Ottoman Government owing to their treachery. There is no evidence that the Ottoman Government planned the massacres, although deportations were well-planned in order to be effective enough to diminish the great danger of a general Armenian uprising." (p.60-61) Sonyel's article also contains a particularly good example of a euphemism. "The whole affair [understand genocide] was spontaneous and the result of extreme provocation on the part of the Armenians." (p.61) Like all rationalizers, Sonyel finds no contradiction between the claim that the Armenian population was in a state of rebellion and yet the deporations proceeded expeditiously, with little resistance, and according to plan.

* 5.12 *
Uras, Esat. *The Armenians in History and the Armenian Question*. Istanbul: Foundation for the Establishment and Promotion of Centers for Historical Research and Documentation, and Istanbul Research Center, 1988.

This massive tome running into a thousand pages is the prototype of revisionist historiography on the Armenians produced in Turkey. The translation of a work first published in 1950 in Turkish, the Uras volume is in the main a collection of documents and lengthy quotations strung together with the sketchiest of background information. It leaves the impression that the history of the Armenians can be discerned by reproducing diplomatic correspondence and official edicts. The distinguishing feature of the book is its reliance on Armenian sources. The first section of the book contains chapters on geography, ethnography, mythology, language, church, and population. All these subjects are constructed on the basis of works by French historians of Armenia, works which are now, in most instances, a hundred years outdated. The principal concern of the Uras book is the legitimacy of Armenian rights to a homeland, a matter which he saw as "a very serious problem in the history of Anatolia." (p.219)

The largest section of the book is devoted to the question of the Ottoman reforms in the nineteenth century and the Armenian Question, topics covered by producing memorandum after memorandum supported by quotations from participants and observers. The chapter headed "Revolts and Relocation" covers the genocide. For all that is said in this chapter, Uras actually devotes just a single paragraph to the genocide, attributing Armenian deaths to "hunger, epidemics, anarchy, robbery, lack of transportation, desertions, enemy occupation...[and] the helplessness of the government." (p.879). The Uras thesis on justifiable genocide speaks for itself: "It should not be forgotten that when the survival of a nation and of a state is threatened, the principle of 'ends justify means' comes into effect." (p.864)

Despite its size, the Uras work is only the backdrop to the update written by Cengiz Kürşad which covers the period from 1923 to 1985, and which is placed at the front of the publication. The section largely addresses the issue of Armenian terrorism which occurred between the years 1975 to 1985. Armenian efforts since 1923 to gain recognition for the genocide are dismissed as propaganda. Everything ranging from the effort to "keep alive the identity and culture of the Armenians" in diaspora to the founding of university chairs in Armenian studies also is labeled propaganda. (pp. 26, 79)

The Revisionists

* 5.13 *
Institute for Ataturk's Principles and the History of Turkish Renovation. *Armenians in the Ottoman Empire and Modern Turkey (1912-1926)*. Istanbul: Bogazici University, 1984.

The book contains four articles "submitted to the 17th Annual Meeting of the Middle East Studies Association in Chicago, 3-6 November, 1983." The anonymous "Introduction" claims that the contents of the publication are part of the effort at a "re-evaluation of the Armenian issue. Even if it meant the re-writing [of] the entire Armenian history..." (p.15) It singles out educators of Armenian background by suggesting that their work is part of an effort by Armenians to vent their "discontent in various forms of expression, scholarship and terrorism not excluded." (p.10) Justin McCarthy's "The Anatolian Armenians, 1912-1922" summarizes his book on the demography of Anatolia. Bilâl N. Şimşir, "The Deportees of Malta and the Armenian Question," is a condensed version of the booklet by the same title. Heath W. Lowry's "American Observers in Anatolia ca. 1920: the Bristol Papers," casts Admiral Mark Bristol, the U.S. High Commissioner in post-war Turkey, as an objective observer of the Anatolian scene because of his equal contempt for both Armenians and Turks. By a selective reading of information preserved in Bristol's papers, Lowry attempts to disprove the report of a massacre upon the capture of the city of Kars from the Armenians by the Turkish Nationalist forces on 30 October 1920.

Mim Kemâl Öke's "The Responses of Turkish Armenians to the 'Armenian Question', 1919-1926" describes the effort by Armenians in Turkey in 1920 to organize the Turkish-Armenian Friendship Association. Reportedly the association sought to establish Armenian amity with Turks by "accepting the guilt of their revolutionary brethren." (p.71) Thereafter Oke quotes from a "brochure" purportedly produced by this organization which lists all the faults of the Armenians and justifies all the actions taken by the Turks: 1) "The author considered that this extraordinary measure [of deportation] was taken in 'self-defence'. He further added that the histories of all nations are filled with legitimate reasons to justify such decisions" (p.74); 2) "the real responsibility lay with the imperialist powers of the late nineteenth century" (p.74); 3) Armenians "were brainwashed to believe in Turkish oppression" (p.75); 4) "Armenian massacres could only be explained in terms of the 'oppression of Armenians by Armenians'" (p.75); 5) "Overambitious as they were, the Armenians launched a military-genocidal campaign penetrating deep into Turkish territory" (pp. 77-78); and so on.

* 5.14 *
Lowry, Heath W. "The U.S. Congress and Adolf Hitler on the Armenians." *Political Communication and Persuasion: An International Journal* 3:2 (1985): 111-140.

This article by the Director of the Washington, DC-based Institute of Turkish Studies attempts to disprove that Hitler made the oft-repeated statement, "Who, after all, speaks today of the annihilation of the Armenians." Basing his position on the argument that the document containing the statement was not introduced as evidence at the Nuremberg trials because it had been leaked to the press earlier, Lowry casts doubt on the authenticity of the statement. He emphasizes the fact that the statement was made in the context of Hitler's preparations for the conquest of Poland and did not allude to plans for the extermination of the Jews. Lowry claims that the quotation is "spurious" because in other records of the speech, and there are at least three variants, no reference is made to Armenians. This attempt to revisit the Hitler quotation was aimed at questioning the linkage between the Armenian genocide and the Holocaust.

* 5.15 *
Gunter, Michael M. "Turkey and the Armenians." In *Multidimensional Terrorism*. Ed. by Martin Slann and Bernard Schechterman. Boulder, CO, and London: Lynne Rienner Publishers, 1987. LC 87-4898. ISBN 1-55587-030-9. See pp. 57-71.

The article responds to a series of charges made by the English-language Armenian popular media in the United States regarding "counterterror" by Turkey and the "harassment" of the Armenian community in Turkey. It also recites the "Turkish response" and concludes with the author's "synthesis:" 1) "Turkish sensitivities about minorities and a desire to have a Turkey for the Turks is understandable ..." (p.67); 2) "Unofficial pressures to conform culturally and religiously undoubtedly exist in Turkey today, but how is this different than in any other country?" (p.67); 3) "there is no evidence that the Turkish government is destroying historical Armenian churches and monuments as an official policy..." (p.68). He dismisses the last matter as specious allegations in the Armenian "diet of disinformation."

* 5.16 *
Sonyel, Salâhi R. *The Turco-Armenian 'Adana Incidents' in the Light of Secret British Documents (July 1908-December 1909)*. Ankara: Turkish Historical Society, 1988. Originally issued in *Belleten* 51, no. 201 (1987): 1,291-1,338.

One of the more carefully crafted works of revisionism on the massacre of Armenians in the region of Adana in 1909, the work strives to depict the series of killings which visited all the towns of the area as the result of armed conflict between Armenians and Turks. Based in part on British sources, secret only to the extent that they constitute Foreign Office documents, Sonyel places the massacre in the context of the 1909 palace counterrevolution and the consequent serious disruptions of civil society in Turkey. However, Sonyel finds that the Armenian reaction to the Young Turk Revolution of 1908 and the counterrevolution was so provocative that the Turks became frightened by the prospect of the Armenians overthrowing the government in Adana, and therefore retaliated.

* 5.17 *
Corsun, Andrew. "Armenian Terrorism: A Profile." *Department of State Bulletin* 82, no. 206 (August 1982): 31-35.

Although this article focused on the threat of Armenian terrorism, it became the source of the language used to characterize the Armenian genocide in the American media. For instance, the "mass deportation" of the Armenians is presented as fact; the death toll, however, is qualified as "alleged." Since that time this qualification has stuck and the use of the phrase "alleged genocide" gained currency. More critical in enunciating the position of the Reagan administration was the final "Note" appended to the article, which even further qualified the allegedness of the Armenian genocide. "Because the historical record of the 1915 events in Asia Minor is ambiguous, the Department of State does not endorse allegations that the Turkish Government committed a genocide against the Armenian people. Armenian terrorists use their allegation to justify in part their continuing attacks on Turkish diplomats and installations..." In the September 1982 issue of the *Bulletin*, further ambiguity was inserted in an "Editor's Note" which stated that the Corsun article "does not necessarily reflect an official position of the Department of State, and the interpretative comments in the article are solely those of the author." However, the subheading of the *Bulletin* reads "The Official Monthly Records of United States Foreign Policy." Since that time the U.S. government has avoided the use of the term "genocide."

* 5.18 *
Ankara University. *Symposium on International Terrorism: Armenian Terrorism, Its Supporters, the Narcotic Connection, the Distortion of History*. Ankara: Ankara University Press, 1984.

This is a collection of some twenty presentations which purportedly describes the problem of Armenian terrorism and demonstrates that it is supported by drug trafficking and the misrepresentation of historical truth. Some of the papers on terrorism by Western analysts contain useful information for understanding the problem. These contrast sharply with the remaining papers whose main thrust is historical revisionism under the guise of studying a contemporary problem. These include: Heath W. Lowry, "Nineteenth and Twentieth Century Armenian Terrorism: 'Threads of Continuity'"; Justin McCarthy, "Armenian Terrorism: History as Poison and Antidote"; Michael M. Gunter, "Contemporary Aspects of Armenian Terrorism"; Türkkaya Ataöv, "Procurement of Arms for Armenian Terrorism:

Realities Based on Ottoman Documents"; and Kâmuran Gürün, "Causes and Prevention of Armenian Terrorism." Paul Henze, in "The Roots of Armenian Violence: How Far Back Do They Extend?," articulates best the main purpose of the above papers. He begins by asking: "Is there something unusual about Armenians as a people, or about their historical experience, that has made them prone to violence?" (p.179) He goes back to the beginning of history to search for an answer to this question. Henze finds it in the defects of historiography. "Armenian history has been studied and written almost entirely by Armenians. The same can be said, though perhaps not to the same degree, of many other peoples, such as the Georgians, Bulgarians, and Hungarians, who have tenaciously survived the vicissitudes of history. But Armenians seem to represent an extreme case, much more so than Jews, e.g. People [sic] who write their own history tend to glorify their past and avoid objective examination of controversial features of it." (p.180)

* 5.19 *

British Documents on Ottoman Armenians, Volume I (1856-1880), Volume II (1880-1890). Ed. by Bilâl N. Şimşir. Ankara: Turkish Historical Society, 1982, 1983. LC 83-217095. The introduction to volume I was issued separately as *The Genesis of the Armenian Question*.

This publication contains a large collection of British documents from the Foreign Office. It includes reports by consuls in the interior of Turkey, dispatches by the Ambassador in Constantinople, and instructions by the Secretary of State for Foreign Affairs. The documents paint a good picture of the lawlessness in the countryside, the shortcomings of the Ottoman government, the venality of the justice system, the extent of brigandage by Kurdish tribesmen, and the helplessness of the unarmed Christian population in general. Yet in a transparent exercise in selectivity, Şimşir writes an introduction to the collection that relies solely on reports critical of, or unflattering to, the Armenians. In a thesis belied by the majority of the documents, the editor argues that the reform measures the British encouraged were an avenue whereby the Christian minorities improved their lot economically to the detriment of the Muslim majority. Still the British purposefully agitated discontent in the Armenian communities as an excuse for intervention. As a result of the War of 1877-78, the Armenians also entered into secret relations with the Russians. The latter encouraged the idea of autonomy for the Armenians who only formed a minority in the provinces. According to Şimşir, the Armenians "were a mere pawn" in the "Anglo-Russian rivalry over Eastern Turkey." The Armenian leaders who advocated reform or western patronage were responsible for "bringing unrest and suffering to their own people." (p.22) The Şimşir volumes are part of a trend in revisionist historiography which aspires to accomplish two things: 1) to be credited with objectivity by publishing documents; and 2) to deflect attention from the genocide by widening the field of controversy to encompass the entire last century of Armenian existence in the Ottoman Empire.

The Disinformers

* 5.20 *

Ataöv, Türkkaya. *A Brief Glance at the "Armenian Question"*. Ankara: Ankara Chambre of Commerce, 1984. *Hitler and the "Armenian Question"*. Ankara, 1984. *The Andonian "Documents" Attributed to Talaat Pasha Are Forgeries!* Ankara: Ankara Üniversitesi Siyasal Bilgiler Fakultesi, 1984. *A 'Statement' Wrongly Attributed to Mustafa Kemâl Atatürk*. Ankara: Ankara Üniversitesi Siyasal Bilgiler Fakultesi, 1984.

This set of booklets was written by the chair of the International Relations Division of the Faculty of Political Science at Ankara University. Meant for popular consumption, the publications revisit the themes of denial in a condensed form. They were all produced in response to the wave of Armenian terrorism and the publicity surrounding it.

The first booklet, after quickly summarizing all of Armenian history in a few pages and demonstrating the extent of Ottoman reliance on Armenian civil servants, begins discussion of the genocide in the following manner: "The events surrounding the *transfer* [sic] of the Armenian population in 1915 had to be examined in the light of active Armenian collaboration with the Tsarist Russian forces, Turkey's enemy during the First World War." (p.33)

The second pamphlet disputes Hitler's statement on the extermination of the Armenians on the grounds that Hitler was "no historian." (p.5) Ataöv maintains that by using the Hitler statement "militant Armenians are exerting every effort to make the Jews and others believe that they are also another persecuted minority." (p.8) Thereafter Ataov attempts to demonstrate "the inclinations of [Armenian] anti-semitism," (p.8) including the charge that "volunteer Armenian troops under the wings of Hitler's Germany during the Second World War were used in rounding up Jews and other 'undesirables' destined for the Nazi concentration camps." (p.9)

The third booklet reviews the Şinasi Orel work on the same subject. In the preface, the work is described by Prof. Necdet Serin, Dean of the Faculty of Political Science at Ankara University, as "the first volume of a series of books and booklets on certain aspects of Turkish-Armenian relations." (p.3)

The fourth booklet discusses the confusion between Mustafa Kemal Ataturk and a certain "Nemrud" Mustafa Kemal to whom a statement admitting the massacres is attributed. The error was detected by two Armenian authors who over the years waged a struggle to halt the proliferation of the misattribution. For Ataöv the subject served as an opportunity to write a paen to Ataturk and criticize the facile tendency to sensationalize quotes, or misquotations, from world leaders.

* 5.21 *
Ataöv, Türkkaya. *Deaths Caused by Disease in Relation to the Armenian Question*. Ankara: Sevinç Matbaasi, 1985. *Documents on the Armenian Question: Forged and Authentic*. Ankara: Barok Ofset, 1985. *An Armenian Falsification*. Ankara: Sevinç Matbaasi, 1985.

The title of the first booklet speaks for itself. It is Ataöv's contention that the high death toll of Armenians during World War I can be explained by the spread of epidemics which also affected the Turks in a similar pattern.

The second booklet revisits the Andonian telegrams as forgeries and reproduces "authentic" Ottoman documents including a 15 March 1916 original signed by Talaat Pasha ordering that "no more displacement of Armenians, on whatever reason, were to take place" (p.20), or a 23 May 1915 document "stating that the displaced Armenians be re-settled to the East of Damascus and the East and South-east of Aleppo" (p.24), while failing to note that what lies in the directions indicated from those two cities in Syria is in the main uninhabitable wasteland.

The third booklet identifies instances of the careless use, in works on the Armenian genocide, of a painting done by a Russian artist in 1871 called the "Apotheosis of War," which shows a heap of skulls in a desert, with its reproduction without proper attribution resulting in a number of publications claiming that the picture depicts an actual scene. Ataöv then reviews the presumably forged Andonian documents again with the intent of leaving the impression that the Armenian genocide is based on falsified evidence.

* 5.22 *
Gürün, Kâmuran. *The Armenian File: The Myth of Innocence Exposed*. London, Nicosia, and Istanbul: K. Rustem & Bro. and Weidenfeld & Nicolson Ltd, 1985. LC 85-31393. ISBN 0-097-78705-5.

Probably the most sophisticated work of revisionism to appear to date, *The Armenian File* was written by a former high ranking official of the Turkish Foreign Ministry with extensive experience at the ambassadorial level. By virtue of his background, Gürün may be regarded formally as one of the key articulators of Turkish government policy. This book purports to trace the political history of the Armenian people from its beginnings until the founding of the Republic of Turkey. Most of it is dedicated to demonstrating that Armenians engaged in a long series of terrorist activities and rebellions from 1860 to 1923, a period wherein virtually every new Armenian organization is assumed to have been founded with the intention of breaking up the Ottoman Empire including ones committed to charity. The provocation thesis is made all-ambracing. The genocide is characterized by Gürün as largely an emigration policy. He finds it specially significant therefore that the Ottoman directives spoke only of "relocation," of "transferring," and of "settling." As for the deaths, besides the usual causes, epidemics and climatic factors, Gürün inserts an original comparison: "The Armenians were forced to emigrate because they had joined the ranks of the enemy. The fact that they were civilians does not change the situation. Those who were killed in Hiroshima and Nagasaki during the Second World War were also civilians. Those who were killed during the First World War in France, Belgium, and Holland were also civilians. Those who died in London during the Battle of Britain were also civilians." (p.216) The Gürün thesis is a rather simple one the entire Armenian population of the Ottoman Empire was a casualty of war.

* 5.23 *
Orel, Şinasi. "The Fact Behind the Telegrams Attributed to Talaat Pasha by the Armenians." *Turkish Review Quarterly Digest* (Winter 1985-86): 83-102. See also his *The Talaat Pasha Telegrams: Historical Fact or Armenian Fiction?* London: K. Rustem & Brother, 1986.

Basing his position largely on the inherent difficulty of authenticating telegrams, Orel attempts to cast doubt on a set obtained by an Armenian named Aram Andonian from an Ottoman civil servant known as Naim Bey. The telegrams in question contained orders for deportation and massacre. Because the documents were obtained surreptitiously, and because Andonian has left two differing accounts on how he came into possession of the telegrams—first depicting Naim Bey as a man having pangs of conscience and delivering the telegrams to ease his guilt, and then describing him more cynically, and accurately, as a gambler and a drunkard who sold him the telegrams—these problems have made the documents vulnerable to questions of authenticity. Thus, they give Orel sufficient cause to submit that the telegrams are part of the "conspiracy" designed to falsely accuse Ottoman officials of responsibility "for the alleged Armenian-related events," Orel's euphemism for genocide. (p.98)

* 5.24 *

The Assembly of Turkish American Associations. *Armenian Allegations: Myth and Reality, a Handbook of Facts and Documents*. 2d ed. Washington, DC: The Assembly, 1987.

In its preface, the former Ambassador of the Turkish Republic to the United States, Şükrü Elekdağ, describes this publication as the "first effort [by Turkish Americans] at setting the record straight vis-a-vis a wide variety of Armenian charges...[and as a] compilation of materials which demonstrates that no Ottoman Government ever planned or carried out a policy of genocide against its Armenian or any other minority population." (p.v) Among a range of U.S. documents or statements outlining Turkish-Armenian relations, articles from the periodical press and selections from the Armenian-American media, included are also a series of reprints: 1) Heath W. Lowry, "Nineteenth and Twentieth Century Armenian Terrorism: Threads of Continuity"; 2) Paul Henze, "The Roots of Armenian Violence: How Far Back Do They Extend?"; 3) Justin McCarthy, "Armenian Terrorism: History as Poison and Antidote;" 4) Stanford J. Shaw and Ezel Kural Shaw, *History of the Ottoman Empire and Modern Turkey*, the chapter entitled "The Northeastern Front 1914-1916"; 5) Justin McCarthy, "The Anatolian Armenians, 1912-1922;" and 6) Heath W. Lowry, "The U.S Congress and Adolf Hitler on the Armenians." The handbook was issued for the purpose of blunting congressional support for commemorative resolutions on the Armenian genocide by claiming that they would endorse "a falsehood as truth," and would "reward the Armenian terrorists." (p. ix)

* 5.25 *

Foreign Policy Institute. *The Armenian Issue in Nine Questions and Answers*. Ankara, The Institute, 1982. LC 83-217095.

This document is an official response to the historical debate engendered by Armenian terrorism. More important, however, is the case made by the institute that the terrorism was preceded by a campaign of "defamation" and "vilification." The obligation to respond to the propaganda became compelling when the "propaganda identified itself with the terrorist movements." The argument is an unintended admission that public discussion about the Armenian genocide in and of itself did not present a sufficient threat. The radicalization of the issue through political violence, on the other hand, was alarming. Both the terrorist threat and the issue of the genocide associated with it required an answer. The standard denials about the Talaat telegrams, about a "planned and systematic" genocide, or about the number of victims are reproduced.

* 5.26 *

Institute for the Study of Turkish Culture. *The Eastern Question: Imperialism and the Armenian Community*. Ankara: Ankara University Press, 1987.

This collection of articles covers various aspects of Armenian-Turkish relations. Its overall purpose is to demonstrate that Armenians aligned themselves with the Western powers that were conspiring to dismember the Ottoman Empire. They encouraged Armenian terrorism against the Muslim population of Anatolia and Transcaucasia, and this resulted in the Armenians committing atrocities.

The Distorters

* 5.27 *

Feigl, Erich. *A Myth of Terror. Armenian Extremism: Its Causes and Its Historical Context*. Freilassing and Salzburg: Edition Zeitgeschichte, 1986.

Ostensibly a book on Armenian terrorism, the Feigl tome perhaps can best be described as an extensively illustrated attempt to distort all of Armenian history. Everything Armenian—history, literature, art, archaeology, geography, is subjected to revisionist reinterpretation and, according to the author, demythologized, whereby virtually nothing is left having any resemblance to the established record of Armenian history. He maintains that Armenia is a geographical name. Therefore the suggestions that the Armenians are original inhabitants of this land is only a historical myth. Throughout their existence Armenians were a minor religious sect. Nationalism reached them through Protestant missionaries and spread from the church to other organizations. There was only a relocation policy in 1915 and the Armenians murdered the Ottoman ruling elite in retaliation. Feigl finally concludes with graphic coverage of the wave of political violence in the seventies and early eighties under "Terrorism as Bloody, Real Fantasy-War." The Feigl volume integrates all the distortions pressed on Armenian history by revisionists and deniers into a comprehensive synthesis.

* 5.28 *

Ottoman Archives. *Yildiz Collection: The Armenian Question, Talori Incidents*. Istanbul: The Foundation for Establishing and Promoting Centers for Historical Research and Documentation, and Istanbul Research Center, 1989.

The collection contains documents from the palace of the Sultan Abdul Hamid II relating to the Ottoman military operations against a remote mountaintop cluster of Armenian villages charged with insurrection in 1894. Original Ottoman documents, dated from 19 May 1894 to 6 October 1894, are reproduced, transliterated into Latin script, translated into Turkish and English. The documents are introduced by four essays, three on terrorism, two of which are reprints of earlier works by Lowry and McCarthy. The third by Dr. Cengiz Kürşad entitled "Armenian Terrorism," is a section from his update to the Uras volume. The introductory essay, wherein the aim of the foundation is given as the prevention of "the further distortion of events" (p. xxxiii), is also in large part a reprint of the section on this period from Uras. Under the guise of describing the episodes of political terrorism from Armenian history, Kürşad's work engages in another exercise in denial. Kürşad's framework, however, virtually reduces the last hundred years of Armenian-Turkish relations to one of terrorism inflicted by Armenians on Turks. The genocide is only "a theme in the campaign of propaganda and psychological warfare." (p. 21) The Ottoman-Russian campaigns during World War I were a war by Armenians against Turks. Besides describing the "resettlment" policy as a "countermeasure," Kürşad, taking his cue from Gürün, is adamant on the matter of the deportations. "Not a single Armenian was deported." (p. 25)

* 5.29 *
Sonyel, Salâhi R. "How Armenian Propaganda Nurtured a Gullible Christian World in Connection with the Deportations and 'Massacres'." *Belleten* 51, no. 161 (1977): 157-175.

"The betrayal of the relatively prosperous Armenian people of the Ottoman Empire by their own self-seeking, self-centered and foreign-inspired leaders, and in return, the treachery of some of the Armenians against their own country, Turkey, when that country was engaged in a life-and-death struggle against its enemies during the First World War and after..." is the opening sentence of this article. Apart from betrayal, Sonyel asserts that Armenian leaders were skillful in the use of propaganda, themselves "indulged in a wide campaign of terror and massacre against the Muslims and then persuaded the West that it was the Armenians who were massacred." Sonyel catalogs all the different kinds of treachery the Armenians engaged in: espionage, collaboration with enemy powers, propaganda, and atrocities. The journal *Belleten* is published by the Turkish Historical Society.

* 5.30 *
Sonyel, Salâhi R. *Displacement of the Armenians Documents*. Ankara: Turkish Historical Society, 1978.

This collection of Ottoman documents—reproduced in facsimile and translated into English, French, and Turkish, including a number of telegrams from 1915 signed by Talaat—shows that the displacement of the Armenians was a well-organized, closely monitored, and carefully implemented policy. The documents give the semblance that the entire process was peaceful, orderly, and with no harm brought to the "immigrants." According to Sonyel the evidence verifies that "the Ottoman Empire planned to displace some of the Armenian citizens temporarily to other parts of the country taking the most humane measures..." (preface) The editor fails to note that, without geographical specification, instructions for "transport" are virtually meaningless. For example, one communique from Talaat reads: "The Armenians within the province should be transported to the areas previously determined." (p. 1) Another signed by the Chief of General Staff glumly states: "It is decided that the Armenians should be moved to the interior of the country." (p. 1) Virtually all the instructions are equally vague about the destination of the people "transported." Nor are there any indications of the scope of the measures, or the numbers of persons supposedly relocated. All the directives produced refer to the province of Hudavendigar, the area around Bursa which saw no fighting during World War I. This detail is overlooked by the editor as it contradicts one of the main arguments by rationalizers and revisionists which insists that only Armenians from the "war zones" were deported.

* 5.31 *
Sonyel, Salâhi R. *The Ottoman Armenians: Victims of Great Power Diplomacy*. London and Nicosia: K. Rustem & Brothers, 1987.

Sonyel attributes the disintegration of Turkish-Armenian relations to the interventionist policies of England and Russia. As they alternated in their sponsorship of "reforms" on behalf of the Armenians, the European Powers only propelled Armenian nationalism. Consequently, they contributed to the emergence of Armenian revolutionary organizations. Sonyel characterizes the massacres from the 1890s on as episodes of civil war, and the genocide of 1915 is called a "Turco-Armenian tragedy." He maintains that Armenian extremists "succeeded in deceiving the public of the Christian world simply because they posed as a 'martyred' nation in the cause of Christ and clamoured that they had been 'massacred.'" Sonyel advances the interesting notion of a double irrationality as the reason behind the suggestion of genocide: Armenian distortion and Western gullibility and predilection to believe other Christians.

* 5.32 *
Şimşir, Bilâl N. *The Deportees of Malta and the Armenian Question*. Ankara: Foreign Policy Institute, 1984.

During the Allied occupation of Constantinople after World War I, the British arrested over a hundred former Young Turk leaders. Originally incarcerated in the city, they were moved to Malta to prevent their escape. The intention of the British government was to try these individuals for crimes against civilian Armenians and British prisoners of war. The reluctance of British jurists to try the accused because of the legal difficulties involved with the case of foreign nationals, the disagreement among the Allies about prosecution, and hostage-taking by the Kemalists unraveled the effort to haul the Young Turks to court. Şimşir uses the failure of the Allied effort to affix criminality as evidence of the absence of proof, the falsehood of the charges, the innocence of the accused, and vindication of the denial that intentional violence had been inflicted on the Armenian population. Şimşir fails to point out, however, that some of the accused were turned over to the Turkish courts, which tried them on the basis of government evidence and which delivered guilty verdicts to a number of them. The key CUP figures tried in absentia were given death sentences.

* 5.33 *
McCarthy, Justin, and Carolyn McCarthy. *Turks and Armenians: A Manual on the Armenian Question*. Washington, DC: Committee on Education, Assembly of Turkish American Associations, 1989.

"There was no genocide, unless one considers what transpired in Anatolia to have been a genocide carried out by both sides on each other." (p. 98) This contradictory conclusion is one of the main arguments of this book. Once again the specter of "mutual extermination" is elaborated upon at some length. More attention is paid to developing the argument that the massacre stories were a propaganda ploy. Throughout, a great deal of emphasis is placed on the supposition that there was so much prejudice against Turks in the West that Christians were apt to believe every stereotype unfavorable to the Turks and favorable to the Armenians. As is common practice with the proponents of the mutuality theory, the role of the Young Turk regime is thoroughly minimized and the Ottoman government is excused by depicting it as inept or distracted.

* 5.34 *
Documents on Ottoman-Armenians, 2 vols. Ed. by Bilâl N. Şimşir. Ankara: Prime Ministry Directorate General of Press and Information, 1982, 1983. LC 85-183095.

A collection of Ottoman documents from the Turkish Military History Archives which are reproduced in facsimile and translated into English, it covers the period 1914-1918, when, according to the editor, Armenians engaged in two series of "aggressions" against Turks in 1915 and from 1917 on. Sixty-three of the one hundred and forty-two documents date from 1918 when the collapse of the Russian front pitted the Ottomans against armed Russian-Armenians fighting on their own. The entire warfare of that period is characterized in the cables from the front as a series of massacres by Armenian "gangs" against civilian Turks. The internal inconsistency of the information provided in the cables dated 1915, however, is more interesting. Reportedly they convey an idea of the extent of Armenian infiltration and sabotage. Yet the context of the war with Russia is not provided, nor is indication given of the Ottoman military's response to the specific instances of infiltration or desertion which are reported in such detail. Instead these reports are used, for instance, to justify taking summary actions "to disperse the Armenians." Similarly, contradictions are concealed in the reports on the rare cases of resistance. One dispatch dated 15 June 1915 talks of "500 Armenian bandits" who had sealed themselves in the castle of Shabin-Karahisar. Another dated 18-19 June reports "500 Armenians" including women and children. There is no mention of the deportation order which had been issued earlier, though the first report says that "security forces were burning down all the Armenians' houses around the castle," without giving a reason. Lastly, a cable dated 28 July reports that "all remaining Armenian bandits in Karahisar have been punished." The form of punishment is not explained. However, no one is known to have survived the siege of the castle. No documents are reproduced, incidentally, on the course of the deportations. The selection of documents therefore is designed to provide ex post facto justification for Ottoman actions by comparing 1915 with 1918. According to Nicati Özkaner, the Director General of Press and Information, who writes in his preface, the documents show "the hostility provoked by the Armenian militants and the atrocities committed by them toward the Ottoman State and the Turkish Muslims of Anatolia during the First World War years."

Chapter 6

THE UKRAINIAN FAMINE

by Lyman H. Legters

In the mind of Stalin, the problem of the Ukrainian peasants who resisted collectivization was linked with the problem of Ukrainian nationalism. Collectivization was imposed on the Ukraine much faster than it was on other parts of the Soviet Union. The resulting hardship in the Ukraine was deliberately intensified by a policy of unrelenting grain procurement. It was this procurement policy that transformed hardship into catastrophe. Famine by itself is not genocide, but the consequences of the policy were known and remedies were available. The evidence is quite powerful that the famine could have been avoided, hence the argument turns on Stalin's intentions.

On the eve of the Bolshevik Revolution, European Social Democrats, including their Russian branch, held generally to two items of received doctrinal wisdom that would bear ultimately on the calamity of the early 1930s in the Ukraine. One of these was the belief that the rural agricultural economy, along with its associated social order, was to undergo capitalist kinds of development as a necessary prelude to the introduction of socialism in the countryside. That expectation could be traced directly back to Marx and Engels. The other belief had been fashioned more recently in the multinational empires of Habsburg and Romanov and taught that ethnic diversity, presumed to be a vestigial social fact that would eventually disappear, might be accommodated in a centralized political system by permitting, perhaps even encouraging, cultural autonomy.[1]

In the Russian case, the first of these propositions was confounded initially in two ways. Capitalist development had not occurred to any significant degree in rural areas, so a socialist program could only be premature at the time of the Bolshevik seizure of power. And, more decisively, Lenin's revolutionary strategy was based in part on appealing to the immediate interests of the peasantry, and the peasants for their part responded by simply seizing the land, making in effect a smallholder's revolution. Consequently, the Bolsheviks in power, at least as soon as initial socializing fervor had abated, could contemplate socialism in the countryside only as a long-term development.

The matter of ethnic diversity, the nationality problem, was also complicated by tension between the proclaimed principle of self-determination and the ambition to retain as much of Russian territory as possible for the impending socialist experiment. The result, which was attained only with Bolshevik success in the Civil War of the post-revolutionary period, was that self-determination gave way to territorial expansion. The urge to secure the greatest possible terrain for the socialist cause was thwarted in such places as Poland and Finland, but not so in other peripheral lands of the USSR such as the Ukraine.[2] Once the boundaries were secure and the party apparatus in place throughout the federation, however, policy could revert to a less contentious approach to nationality, except of course in places where active resistance continued.

Lenin's New Economic Policy

Broadly speaking, then, most of the decade of the 1920s, characterized by Lenin's New Economic Policy (NEP), featured a comparatively permissive attitude on the part of the Bolshevik leadership toward both peasants and the nationalities in their respective republics. As between these two strands of thinking and policy, the nationalities problem seemed the more settled in this period. The Ukraine, for example, enjoyed a veritable flowering of its national culture under the program of "Ukrainization" led by party leader Mykola Skrypnyk from 1927 to 1933.[3] On the other hand, there was a more or less continuous debate about economic policy, notably between those favoring the abandonment of NEP for the sake of socialization of the countryside and the defenders of a very gradual departure from NEP, thereby making it clear that the respite of NEP for the peasantry would be reversed sooner or later.[4] At the same time, some party leaders, Stalin prominent among them, regarded the two issues as indissolubly linked, suggesting that measures designed to cope with the peasantry and agricultural sector would address the nationality question also.

Even the defenders of NEP could not deny the continuing problem of grain procurement in the countryside, a problem the intensity of which varied with success or failure of harvest and with the uncertain tractability of the peasants. A downward trend in procurements in 1927-28, sufficiently drastic to threaten supplies to the cities and to other sectors of the economy, set in motion a campaign to extract the needed agricultural products, employing techniques that were reminiscent in their severity of the Civil War period. Peasants found to be withholding surplus grain were treated as speculators and their supplies subject to confiscation. The rhetoric accompanying the campaign tended to be couched in the terms of class struggle, focusing on allegations that the more favored agricultural producers were profiting at the expense of poorer peasants and of urban workers. This made the procurement struggle a kind of preview of, and dress rehearsal for, the collectivization drive that Stalin launched the following year.

"Primitive Accumulation"

The argument for proceeding with measures of socialization in the countryside had so far come mainly from elements of the party usually referred to as the Left and associated with opposition to Stalin's increasing control over the party. Preobrazhensky in particular had advocated a deliberate exploitation of the peasantry, what in Marxian terms would be called "primitive accumulation," as the best way to finance economic development in general. His ideas had been renounced by the party officially, and Stalin was supposed to be among those rejecting such measures. By the time of the procurement crisis, Stalin's dominance within the party had been secured, as demonstrated by the reluctance of party leaders to do or say anything that might identify them as defenders of the *kulak*s, the more prosperous peasants who now figured as the enemy in this phase of class struggle. And Stalin's shift in position by 1928-29 was perhaps less abrupt than it seemed.

That shift revealed itself as a sudden adoption of the Preobrazhensky line, whereby peasants would be underpaid for their output while paying excessive prices for the purchases they had to make, the whole enterprise masked as an attack on the *kulak*s for their exploitation of less favored segments of the peasant population. The emergency measures of 1928 produced a deepening division within the party, Bukharin joined by Tomsky, Rykov, and others in advocating moderation while Molotov and Kaganovich supported Stalin in his draconian approach to procurement.[5] The split became more evident toward the end of the year and early in 1929 as Stalin took an increasingly explicit stand on rapid industrialization at the expense of agriculture, as reflected in the upward movement of the targets stipulated in the Five Year Plan, drafted in 1927 and intended to run through 1931-32. At the same time, he intensified his effort to isolate the opposition and mobilize the party behind his program. Yet as late as April 1929, the crucial Sixteenth Party Conference appeared to maintain the essence of NEP with respect to agriculture. Though the socialized sector, state and collective farms, was to be developed further, ninety percent of agricultural production was still expected from individual farmers. Given the renewed emphasis on industrial development, this cautious outlook for agriculture contained a serious contradiction.

Collectivization

The contradiction began to be resolved late in 1929 as the party moved to a more coercive campaign of collectivization. Until then, although collectivization had been favored officially, it had been largely voluntary and involved mostly the poorer peasants. But as the campaign of dekulakization intensified, larger numbers joined the collective farms out of fear that they might be labeled *kulak*s and become subject to dispossession. At this stage, too, the "encouragement" of collectivization fell increasingly to police organs and to the brigades of militant workers sent out to the countryside from the cities.[6] The result, in which political motives and perceived economic requirements can scarcely be disentangled, was a massive overfulfillment of Five Year Plan goals for collectivization and the effective destruction of the NEP orientation of agricultural policy. Stalin appeared to acknowledge the shortcomings of the campaign with his "Dizzy with Success" article of March 1930, in which he deplored certain excesses and, in effect, introduced a pause in the process of collectivization. In the confusion that followed for most of 1930, and in the face of uncertainty among the agents of collectivization who had not been warned of Stalin's shift, Stalin's admissions were confirmed as to the shallowness of peasant "conversion" by the movement of vast numbers out of the kolkhozes. Nevertheless, after this interlude the drive for further collectivization resumed.

Peasantry and Nationality

From the Ukrainian point of view, there was much to confirm Stalin's linkage of peasantry and nationality as problems to be addressed. Indeed, despite the autonomy that the Ukraine continued to enjoy in the cultural realm, it was very possible to view the policies pronounced in Moscow as twin onslaughts on Ukrainian nationality and peasantry. The percentage of Ukrainian farms collectivized rose from 8.6 in December 1929 to 65.0 in March 1930 to 70.0 in mid-1932; corresponding percentages for Russia were 7.4, 59.0, and 59.3. The 90 percent mark was reached by 1935 in the Ukraine, not until late 1937 in Russia. Moreover, the urban workers sent forth to implement collectivization introduced an ethnic issue; many came from outside the Ukraine, and even in Ukrainian cities many workers were Russian, or at any rate non-Ukrainian. With collectivization taking priority over Ukrainization, the Ukrainian party organization was profoundly affected. Skrypnyk's regime was undermined, and lower party echelons were transformed as party secretaries were purged, often for real or imagined opposition to collectivization. At the same time, Ukrainian resistance seems to have been exceptionally strong, as indicated by numbers of punishable offenses.

Questionable as the forced collectivization program may have been from an economic point of view, by itself it would not necessarily have led to famine. Enormous hardship was inflicted on the peasantry in the course of it, especially in the winter of 1929-1930, and of course not only in the Ukraine. Enormous losses were also recorded as the peasants responded with sabotage, destruction of grain and livestock. Furthermore, the impact was by no means restricted to the *kulak*s, for the sheer scale and recklessness of the drive inflicted severe damage on whole regions, including many middle and even poor peasants who were caught up in the "dizziness" of unchecked coercion. Nevertheless, famine was not inevitable.

Unrelenting Grain Procurement

A policy of unrelenting grain procurement made the critical difference between hardship and catastrophe. The Ukrainian harvest of 1930 was exceptionally good and could meet the quota (of about one-third) imposed by Moscow with no great difficulty. The same 7.7 million ton quota for 1931 could not be met, however, because of the poorer harvest, and central authorities, while applying great pressure, began to attribute the shortfall to deliberate withholding of grain. The 1932 harvest was poorer still but, even with a modest reduction in the quota, Moscow demanded nearly half of the total—which by itself would have met bare requirements in the Ukraine for people and livestock. Ukrainian party officials issued numerous warnings about the dire consequences to be expected if Moscow did not relent, recounting stories of villages where nothing had been left for the populace to eat, and this at a time when the Soviet Union was exporting grain.

The official response to all warnings was indifference or disbelief, coupled with new regulations imposing stern penalties for withholding or pilfering. In November 1932 the Ukrainian Soviet regime prohibited the distribution of food and the creation of reserves (seed grain) until quotas were met. Even so, effective control over the Ukraine was transferred to Stalin's non-Ukrainian lieutenant, Pavel Postyshev, who ruled against the provision of aid to the starving countryside and sent brigades to collect what little was left of grain distributed to collective farm members. At the same time, Postyshev brought the nationality issue into play by blaming shortfalls in collections on Skrypnyk and other Ukrainian "nationalist wreckers."[7]

Terror-Famine

Memoir literature and interviews conducted long after provide a grim picture of the consequences: corpses in the streets of the villages, deliberate cruelty by enforcement authorities, starving children, cannibalism, in short, all of the accompaniments of deep and prolonged famine.[8] Demographic evidence yields less graphic but no less startling demonstration of the terrible outcome of Stalin's policies. One estimate, by Maksudov, arrives at a figure of 4.5 million deaths in the Ukraine as a result of famine, a bit over half of the premature deaths he estimates for the Soviet Union as a whole.[9] Noting that this estimate disregards the resettlement of depopulated villages by non-Ukrainians, Mace suggests the higher figure of 7.5 million.[10] Demographic evidence also helps to locate the areas of greatest suffering, the Ukraine ranking first according to most accounts. Also telling is a comparison of two districts facing each other across the Russian-Ukrainian boundary, the Ukrainian side showing extreme devastation and the Russian side roughly normal mortality.

"Terror-famine" is the term Robert Conquest uses for the whole episode, suggesting not just the nature of the events but also the deliberate intent that pushed the misery associated with collectivization across the line to outright devastation.[11] Famine by itself is of course not a genocide, nor is massive loss of life. But by demonstrating that the consequences of policy were known and remedies available, the argument turns on the intentions of those responsible. The evidence is quite powerful that the famine could have been avoided; it is overwhelming that the worst consequences could have been ameliorated at least. It is equally hard to disregard the evidence, not least from the statements of Stalin and other party leaders, that the entire policy had a nationality dimension as well as an economic one. The Ukraine would have suffered terribly, by its very nature as an agricultural stronghold, from collectivization and the manner of its imposition. But there is no adequate explanation, apart from the nationality question, for the singling out of the Ukraine for exceptionally dire consequences.[12]

The UN Definition of Genocide

It can be argued that the UN definition of genocide is deficient in its failure to allow for murderous onslaughts on strata—such as the *kulak*s—of a given population, whether real or invented.[13] Were this extension to be admitted, then the program of dekulakization, given the extreme loss of life that its implementation entailed, would count as a genocide. In any event, what is beyond doubt is that the Ukrainian famine does fall within the UN definition as an attempt to destroy the basis for continued existence of a nationality. The Ukraine survives as a self-conscious ethnic community, but a genocidal policy does not have to succeed in its final aim before it can be counted as a genocide.

NOTES

1. In the Marxian tradition the classic treatment of the subject is Otto Bauer, *Die Nationalitätenfrage und die Sozialdemokratie* (Wien: I. Brand, 1907); Joseph Stalin, *Marxism and the National-Colonial Question* (New York: International Publishers, 1935) is a theoretically inferior effort, partly derived from and partly at odds with Bauer; for a modern study, see Ian Cummins, *Marx, Engels and National Movements* (New York: St. Martin's Press, 1980).

2. On these events, see Richard Pipes, *The Formation of the Soviet Union; Communism and Nationalism, 1917-1923* (Cambridge, MA: Harvard University Press, 1954).

3. James E. Mace, "Famine and Nationalism in Soviet Ukraine," *Problems of Communism* (May-June 1984): 41 ff.

4. M. Levin, *Russian Peasants and Soviet Power* (New York: W.W. Norton, 1975), 148-158.

5. The episode is described in detail against the background of the leadership struggle in Stephen F. Cohen, *Bukharin and the Bolshevik Revolution* (New York: A. A. Knopf, 1973), 270 ff.

6. Lynne Viola, *The Best Sons of the Fatherland; Workers in the Vanguard of Soviet Collectivization* (New York: Oxford University Press, 1987).

7. The foregoing account relies heavily on James E. Mace, *Communism and the Dilemmas of National Liberation* (Cambridge, MA: Harvard Ukrainian Research Institute, 1983) and Robert Conquest, *The Harvest of Sorrow* (New York: Oxford University Press, 1986).

8. For example, Miron Dolot, *Execution by Hunger* (New York: W.W. Norton, 1987).

9. Cited in Mace, "Famine," 38.

10. Mace, "Famine," 38.

11. Conquest, 322-330.

12. Conquest, 272.

13. An argument made in Lyman H. Legters, "The Soviet Gulag: Is It Genocidal?" in *Toward the Understanding and Prevention of Genocide*, ed. by Israel W. Charny (Boulder, CO: Westview Press, 1984). The discussion is pursued further in Frank Chalk and Kurt Jonassohn, *The History and Sociology of Genocide* (New Haven, CT: Yale University Press, 1990), 12-23.

Chapter 6: Annotated Bibliography

* 6.1 *

Allworth, Edward, ed. *Soviet Nationality Problems*. New York and London: Columbia University Press, 1971. LC 77-166211. ISBN 0-231-03493-8.

The nine papers that make up this volume were originally presented to the Seminar on Soviet Nationality Problems, which was held at Columbia University during the academic year of 1968-1969. In the context of understanding Ukrainian nationalism, Marc Raeff's paper, "Patterns of Russian Imperial Policy Toward the Nationalities," is both the most illuminating and the least dated by recent events in the Soviet Union.

The traditional methods of Imperial territorial expansion were 1) conquest or acquisition of non-Russian territories; 2) incorporation; and 3) assimilation. This three-fold process is unexceptionably applicable to the Ukraine. In 1654 Ukrainian leaders turned to Petersburg in an appeal for protection against the aggressive designs of Poland. Thus at first the Ukraine was a protectorate of Imperial Russia. In one hundred-twenty-one years, Russia was able to consummate the Ukraine's incorporation into the Czardom of Muscovy. Raeff sets forth the steps which led to eventual incorporation:

> ...[I]n the Ukraine the Cossack Host managed to preserve its autonomy and organization at least until 1709, and it even lingered on in a limited way until 1775. In 1709, as a consequence of Hetman's Mazepa's siding with Charles XII [of Sweden] at Poltava, the autonomy of the Dnieper Cossack Host was drastically curtailed. In 1775—following the Pugachev rebellion—Catherine II abolished the Zaporozhian *Sich* altogether.

The Czars sought to assimilate the Ukraine through policies of Russification. Of primary importance for Russification was the imposition of the Russian language on the Ukrainians, along with the prohibition of the Ukrainian language as a publishing vehicle. Russians have persisted in what is a delusion, namely, that the Ukrainian language is only a peasant dialect. In the 1820s, folklorists and poets, among others, mounted a successful effort to transform the "peasant dialect" into a fully developed literary language, a language that could claim equality with Russian in all respects. It will be recalled that in the late 1920s, Strypnyk, the Ukrainian commissar of education, called a conference to rid the Ukrainian language of Russianisms. This is a measure of the extent to which Ukrainian was not a mere peasant dialect.

* 6.2 *

Conquest, Robert. *The Great Terror, a Reassessment*. London, Sydney, Auckland, and Johannesburg: Hutchinson, 1990. ISBN 0-09-174293-5.

In Chapter 10 of this revised edition of his 1968 publication, Conquest designates the era of the Great Terror as "a holocaust of the things of the spirit." By "things of the spirit," he refers to the cultural and scientific institutions, and their representatives, that flourished in pre-1917 Ukraine. The Stalinist purpose was to purge and then to destroy the Ukrainian intelligentsia, universities, and publishers. The Stalinist method consisted of widespread arrests, interrogations, and torture. Conquest also examines the horror of labor camps as ideological re-education centers for ideologically unsound peasants and intellectuals.

* 6.3 *

Conquest, Robert. *The Harvest of Sorrow; Soviet Collectivization and the Terror-Famine*. New York: Oxford University Press, 1986. LC 86-2437. ISBN 0-19-504054-6.

Conquest makes use of a wide range of evidence to substantiate claims, including testimonies from survivors and primary demographic data. He identifies two distinct Stalinist policies that, being merged, resulted in the decision to impose famine and ethnocide on the Ukraine in 1932-33. Dekulakization and collectivization from 1929-1932 was a policy in agricultural production designed to achieve socialism in the countryside in accordance with Marxist-Leninist doctrine; the second policy was put in place to reverse Stalin's previous leniency toward the renewal and revitalization of Ukrainian nationalism. The famine, preceded by the conspiracy trial in 1931, was imposed to destroy the independence and viability of the Ukrainian language, culture, intelligentsia, and autocephalous church.

Ukrainian nationalism has had a long history. The birth of the Ukrainian people, as distinct from the Russian people, can be dated from 1240 when Kiev, the capital of all the East Slavs, fell to the advancing Mongols. Those of the east Slavs who were pushed west became Ukrainians while those who lived North of Kiev became the great Russians.

Stalin succeeded in his designs to crush Ukrainian nationalism, but only temporarily. "With the extirpation of so many of its natural leaders and adherents at every level," national feeling was numbed during the remaining years of the 1930s. Yet ultimately the Stalinist drive failed, as events in 1990 and 1991 have unmistakably revealed.

* 6.4 *
Dolot, Miron. *Execution by Hunger; the Hidden Holocaust*. New York and London: W.W. Norton, 1985. LC 84-16568. ISBN 0-393-30416-7.

Execution by Hunger is his horrifying memoir of the Ukrainian famine. Dolot, a survivor of the famine, strongly suggests that it was artificially induced as a special Stalinist measure to eradicate Ukrainian national aspirations.

* 6.5 *
Kingston-Mann, Esther. *Lenin and the Problem of Marxist Peasant Revolution*. New York and Oxford: Oxford University Press, 1985. LC 82-14314. ISBN 0-19-503278-0.

Kingston-Mann offers a scholarly and theoretically sophisticated examination of the relationship between Leninist and Bolshevik thought and the role and status of the peasantry. The book is useful background for the collectivization strategy Stalin adopted at a later stage.

* 6.6 *
Koestler, Arthur. "Soviet Myth and Reality." In *The Yogi and the Commissar and Other Essays*. New York: Macmillan, 1945. LC 45-4437.

Koestler was in Kharkov during the winter of 1932-33, as he tells us in "Soviet Myth and Reality." He was appalled to discover the grotesque incongruity that existed between anyone's observation of mass starvation in the streets and what the local newspapers were reporting about life in the Ukraine. Koestler notes that Stalin's control of the press was total, in contrast to Hitler's, which was only partial. Hence the local newspapers were boasting of over-fulfillment of economic plans. They were filled with pictures of smiling, happy peasants who praised Comrade Stalin on his accomplishments. Koestler contrasts this pretty fantasy with the unspeakably ugly truth:

> Travelling through the countryside was like running the gauntlet: the stations were lined with begging peasants with swollen hands and feet, the women holding up to the carriage windows horrible infants with enormous wobbling heads, sticklike limbs, swollen, pointed bellies.

* 6.7 *
Kravchenko, Victor. *I Chose Freedom: The Personal and Political Life of a Soviet Official*. New York: Scribners, 1946. LC 46-2999 rev.

Kravchenko was a young communist official in the Ukraine at the time of the famine. In Chapter 10, "Harvest in Hell," he explains the decision to deploy trusted communist cadres in the Ukrainian countryside to safeguard the new harvest:

> Everything depended on the new harvest. Would the starving peasantry have the strength and the will to reap and to thresh in the midst of millionfold death. To make sure the crops would be harvested, to prevent the desperate collective farmers from eating the green shoots, to save the *kolkhoze*s from breaking down under mismanagement, to fight against enemies of collectivization, special Political Departments were set up in the villages, manned by trusted communists—militarymen, officials, professionals, N.K.V.D. men, students. An army of more than a hundred thousand stalwarts, selected by the Central Committee of the Party, was thus deployed through the collectivized areas, charged with the duty of safeguarding the new harvest.

He then describes the consequences of "safeguarding the harvest" as they affected the most vulnerable part of the Ukrainian population:

> The most terrifying sights were little children with skeleton limbs dangling from balloon-like abdomens. Starvation had wiped every trace of youth from their faces, turning them into tortured gargoyles; only in their eyes still lingered the reminder of childhood. Everywhere we found men and women lying prone, their faces and bellies bloated, their eyes utterly expressionless.

In 1943, Kravchenko was assigned to duty in the United States as a member of the Soviet Purchasing Commission. In 1944, he defected while on a trip to New York. He says that he began to lose faith in the Party when he was ordered to safeguard "the harvest in hell."

* 6.8 *
Legters, Lyman H. "The Soviet Gulag: Is It Genocidal?" In *Toward the Understanding and Prevention of Genocide*. Ed. by Israel W. Charny. Boulder, CO: Westview Press, 1984. LC 84-15241. ISBN 0-86531-843-3.

Legters argues that the Gulag meets the UN definition of genocide by reason of its disproportionate involvement of national minority groups, but also that the UN definition is deficient when applied to a society that uses class categories, such as *kulak*s, as a basis for differential, murderous treatment of citizens:

> If an allegedly socialist society, whose primary form of classification is that of class, either targets or invents a class with extermination in prospect, that program must count as genocide lest the term lose its continuing pertinence for the contemporary world in all of its variety.

* 6.9 *
Lewin, M. *Russian Peasants and Soviet Power, a Study of Collectivization*. New York: W.W. Norton & Co., 1975. ISBN 0-393-00752-9.

Based to a considerable extent on Soviet sources, Lewin's careful and highly detailed study examines the decision for collectivization and the process of its execution in 1928-1929. Despite the fact that he does not single out the Ukraine and though he ends the treatment before the onset of famine, this is an essential text for the prelude to the famine.

* 6.10 *
Mace, James E. *Communism and the Dilemmas of National Liberation: National Communism in Soviet Ukraine, 1918-1933*. Cambridge, MA: Harvard Ukrainian Research Institute, 1983. LC 83-4361. ISBN 0-916458-09-1.

Mace's book is the fundamental scholarly investigation of the Ukrainian problem in the Soviet Union. He lays the groundwork for an assessment of the genocidal implications of collectivization and the ensuing famine.

* 6.11 *
Mace, James E. "Famine and Nationalism in Soviet Ukraine." *Problems of Communism* 33:3 (May-June 1984): 37-50.

Mace argues that Stalin had singled out the Ukraine for especially harsh treatment because of the secessionist threat it posed for the Soviet Union. Mace reminds us that during the 1918 German occupation of the Ukraine:

> Even Mennonite German communities welcomed their co-nationals and provided volunteers to fight the Bolsheviks, despite old pacifist traditions....The Ukrainians not only formed their own nation-state but after their military defeat and incorporation into the USSR, became what Poland would become in the Soviet bloc after World War II: that part of the larger entity that was most conscious of its national distinctiveness, most assertive of its prerogatives, and least willing to follow Moscow's model in arranging its own affairs.

In 1923, Moscow permitted a certain limited Ukrainization, a policy designed to give the Soviet Ukrainian state a veneer of national legitimacy. Still later in the 1920s Mykola Skrypnyk became the Ukrainian party leader, he being a strong advocate of his Republic's national interests. With respect to the national language, "one of his first acts as education commissar was to chair an orthography conference." He brought experts from Europe, Russia, and the Ukraine together "to standardize Ukrainian spelling and purge the language of Russianisms."

Evidently the movement toward Ukrainian nationalist legitimacy went far beyond what Stalin had ever intended or authorized; it also went far beyond what he would tolerate. The "terror-famine" of 1932-33 was the result of Stalin's decision to reverse his previous policies favoring limited Ukrainization.

* 6.12 *
Mace, James E. "The Man-Made Famine of 1933 in the Soviet Ukraine: What Happened and Why?" In *Toward the Understanding and Prevention of Genocide*. Ed. by Israel W. Charny. Boulder, CO: Westview Press, 1984. LC 84-15241. ISBN 0-86531-843-3.

Mace depicts the Ukrainian famine in which five to seven million perished as a deliberate Stalinist assault on the Ukraine as a center of nationalism and as a potential threat to Moscow's centralizing authority. To document this charge, Mace describes the indictments made in a conspiracy trial held in the Ukraine in 1930:

So many members of the All-Ukraine Academy of Sciences were placed in the dock that whole institutions had to be closed. The Ukrainian Autocephalous Church was also tied into the alleged plot and forced to proclaim its own liquidation....[T]he defendants were accused not only of engaging in a terrorist plot to assassinate top Soviet leaders and lead a *kulak* uprising to establish an independent fascist state with capitalist support, but also with activities labelled "cultural wrecking," consisting of interpreting Ukrainian history as national history, advocating the adoption of non-Russian terms in the Ukrainian language, or establishing an orthography with spelling rules different from Russian.

* 6.13 *
Maksudov, S. "Losses Suffered by the Population of the USSR in 1918-1958." *Cahiers du Monde Russe et Sovietique* 18:3 (1977): 223-265.

The author's demographic study sheds light on the consequences of collectivization and famine for population levels in the Ukraine and elsewhere. Maksudov estimates the number of deaths caused by the famine to be 4.5 million. This estimate is low. Mace places the number of deaths at 7.5 million.

* 6.14 *
Medvedev, Roy A. *Let History Judge; the Origins and Consequences of Stalinism.* Trans. by Colleen Taylor. New York: Vintage Books, 1971, 1973. LC 75-5843. ISBN 0-394-71928-X.

Medvedev says that Stalin gave evidence of having, from the earliest days of his career as a revolutionary leader, many grave faults of character. According to Medvedev, among Stalin's negative traits were "boorishness and self-importance, pathological conceit and callousness, mistrust and stealth, an inability to take the criticism of his comrades, and a craving for influence and power." All or most of these traits came into play in Stalin's handling of the criticism of the Ukrainian party leader, Strypnyk. Thus at the Tenth Party Congress, held in March of 1921, Strypnyk roundly criticized Stalin's speech on the nationality problem, calling it "inane and abstract" and offering no solution to the problem whatsoever. Instead of engaging Strypnyk in serious argumentation, Stalin launched a smear campaign against his opponent; he virtually accused him of giving conscious support to class enemies on "the cultural front." Twelve years later, in 1933, Strypnyk committed suicide.

Medvedev writes as a reform-minded communist. In commenting on Stalin's performance as a dictator, he constantly juxtaposes Stalin's "mistakes" and Stalin's "crimes," with mistakes being construed as errors of calculation or reasoning. In the example given above, Medvedev does not say that Stalin's views on nationalities were wrong, but only that one particular speech on the subject was poorly expressed and inadequately argued. Stalin's crime in this instance was to vengefully crush Strypnyk, his critic, rather than to refute him in open debate. Thus Medvedev sees the criminality of the Stalinist period as arising not from the communist system, not from an absolute dictatorship, but from the deep character flaws of Stalin the man.

* 6.15 *
Mitrany, David. *Marx Against the Peasant; a Study in Social Dogmatism.* Chapel Hill, NC: University of North Carolina Press, 1951. LC 61-18128.

Mitrany examines the position of peasantries in traditional Marxian thought, setting Soviet policies, including collectivization, within that context. He suggests that the revolutionary wave of the twentieth century has been primarily agrarian and that Marxism has been both hostile to and exploitative of it.

* 6.16 *
Pipes, Richard. *The Formation of the Soviet Union; Communism and Nationalism, 1917-1923.* Cambridge, MA: Harvard University Press, 1954. LC 54-5183. Harvard University Press published a revised edition in 1964.

Although Pipes examines nationalisms in the Ukraine and Belorussia, the Moslem Borderlands, and the Caucasus, his elucidation of the nationalist movement in the Ukraine during the period of 1917 to 1923 is what concerns us here. From February 1917 to early 1920 when the Soviet conquest was complete, the Ukrainian national movement entered into, and withdrew from, a succession of tentative alliances with the Kerensky government, with the Ukrainian Bolsheviks, with Lenin's government, with the military rule of the White armies, and even, during 1918, with the German and Austro-Hungarian armies that occupied the country. Over these three years, as Pipes says, "no fewer than nine governments attempted to assert their authority over the land." None was successful in a struggle in which the main protagonists were the Ukrainian nationalists and the Russian communists.

The Ukrainian nationalists were strong in the villages but weak in the cities, like Kiev and Kharkov, which meant that they were dependent on the "politically disorganized, ineffective, and unreliable village." Moreover they were politically immature and inexperienced, not having had any practice in the art of administration. The fate of the Ukraine, therefore, was decided in the cities where the culture was predominantly Russian and where there was an active hostility to Ukrainian nationalism. Nonetheless the Ukrainian movement which emerged in the course of the Russian Revolution was, despite its ultimate failure, a political expression of genuine interests and loyalties. Its roots were manifold; a specific Ukrainian culture, resting on peculiarities of language and folklore; a historic tradition dating from the seventeenth-century Cossack communities; an identity of interests among the members of the large and powerful group of well-to-do peasants of the Dnieper region; and a numerically small but active group of nationally conscious intellectuals, with a century-old heritage of cultural nationalism behind them.

Briefly Annotated Works

* 6.17 *
Bellis, Paul. *Marxism and the U.S.S.R.; the Theory of Proletarian Dictatorship and the Marxist Analysis of Soviet Society*. Atlantic Highlands, NJ: Humanities Press, 1979. LC 79-11801. ISBN 0-391-01007-7.

Bellis provides background on Soviet Marxism and its theoretical and ideological justifications for economic measures and policies, including the policy of collectivization.

* 6.18 *
Bettelheim, Charles. *Class Struggles in the USSR; Second Period: 1923-1930*. New York: Monthly Review Press, 1978. LC 76-28976. ISBN 0-85527-9.

Applying Marxian categories critically to the Soviet experience of the later 1920s, Bettelheim offers a trenchant analysis of the prelude to, and processes of, collectivization which he views as a species of appropriation.

* 6.19 *
Carr, Edward Hallett, and R.W. Davies. *Foundation of a Planned Economy, 1926-1929 Vol. 1, Parts 1 and 2, of* A History of Soviet Russia. New York: Mac-Millan Co., 1969. LC 71-80789.

The continuation of the monumental history begun by Carr alone, this is *the* history of the period immediately preceding collectivization; it details the circumstances that led up to Stalin's decision to collectivize the rural economy.

* 6.20 *
Carrere d'Encausse, Helene. *Decline of an Empire; the Soviet Socialist Republics in Revolt*. New York: Harper Colophon, 1981. ISBN 0-06-090844-0.

An important examination of relations between Soviet central authority and the constituent republics in the post-Stalinist era, this book treats the Ukraine alongside the other republics. The focus is not only on discontent and other centrifugal factors but also on the implications of contemporary demographic trends.

* 6.21 *
Carynyk, Marco, Luyblubomyr Y. Luciuk, and Bohdan S. Kordan, eds. *The Foreign Office and the Famine: British Documents on Ukraine and the Great Famine*. Kingston, Ontario, and Bestal, NY: Limestone Press, 1988. ISBN 0-919642-29-2.

The British Foreign Office documents in this collection afford a useful external perspective on the character of the famine.

* 6.22 *
Chalk, Frank, and Kurt Jonassohn. *The History and Sociology of Genocide*. New Haven and London: Yale University Press, 1990. LC 89-27381. ISBN 0-300-04445-3.

By means of comparison and synthesis, Chalk and Jonassohn seek to refine the definition of genocide and our understanding of the phenomenon.

* 6.23 *
Davies, R.W. *The Industrialization of Soviet Russia*, Vol. 1, *The Socialist Offensive; the Collectivization of Soviet Agriculture, 1929-1930*, and Vol. 2, *The Soviet Collective Farm, 1929-1930*. Cambridge, MA: Harvard University Press, 1980. LC 79-15263, 79-15273. ISBN 0-674-81480-0 v1, 0-674-82600-0 v2.

The author's continuation of Carr's *History of Soviet Russia*, these books trace the drive for collectivization, in the Ukraine and elsewhere, in the framework of shifting policies and with the status of the collective farm that resulted.

* 6.24 *
Dmytryshyn, Basil. *Moscow and the Ukraine, 1917-1953*. New York: Bookman Associates, 1956. LC 57-1284.

Dmytryshyn offers a general history of relations between the Soviet center and the Ukrainian periphery. He includes the shifting policies designed to address the nationality problem.

* 6.25 *
Ellison, Herbert J. "The Decision to Collectivize Agriculture." In *Russian Economic Development*. Ed. by William L. Blackwell. New York: New Viewpoints, 1974. LC 73-11162. ISBN 0-531-06363-1.

Ellison examines the decision of the Fifteenth Party Congress of 1927 to collectivize agriculture, emphasizing the interplay of forces within the party that conditioned the decision.

* 6.26 *
Heller, Mikhail, and Aleksander M. Nekrich. *Utopia in Power; the History of the Soviet Union from 1917 to the Present*. New York: Summit Books, 1986. LC 86-5792. ISBN 0-671-46242-3.

In Chapter 5 of their history, two Soviet-trained scholars deal extensively with collectivization and the ensuing famine, including a summary of estimated population losses. They do not single out the Ukraine or address the question of genocide.

* 6.27 *
Millar, James R. "Mass Collectivization and the Contribution of Soviet Agriculture to the First Five Year Plan." *Slavic Review* 33 (1974): 750-766.

Millar offers an economist's examination of the performance of the agricultural sector during the collectivization that was a salient part of the First Five Year Plan.

* 6.28 *
Solomon, Susan Gross. *The Soviet Agrarian Debate; a Controversy in Social Science, 1923-1929*. Boulder, CO: Westview Press, 1977. LC 77-21555. ISBN 0-89158-339-4.

Soloman details the debate among Marxist and non-Marxist economists concerning appropriate policies to be pursued in the countryside to promote agricultural production. The debate led up to, and was terminated by, the decision to collectivize rapidly and, in the event, brutally.

* 6.29 *
Viola, Lynne. *The Best Sons of the Fatherland; Workers in the Vanguard of Soviet Collectivization*. New York and Oxford: Oxford University Press, 1987. LC 86-17987. ISBN 0-19-504262-X.

Viola examines the employment of workers as militant agents of collectivization in the period leading up to the resulting famine in the Ukraine and elsewhere.

CHAPTER 7

GENOCIDE AND MODERN WAR

by Eric Markusen

It is the governments of the world that either carry out or condone genocide, modern war, and other forms of mass killing. Although genocide and warfare are often regarded as distinctly different phenomena, there are in fact a number of important connections and commonalities between them, among which are several psychosocial facilitating factors. Markusen gives special attention to three of these: dehumanization of the victims, the systematic use of euphemistic language in describing the violence that is inflicted on victims, and bureaucratic organization of the overall effort. These three factors are of approximately equal importance in the waging of both wars and genocides. "The scale of man-made death is the central moral as well as material fact of our time." In the light of this fact, it is particularly unfortunate that the energy and resources devoted to understanding and preventing mass killing have been negligible.

INTRODUCTION

Four generalizations emerge from a review of the scholarly literature on genocide, warfare, and other forms of mass killing that governments have conducted or condoned: 1) the twentieth century is the most violent and murderous in history; 2) genocide and warfare are by no means the only significant forms of governmental mass killing; 3) although genocide and warfare are often regarded as distinctly different phenomena, there are in fact a number of important connections and commonalities between them; 4) the scholarly attention devoted to these issues is negligible relative to their significance.

THE VIOLENCE OF THE TWENTIETH CENTURY

The discussion of genocide and modern war must, at the outset, be placed in the overall context of collective violence and mass killing. As William James observed in his 1910 essay, "The Moral Equivalent of War," "History is a bath of blood."[1] Likewise, in his pioneering study, *Taking Lives: Genocide and State Power*, sociologist Irving Louis Horowitz asserts: "Mass murder and warfare among peoples is an ever-present truth of humankind."[2] And in an article on human cruelty throughout history, another sociologist, Randall Collins, concludes that "The prevailing reality of world history is violence."[3]

According to a number of scholars, the violence of past centuries pales before the violence and murderousness of the present one. In his pioneering work, *Twentieth Century Book of the Dead*, Scottish sociologist Gil Elliot estimated that more than 110,000,000 people were killed by their fellow human beings between 1900 and 1972. "To set such a figure against the scale of violence in previous times," he stated, "involves the difficulties of comparing like periods and allowing for population increase. However, every attempt to do so shows the twentieth century to be incomparably the more violent period."[4] Such findings led Elliot to conclude that "the scale of man-made death is the central moral as well as material fact of our time."[5]

Efforts to compare the magnitude of "man-made death" in the twentieth century with that in prior centuries confront serious methodological obstacles. Among them is the fact that the number of people—particularly civilians—killed in wars, massacres, and other forms of collective violence have seldom been recorded with precision. Also, many deaths caused by warfare result from delayed or indirect effects of the conflict, such as destruction of crops, economic collapse, and disruption of medical care. And, as acknowledged by Elliot in the preceding paragraph, evaluation of the assertion that the twentieth century is the most violent requires that population trends be taken into consideration. This, in turn, requires not only estimates of casualties of violence but also estimates of the population for the place and time in which the violence occurred. Thus, comparisons of the scale of twentieth century violence with violence in previous centuries are necessarily imprecise. The reader should bear this caveat in mind as the following studies are reviewed.

Sociologist Pitirim Sorokin was one of the first modern scholars to trace quantitative trends in collective violence over the centuries.[6] After a lengthy discussion of the numerous methodological difficulties entailed in such a study, he used historical materials to estimate the casualties, that is, both deaths and injuries, of European wars from the eleventh century through 1925. He also used population estimates to calculate the number of war casualties per 1,000 in the population for each century in each of the ten European nations under study. He found that the estimated war casualties per 1,000 population during the first twenty-five years of the twentieth century, fifty-four casualties, were considerably higher than in any other entire century. For example, the war casualties per 1,000 of the population for the twelfth, eighteenth, and nineteenth centuries were two, thirty-three, and fifteen respectively.[7] On the basis of such trends, Sorokin concluded that **"the curse or privilege to be the most devastating or most bloody war century belongs to the twentieth; in one quarter century it imposed upon the populations a 'blood tribute' far greater than that imposed by any of the whole centuries combined."** [emphasis in original][8] In a later book, in which he extended the scope of his comparative study farther back and forward in time, he confirmed his earlier results, finding the twentieth century to be "the bloodiest and most belligerent of all the twenty-five centuries under consideration."[9]

The recent work of William Eckhardt supports Sorokin's conclusions. Eckhardt has continued the effort to quantify the human costs of collective violence.[10] In a recent study, he compared the number of wars and the number of war-related deaths from 3000 B.C. through the first half of the twentieth century.[11] For estimates of the global population, the number of wars, and the number of people killed in wars during each century, he reviewed a wide range of sources, including world population histories and military histories. While acknowledging the limitations of such data, particularly in earlier centuries, Eckhardt argues that rough estimates are nonetheless possible. His findings for recent centuries are summarized in table 1.

It is evident that the number of people killed in wars, per each 1,000 of the population, has increased steadily over the past centuries, culminating in an unprecedented number during the first half of the twentieth.

Summarizing his research, Eckhardt states that "war-related deaths have been increasing over the past fifty centuries. When death estimates were divided by population estimates, this measure was significantly correlated with centuries, so that population growth alone could not explain the increase in war deaths over these fifty centuries. In other words, **war-related deaths were increasing significantly faster than population growth.**" [emphasis added][14] In an earlier study, Eckhardt eliminated the death tolls of World Wars I and II from the estimate of war-deaths during the twentieth century and still found that the rate of war-deaths has been increasing faster than the rate of population growth.[15]

These studies, and others,[16] focused their quantitative historical comparisons on warfare, but they do not consider genocide as another, ostensibly different, form of governmental violence. Unfortunately, the field of genocide studies has not yet produced its counterpart to Sorokin or Eckhardt. Indeed, as is discussed below, genocide scholars are still engaged in debate over the very definition of "genocide." Nonetheless, it is noteworthy that some researchers have suggested that, during the twentieth century at least, the death toll from warfare, as high as it has been, may be significantly lower than the death toll from genocide and genocidal killing. Political scientist R.J. Rummel, for example,

Table 1: War-Related Deaths per 1,000 of the Global Population, by Century, between 1000 and 1950 A.D.[12]

	\multicolumn{10}{c}{Century (A.D.)}
	11	12	13	14	15	16	17	18	19	20*
global pop. (millions)	320	360	360	350	425	500	545	720	1200	2500
# of wars**	47	39	67	62	92	123	113	115	164	120
war deaths per 1000 of the global population	.18	.36	1.14	1.43	2.07	3.23	11.21	9.72	16.19	44.37

* Eckhardt computed figures only for the first half of the twentieth century.

** He defined "war" as "any armed conflict, involving at least one government, and causing at least 1,000 civilian and military deaths per year, including war-related deaths from famine and disease."[13]

has estimated that, while more than thirty-five million people "have died in this century's international and domestic wars, revolutions, and violent conflicts," more than 100 million have been killed "apart from the pursuit of any continuing military action or campaign," mainly at the hands of "totalitarian or extreme authoritarian governments" in "massacres, genocides and mass executions of [their] own citizens."[17] Similarly, Helen Fein has estimated that genocides between 1945 and 1980 killed more than twice as many people as did wars during the same period.[18]

Thus, it appears that, despite serious methodological limitations, there is in fact evidence to support the assertion that our present century is very probably the most violent and lethal in history. When the nuclear weapons currently deployed by several nations are taken into consideration, there can be no doubt that this century has the potential to be unequivocally the most murderous. Nuclear weapons are so destructive that a nuclear war could, in a very real sense, "end history" by destroying civilization.

STRUCTURAL VIOLENCE

While the literature on collective violence focuses predominantly on genocide and warfare, it is important to note that there are other forms of governmental mass killing. One important, though insufficiently appreciated, means by which governmental policies result in large numbers of deaths is the creation or tolerance of harmful social conditions. According to William Eckhardt and Gernot Köhler, "While one group of scholars in the field restricts the term 'violence' to mean armed violence in wars and revolutions, others take a broader view and subsume both armed and structural components under the term 'violence.' Structural violence is the violence created by social, political, and economic institutions and structures which may lead to as much death and harm to persons as does armed violence."[19] Horowitz mentions a related concept, benign neglect, in his important essay, "Functional and Existential Visions of Genocide," where he alludes to "one shadowy area of genocide that permits the state to take lives by indirection, for example by virtue of benign neglect, or death due to demographic causes." Unfortunately, he does not develop this intriguing concept beyond commenting that the efforts a government makes to reduce deaths from malnutrition, disease, and other "natural" causes constitute a "central indication of how a society values life."[20]

As devastating as armed violence has been during the twentieth century, structural violence has resulted in many more deaths. In fact, on the basis of careful demographic analysis, Eckhardt and Köhler conclude that "about ninety-five percent of the total violence in the first three quarters of the twentieth century could be attributed to structural violence."[21] More recently, Eckhardt has estimated that, during the twentieth century, structural violence "has caused a total of some 1600 million deaths, or approximately nineteen million deaths per year."[22]

This form of governmental mass killing requires urgent attention, not only because of the sheer scale of the death tolls, but also because it is directly related to armed violence in at least two ways. First, structural violence, by causing suffering and death as the result of structured social inequality, creates conditions conducive to the outbreak of overt violence, particularly in the form of revolution and civil war. Second, by diverting societal resources from programs to meet human needs and by destroying portions of the economic infrastructure, armed violence tends to aggravate the economic and social conditions that cause structural violence.

THE PREPARATIONS FOR NUCLEAR OMNICIDE

No discussion of governmental mass killing in general, and genocide and modern war in particular, can be complete without reference to the preparations, by a diverse group of nations, for a war waged with nuclear weapons. For nearly fifty years, the United States and the Soviet Union held the world under the threat of nuclear holocaust by their policies of deterrence through the threat of mutually assured destruction, a threat that was backed up by the deployment of more than 50,000 nuclear weapons. As this book goes to press in 1992, the United States and the new leaders of the former Soviet Union, particularly Boris Yeltsin, the president of the Russian Republic, have entered a period of unprecedented cooperation and have made preliminary agreements to dramatically reduce the size of their nuclear stockpiles.[23] There is no doubt that the risk of a massive nuclear war between the U.S. and the former Soviet Union has significantly diminished.

However, complacency is by no means warranted. There are still tens of thousands of nuclear warheads in the arsenals of the United States, Russia, Ukraine, Belarus, and Kazhakstan. These weapons collectively possess the explosive equivalent of more than one million atomic bombs like those that destroyed the Japanese cities of Hiroshima and Nagasaki in the closing days of World War II. Ambitious plans to reduce these arsenals could founder if the current economic chaos in the former Soviet Union provokes the overthrow of the democratically elected governments and their replacement by militaristic hardliners. Yeltsin himself, in a meeting with President Bush early in 1992, warned that the Cold War could return if improvements in the lives of Russians and other former Soviets are not made soon. He was quoted by the *Wall Street Journal* as telling President Bush, "if reform in Russia goes under, that means there will be a cold war—the cold war will turn into a hot war—this is again going to be an arms race."[24]

In addition to the United States and the former Soviet Union, several other nations have acquired nuclear weapons capability, including China, France, Great Britain, India, Israel, Pakistan, and South Africa; and other nations, like Libya, Iraq, and North Korea, are striving to obtain nuclear weapons.[25] Indeed, one of the reasons the United States gave for the use of military force against Iraq in the Persian Gulf War of 1991 was the fear that the Iraqis would soon possess nuclear weapons.[26]

As yet, these nuclear arsenals pose only a potential threat to humankind; those nations that possess nuclear weapons do so in order to deter the use of nuclear and, in some cases, non-nuclear, weapons against them. However, in order for such deterrence to be credible, the nuclear-armed nations must be ready and willing to actually use the weapons. In recent years, a number of authorities, including retired military officers and former government officials, have warned that present nuclear deterrence arrangements are dangerously unstable. They cite the likely spread of nuclear weapons to additional nations in some of the most crisis-prone regions of the world and possibly to terrorist groups[27]; the growing numbers of so-called first strike weapons designed more for fighting nuclear wars than simply deterring them[28]; the existence of nuclear policy makers who argue that it is possible to fight, win, and survive a nuclear war[29]; and serious problems in arrangements for maintaining control over nuclear weapons in the event that deterrence fails and nuclear war breaks out.[30]

If even a fraction of the existing nuclear arsenals were used in combat, it is likely that more people would die than in any genocide or war in history. One study by the United States Congressional Office of Technology Assessment estimated that a "large" Soviet attack on the United States could cause as many as 160,000,000 deaths.[31] A study by the World Health Organization calculated that a war fought with about one-half of the existing Soviet and American nuclear weapons would promptly kill as many as 1,100,000,000 and that another billion would die within the first year as a result of radiation exposure, untreated burns and other injuries, the lack of food and water, and other deprivations.[32] This statement, made in the mid-1980s, is still valid in 1992.

In addition to directly-caused deaths and injuries, nuclear war would cause great damage to the environment. For example, the smoke and soot from fires started by nuclear detonations are likely to drift into the higher levels of the earth's atmosphere and reduce the amount of sunlight and heat that reaches the surface. This would create what scientists have called a "nuclear winter" and drastically reduce the survival chances for anyone who survived the initial effects of the war.[33] Reputable scientists have even warned that the possibility of human extinction cannot be ruled out as a consequence of nuclear war and nuclear winter.[34]

Some scholars have questioned the appropriateness of the term "war" when used in connection with nuclear weapons, given their unprecedented destructiveness. As an alternative to the misleading concept of "nuclear war," philosopher John Somerville has proposed the term "nuclear omnicide," to convey the probability that a war fought with nuclear weapons would constitute a categorically new dimension of mass killing.[35] Somerville coined omnicide from the Latin words *omni* meaning "all" and *cide* meaning "to kill." In recognition of the uniquely destructive nature of nuclear weapons, and the fact that they are deeply embedded in the national security arrangements of several nations, Lifton and Markusen have suggested the concept of a nuclear "genocidal system." "A genocidal system," they write, "is not a matter of a particular weapons structure or strategic concept so much as an overall constellation of men, weapons, and war-fighting plans which, if implemented, could end human civilization in minutes and the greater part of human life on the planet within hours...."[36]

GENOCIDE AND MODERN WAR AS FORMS OF GOVERNMENTAL MASS KILLING

Some scholars regard genocide and war as quite different phenomena. For example, sociologist Horowitz asserts that "it is operationally imperative to distinguish warfare from genocide," and political scientist R.J. Rummel has stated that "There are no common conditions or causes of domestic and foreign conflict behavior."[37] Similarly, in their discussion of definitions of genocide, Frank Chalk and Kurt Jonassohn emphasize that it is "essential...to exclude from our analysis the casualties of war, whether military or civilian."[38] In her recent critique of the available literature on this question, Helen Fein asserts that "The question of whether killings of civilians in war are war crimes, consequences of acts of war admissable under the war convention, or acts of genocide has been clouded by the fact that genocide-labelling of wars today is often a rhetorical strategem for political delegitimation of specific wars which the labeller opposes."[39] However, it is important to note that genocide and modern war are not as distinct and separate as some have asserted them to be; other scholars have discerned important connections between them.[40]

GENOCIDE

According to political scientist Roger Smith, the twentieth century "is an age of genocide in which sixty million men, women, and children, coming from many different races, religions, ethnic groups, nationalities, and social classes, and living in many different countries, on most of the continents of the earth, have had their lives taken because the state thought it desirable."[41] A partial listing of twentieth century genocides includes the killing of more than 1,000,000 Armenians by the Turks in 1915; the Holocaust in which 6,000,000 Jews and 4,000,000 members of other victim groups were killed by the Nazis between 1939 and 1945; the slaughter of approximately 3,000,000 Ibo tribesmen by other Nigerians between 1967 and 1970; the massacre of more than 1,000,000 Bengalis by the the army of East Pakistan in 1971; and the killing of as many as 2,000,000 Cambodians by the Khmer Rouge between 1975 and 1979.[42] An analysis of genocides and closely-related forms of mass killing since 1945 found forty-four "episodes" of genocidal violence that, collectively, took the lives of "between seven and sixteen million people, at least as many who died in all international and civil wars in the period."[43]

Recent scholarship has indicated that death tolls from past cases of genocidal killing may be far greater than has been thought. In a meticulous analysis of just one case—the Soviet Union between 1917 and 1987—R.J. Rummel estimates that during that seventy year period, "Probably 61,911,000 people, 54,769,000 of them citizens, have been murdered by the Communist party, the government of the Soviet Union."[44]

The basic act of defining genocide is problematic and controversial. Despite a plethora of recent scholarship on definitional issues, a widely accepted definition of genocide continues to elude scholars.[45] The definitional dilemma has been complicated by the misapplication of the term. As Jack Nusan Porter notes, the label of "genocide" has been applied, inappropriately, to the following practices: racial integration, methadone maintenance programs, certain features of the medical treatment of Irish Catholics, and the closing of synagogues in the Soviet Union.[46]

Raphael Lemkin coined the term "genocide" in his 1944 book, *Axis Rule in Occupied Europe*, which contained one of the first detailed accounts of Nazi persecution of Jews and other groups. Lemkin derived the term from the Greek word *genos*, which means "race" or "tribe," and the Latin word *cide*, meaning "to kill." Thus, he defined genocide as "the destruction of a nation or ethnic group."[47] In addition to direct mass killing, such "destruction" could assume other forms, including destruction of cultural heritage and prevention of procreation. Lemkin's definition served as the basis for the first formal, legal definition of genocide, which was codified in 1948 in the United Nations Convention on the Prevention and Punishment of the Crime of Genocide. According to the Convention, genocide refers to "acts committed with intent to destroy, in whole or in part, a national, ethnical, racial, or religious group, as such."[48] The UN definition, while generally acknowledged as an important milestone in international jurisprudence, emerged from a contentious process of political compromise and deliberately excluded social and political groups, for example, the millions of Soviet civilians identified as "class enemies" and murdered by the Stalin government between 1920 and 1939. Many scholars of genocide decry this omission.[49]

In comparison with the legal definition of genocide embodied in the Genocide Convention, social science and other scholarly definitions encompass a wider array of targeted groups, destructive actions, and actual cases. For example, Horowitz defines genocide as "a special form of murder: state-sanctioned liquidation against a collective group, without regard to whether an individual has committed any specific and punishable transgression."[50] Another definition, based on in-depth study of more than thirty cases of genocide, is offered by Chalk and Jonassohn: "Genocide is a form of one-sided mass killing in which a state or other authority intends to destroy a group, as that group and membership in it are defined by the perpetrator."[51] Genocide scholar Israel Charny has proposed a "humanistic" definition that greatly expands the range of targeted groups: "the wanton murder of human beings on the basis of any identity whatsoever that they share—**national, ethnic, racial, religious, political, geographical, ideological.**" [emphasis in original][52] More recently, Charny has proposed an even broader, "generic," definition of genocide: "mass killing of substantial numbers of human beings, when not in the course of military action against the military forces of an avowed enemy, under conditions of the essential defenselessness and helplessness of the victims."[53]

From the welter of competing definitions of genocide, we can discern several common features. First, genocide is a crime of governments, either directly, as when a government officially undertakes a campaign of extermination against a targeted group, or indirectly, when a government permits a subnational group to slaughter members of another subnational group. Put in different terms, genocide is a national security policy.[54] Second, the victims are selected for death on the basis of group membership, rather than any transgressions against the killers. Third, while direct killing is the most characteristic form of destruction, for example, mass shooting or burning alive, many deaths result from starvation and disease. Finally, the victims are far less powerful than the perpetrators.

MODERN (TOTAL) WAR

Just as the twentieth century has been described as "an age of genocide," so has it been labeled "the century of total war."[55] William Eckhardt has estimated the death tolls of 471 wars that have occurred since 1700 and arrived at a total of 101,550,000 fatalities.[56] Ruth Leger Sivard, on the basis of Eckhardt's data, notes that "With twelve years to go, this modern century in which we live will account for over ninety percent of the deaths in wars since 1700."[57] In just one year, 1987, Eckhardt counted twenty-two wars underway—more than in any other year in recorded history. In that single year of fighting, an estimated 244,000 people were killed; the overall death toll of the twenty-two wars since their inceptions is more than 2,200,000. Civilians accounted for eighty-four percent of the deaths.[58]

As is the case with the concept of "genocide," there is no single, widely-accepted definition of "war." Indeed, it is not uncommon to find books on the subject of war in which the term itself is left undefined. Among those who do formally define war, there is much variance among definitions. A common starting point for contemporary discussions of war is the 1832 book, *On War*, by the Prussian general and military theoretician, Karl von Clausewitz. Clausewitz saw war as "an act of violence intended to compel our opponent to fulfill our will" and as "an act of violence pushed to its utmost bounds." He also referred to war as a "mere continuation of politics (or policy) by other means."[59] Clausewitz identifies two key dimensions of war. The first is violence since war is violence by definition. The second is more implicit, that is, at least one of the combatants is a government whose foreign or domestic policy goals are served by violence. These two dimensions of war are also featured in contemporary definitions. For example, William Eckhardt, as noted in table 1 above, defines war as "any armed conflict which includes one or more governments, and causes deaths of 1,000 or more people per year."[60] Ronald Glossop similarly states that "War is large-scale violent conflict between organized groups that are or that aim to establish governments."[61] And Arthur Westing defines war as "armed conflict between nations or between groups within a nation."[62]

Traditionally, there have been two principle types of war: international war, in which two or more nations engage directly in armed conflict, and civil war, in which a government fights against a subnational group or two or more subnational groups fight against each other. In the post-World War II era, a third type of war—proxy war—has become increasingly common. In this type of war, nations, particularly the United States and the Soviet Union, avoid direct conflict with each other but instead fight each other indirectly through each other's allies, as was the case with the United States in Vietnam. Thomas M. Franck has described proxy wars as "wars of agitation, infiltration, and subversion carried on by proxy through national liberation movements."[63]

Each of these types of war can develop either or both of the two features associated with the concept of total war. The first feature of total war—extensive mobilization of the warring nations—is accomplished in several ways, including the conscription of citizens to serve in mass armies, the use of propaganda to maintain morale and support for the war, and the exploitation of large sectors of the national economy for the war effort. The second feature of total war—an extremely high level of death and destruction in general and deliberate targeting of civilians in particular—reflects both advances in weapons technology and a steady expansion in the types of targets considered legitimate by military and political leaders.[64]

The actual term "total war" was invented in 1918 and inspired by the Napoleonic wars of the late 1700s and the early months of World War I, both of which featured mass armies raised by conscription and the application of science to develop highly destructive weapons.[65] No recent war, even World Wars I and II, has been completely "total" in the sense that all of the available resources of the combatant nations have been devoted to the conflict or that the destruction of the enemy has been complete. Rather, as Marjorie Farrar has suggested, "totality can be interpreted as one extreme in a spectrum of possibilities. Distinction is then made among degrees of totality...war is total in the degree to which it approaches the extreme of totality."[66] Thus, in practice, the term "total war" is applied to conflicts in which extensive societal involvement and/or indiscriminate destruction are evident.

While many wars in history have been characterized by one or both dimensions of total war, a number of features of modern war have created an especially strong tendency in the direction of totality. In his study of historical and modern war, Quincy Wright emphasized the following trends in modern war: the increased size of military force, primarily as the result of conscription; the mechanization of society in general and warfare in particular, with the latter resulting in escalating destructiveness of weapons; and the breakdown of the distinction between soldiers and civilians.[67]

The lethality of weapons has increased tremendously during the modern era. Whereas in World War I, about three people were killed by each ton of bombs dropped on London by German airplanes, during World War II, the American use of fire bombs against Japan raised the deaths per ton to about fifty. By the end of World War II, the invention of the atomic bomb raised the rate far higher, up to "about 10,000 persons killed per ton of normal bomb load for the B-29 that made the raid."[68] According to sociologist Hornell Hart, "The five centuries from 1346 to 1875 saw several times as much increase in explosive power as had been achieved in the previous million years. The seventy years from 1875 to March 1945 saw several times as much increase in explosive power as the previous five centuries."[69]

Also, the targeting of population centers with very destructive weapons, for example the Nazi bombardment of London and Belgium with V-1 buzz bombs and V-2 ballistic missiles, and the British and American incendiary bombing campaigns against German and Japanese cities during World War II, greatly heightened the risk to civilians. In World War I, civilians accounted for only one in twenty deaths; by World War II, in contrast, approximately two-thirds of the deaths were of civilians.[70] This trend has continued and increased since 1945. According to Sivard, "By the 1970s, civilians accounted for seventy-three percent of war deaths; thus far in the 1980s, civilians have accounted for eighty-five percent of war deaths."[71]

The destructive power of modern weapons, combined with the fact that many people are crowded into cities, can mean that even when efforts are made to avoid direct attacks against civilians, many noncombatants may nonetheless be killed or injured. A case in point is the recent Persian Gulf War of 1991, in which the United States and about thirty other nations fought against Iraq in order to end the Iraqi occupation of Kuwait and destroy the Iraqi projects to develop and deploy nuclear, chemical, and biological weapons of mass destruction. Although the U.S. and allied forces asserted a clear policy of targeting only military targets, many civilians were killed when bombs went off course and when nearby buildings, including homes, were smashed and burned. The U.S. Air Force, as reported in the *New York Times*, estimated that seventy percent of bombs dropped missed their targets.[72]

No official U.S. estimate of the number of civilians killed has been announced to date, but one unofficial estimate put the toll at between 5,000 and 16,000 Iraqi civilians killed during the war and an additional 4,000 to 6,000 who died in the months immediately following the war as the result of untreated wounds and the lack of medical attention.[73] So great was the destruction of the capital city, Baghdad, and other cities, that a United Nations report issued in March 1991 described the damage as "near apocalyptic" and stated that Iraq had been moved back to a "pre-industrial age."[74] Further evidence of the toll on civilians was gathered in May 1991 by a medical team from Harvard University that visited several Iraqi cities. They estimated that the destruction of hospital facilities and the general degradation of public services were likely to cause the deaths of tens of thousands of Iraqi infants in the coming months.[75]

CONNECTIONS AND COMMONALITIES BETWEEN GENOCIDE AND MODERN WAR

Although, as noted above, there has been a tendency to differentiate between genocide and warfare as distinct forms of collective violence, there are in fact a number of connections between them. First, modern war often creates political, organizational, and psychological conditions that are highly conducive to the outbreak of genocide. Second, the techniques of modern war—specifically, the targeting of noncombatants with very destructive weapons—tend to blur the line between genocide and war. Third, there is evidence that similar psychological and social processes operate in both forms of mass killing. Each of these connections is briefly examined below.

MODERN WAR EXPEDITES GENOCIDE

Leo Kuper has noted that "international warfare, whether between 'tribal' groups or city states, or other sovereign states and nations, has been a perennial source of genocide."[76] Referring to the Armenian genocide of 1915 and the Nazi Holocaust against the Jews, Vahakn Dadrian observes that "It is no accident that the two principal instances of genocide of this century coincided with the episodes of two global wars."[77] Civil wars also create the potential for genocide, as was the case with "auto-genocide" in Cambodia between 1975 and 1978.[78]

Several dimensions of modern war expedite genocide. First, by posing a dire threat to the society, war serves, according to Dadrian, as "a cataclysmic agent of disequilibrium entailing manifold crises...."[79] The threat of disruption not only is blamed on the external enemy but also can be blamed on members of a minority group within the society. The minority group may be accused of collaborating with the enemy or used as a scapegoat for the frustrated aggression of the dominant group, especially when the war begins to go badly. Second, during modern war, the government, whether democratic or totalitarian, becomes more centralized and powerful, using censorship and propaganda to increase support for its belligerent policies.[80] This can diminish popular resistance to intensified ruthlessness against enemies, both external and internal. Third, the government at war can utilize the military forces—men who have been trained to kill in the service of their nation—for the perpetration of genocide. This occurred in both the Armenian genocide[81] and the Holocaust.[82] Fourth, just as conditions of war significantly increase the power of the genocidal government, they also tend to increase the vulnerability of the targeted victim groups, which tend to be, as Dadrian notes, "isolated, fragmented, and nearly totally emasculated through the control of channels of communication, wartime secrecy, the various sections of the wartime apparatus, police, and secret services, and the constant invocation of national security."[83] Finally, modern war creates a climate of moral and psychological numbing or desensitization that increases popular tolerance of cruelty, whether directed against an external or internal enemy.[84]

BLURRING OF THE LINE BETWEEN WAR AND GENOCIDE

Genocide and warfare have been differentiated on a number of grounds. Morally, genocide is universally regarded as unequivocally evil, while warfare is widely regarded as a necessary and valid "continuation of politics," to paraphrase Clausewitz. Also, the two forms of mass killing may be distinguished with respect to the relation between ends and means. While both use similar means—mass killing—the end or goal is quite different. Genociders aim to kill for the sake of killing; in war, killing is done in order to end the war. Had the Nazis not lost World War II, for example, they would have continued their genocide against the Jews. In contrast, the Allies immediately discontinued the practice of firebombing cities when the enemy surrendered. Finally, there is an apparent difference in the nature of the victims. The victims of genocide are usually defenseless members of a minority group, while the victims of war are generally citizens of a society engaged in armed conflict.

Nonetheless, on close examination these differences become narrower or blurred. With respect to the moral dimension, one of the traditional criteria for a "just war" has been the careful discrimination between soldiers and civilians.[85] The deliberate targeting of civilians violates this important criterion. As Lewis Mumford has observed, "in principle, the extermination camps where the Nazis incinerated over six million helpless Jews were no different from the urban crematoriums our air force improvised in its attacks by napalm bombs on Tokyo...our aims were different, but our methods were those of mankind's worst enemy."[86] Leo Kuper, in a discussion of "the changing nature of warfare," notes how, in the Second World War, "Germany employed genocide in its war for domination." He goes on to say, however, "but I think the term [genocide] must also be applied to the atomic bombing of the Japanese cities of Hiroshima and Nagasaki by the U.S.A. and to the pattern bombing by the Allies of such cities as Hamburg and Dresden."[87] It should be noted that some scholars strongly disagree with such a comparison.[88]

Also, in certain cases of war and genocide, the distinction between ends and means also breaks down. Some genocide scholars suggest that not all genocides aim to destroy the entire victim group as the primary goal, but that killing part of the group may be used to deter the survivors from resisting oppression by the perpetrators; in other words, killing is the means to an end other than total annihilation. Dadrian, for example, discusses retributive genocide, in which a portion of a minority group is killed as a warning to the remainder of the consequence of non-compliance with dominant group policies, and utilitarian genocide, in which part of a group is decimated in order to confiscate their property or to exploit the labor of the demoralized survivors.[89] Modern total war, by slaughtering enemy civilians, also seeks to exploit the survivors, in this case by inducing them to withdraw their support from their government's war effort and thereby hasten surrender.

Finally, the distinction based on the nature of the victims is often blurred. In many cases of total war, the victims, despite being citizens of an armed sovereign state, are every bit as defenseless and helpless as the victims of genocide. The majority of victims of modern war are civilians—including the elderly, women, and children—who have scant chance of escaping bombs dropped from airplanes or high explosives or chemical weapons shot from heavy artillery.

Psychosocial Facilitating Factors Common to Both Genocide and Modern War

A further connection between genocide and modern war is that similar psychological and social processes facilitate both. These psychosocial facilitating factors operate at all levels of the killing projects to neutralize potential moral qualms, minimize empathy with the victims, and negate doubts that might otherwise interfere with smooth, guilt-free, even enthusiastic, performance of tasks. They help account for the fact, observed by a number of scholars of collective violence, that the vast majority of perpetrators and implementors of mass killing are not sadistic or psychopathic, but are, instead, quite "normal" psychologically.[90]

There are several psychosocial factors common to both genocide and modern war. The *healing-killing paradox*, a concept developed by Robert Jay Lifton in his study of Nazi doctors, refers to the justification of mass killing as being in the service of a noble, and even heroic, cause. Thus, at the Auschwitz death camp, Lifton found that "killing was done in the name of healing...For the SS doctor, involvement with the killing process became equated with healing."[91] Israel Charny has observed a similar process in other genocides: "Incredible as it may seem," he writes, "virtually every genocide is defined by its doers as being on behalf of the larger purpose of bettering human life."[92] Historian Ronald Schaffer has observed a comparable process in the justification of strategic bombing of cities during World War II: the advocates of city bombing argued that such attacks would demoralize the civilian population and thus hasten the end of the war, thereby sparing high casualties on the battlefields.[93] It should be emphasized in this context that both genocide and modern war are national security policies authorized by the highest government officials. Many, if not most, of those who follow the orders to engage in mass killing are likely to regard themselves, therefore, as dedicated patriots serving their nation by assuming a grim but necessary responsibility.

Dehumanization of the victims of the violence is an extremely important contributing factor in mass killing projects. Kuper defines dehumanization as "the relegation of the victims to the level of animals or of objects."[94] Dehumanization dramatically reduces inhibitions against killing by destroying moral concerns and empathy. It can take at least two forms—ideological and technological—both of which operate in genocide and modern war.[95]

Ideological dehumanization relies on government propaganda and indoctrination to portray the targets of violence as subhuman and evil, thereby deserving of any degree of ruthlessness. For example, Lifton points out that in the Holocaust, the Jewish victims were frequently characterized as "bacteria" and "vermin."[96] And Dower notes that in World War II, the Americans and Japanese engaged in what could be called reciprocal dehumanization. Thus, "the Japanese were perceived as animals, reptiles, or insects."[97] The Japanese, in turn, stereotyped their American enemies as "unclean and wrong-hearted men, as beasts, and ultimately—in the most prevalent Japanese idiom of all—as demons."[98]

Technological dehumanization erases the individual identity of the victims by imposing physical distance between them and the killers. Thus, in the Holocaust, the psychological stress on the killers was greatly reduced when the Nazis shifted from the earlier technique of face-to-face mass shooting of victims to the far more impersonal technique of huge gas chambers.[99] Likewise, Lee Kennett has observed of World War II that "The escalation of the air war was made easier by the fact that those who directed the bombing offensives and those who carried them out remained curiously insulated and detached from the consequences of their work. Photographs taken at thirty thousand feet gave no clue to the human effects of a raid, nor did other sources."[100]

Euphemistic language plays an important role in enabling ordinary people to be involved in killing projects.[101] As Kelman has noted, "Moral inhibitions are less easily subdued if the functionaries, in their own thinking and in their communication with each other, have to face the fact that they are engaged in organized murder...The difficulty is handled by the well-known bureaucratic inventiveness in the use of language."[102] In the Holocaust, for example, deportation to the death camps was code-named "evacuation to the East," and the actual killing was termed "special action" and "special treatment."[103] In World War II, likewise, the deliberate fire bombing of cities crowded with civilians was known as "strategic bombing," and the specific attacks on neighborhoods filled with German factory workers, which killed thousands and women and children, was intended, in the official jargon, to "de-house" those workers.[104] The Persian Gulf War of 1991 was no exception to the tendency to "sanitize" the killing by the use of euphemisms. Hence, bombing raids were called "sorties"; inadvertent killing of civilians was "collateral damage"; bombs of various kinds were referred to as "ordnance"; and the accidental killing of American and British soldiers by their compatriots was termed "death by friendly fire."[105]

The *bureaucratic organization* of modern genocides and wars plays an extremely important role in facilitating the participation of psychologically normal individuals in projects designed to mass murder innocent men, women, and children. As Richard Rubenstein has observed: "Usually the progress in death-dealing capacity in the twentieth century has been described in terms of technological advances in weaponry. Too little attention has been given to the advances in social organization that allowed for the effective use of the new weapons. In order to understand how the moral barrier was crossed that made massacre in the millions possible, it is necessary to consider the importance of bureaucracy in modern political organization."[106]

Four features of bureaucratic organizations serve to promote the overall efficiency of modern genocide and warfare as well as to enable individual contributors to carry out their tasks with a minimum of questioning or doubt. These four features are: hierarchical authority, division of labor, amoral rationality, and organizational loyalty.

Hierarchical authority refers to the formal, top-down decision-making arrangements of bureaucracies which enable people at lower levels to have a reduced sense of personal responsibility for either the policy they are helping to implement or its final outcome. They are, after all, only "following orders" that have descended through all the levels of the organization above their own.[107]

Division of labor involves the breaking down of complex tasks into compartmentalized sub-tasks. As sociologist Fred Katz observes, "Bureaucracies are social machineries for accomplishing complex objectives in relatively orderly fashion...The individual bureaucrat typically focuses on a particular task, without considering the wide implications, including broader moral issues."[108]

Amoral rationality involves preoccupation with the best means of attaining a particular goal, or completing a given task, while tending to ignore moral or human implications of the goal or task. Bureaucracies deliberately strive to render moral and human considerations irrelevant with respect to the task at hand.[109] As sociologist Helen Fein suggests, "Bureaucracy is not itself a cause of the choice of destructive ends, but it facilitates their accomplishment by routinizing the obedience of many agents, each trained to perform his role without questioning the ends of action."[110]

Finally, organizational loyalty refers to the tendency for members of bureaucratic organizations to become preoccupied with maintaining or expanding their particular organization as an end in itself. Such concerns may obscure moral and human implications of given policies. Markusen has examined the role of organizational loyalty in both the Holocaust and the British and American strategic bombing campaigns in World War II, as well as in the preparations for nuclear war.[111]

In closing this section, it should be emphasized that all of the psychological and organizational forces discussed above can mutually reinforce each other to create a powerful momentum toward genocidal killing.[112]

Conclusions

Gil Elliot, one of the pioneers in the study of collective violence, was quoted above as saying that "the scale of man-made death is the central moral as well as material fact of our time." Unfortunately, the energy and resources devoted to understanding and preventing mass killing have been negligible. As Israel Charny has written, "At this point in its evolution, mankind is deeply limited in its readiness to experience and take action in response to genocidal disasters. Most events of genocide are marked by massive indifference, silence, and inactivity."[113] Our understanding of this crucial realm of human behavior, despite the efforts of a relative handful of dedicated scholars and activists, remains rudimentary and dangerously inadequate.[114]

Finally, in view of the fact that the preparations for nuclear omnicide could well lead to the worst catastrophe of human history, it is extremely important to note that psychological and social factors similar to those operating in more "ordinary" forms of mass killing, like genocide and modern war, have been observed in the individuals and organizations responsible for inventing, building, operating, and planning for the use of nuclear weapons.[115] Thus, some of the same processes that have accounted for mass killing in the past, and that have made the present century the most lethal ever, are also at work in creating the potential end of history.

NOTES

1. William James, "The Moral Equivalent of War," in *War and Morality*, ed. by Richard A. Wasserstrom (Belmont, CA: Wadsworth, 1970), 4. James' essay was originally published in 1910.

2. Irving Louis Horowitz, *Taking Lives: Genocide and State Power*, 3d ed. (New Brunswick, NJ: Transaction Books, 1982), 2.

3. Randall Collins, "Three Faces of Cruelty: Towards a Comparative Sociology of Evil," *Theory and Society* 1 (1974): 32.

4. Gil Elliot, *Twentieth Century Book of the Dead* (New York: Charles Scribner's Sons, 1972), 1.

5. Elliot, 6.

6. Pitirim Sorokin, *Social and Cultural Dynamics, V. III: Fluctuations of Social Relationships, War, and Revolution* (New York: The Bedminister Press, 1962), 37. Originally published in 1937.

7. Sorokin's data are summarized in Quincy Wright, *A Study of War V.I.* (Chicago: University of Chicago Press, 1942), 656.

8. Sorokin, 342.

9. Pitirim Sorokin, *The Crisis of Our Age* (New York: E.P. Dutton, 1954), 203.

10. William Eckhardt and Gernot Köhler, "Structural and Armed Violence in the 20th Century: Magnitudes and Trends," *International Interactions* 6, no. 4 (1980): 347-375 and William Eckhardt, "Civilian Deaths in Wartime," *Bulletin of Peace Proposals* 20, no. 1 (1989): 89-98.

11. William Eckhardt, "War-Related Deaths Since 3000 BC," a paper presented to the 1991 annual meeting of the International Society for the Comparative Study of Civilizations, Santo Domingo, the Dominican Republic.

12. Table derived from data in Eckhardt, "War-Related Deaths," 7.

13. Eckhardt, "War-Related Deaths," 1.

14. Eckhardt, "War-Related Deaths," 2.

15. Eckhardt, "Civilian Deaths," 90.

16. See, for example, Roy L. Prosterman, *Surviving to 3000: An Introduction to the Study of Lethal Conflict* (Belmont, CA: Duxbury Press, 1972).

17. R.J. Rummel, "War Isn't This Century's Biggest Killer," *Wall Street Journal* (7 July 1986): Op-Ed page.

18. Helen Fein, "Genocide: A Sociological Perspective," *Current Sociology* 38, no.1 (1990): 83.

19. Eckhardt and Köhler, 348.

20. Horowitz, 34.

21. Eckhardt and Köhler, 365.

22. Eckhardt, "Civilian Deaths," 97; see also R.J. Johnston, et al., "The Geography of Violence and Premature Death: A World-Systems Approach," in *The Quest for Peace*, ed. by Raimo Varyrnen, et al. (London: Sage Publications, 1987), 241-259.

23. Russell Watson, "A Farewell to Arms?" *Newsweek* (10 February 1992): 32-33.

24. Quoted in Michael McQueen, "Bush and Yeltsin, at Camp David, Forge Closer Ties but Reach No Specific Pacts," *Wall Street Journal* (3 February 1992): A-12.

25. Leonard S. Spector, *The Undeclared Bomb: The Spread of Nuclear Weapons, 1987-88* (Cambridge, MA: Ballinger Publishing Co, 1988).

26. William Safire, "Object: Survival," *The New York Times* (11 November 1990): Op-Ed page.

27. Tom Harkin, with C.E. Thomas, *Five Minutes to Midnight: Why the Nuclear Threat Is Growing Faster Than Ever* (New York: Carol Publishing Group, 1990); see also Spector.

28. Robert Aldridge, *First Strike: The Pentagon's Strategy for Nuclear War* (Boston: South End Press, 1983); see also Michio Kaku and Daniel Axelrod, *To Win a Nuclear War: The Pentagon's Secret War Plans* (Boston: South End Press, 1987).

29. See, as examples: Colin Gray and Keith Payne, "Victory Is Possible," *Foreign Policy* 39 (1980): 14-27; Morton Halperin, *The Nuclear Fallacy: Dispelling the Myth of Nuclear Strategy* (Cambridge, MA: Ballinger Publishing Co., 1987); Desmond Ball and Robert Toth, "Revising the SIOP: Taking War-Fighting to Dangerous Extremes," *International Security* 14, no.4 (1990): 65-92.

30. Daniel Ford, *The Button: The Pentagon's Command and Control System* (New York: Simon & Schuster, 1985); Ashton Carter, John D. Steinbrunner, and Charles Zraket, eds., *Managing Nuclear Operations* (Washington, DC: Brookings, 1986).

31. U.S. Office of Technology Assessment, *The Effects of Nuclear War* (Washington, DC: U.S. Government Printing Office, 1979).

32. World Health Organization, *Effects of Nuclear War on Health and Health Services* (Geneva: World Health Organization, 1984).

33. Carl Sagan and Richard Turco, *A Path Where No Man Thought: Nuclear Winter and the End of the Arms Race* (New York: Random House, 1990).

34. Paul Ehrlich, et al., "Long-Term Biological Consequences of Nuclear War," *Science* 222 (1983): 1,293-1,330.

35. John Somerville, "Nuclear 'War' Is Omnicide," in *Nuclear War: Philosophical Perspectives*, ed. by Michael Allen Fox and Leo Groarke (New York: Peter Lang Publishing Company, 1985), 4.

36. Robert Jay Lifton and Eric Markusen, *The Genocidal Mentality: Nazi Holocaust and Nuclear Threat* (New York: Basic Books, 1990), 3.

37. Horowitz, 32; Rummel quoted in Horowitz, 32.

38. Frank Chalk and Kurt Jonassohn, *The History and Sociology of Genocide: Analyses and Case Studies* (New Haven: Yale University Press, 1990), 23.

39. Fein, 22.

40. See, for example, Vahakan N. Dadrian, "A Typology of Genocide," *International Review of Modern Sociology* 5, no. 2 (1975): 201-212; Leo Kuper, *Genocide: Its Political Use in the Twentieth Century* (New Haven: Yale University Press, 1981), 46; Leo Kuper, "Other Selected Cases of Genocide and Genocidal Massacres: Types of Genocide," in *Genocide: A Critical Bibliographic Review, V. I.*, ed. by Israel W. Charny (London: Mansell and New York: Facts on File, 1980), 158; Eric Markusen, "Genocide and Total War: A Preliminary Comparison," in *Genocide and the Modern Age: Etiology and Case Studies of Mass Death*, ed. by Isidor Wallimann and Michael Dobkowski (New York: Greenwood Press, 1987), 106-117; Eric Markusen, "Genocide, Total War, and Nuclear Omnicide," in *Genocide: A Critical Bibliographic Review, V. II.*, ed. by Israel W. Charny (London: Mansell and New York: Facts on File, 1991), 236-243; Eric Markusen and David Kopf, *The Holocaust and Strategic Bombing: Genocide and Total War in the Twentieth Century* (Boulder, CO: Westview Press, forthcoming).

41. Roger Smith, "Human Destructiveness and Politics: The Twentieth Century as an Age of Genocide," in *Genocide and the Modern Age: Etiology and Case Studies of Mass Death*, ed. by Isidor Wallimann and Michael Dobkowski (New York: Greenwood, 1987), 21.

42. Barbara Harff, "The Etiology of Genocides," in *Genocide and the Modern Age: Etiology and Case Studies of Mass Death*, ed. by Isidor Wallimann and Michael Dobkowski (New York: Greenwood, 1987), 46.

43. Barbara Harff and Ted Robert Gurr, "Toward Empirical Theory of Genocides and Politicides: Identification and Measurement of Cases since 1945," *International Studies Quarterly* 32 (1988): 359.

44. R. J. Rummel, *Lethal Politics: Soviet Genocide and Mass Murder since 1917* (New Brunswick, NJ, and London: Transaction Books Publishers, 1990), 1.

45. See, for example, Ward Churchill, "Genocide: Toward a Functional Definition," *Alternatives* 11 (1986): 403-430; Henry R. Huttenbach, "Locating the Holocaust on the Genocide Spectrum: Towards a

Methodology of Definition and Categorization," *Holocaust and Genocide Studies* 3, no. 3 (1988): 289-303; Chalk and Jonassohn, 12-27.

46. Jack N. Porter, ed., *Genocide and Human Rights: A Global Anthology* (Washington, DC: University Press of America, 1982), 9-12.

47. Raphael Lemkin, *Axis Rule in Occupied Europe* (New York: Columbia University Press, 1944), 79.

48. Cited in Kuper, *Genocide: Its*, 210.

49. Kuper, *Genocide: Its*, 93-94 and Chalk and Jonassohn, 10-12.

50. Horowitz, 1-2.

51. Chalk and Jonassohn, 23.

52. Israel W. Charny, "The Study of Genocide," in *Genocide: A Critical Bibliographic Review*, vol. 1, ed. by Israel W. Charny (London: Mansell and New York: Facts on File, 1980), 4.

53. Israel W. Charny, "A Proposal for a New Encompassing Definition of Genocide: Including New Legal Categories of Accomplices to Genocide, and Genocide as a Result of Ecological Destruction and Abuse." A paper prepared for the First Raphael Lemkin Symposium on Genocide, Yale University Law School, February 1991.

54. Markusen, "Genocide and Total War," 237-238.

55. Raymond Aron, *The Century of Total War* (Boston: Beacon Press, 1954).

56. *World Military and Social Expenditures, 1987-88*, ed. by Ruth Leger Sivard (Washington, DC: World Priorities, 1987), 28.

57. *World Military*, 28.

58. *World Military*, 28.

59. Karl von Clausewitz, *Vom Krieg*. (Bonn, Germany: Ferd. Dümmlers Verlag, 1966), Section no. 24. First published in 1832. The pertinent sentence in the German original reads: "Der Krieg ist eine blosse Fortsetzung der Politik mit anderen Mitteln." The sentence is to be literally translated as: War is a mere continuation of politics (or policy) by other means. *Politics* seems to us to be a better translation of *Politik* than *policy*. More idiomatic, perhaps, would be the phrase *foreign policy*. Hence the sentence in English probably should read: War is a mere continuation of foreign policy by other means.

60. Eckhardt, "War-Related Deaths," 1.

61. Ronald Glossop, *Confronting War: An Examination of Humanity's Most Pressing Problem*, 2d. ed. (Jefferson, NC: MacFarland, 1987), 7.

62. Arthur Westing, "War as Human Endeavor: The High-Fatality Wars of the Twentieth Century," *Journal of Peace Research* 3 (1982): 261.

63. Thomas M. Franck, "Who Killed Article 2(4)? Or: Changing Norms Governing the Use of Force by States," *American Journal of International Law* 64 (1970): 812.

64. Markusen, "Genocide and Total War," 103-105 and Markusen and Kopf.

65. Berenice A. Carroll, "'Total War,' the Self-Fulfilling Prophecy?" in *Design for Total War: Arms and Economics in the Third Reich*, ed. by Berenice A. Carroll (The Hague: Mouton, 1968), 17-36.

66. Marjorie Farrar, "World War II as Total War," in *War: A Historical, Political, and Social Study*, ed. by L.L. Farrar, Jr. (Santa Barbara, CA: ABC-Clio, 1978), 171.

67. Quincy Wright, *A Study of War, with a Commentary on War since 1941*. 2d ed. (Chicago: University of Chicago Press, 1942, 1965), 75.

68. Hornell Hart, "Acceleration in Social Change," in *Technology and Social Change*, ed. by Francis R. Allen, et al. (New York: Appleton-Century-Crofts, 1957), 42-43.

69. Hart, 42-43.

70. Gordon Wright, "The Impact of Total War," in *The Ordeal of Total War, 1939-1945* (New York: Harper and Row, 1968), 236 and Elliot, 88.

71. *World Military*, 28.

72. "The Damage Was Not Collateral," *New York Times* (24 March 1991): Op-Ed page.

73. George Lopez, "The Gulf War: Not So Clean," *Bulletin of the Atomic Scientists* 47, no. 7 (1991): 32.

74. Quoted in Paul Walker and Eric Stambler, "...and the Dirty Little Weapons," *Bulletin of the Atomic Scientists* 47, no. 4 (1991), 22.

75. Patrick Tyler, "Health Crisis Said to Grip Iraq in Wake of War's Destruction," *New York Times* (22 May 1991): A6.

76. Leo Kuper, *The Prevention of Genocide* (New Haven: Yale University Press, 1985), 157.

77. Vahakn N. Dadrian, "The Structural-Functional Components of Genocide: A Victimological Approach to the Armenian Case," in *Victimology: A New Focus*, vol. IV. edited by Israel Drapkin and Emilio Viano (Lexington, MA: Lexington books, 1975), 123; see also Helen Fein, *Accounting for Genocide* (New York: The Free Press, 1979), 25-30; and James J. Reid, "The Concept of War and Genocidal Impulses in the Ottoman Empire, 1821-1918," *Holocaust and Genocide Studies* 4, no. 2 (1989): 175-191.

78. David Hawk, "The Cambodian Genocide," in *Genocide: A Critical Bibliographic Review*, vol. 1, ed. by Israel W. Charny (London: Mansell and New York: Facts on File, 1988), 137-154.

79. Dadrian, "The Structural-Functional," 129.

80. Farrar, 175.

81. Reid, 175-191.

82. Arno Mayer, *Why Did the Heavens Not Darken?: The "Final Solution" in History* (New York: Pantheon, 1988).

83. Dadrian, "The Structural-Functional," 132.

84. Yehuda Bauer, *A History of the Holocaust* (New York: Franklin Watts, 1982), 58.

85. Michael Walzer, *Just and Unjust Wars* (New York: Basic Books, 1977).

86. Lewis Mumford, "The Morals of Extermination," *The Atlantic* 204, no.4 (1959): 39.

87. Kuper, *Genocide: Its*, 46.

88. See, as a good example, Huttenbach, "Locating," 292-293.

89. Dadrian, "The Structural-Functional," 206-207.

90. See, for example, Israel W. Charny, "Genocide and Mass Destruction: Doing Harm to Others as a Missing Dimension in Psychopathology," *Psychiatry* 49, no. 2 (1986): 144-157 and Eric Markusen, "Professions, Professionals, and Genocide," in *Genocide: A Critical Review*, vol. II, ed. by Israel W. Charny (London: Mansell and New York: Facts on File, 1991), 264-298.

91. Robert Jay Lifton, *The Nazi Doctors: Medical Killing and the Psychology of Genocide* (New York: Basic Books, 1986), 456.

92. Israel W. Charny, in collaboration with Chanan Rapaport, *How Can We Commit the Unthinkable? Genocide, the Human Cancer* (Boulder, CO: Westview Press, 1982), 113.

93. Ronald Schaffer, *Wings of Judgement: American Bombing in World War II* (New York and Oxford: Oxford University Press, 1985), 80-106.

94. Kuper, *Genocide: Its*, 86. See also Herbert C. Kelman and V. Lee Hamilton, *Crimes of Obedience: Toward a Social Psychology of Authority and Responsibility* (New Haven and London: Yale University Press, 1989), 19-20; and Fein, *Accounting*, 4.

95. Markusen, "Genocide and Total War," 111-112 and Markusen and Kopf.

96. Lifton, 16.

97. John W. Dower, *War without Mercy: Race and Power in the Pacific War* (New York: Pantheon Books, 1986), 81.

98. Dower, 216.

99. Lifton and Markusen, 126.

100. Lee Kennett, *A History of Strategic Bombing* (New York: Charles Scribner's Sons, 1982), 187.

101. Herbert Hirsch and Roger Smith, "The Language of Extermination in Genocide," in *Genocide: A Critical Review*, vol. II, ed. by Israel W. Charny (London: Mansell and New York: Facts on File, 1991), 386-403.

102. Herbert Kelman, "Violence without Moral Restraint: Reflections on the Dehumanization of Victims and Victimizers," *Journal of Social Issues* 29, no. 4 (1973): 48.

103. Lifton, 445.

104. Max Hastings, *Bomber Command* (New York: The Dial Press, 1979), 122-140.

105. Jeremy Iggers, "Euphemisms Can Impair Clear Thinking about War," *Minneapolis Tribune* (6 February 1991): 1E, 2E; for a critical analysis of the media coverage of the Gulf war, see Daniel Hallin "TV's Clean Little War," *Bulletin of the Atomic Scientists* 47, no. 7 (1991): 17-19.

106. Richard L. Rubenstein, *The Cunning of History: The Holocaust and the American Future* (New York: Harper Colophon, 1978), 22.

107. Kelman and Hamilton, 103-105.

108. Fred E. Katz, "A Sociological Perspective to the Holocaust," *Modern Judaism* 2 (1982): 274. See also: Zygmunt Bauman, *Modernity and the Holocaust* (Ithaca, NY: Cornell University Press, 1989), 98-107.

109. Max Weber, "Bureaucracy," in *From Max Weber: Essays in Sociology*, ed. by H.H. Gerth and C. Wright Mills (New York: Oxford University Press, 1958), 215-216.

110. Fein, *Accounting*, 22.

111. Markusen, "Genocide, Total War," 241-244 and Markusen and Kopf.

112. Lifton and Markusen, 156-191.

113. Charny, *How Can We Commit*, 284.

114. Kuper, *Genocide, Its*, 40; for some of the reasons for the neglect of these issues, see: Chalk and Jonassohn, 40-42.

115. Lisa Peattie, "Normalizing the Unthinkable," *Bulletin of the Atomic Scientists* 40, no. 3 (1984): 32-36; Kuper, *The Prevention*, 235; Lifton and Markusen; Markusen, "Genocide, Total War," 236-243.

CHAPTER 7: ANNOTATED BIBLIOGRAPHY

The bibliography that follows is divided into five sections. The first section contains materials on trends in collective violence and mass killing during the twentieth century. Sections two, three, and four focus on genocide, modern war, and nuclear omnicide respectively. The fifth section contains materials on connections and commonalities among the three types of governmental mass killing projects.

The Murderousness of the Twentieth Century

* 7.1 *
Dando, William A. *The Geography of Famine*. New York: John Wiley and Sons, 1980. LC 80-11145. ISBN 0-470-26956-1.

In the modern era, famine increasingly reflects governmental policy choices, either to allow people to starve or to deliberately create conditions that result in famine. This book is a primer on mass starvation from 4000 B.C. to 1978.

* 7.2 *
Eckhardt, William, and Gernot Köhler. "Structural and Armed Violence in the 20th Century: Magnitudes and Trends." *International Interactions* 6, no.4 (1980): 347-375.

The authors explore the important concept of structural violence, which refers to deaths caused by social and economic conditions that impair the health and reduce the life expectancy of vast numbers of disadvantaged people throughout the world. Armed violence, in contrast, involves overt destruction, and is caused primarily by warfare. The authors conclude that "structural violence was about seventeen times greater than behavioral, that is, armed, violence in the twentieth century...." (p.365) The essay contains several useful tables and charts, as well as a good bibliography. See also 7.36.

* 7.3 *
Elliot, Gil. *Twentieth Century Book of the Dead*. New York: Charles Scribner's Sons, 1972. LC 72-7584. ISBN 0-684-13115-3.

Anyone seriously concerned about the subject of governmental mass killing should read this book carefully. "The aim of this work, precisely, is to identify, against a background of knowable fact, the violent dead of the twentieth century...." (p.11) As noted in the narrative above, Elliot estimated that more than one hundred million human beings were victims of "man-made death" in the first seven decades of this century; he compares this scale "with the scale on which a modern nation operates and lives. The obvious reason for the comparison is simply that the figure of a hundred million represents the size in population of a large modern nation, and as a familiar image it may help us to visualize the scale and complexity of man-made death." (p.6) In Book One, titled, "Sketches: People in the Machines of Death," Elliot examines a number of cases, including "The European Soldier in the First World War," "The Russians in the Twentieth Century," "China in the Twentieth Century," "The Jews of Europe," "The Rest of the Second World War," and "Other Twentieth Century Conflicts." In Book Two, titled, "Analyses: Parts of the Machine," he explores how ideology, technology, and other factors have contributed to the shocking death tolls. The book ends with a detailed statistical appendix in which the author documents the sources for his figures and assumptions. For a useful review of Elliot's book which criticizes its flaws while acknowledging its contributions, see Victor Marshall, "Notes on a New Necrology." *Omega* 4, no.4 (1973): 267-273.

* 7.4 *

Leviton, Daniel, ed. *Horrendous Death, Health, and Well-Being*. New York: Hemisphere Publishing Corp, 1991. LC 90-4652. ISBN 1-56032-033-8.

Leviton's collection makes an important contribution to the recognition and understanding of the problem of collective violence. It contains excellent articles on homicide, genocide, terrorism, war, destruction of the enviroment, poverty and unemployment, hunger, and the threat of nuclear war.

* 7.5 *

Rhodes, Richard. "Man-Made Death: A Neglected Mortality." *Journal of the American Medical Association* 260 (1988): 686-687.

In this succinct article, Rhodes makes a persuasive case for allocating more resources to the understanding, and prevention, of man-made death. Citing Gil Elliot's pioneering work [7.3], as well as recent statistical analyses of the deathtolls of modern war, the author concludes that "The scale of public man-made death in modern times is comparable with the scale of death in former times from epidemic disease." (p.686) Rhodes suggests that the public health movement that dramatically reduced the toll of epidemic disease may provide an analogue, or model, for efforts to bring man-made death under rational control.

* 7.6 *

Rubenstein, Richard L. *The Age of Triage: Fear and Hope in an Overcrowded World*. Boston: Beacon Press, 1983. LC 82-9407. ISBN 0-8070-4376-1.

In an important, provocative, and disturbing study of govermental mass killing, Rubenstein argues that an important underlying motive for oppression and genocidal violence is the elimination of "surplus populations," which are increasing in numbers and significance in recent decades of the twentieth century. According to the author, "A surplus population is one that for any reason can find no viable role in the society in which it is domiciled. Because such people can expect none of the normal rewards of society, governments tend to regard them as potential sources of disorder and have often attempted to control them or to remove them from the mainstream of society altogether." (p.1) Rubenstein examines several case studies, including the Irish Potato Famine, the Holocaust, and the genocide in Cambodia in order to explicate his controversial thesis. His concluding chapter, titled "Is There a Way Out?," advocates fundamental changes in social values and economic arrangements.

* 7.7a *

Rummel, R.J. *Lethal Politics: Soviet Genocide and Mass Murder since 1917*. New Brunswick, NJ, and London: Transaction Books, 1990. LC 89-28836. ISBN 0-88738-333-5.

* 7.7b *

Rummel, R.J. *China's Bloody Century: Genocide and Mass Murder since 1900*. New Brunswick, NJ, and London: Transaction Books, 1991. ISBN 0-88738-417-X.

In these two volumes in a projected three-volume series on governmental mass killing during the twentieth century, Rummel uses the concept of "democide" to refer to cases where governments deliberately slaughter masses of civilians. He concludes that "Such democide has been far more prevalent than people have believed, even several times greater than the number killed in all of this century's wars." (p.ix) Another important conclusion is that democracies are much less likely to engage in democide and related froms of mass killing than are totalitarian governments.

* 7.8 *

Stohl, Michael, and George A. Lopez, eds. *Government Violence and Repression: An Agenda for Research*. New York: Greenwood Press, 1986. LC 85-24741. ISBN 0-313-24651-3.

The contributors to this important study of governmental violence argue that terrorism is practiced not only by non-governmental groups, but also by governments. Thus, Barbara Harff, in "Genocide as State Terror," argues that "genocide is the most extreme policy option available to policymakers bent on state terror, and is likely to be used to eliminate opposition groups." (p.183) Equally provocative are George Lopez's chapter on "National Security Ideology as an Impetus to State Violence and State Terror" and Ted Gurr's chapter on "The Political Origins of State Violence and Terror: A Theoretical Analysis."

* 7.9 *

Westing, Arthur H., ed. *Environmental Warfare: A Technical, Legal, and Policy Appraisal*. New York: Taylor and Francis, 1984. LC 84-8895. ISBN 0-85066-278-8.

The ancient practice of deliberately destroying the "enemy's" habitat has become vastly more harmful due to modern technology. For a focused case study of environmental warfare as a form of governmental mass killing see Weisberg, Barry. *Ecocide in Indochina: The Ecology of War*. San Francisco: Canfield Press, 1970.

Genocide

* 7.10 *

Chalk, Frank, and Kurt Jonassohn. *The History and Sociology of Genocide*. New Haven: Yale University Press, 1990. LC 89-2738. ISBN 0-300-04445-3 pa.

Part I of Chalk and Jonassohn presents the conceptual framework and includes a detailed discussion of the concept of genocide, a review of scholarly literature on genocide, the authors' own definition and typology of genocide, and a brief historical survey of genocides from antiquity through the twentieth century. Part II features succinct case studies of genocides, ranging from the Roman destruction of Carthage in 176 B.C. to the Turkish-Armenian genocide; the U.S.S.R. under Stalin; the Holocaust; and post-World War II genocides in Indonesia, Burundi, Bangladesh, Cambodia, East Timor, and the Amazon jungles of South America. Of particular note are the readings on the slaughter of Indians in North America. Part III consists of non-annotated bibliographies on conceptual and background issues as well as each of the case studies examined in Part II. This book can serve as a core text for courses on the genocide.

* 7.11 *

Charny, Israel W., ed. *Toward the Understanding and Prevention of Genocide*. Boulder, CO: Westview Press, 1984. LC 84-15241. ISBN 0-86531-843-3.

Comprising a selection of papers that were presented at the International Conference on the Holocaust and Genocide in Israel in 1982, the book is divided into five parts. Part I, "Scenarios of Genocide Past and Future," features two important articles: Helen Fein's "Scenarios of Genocide: Models of Genocide and Critical Responses" and Leo Kuper's "Types of Genocide and Mass Murder." Part II includes a number of case studies, including Pol Pot's Cambodia, the Soviet Gulag, the Armenian genocide, the Holocaust, and genocidal killings in Tibet. Part III focuses on "Dynamics of Genocide"; Part IV on "Arts, Religion, and Education"; and Part V on "Toward Intervention and Prevention."

* 7.12 *

Charny, Israel W., ed. *Genocide: A Critical Bibliographic Review*. London: Mansell and New York: Facts on File, 1988. ISBN 0-7201-186-X (Mansell).

Charny has compiled a vital contribution to research and education about genocide and genocidal killing. Scholars from a wide range of disciplines have written the thirteen critical reviews and accompanying bibliographies. Their topics include the psychology of genocidal killing; specific genocides, the Holocaust, the Armenian genocide, genocide in the U.S.S.R, the Cambodian genocide, and other selected cases; and philosophical aspects of mass killing.

* 7.13 *

Charny, Israel W., ed. *Genocide: A Critical Bibliographic Review V. II*. London: Mansell and New York: Facts on File, 1991. ISBN 0-7201-2053-5 (Mansell).

The second volume contains critical reviews and annotated bibliographies on subjects not covered in the first. There is a special section on denial of the Holocaust and the Armenian genocide that includes a remarkable article by Vahakn Dadrian, "Documentation of Armenian Genocide in Turkish Sources," as well as sections on "Law and Genocide" and "Educating about the Holocaust and Genocide." Another section contains articles on a comparative analysis of genocide, war, and the preparations for nuclear omnicide; the role of professions and professionals in genocidal killing. Other topics are the memorialization of the Holocaust; first person accounts of genocide; contributions of rescuers in the Holocaust; and the role of language in genocide.

* 7.14 *

Churchill, Ward. "Genocide: Toward a Functional Definition." *Alternatives* 11 (1986): 403-430.

In this helpful review of earlier attempts to define genocide, Churchill states, "While it can be said with virtual certainty that genocide today exists on a widespread and possibly growing basis, it cannot be correspondingly contended that the phenomenon is understood." (p.403) As contributions toward such understanding, the author points out how political issues intrude on the study of genocide, offers useful reflections on the concept of "cultural genocide," and proposes his own typology of genocide.

* 7.15 *

Dadrian, Vahakn N. "A Typology of Genocide." *International Review of Modern Sociology* 5, no. 2 (1975): 201-212.

* 7.16 *
Dadrian, Vahakn N. "A Theoretical Model of Genocide with Particular Reference to the Armenian Case." *Sociologica Internationalis* 14, no. 1/2 (1976): 99-126.

* 7.17 *
Dadrian, Vahakn N. "The Convergent Aspects of the Armenian and Jewish Cases of Genocide: A Reinterpretation of the Concept of Holocaust." *Holocaust and Genocide Studies* 3, no. 2 (1988): 151-170.

* 7.18 *
Dadrian, Vahakn N. "The Anticipation and Prevention of Genocide in International Conflicts: Some Lessons from History." *International Journal of Group Tensions* 18, no. 3 (1988): 205-214.

Dadrian is a sociological pioneer who has contributed to the conceptual and theoretical understanding of genocide and has demonstrated important parallels between the Holocaust and the Armenian genocide of 1915.

* 7.19 *
Fein, Helen. "Genocide: A Sociological Perspective." *Current Sociology* 38, no.1 (1990): 1-126.

Fein's analysis of the important scholarly literature on genocide is comprehensive. Among the issues that she surveys and comments on are "social recognition and criminalization of genocide"; "defining genocide as a sociological concept"; and "explanations of genocide." She also includes two sections on "contextual and comparative studies," in which she addresses such issues as the alleged uniqueness of the Holocaust, misuses of genocide comparisons, relationships between genocide and other forms of mass killing, and the role of helpers and rescuers. Her final section examines literature on punishment and prevention and ends with a research agenda for sociology.

* 7.20 *
Harff, Barbara, and Ted Robert Gurr. "Toward Empirical Theory of Genocides and Politicides: Identification and Measurement of Cases since 1945." *International Studies Quarterly* 32 (1988): 359-371.

After critically reviewing previous definitions and typologies of genocide, the authors propose a typology "which distinguishes between two categories of genocide, in which victim groups are defined primarily in terms of communal characteristics, and four types of politicide, in which victim groups are defined in terms of their political status or opposition to the state." (p.359) They then identify, and estimate the death tolls of, genocides and politicides since World War II.

* 7.21 *
Horowitz, Irving Louis. *Taking Lives: Genocide and State Power*. 3d ed. New Brunswick, NJ: Transaction Books, 1982. LC 79-66341. ISBN 0-87855-751-2 pa.

After decrying the neglect of genocide by the social science community, Horowitz examines a number of definitions of genocide and presents a valuable discussion of "eight basic types of societies that can be defined on a measurement scale of life and death" (p. 43), that is, the extent to which they resort to mass killing, torture, and other forms of violence as means of social control. Horowitz is one of the sociological pioneers in this field.

* 7.22 *
Huttenbach, Henry R. "Locating the Holocaust on the Genocide Spectrum: Towards a Methodology of Definition and Categorization." *Holocaust and Genocide Studies* 3, no. 3 (1988): 289-303.

The author examines the concept of genocide, per se, as well as the question of the uniqueness of the Holocaust as an example of genocide. He advocates and initiates the development of "a spectrum of genocide....within which the Holocaust will occupy a distinct niche, flanked in proximity by those events with which it shares the greatest similarity..." (p.291)

* 7.23 *
Katz, Steven T. "Essay: Quantity and Interpretation—Issues in the Comparative Historical Analysis of the Holocaust." *Holocaust and Genocide Studies* 4, no. 2 (1989): 127-148.

Katz addresses the issue of the uniqueness of the Holocaust by comparing it with several other cases of governmental violence, including the witch hunts of the 15th, 16th, and 17th centuries; black slavery and the slaughter of Indians in the United States; and the Nazi persecution of Gypsies, homosexuals, and other groups. He concludes that "fundamental distinctions, elemental differences, mark off the Holocaust phenomenologically from these other, similarly immoral and abhorent, cases." (p.127)

* 7.24 *
Kuper, Leo. *Genocide: Its Political Use in the Twentieth Century*. New Haven: Yale University Press, 1981. LC 81-16151. ISBN 0-300-02795-8.

In what is perhaps the definitive social scientific analysis of genocide currently available, Kuper reviews the literature on theories of genocide and provides a number of succinct case histories of specific genocides and related atrocities. He argues that decolonization can create preconditions for genocide when ethnic and tribal rivalries that had been suppressed by the colonizing power are permitted to flare into violence, a thesis that augurs ill for several nations in newly-independent Eastern Europe, like Romania and Yugoslavia. Another of his conclusions, one that has provoked considerable controversy as indicated above, is that the highly destructive nature of modern weapons, combined with the willingness to target civilians in war, has blurred the line between genocide and warfare. His criticisms of the inability of the United Nations to prevent or interrupt genocide, and his concluding chapter on "The Non-Genocidal Society," set the stage for 7.25.

* 7.25 *
Kuper, Leo. *The Prevention of Genocide*. New Haven: Yale University Press, 1985. LC 81-16151. ISBN 0-300-02795-8.

Kuper builds on his 1981 book. He supplies additional cases and examines in detail the prospects for early recognition, intervention, and prevention of genocidal violence. His main argument is that the international community in general, and the United Nations in particular, have been disgracefully negligent and weak when confronted by cases of genocidal killing, for example, Cambodia between 1975 and 1978. After reviewing the inadequacies of the United Nations response in Cambodia and elsewhere, Kuper presents a number of suggestions for strengthening the UN's capacity for effective intervention.

* 7.26 *
Lang, Berel, ed. "Philosophy and the Holocaust." *The Philosophical Forum* 16, nos. 1-2 (1984-85): 1-140.

This special issue devoted to the Holocaust and genocide contains a number of provocative essays. Among these are "The Concept of Genocide," by Berel Lang, on the meanings of the term "genocide" and the psychological processes that operate among the perpetrators; "The Origins of Extermination in the Imagination," by William Gass; and "Measuring Responsibility," by A. Zvie Bar-On.

* 7.27 *
Lifton, Robert Jay. *The Nazi Doctors: Medical Killing and the Psychology of Genocide*. New York: Basic Books, 1986. LC 85-73874. ISBN 0-465-04904-4.

Basing his detailed case study on extensive interviews with former Nazi doctors as well as several dozen Auschwitz survivors, Lifton examines the role of the German medical profession in the Holocaust. The final section of the book, titled "The Psychology of Genocide," develops a number of psychological and historical concepts to explain how "ordinary" men could become implicated in "demonic" actions. Lifton argues that genocides like the Holocaust may be seen as desperate attempts to find a "cure" to massive psychological and social upheavals, and that violence against designated victim groups may give the perpetrating group the illusion of security and safety. Lifton also demonstrates the roles of euphemistic language, bureaucractic compartmentalization of tasks, and the distancing effects of technology in facilitating genocidal killing.

* 7.28 *
Markusen, Eric. "Professions, Professionals, and Genocide." In *Genocide: A Critical Bibliographic Review, V. II*. Ed. by Israel W. Charny. London: Mansell and New York: Facts on File, 1991. ISBN 0-7201-2053-5 (Mansell).

Markusen examines how members of such professions as medicine, law, education, the church, and the military have contributed to the Holocaust, the Armenian genocide, and other types of mass killing as bystanders, accomplices, and perpetrators.

* 7.29 *
Mazian, Florence. *Why Genocide? The Armenian and Jewish Experiences in Perspective*. Ames, IA: Iowa State University Press, 1990. LC 89-15268. ISBN 0-8138-0143-5.

The author states that the purpose of the book is "to answer a very basic question: Why is genocide, rather than any other alternative, selected by a people or state as the solution to a real or imagined problem?" (p.ix) In order to answer this question, Mazian analyzes, in a comparative mode, two major genocides of the twentieth century by means of a conceptual framework consisting of six determinants: 1) the creation of "outsiders"; 2) internal strife in the perpetrating group; 3) destructive uses of communication, including the use of propaganda to promote an aggressive ideology; 4) powerful leadership; 5) organization of the destruction process (i.e., recruitment and training of the perpetrators); and 6) the "failure of multidimensional levels of social control." (p.ix)

* 7.30 *
Rubenstein, Richard L. *The Cunning of History: The Holocaust and the American Future*. New York: Harper and Row, 1975, 1978. LC 75-9334. ISBN 0-06-067013-4.

Rubenstein argues that "we are more likely to understand the Holocaust if we regard it as the expression of some of the most profound tendencies in Western civilization in the twentieth century." (p.21) Among these tendencies, according to Rubenstein, are secularization, rationality, bureaucracy, and growing numbers of politicaly stateless and economically superfluous people. His chapters on "The Modernization of Slavery" and "The Health Professions and

Corporate Enterprise at Auschwitz" are particularly noteworthy.

* 7.31 *
Wallimann, Isidor, and Michael M. Dobkowski, eds. *Genocide and the Modern Age: Etiology and Case Studies of Mass Death*. New York: Greenwood Press, 1987. LC 86-9978. ISBN 0-313-24198-8.

The editors have divided their valuable collection of essays into two major parts. The first contains essays that conceptualize, classify, define, and explain genocide. The second contains case studies, such as the Holocaust, the Armenian genocide, and the killing of aboriginal peoples in Australia. Richard L. Rubenstein provides a provocative afterword entitled "Genocide and Civilization."

Modern War

* 7.32 *
Adams, James. *Engines of War: Merchants of Death and the New Arms Race*. New York: Atlantic Monthly Press, 1990. LC 90-197. ISBN 0-87113-352-0.

In a sobering survey of the global arms traffic, Adams shows how some of the most unstable regions of the world are acquiring large arsenals of nuclear, chemical, and biological weapons.

* 7.33 *
Carroll, Berenice A. "'Total War,' the Self-Fulfilling Prophecy?" In *Design for Total War: Arms and Economics in the Third Reich*. Ed. by Berenice A. Carroll. The Hague, Netherlands: Mouton, 1968. LC 68-15527.

Carroll offers a useful survey of the origins of the term "total war," as well as its precursors in the writings of Clausewitz and others. Another valuable discussion is Richard Hobbs' "The Growth of the Idea of Total War" that appears in his book, *The Myth of Victory: What is Victory in War?* (Boulder, CO: Westview Press, 1979).

* 7.34 *
Dyer, Gwynne. *War*. New York: Crown Publishers, 1985. LC 85-5704. ISBN 0-517-55615-4.

War is a readable, richly illustrated historical overview of warfare from primitive conflict through contemporary proxy wars and nuclear deterrence. Dyer's chapters, "The Road to Mass Warfare" and "Reductio Ad Absurdum: Total War," as well as his two chapters on nuclear war, are particularly noteworthy.

* 7.35 *
Dower, John W. *War without Mercy: Race and Power in the Pacific War*. New York: Pantheon Books, 1986. LC 85-43462. ISBN 0-394-50030-X.

Racism and "race hate" were important in the war between the United States and Japan. Noting that "it was a common observation of Western war correspondents that the fighting in the Pacific was more savage than in the European theater," Dower suggests that "Race hate fed atrocities, and atrocities in turn fanned the fires of race hate. The dehumanization of the Other contributed immeasurably to the psychological distancing that facilitated killing, not only on the battlefield but also in the plans adopted by strategists far removed from the actual scene of combat...The natural response...was an obsession with extermination on both sides—a war without mercy." (p.11) In his final chapter, Dower explores possible reasons for the "speed with with which a war of seemingly irreconcilable hatred gave way to cordial relations once the fighting had ceased." (p.311)

* 7.36 *
Eckhardt, William. "Civilian Deaths in Wartime." *Bulletin of Peace Proposals* 20, no.1 (1989): 89-98.

Eckhardt succinctly summarizes war casualties during the last three centuries. He concludes that "wars have increased in frequency, duration, and deaths from the 18th to the 20th centuries. The increase in deaths was four times the increase in world population." (p.97) His discussions of "hunger-related deaths in wartime" and "structural violence" are notable.

* 7.37 *
Farrar, Marjorie. "World War II as Total War." In *War: A Historical, Political, and Social Study*. Ed. by L.L. Farrar, Jr. Santa Barbara, CA: ABC-Clio, 1978. LC 77-16620. ISBN 0-87436-221-0.

Among Farrar's conclusions in this useful essay is that total wars, like World War II, tend to blur the distinction, both politically and morally, between democratic and totalitarian governments that wage them. "The war," asserts Farrar, "pushed Western civilization toward totalitarianism." (p.179)

* 7.38 *
Fetter, Steve. "Ballistic Missiles and Weapons of Mass Destruction: What Is the Threat? What Should Be Done?" *International Security* 16, no. 1 (1991): 5-42.

Fetter examines the proliferation of highly destructive weaponry to nations in unstable, violence-prone regions of the world. He provides technical information on such weapons, a discussion of why nations may seek to acquire them, and suggestions for impeding such acquisition.

* 7.39 *
Fuller, J.F.C. *The Conduct of War, 1789-1961*. New Brunswick, NJ: Rutgers University Press, 1961. LC 61-1026.

In this widely-cited book, Fuller argues that the era of modern, total war began with the use of the military draft to raise mass armies during the Napoleonic wars of the late 1700s. He traces the evolution of totalistic tendencies in subsequent wars, particularly the breakdown of the distinction between soldiers and civilians. He includes a fascinating discussion of the American Civil War as an example of total war.

* 7.40 *
Gabriel, Richard. *The Painful Field: The Psychiatric Dimension of Modern War*. New York: Greenwood Press, 1989. LC 87-31785. ISBN 0-313-24718-8.

The vulnerability of the human mind to the stresses of military combat is a crucial, yet all too frequently ignored or under-appreciated, aspect of modern warfare. Pointing out in detail how mental breakdowns among soliders have been very common throughout history, Gabriel argues that modern war, with its vastly more destructive weapons, is far more likely to cause psychiatric casualties than its precursors. In his final chapter, Gabriel examines efforts by U.S. and Soviet researchers to develop drugs that "will prevent or reduce anxiety while allowing the soldier to retain his normal and vitally needed acute levels of mental awareness." (p.168) However, according to Gabriel, "The real horror lurking behind the attempt to use chemical means for preventing psychiatric collapse in battle is that in order for a soldier to function in the environment of modern war, he must be psychically reconstituted in a manner precisely identical to what we have traditionally defined as being mentally ill. He must be chemically made over to become a sociopathic personality in the clinical sense of the term." (p.172)

* 7.41 *
Gander, T. J. *Nuclear, Chemical, and Biological Warfare*. London: Ian Allen, Ltd., 1987. ISBN 0-7110-1722-0.

Gander presents, clearly and succinctly, the basic facts about these three types of weapons of mass destruction, and includes a great many excellent photographs, of which those depicting aspects of chemical warfare are particularly striking.

* 7.42 *
Hartigan, Richard Shelly. *The Forgotten Victim: A History of the Civilian*. Chicago: Precedent Publishing, 1982. LC 83-134732. ISBN 0-913750-19-0.

The author asks: "Is the idea of the civilian an anachronism? Have nuclear weapons and guerilla warfare forever obliterated the distinction between combatant and noncombatants?" (p.1) Reluctantly, Hartigan answers in the affirmative and then proceeds to trace the history of the erosion of this crucial distinction.

* 7.43 *
Keegan, John. *The Face of Battle*. New York: The Viking Press, 1976. LC 76-10611. ISBN 0-670-30432-8.

Keegan examines the changing nature of warfare by means of a detailed portrayal of three battles: Agincourt, in 1415; Waterloo, in 1815; and the Somme, in 1916. A central theme is that advances in destructive technology have made warfare progressively more lethal and impersonal. In his concluding chapter, titled "The Future of Battle," Keegan notes that, "Impersonality, coercion, deliberate cruelty, all deployed on a rising scale, make the fitness of modern man to sustain the stress of battle increasingly doubtful." (p.325) See also 7.40.

* 7.44 *
Kennett, Lee. *A History of Strategic Bombing*. New York: Charles Scribner's Sons, 1982. LC 82-10673, ISBN 0-684-17781-1.

Kennett succinctly reviews the evolution of strategic bombing. The final two chapters, "Japan: Ordeal by Fire," and "The Bombing War in Retrospect," are especially recommended.

* 7.45 *
Lifton, Robert Jay. *Death in Life: Survivors of Hiroshima*. New York: Random House, 1967. LC 67-22658. Reissued in 1984.

Based on extensive interviews with seventy-five survivors of the Hiroshima bomb, Lifton's study of the psychological, cultural, and social impacts of the atomic bombings is the definitive one. In the final chapter, Lifton extends his analysis to other cases of mass killing and mass death and introduces such seminal concepts as "death guilt" and "psychic numbing."

* 7.46 *
Lopez, George. "The Gulf War: Not So Clean." *Bulletin of the Atomic Scientists* 47, no. 7 (1991): 30-35.

The author argues that, despite public claims and a sincere effort to avoid direct targeting of civilians by the U.S. and its allies in the Persian Gulf War of 1991, "collateral damage" and civilian deaths were nonetheless very widespread.

* 7.47 *
Nolan, Janne E., and Albert D. Wheelon. "Third World Ballistic Missiles." *Scientific American* 274, no. 2 (1990): 34-40.

Missiles capable of delivering nuclear, chemical, and biological warheads have spread rapidly to such nations as Israel, Egypt, Iran, Iraq, Libya, South Africa, and Argentina. The authors warn that "The Third World military buildup is perhaps even more worrisome than its First World prototype, for it is far more likely to find expression in war." (p.34)

* 7.48 *
O'Connell, Robert L. *Of Arms and Men: A History of War, Weapons, and Aggression*. New York and Oxford: Oxford University Press, 1989. LC 88-19526. ISBN 0-19-505359-1 pa.

O'Connell offers an eloquent account of the evolution of weapons and warfare from antiquity through the nuclear age. Among the important themes that pervade this chronologically organized survey are dehumanization; increased distance between killers and killed; and the breakdown of the traditional distinction between soldiers and civilians during wars of the twentieth century. O'Connell exemplifies the meaning of dehumanization in this statement, "new armaments were most easily employed if their victims could be conceptualized, however implausibly, as belonging to another species." (p.190)

* 7.49 *
Sallagar, Frederick. *The Road to Total War*. New York: Van Nostrand Reinhold, 1969. LC 74-22389. ISBN 0-442-25074-6.

"What characterizes an all-out, or total, war is that it is fought for such high stakes that the belligerents are willing, or compelled, to employ, not all weapons they possess, but any weapons they consider appropriate and advantageous to them." (p.3) Sallagar asserts that "It was the adoption of indiscriminate air warfare which signaled the transition to total war...." [in World War II) (p.4) After tracing the process by which misunderstandings, as well as deliberate decisions, led to a policy of bombing cities by Germany, Great Britain, and the United States, he concludes with speculations on the implications of his study for future wars.

* 7.50 *
Schaffer, Ronald. *Wings of Judgment: American Bombing in World War II*. New York and Oxford: Oxford University Press, 1985. LC 85-4861. ISBN 0-19-503629-8.

In an outstanding examination of the American practice of bombing cities during World War II, Schaffer reviews the shift from an initial aversion to attacks against cities in Europe to the policy of direct, incendiary attacks against Japanese cities. He includes two valuable chapters on moral dimensions of the bombing of cities and concludes with an epilogue in which he asserts that, "despite enormous qualitative changes in the potential of weapons [with the invention of nuclear weapons], the thinking of American military leaders, scientists, and statesmen in the postwar years contained important vestiges of earlier views about air warfare and its moral consequences." (p.190) In fact, the men responsible for the planning and implementation of the incendiary raids against Japanese cities were among those in charge of early American nuclear weapons policy.

* 7.51 *
Sherry, Michael S. *The Rise of American Air Power: The Creation of Armageddon*. New York and London: Yale University Press, 1987. LC 86-19003. ISBN 0-300-03600-0.

Sherry delves deeply into the historical, political, ideological, cultural, and social-psychological dimensions of the embrace of the policy of attacking cities. The chapters on "The Sociology of Air War," "The Sources of Technological Fanaticism," and "The Triumph of Technological Fanaticism" are of particular interest. Like Schaffer [7.50], Sherry concludes with important reflections on early U.S. nuclear weapons policy, which evolved from strategic bombing policies and practices. While the Schaffer and Sherry books inevitably contain considerable common information, differences in focus make them usefully complementary, rather than redundant. Together with Richard Rhodes' *The Making of the Atomic Bomb* [7.76], they provide a solid historical foundation for an understanding of the early evolution of American nuclear weapons policy.

* 7.52 *
Stockholm International Peace Research Institute. *Incendiary Weapons*. Cambridge, MA, and London: The MIT Press, 1975. LC 75-11515. ISBN 0-262-19139-3.

This SIPRI volume examines the uses of fire as a military weapon throughout history; fire weapons include flamethrowers and incendiary bombs in World War II and napalm in Vietnam. There is a summary of existing international laws that purport to limit the use of such weapons. Also several harrowing chapters relate the effects of incendiary weapons on human beings.

* 7.53 *
Van Creveld, Martin. *Technology and War: From 2000 B.C. to the Present*. London: Collier Macmillan Publishers and New York: The Free Press, 1989. LC 88-16405. ISBN 0-02-933151-X.

That "war is completely permeated by technology and governed by it" is Van Creveld's basic thesis. The author, whose other books on warfare are required texts in military academies throughout the world, divides both his book and the history of warfare into four periods, each characterized by the nature of the technology that dominated it. Thus, during the first period, from 2000 B.C. to 1500 A.D., human and animal muscle-power constituted the chief means of waging war. The second period, which the author labels "the Age of Machines," extended from the Renaissance to about 1830. Key technological developments during this period were the exploitation of gunpowder and the widespread use of firearms. Third, from 1830 to 1945, such inventions as the railway and the telegraph, and the rise of complex bureaucratic organizations, gave rise to "the Age of Systems." Fourth and finally, the invention of nuclear weapons and computers created the present age, which Van Creveld terms "the Age of Automation." Van Creveld concludes with a useful bibliographic essay. Compare with 7.94 below.

* 7.54 *
Walker, Paul, and Eric Stambler. "...and the Dirty Little Weapons." *Bulletin of the Atomic Scientists* 47, no. 4 (1991): 21-24.

Media coverage of the Persian Gulf War of 1991 created "the impression that the war was a bloodless, push-button battle in which only military targets were destroyed."(p.21) The reality, according to the authors, was very different. In addition to providing details of the destructive power of some of the weapons that were used against Iraq, they note that "of the 88,500 tons of bombs dropped, only 6,520 tons—7.4 percent—were precision-guided ordnance, according to official Pentagon figures."(p.22)

* 7.55 *
Williams, Peter, and David Wallace. *Unit 731: Japan's Secret Biological Warfare in World War II*. New York: The Free Press, 1989. LC 88-39072. ISBN 0-02-935301-7.

At the end of the war, the United States government agreed not to prosecute the responsible Japanese as war criminals in return for their cooperation in providing American scientists with technical information that was used to develop American biological weaponry. The authors have based their account of Japan's use of biological warfare on long-secret documents obtained through the Freedom of Information Act. For a brief account, see: John W. Powell, "A Hidden Chapter in History." *Bulletin of the Atomic Scientists* 37, no.8 (1981): 44-52.

* 7.56 *
World Military and Social Expenditures. 1974-. A. Ed.: Ruth Leger Sivard. Washington, DC: World Priorities. ISSN 0363-4795. 1991 edition has ISBN 0-918281-07-5.

Sivard's annually published compendium compares expenditures of national governments around the world for war and armaments with those for the social needs of education, medical care, and housing, among others. It also provides key indicators of a nation's quality of life such as the infant mortality rate. A consistent theme of the series has been the great disparity between the prodigious resources devoted to the military and the relatively scanty funds committed to human needs. The annual editions are an excellent resource for students of collective violence, both behavioral and structural.

* 7.57 *
Wright, Gordon. "The Impact of Total War." In *The Ordeal of Total War, 1939-1945*. New York: Harper and Row, 1968. LC 68-28221.

In the final chapter of his important study of World War II, Wright examines the political, social, and psychological impacts of the war on Western society. A major conclusion is that there is a tendency for democratic political institutions to weaken when they are engaged in a war against totalitarian powers.

* 7.58 *
Wright, Quincy. *A Study of War*. With a commentary on war since 1941. 2d ed. Chicago: University of Chicago Press, 1965. LC 65-5396.

Wright coordinated this vast compendium of data on trends in warfare throughout history at the University of Chicago. This edition, in 1,637 pages, is a one-volume, updated abridgement of the work that was originally published in two volumes in 1942.

Nuclear Omnicide

* 7.59 *
Ball, Desmond, and Jeffrey Richelson, eds. *Strategic Nuclear Targeting*. Ithaca, NY, and London: Cornell University Press, 1986. LC 85-48195. ISBN 0-8014-1898-4.

In the preface to this truly remarkable collection of authoritative articles on American, Soviet, British, and French nuclear targeting plans, the editors state that "Declassified U.S. nuclear war plans of the late 1940s and early 1950s showed that the target planning process had frequently been arbitrary and inefficient and sometimes irrational." (p.7) The chapters that follow indicate that later American nuclear war plans are by no means free of such problems; nor are those of other nuclear-armed nations. Of particular importance are the chapters by David Rosenberg, "U.S. Nuclear War Planning, 1945-1960;" Ball, "The Development of the SIOP, 1960-1983;" Richelson, "Population Targeting and U.S. Strategic Doctrine;" and David Cattell and George Quester, "Ethnic Targeting: Some Bad Ideas." "Ethnic targeting" refers to the deliberate targeting of specific population groups in the Soviet Union, notably the "Great Russians," as opposed to members of other Republics. This approach, note the authors, was advocated by key advisors to the Carter and Reagan administrations. Cattell and Quester assert that the employment of such a targeting scheme would constitute "genocide." (p.281)

* 7.60 *

Bundy, McGeorge. *Danger and Survival: Choices About the Bomb in the First Fifty Years*. New York: Random House, 1988. LC 88-42824. ISBN 0-394-52278-8.

A well-informed former presidential advisor relates the history of the nuclear age, from the decisions to build and then use the first atomic bombs to the present period. Bundy not only examines key actions by the United States and the Soviet Union, but also explores why other nations, like Great Britain and Israel, decided to acquire their own nuclear weapons.

* 7.61 *

Carter, Ashton, John D. Steinbrunner, and Charles A. Zraket, eds. *Managing Nuclear Operations*. Washington, DC: Brookings, 1986. LC 86-32655. ISBN 0-8157-131-4 pa.

Like 7.59, this startling book goes beyond the verbiage and rhetoric of much of the writing on nuclear strategy to focus on details about actual arrangements for the weapons, both during peace and in the event of war. The editors, in their introduction, assert that "All the widely accepted notions about the role of nuclear weapons in security make strong, but frequently tacit and sometimes unjustified, assumptions about the ability of the command system to manage nuclear weapons." (p.2) Indeed, an important theme running through the book is the doubtful ability of maintaining control over nuclear weapons in the event that a nuclear war breaks out. The titles of some of the chapters give an idea of the array of issues that are examined: "Alerting in Crisis and Conventional War," "War Termination," "Delegation of Nuclear Command Authority," "Targeting," "The Psychological Climate of Nuclear Command," and "Sources of Error and Uncertainty." See also 7.62.

* 7.62 *

Ford, Daniel. *The Button: The Pentagon's Command and Control System*. New York: Simon & Schuster, 1985. LC 84-27616. ISBN 0-671-50068-6.

On the basis of extensive interviews with key policymakers and decision makers, Ford identifies many fundamental problems in the arrangements for maintaining control over nuclear weapons during both intense international crises and actual conflict. He asserts that there is a sizeable "gap between official rhetoric and Pentagon plans" for nuclear war. (p.17) The rhetoric calls for the use of American nuclear weapons only in retaliation for an enemy attack, but the actual plans involve the capacity for a pre-emptive, first strike with U.S. nuclear weapons. Ford also exposes the tendency of presidents to be quite ignorant of the nuclear weapons and war plans for which they are responsible as Commander in Chief of all U.S. military forces. (p.89-90) And he critically examines the "technological illiteracy" of senior military officers responsible for nuclear weapons: "The military commanders' lack of knowledge about the new technology at their disposal makes it very difficult for them to make sensible choices...." (p.186)

* 7.63 *

Gay, William C., and Michael Pearson. *The Nuclear Arms Race*. Chicago and London: The American Library Association, 1987. LC 86-32087. ISBN 0-8389-0467-X.

The authors have written excellent essays on the history of the arms race, consequences of nuclear war, and alternatives to present policies. They have provided annotated bibliographies on a wide range of issues, and appended a helpful section on how to obtain additional information. Their chapter on "The Probability of Nuclear War" is particularly noteworthy.

* 7.64 *

Gay, William C., and Ronald E. Santoni. "Philosophy and Contemporary Faces of Genocide: Multiple Genocide and Nuclear Destruction." In *Genocide: A Critical Bibliographic Review. V. I.* Ed. by Israel W. Charny. London: Mansell and New York: Facts on File, 1988. ISBN 0-7201-186-X (Mansell).

The authors begin this essay on the philosophical dimensions of mass killing in the nuclear age by noting that "For the first time in human history, the issue of whether or not human beings possess the capacity to destroy all life on the planet Earth is being debated." (p.172) They then examine a number of topics, including the possibility of human extinction in a nuclear holocaust and traditional moral criteria for so-called "just-wars." The essay is followed by an excellent annotated bibliography that will be useful to anyone, not just philosophers, seriously concerned about the nuclear threat.

* 7.65 *
Halperin, Morton. *The Nuclear Fallacy: Dispelling the Myth of Nuclear Strategy*. Cambridge, MA: Ballinger Publishing Co., 1987. LC 86-32255. ISBN 0-88730-114-2.

A former deputy assistant secretary of defense has written a strong critique of past and present U.S. policies on nuclear weapons. Halperin identifies what he sees as many fallacies in recent strategic thinking and suggests that the most important fallacy is the tendency to think of "nuclear explosive devices" as weapons that can actually be used in war.

* 7.66 *
Harkin, Tom, with C. E. Thomas. *Five Minutes to Midnight: Why the Nuclear Threat Is Growing Faster Than Ever*. New York: Birch Lane Press—Carol Publishing Group, 1990. LC 90-19405. ISBN 1-5597-042-5.

Although the recent improvement in U.S.-Soviet relations and the presumed end of the Cold War may have induced some observers to dismiss the nuclear threat to a low priority concern, these authors, the senior of whom is a Democratic U.S. Senator from Iowa, argue persuasively that the danger posed by nuclear weapons is still all too real and urgent. In their chapter, "The Growing Threat of Nuclear War," Harkin and Thomas expose the continuing dangers posed by the spread of nuclear weapons to additional nations. In addition to sounding a warning, they also include several provocative chapters in a section titled "Alternative National Security Strategies." See also 7.80.

* 7.67 *
Herken, Gregg. *Counsels of War*. Expanded ed. New York: Oxford University Press, 1987. LC 86-31296. ISBN 0-19-504986-1.

Herken conducted interviews with dozens of key policymakers and delved through many primary and secondary documents in order to create this revealing, and frequently disturbing, historical study. Like Ford in 7.62, he exposes the fact that, while our leaders have stated publicly that American nuclear weapons would be used only in retaliation for a nuclear attack against us, the actual war plans have called for U.S. first strikes. Herken also documents the role of "inter-service rivalry," where the several branches of the U.S. military forces compete for shares of the defense budget and for new weapons technologies, in driving the nuclear arms race forward.

* 7.68 *
Kaku, Michio, and Daniel Axelrod. *To Win a Nuclear War: The Pentagon's Secret War Plans*. Boston: South End Press, 1987. LC 86-27974. ISBN 0-89608-321-7 pa.

Recently declassifed Pentagon documents, many obtained through the Freedom of Information Act, are the basis of the authors' examination of secret U.S. nuclear plans from 1945 through the mid-1980s. Kaku and Axelrod assert that "These secret documents demonstrate in detail that, contrary to public statements and widespread popular belief, in periods of crisis the Pentagon has indeed threatened the use of nuclear weapons against Third World nations and has seriously considered launching a first strike against the Soviet Union." (p.3)

* 7.69 *
Kaplan, Fred. *The Wizards of Armageddon*. New York: Simon & Schuster, 1983. LC 83-369. ISBN 0-671-42444-0.

This is perhaps the best single historical narrative of the development of American nuclear weapons policy from the end of World War II through the early 1980s. In-depth interviews with dozens of key figures, ranging from former secretaries of defense through retired generals to still-active nuclear policymakers, enabled Kaplan to produce a fascinating, intimate portrait of the key individuals and organizations responsible for nuclear war plans that reads almost like a novel. Of particular note is his account of the continuity in personnel and philosophy between the firebombing of Japanese cities during World War II and early post-war atomic warfare policy. (p.33-50) Kaplan also reveals how the ostensibly "scientific" basis of nuclear policy making often masks personal bias and organizational interests; for example, claims that the United States was dangerously behind the Soviet Union with respect to bombers and missiles, the so-called "bomber gap" of the 1950s and "missile gap" of the 1960s, respectively, were based on demonstrably weak and even deliberately distorted evidence, but led nonetheless to increases in defense spending and nuclear weapon deployments. (p.155-173)

* 7.70 *
Kolkowicz, Roman, ed. *The Logic of Nuclear Terror*. Boston: Allen & Unwin, 1986. LC 86-22317. ISBN 0-04-497032-3 pa.

During the last few years, there has been a plethora of books published on the subject of nuclear deterrence. This is one of the very best. Kolkowicz, in a chapter titled "Intellectuals and the Deterrence System," traces the evolution of a new academic speciality, "nuclear strategists," which purported to be able to evaluate various nuclear weapons policies in objective, nonpolitical, scientific terms, a claim which Kolkowicz finds debatable. (p.26) The essay by Ken Booth, "Nuclear Deterrence and 'World War III': How Will History Judge?" emphasizes the disastrous consequences of the actual use of nuclear weapons and forcefully reminds the reader that deterrence, to be credible, rests on the ability and willingness to slaughter millions of innocent people. Also noteworthy are the essays by Robert Jervis, "Strategic Theory: What's New and What's True;" and Joseph Nye, "The Long-Term Future of Nuclear Deterrence."

* 7.71 *
Kovel, Joel. *Against the State of Nuclear Terror*. Boston: South End Press, 1983. LC 84-50942. ISBN 0-89608-219-9 pa.

In an impassioned, but carefully-documented, attack on American nuclear weapons policies, Kovel explores the psychological, cultural, and political reasons that the American public has been so passive in the face of threatened annihilation. Among his important conclusions are that nuclear weapons are antithetical to democracy, and that "nuclear states" utilize a variety of methods to "terrorize" their citizens into compliance with national security policies. In Part II, he explores the provocative theme of technocracy, "domination projected through science," as an important factor in the nuclear predicament. Finally, he suggests principles and directions for anti-nuclear politics.

* 7.72 *
Kramer, Ronald C., and Sam Marullo. "Toward a Sociology of Nuclear Weapons." *The Sociological Quarterly* 26, no. 3 (1985): 277-292.

The authors criticize recent neglect of the nuclear threat by sociologists, review earlier contributions that sociologists did make toward understanding it, and suggest directions for further research. Theirs is the lead article of a special section of four pieces on "The Sociology of the Nuclear Threat."

* 7.73 *
Kurtz, Lester R. *The Nuclear Cage: A Sociology of the Arms Race*. Englewood Cliffs, NJ: Prentice Hall, 1988. LC 87-19296. ISBN 0-13-625396-5 pa.

Kurtz applies sociology and other behavioral sciences to explain how we have become trapped in "the nuclear cage" (i.e. a world threatened by the spectre of nuclear holocaust). The three chapters in Part II, "Reciprocity, Bureaucracy, and Ritual," "The Social Psychology of Warfare," and "Economic and Social Roots of the Arms Race," examine concepts and processes that are often ignored or given short shrift in books on nuclear weapons issues. Kurtz concludes with four chapters on the subject of "Preventing the Holocaust." His book would serve well as a core text for courses on nuclear weapons and nuclear war.

* 7.74 *
Lifton, Robert Jay, and Richard Falk. *Indefensible Weapons: The Political and Psychological Case Against Nuclearism*. New York: Basic Books, 1982. LC 82-76850. ISBN 0-465-03237-0 pa.

Lifton and Falk identify and critique the phenomenon of nuclearism, which they define as "…psychological, political, and military dependence on nuclear weapons, the embrace of the weapons as a solution to a wide variety of human dilemmas, most ironically that of 'security.'" The first part, written by Lifton, a psychiatrist, examines a wide range of psychological aspects of nuclearism, while the second, written by Falk, a scholar in international law and politics, traces its political causes and consequences. Both authors make recommendations for changes and reforms at the individual and political levels.

* 7.75 *
McLean, Scilla, ed. *How Nuclear Weapons Decisions Are Made*. New York: St. Martin's Press, 1986. LC 85-27869. ISBN 0-312-39530-2.

The chapters in this important compendium describe the organizations and procedures responsible for nuclear weapons policy in the United States, the Soviet Union, and other nuclear-armed nations.

* 7.76 *
Rhodes, Richard. *The Making of the Atomic Bomb*. New York: Simon & Schuster, 1986. LC 86-15445. ISBN 0-671-44133-7.

In this massive and richly detailed history of the development of the first atomic bombs and the decisions to drop them on the Japanese cities of Hiroshima and Nagasaki, Rhodes uses excerpts from diaries and memoirs to create vivid portraits of the individuals involved in one of the most significant enterprises in history. Rhodes provides a thorough explanation of the advances in nuclear physics that led to the atomic bomb and describes the violent wartime context in which it was used. He also uses accounts by Japanese survivors in order to reveal the nature of atomic destruction. His book won both the National Book Award and the Pulitzer Prize.

* 7.77 *
Sagan, Carl, and Richard Turco. *A Path Where No Man Thought: Nuclear Winter and the End of the Arms Race*. New York: Random House, 1990. LC 89-4315. ISBN 0-394-58307-8.

Two scientists who were involved in the discovery of the nuclear winter phenomenon make a major contribution to informed awareness of the nuclear threat. They assess recent scientific efforts to evaluate the probability that nuclear war would cause nuclear winter and conclude that even a "small" nuclear war would probably cause disastrous damage to the earth's ecosystem. They also criticize existing policy making about nuclear weapons for failing to adequately appreciate the danger of nuclear winter. And they offer a number of thoughtful proposals for reducing the risk of nuclear omnicide. Like Harkin and Thomas in 7.66, they argue against complacency about the nuclear threat even in a post-Cold War era: "Altogether there are nearly 60,000 nuclear weapons in the world. Behind the welcome improvements in rhetoric and relations, the machinery of mass murder still waits, purring and attentive." (p.xviii)

* 7.78 *
Sederberg, Peter C., ed. *Nuclear Winter, Deterrence and the Prevention of Nuclear War*. New York: Praeger, 1986. LC 86-8412. ISBN 0-275-92160-3 pa.

The contributors to this excellent collection were asked to discuss the implications for nuclear weapons policy of the so-called "nuclear winter" phenomenon, that is, the probability that even a "small" nuclear war would probably cause far greater damage to the planetary ecosystem than previously assumed. Their conclusions range from the conviction that nuclear winter has made nuclear deterrence obsolete to a reluctant acceptance of the fact that deterrence will remain a necessary policy into the distant future. Among the most noteworthy essays are Sederberg's on "Nuclear Winter: Paradoxes and Paradigm Shifts;" William Baugh's on "Dilemmas of Deterrence Policy;" and Robert Kennedy's on "Nuclear Winter, War Prevention, and the Nuclear Deterrent."

* 7.79 *
Somerville, John. "Nuclear 'War' Is Omnicide." In *Nuclear War: Philosophical Perspectives*. Ed. by Michael Allen Fox and Leo Groarke. New York: Peter Lang Publishing Co., 1985. LC 85-4274. ISBN 0-8204-0209-5.

Somerville was one of the first to use the concept of "omnicide" to refer to nuclear war.

* 7.80 *
Spector, Leonard S. *The Undeclared Bomb: The Spread of Nuclear Weapons, 1987-88*. Cambridge, MA: Ballinger Publishing Co, 1988. LC 88-28726. ISBN 0-88730-303-X.

Spector is one of the most widely respected authorities on the spread of nuclear weapons. Here he examines the political and military motives, as well as the technical means, for the proliferation of nuclear weapons. See also his more recent article, "The New Nuclear Nations," *Social Education* (March 1990): 143-145.

* 7.81 *
White, Ralph K., ed. *Psychology and the Prevention of Nuclear War: A Book of Readings*. New York: New York University Press, 1986. LC 85-15520. ISBN 0-8147-9203-0.

Edited by one of the pioneers in the psychological study of war and peace issues, this excellent collection of readings covers a wide range of topics, including psychological effects of the nuclear threat; psychological dimensions of nuclear deterrence; attitudes of "ordinary" citizens and leaders; sources of impaired perception and judgment by decision makers; management of crises; and approaches to resolving conflicts without resort to violence by negotiation, bargaining, and mediation.

* 7.82 *
Zuckerman, Edward. *The Day after World War III*. New York: The Viking Press, 1984. LC 83-040230. ISBN 0-670-25880-6.

Zuckerman provides a detailed account of past and present American plans for surviving nuclear war, with many fascinating details about actual arrangements. He also offers insights into the mindsets of individuals responsible for making the plans.

Commonalities and Connections between Genocide and Modern War

* 7.83 *
Aronson, Ronald. *The Dialectics of Disaster: A Preface to Hope*. London: Verso, 1983. (Dist. by Schocken Books.) ISBN 0-86091-075-X.

In this important book, Aronson makes a comparative analysis of the Nazi Holocaust, purges and other forms of mass killing under Stalin in the Soviet Union, and the American war in Vietnam. After examining commonalities and differences among these three historical cases, he analyzes two ongoing cases involving actual or potential violence, the Arab-Israeli conflict and the nuclear arms race. The overall goal of this creative book is to suggest answers to the question with which it begins: "Is there reason to hope today?" (p.ix) Three of the eight chapters directly address the question of hope in an age of violence.

* 7.84 *
Askenasy, Hans. *Are We All Nazis?* Secaucus, NJ: Lyle Stuart, 1978. LC 77-13596. ISBN 0-8184-0248-2.

In an angry, stimulating book, Askenasy asserts that some of the same psychological and social factors that made the Holocaust possible are still active and influential in modern nations, including the United States.

* 7.85 *
Bedau, Hugo Adam. "Genocide in Vietnam?" In *Philosophy, Morality, and International Affairs.* Ed. by Virginia Held, Sidney Morgenbesser, and Thomas Nagel. New York: Oxford University Press, 1974. LC 73-90349. ISBN 0-19-501759-5.

In an erudite paper, Bedau denies allegations that U.S. actions during its war in Vietnam, such as mass bombing, free-fire zones, and defoliation, constituted a case of genocide. He concludes that while such actions resulted in indiscriminate mass killing of civilians, there was not clear evidence of intent to destroy a group, in whole or in part, as required by the Genocide Convention for a finding of genocide. Bedau does suggest, however, that "The gap between the results of the present discussion and a verdict of genocide is not very wide" (p.45)

* 7.86 *
Bauman, Zygmunt. *Modernity and the Holocaust.* Ithaca, NY: Cornell University Press, 1989. LC 89-7274. ISBN 0-8014-2397-X.

Bauman's sociological analysis of the Holocaust illuminates other cases of twentieth century genocide and other forms of mass killing, like modern warfare. After decrying the relative neglect of the Holocaust by sociologists, Bauman states that he will *"treat the Holocaust as a rare but significant and reliable test of the hidden possibilities of modern society."* (emphasis in the original, p.12) In the remainder of the chapter, he proceeds to examine "the meaning of the civilizing process," the "social production of moral indifference," the "social production of moral invisibility," and the "moral consequences of the civilizing process." (p.18-30) In later chapters, he examines such themes as the "peculiarity of modern genocide," "dehumanization of bureaucratic objects," "the role of bureaucracy in the Holocaust," and "inhumanity as a function of social distance."

* 7.87 *
Charny, Israel W., in collaboration with Chanan Rapaport. *How Can We Commit the Unthinkable? Genocide, the Human Cancer.* Boulder, CO: Westview Press, 1982. LC 81-19784. ISBN 0-86531-358-X.

In this indispensable work, a pioneer in the field of genocide studies explores in detail social and psychological forces that enable ostensibly normal men and women to participate in genocides and other forms of mass killing. One of his provocative psychological conclusions is that mass murder of designated victims may be an attempt to cope with and master death-anxiety and other forms of insecurity in the victimizing group. (p.91-182) The final section of the book is titled, "Why Can There Still Be Hope?" and includes two chapters that explore the concept of "nonviolent aggression" and one that advocates a "genocide early warning system." The text is followed by a lengthy section of richly annotated footnotes.

* 7.88 *
Charny, Israel W. "Understanding the Psychology of Genocidal Destructiveness." In *Genocide: A Critical Bibliographic Review.* Ed. by Israel W. Charny. London: Mansell and New York: Facts on File, 1988. ISBN 0-7201-186-X (Mansell).

This concise account of Charny's thought on psychological and social factors in mass killing updates the entry above, 7.87. It consists of a narrative essay, followed by an annotated bibliography.

* 7.89 *
Collins, Randall. "Three Faces of Cruelty: Towards a Comparative Sociology of Evil." *Theory and Society* 1 (1974): 415-440.

In a crucial theoretical and empirical contribution to the understanding of collective violence and mass killing, Collins examines three dimensions of human cruelty: ferociousness—"This is the dimension of overt brutality...;" callousness—"brutality routinized and bureaucratized, cruelty without passion;" and asceticism—"the turning of cruelty against oneself and against others with whom one has solidarity." (p.419) Of the three, callousness is most characteristic of modern society, in large part because modern societies tend to be bureaucratically organized, and because "the structural organization of bureaucracy seems uniquely suited for the perpetration of callous violence" (p.432)

* 7.90 *
Coser, Lewis. "The Visibility of Evil." *Journal of Social Issues* 25, no. 1 (1969): 101-109.

In a pioneering, and still timely, contribution, Coser examines how "good," "normal" individuals can be induced to inflict cruelty and death on other human beings. A fundamental process, he finds, is the "denial of common humanity" between the killers and their victims. Coser analyzes a number of social and cultural factors that facilitate such dehumanization, including culturally-inculcated stereotypes, "restrictions on the span of sympathy," and simple "denial of knowledge."

* 7.91 *
Falk, Richard. "Ecocide, Genocide, and the Nuremberg Tradition of Individual Responsibility." In *Philosophy, Morality, and International Affairs*. Ed. by Virginia Held, Sidney Morgenbesser, and Thomas Nagel. New York: Oxford University Press, 1974. LC 73-90349. ISBN 0-19-501759-5.

Falk's is another thoughtful assessment of whether U.S. actions in the Vietnam war constituted genocide. Falk also considers parallels between genocide and ecocide, the deliberate destruction of habitat. See also 7.85 and 7.9.

* 7.92 *
Gault, William Barry. "Some Remarks on Slaughter." *American Journal of Psychiatry* 128, no. 4 (1971): 450-455.

On the basis of interviews with returning Vietnam combat veterans who had observed or participated in massacres of defenseless Vietnamese, the author, an Army psychiatrist, identifies several "principles contributing to slaughter." (p.451) These "devices...through which relatively normal men overcame and eventually neutralized their natural repugnance toward slaughter" included the inability to precisely define the enemy in a guerilla war ("the enemy is everywhere"); dehumanization of the victims—Gault uses the apt term "cartoonization;" "dilution of responsibility" through the chain of command; and the "ready availability of firepower." (p.451-452)

* 7.93 *
Group for the Advancement of Psychiatry. Committee on Social Issues. *Psychiatric Aspects of the Prevention of Nuclear War*. Report # 57. New York: American Psychiatric Association, 1964. LC 64-7800.

Dehumanization is the practice of regarding people targeted for violence as less than human and therefore undeserving of any moral or empathic considerations. Dehumanization, as this report documents, is an important factor in both modern warfare and in genocide.

* 7.94 *
Hart, Hornell. "Acceleration in Social Change." In *Technology and Social Change*. Ed. by Francis R. Allen, et al. New York: Appleton-Century-Crofts, 1957. LC 57-5944.

Hart's article is an early, but still very relevant, sociological analysis of the ever-increasing rate of cultural and technological change in the modern era. Of particular interest are Hart's discussions of "the accelerating power to kill and to destroy," accompanied by several excellent charts and graphs, and "why cultural change accelerates." The article by Francis Allen, "Influence of Technology on War," in the same volume is also excellent. Both authors document the massive increase in the destructive power of modern weapons and the consequently increased costs of war, both human and economic.

* 7.95 *
Hughes, Everett C. "Good People and Dirty Work." *Social Problems* 10, no. 1 (1962): 3-11.

Referring to the mass killings of the Holocaust, sociologist Hughes asks: "How and where could there be found in a modern civilized country the several hundred thousand men and women capable of such work?" (p.4) His answers to this question are relevant not only to the Holocaust, but also to other cases of governmental mass killing projects, including total war. Among his important points is his suggestion that "those pariahs who do the dirty work of society, e.g. exterminating society's 'enemies,' are really acting as agents for the rest of us." (p.7)

* 7.96 *
Johnson, Robert. "Institutions and the Promotion of Violence." In *Violent Transactions: The Limits of Personality*. Ed. by Anne Campbell and John J. Gibbs. Oxford and New York: Basil Blackwell, 1986. LC 86-8228. ISBN 0-631-14633-4.

Johnson analyzes some of the processes by which large-scale organizations facilitate contributions to violent outcomes by otherwise "ordinary" employees. These processes include bureaucratic routinization and division of labor, authorization, situational socialization, and dehumanization of both the implementers and victims of violence.

* 7.97 *
Katz, Steven T. "Technology and Genocide: Technology as a 'Form of Life.'" In *Echoes from the Holocaust: Philosophical Reflections on a Dark Time*. Ed. by Alan Rosenberg and Gerald Meyers. Philadelphia: Temple University Press, 1989.

Although this brilliant essay focuses specifically on the Holocaust, it illuminates how technology can facilitate other forms of mass killing, including war. Among the provocative concepts Katz analyses is the "technological mentality" (p.276) See also 7.98.

* 7.98 *
Lang, Berel. "Genocide and Omnicide: Technology at the Limits." In *Nuclear Weapons and the Future of Humanity: The Fundamental Questions*. Ed. by Steven Lee and Avner Cohen. Totowa, NJ: Rowman & Allenheld, 1986.

Lang reflects on how technology facilitated both the perpetration of the Holocaust and the preparations for nuclear omnicide. See also 7.97.

* 7.99 *
Kelman, Herbert C., and V. Lee Hamilton. *Crimes of Obedience: Toward a Social Psychology of Authority and Responsibility*. New Haven and London: Yale University Press, 1989.

Many of those involved in governmental mass killing projects justify their complicity by claiming to have "obeyed authority." Kelman and Hamilton examine several "crimes of obedience," including the cases of William Calley, Klaus Barbie, and Kurt Waldheim, in order to clarify the psychological and social dimensions of such crimes. The authors examine several social-psychological processes that facilitate violence by weakening moral and empathic restraints. Among these processes are authorization, routinization, and dehumanization. They also discuss the infamous "Obedience to Authority" experiments conducted by Stanley Milgram. The final chapter, "On Breaking the Habit of Unquestioning Obedience," is particularly noteworthy.

* 7.100 *
Kuper, Leo. "Epilogue: The Nuclear Arms Race and Genocide." In *The Prevention of Genocide*. New Haven: Yale University Press, 1985. LC 85-40465. ISBN 0-300-03418-0.

Kuper, one of the leading scholars of genocide, comments on "some of the implications of nuclear armaments, which now present an overwhelming threat of genocide, and indeed of omnicide, the extinction of our species." (p.228) Among his points: "Many sources of conditioning to nuclear warfare derive from quite ordinary routines in industry, government bureaucracies, and the armed forces. Some of the implications of their conditioning appear more clearly in the context of Nazi experience." (p.235) See also 7.102.

* 7.101 *
Lifton, Robert Jay. *The Broken Connection: On Death and the Continuity of Life*. New York: Simon and Schuster, 1979. LC 79-12886. ISBN 0-671-22561-8.

Lifton explores psychological issues relevant to genocide, war, and nuclear omnicide. He traces a sequence in genocidal killing from what he terms "psychohistorical dislocation," that is, disconcerting and bewildering confusion and anxiety caused by rapid social change and economic and political instability, to a desperate search for "cure" in the form of a totalitarian ideology that purports to explain the dislocation and provide a means for transcending it. The transcendence usually occurs by radically transforming the society at the expense of designated victims who become scapegoats for the perpetrators' anxieties and fears. Part III, "Death and History: The Nuclear Image" (p.283-387), and the chapters on "Dislocation and Totalism" and "Victimization and Mass Violence" are particularly valuable.

* 7.102 *
Lifton, Robert Jay, and Eric Markusen. *The Genocidal Mentality: Nazi Holocaust and Nuclear Threat*. New York: Basic Books, 1990. LC 89-43101. ISBN 0-465-02662-1.

Lifton and Markusen argue that the actual genocide carried out by the Nazis and the potential genocide inherent in the preparations for nuclear war both reflect an underlying mind-set which the authors term "the genocidal mentality." In the nuclear case, this "can be defined as a mind-set that includes individual and collective willingness to produce, deploy, and, according to certain standards of necessity, use weapons known to destroy entire human populations—millions, or tens or hundreds of millions, of people." (p.3) While recognizing important differences between the two cases, Lifton and Markusen identify and analyze a number of important parallels and commonalities. Among these commonalities are the embrace of a violent national security ideology in response to a sense of threat to the society; the use of science, and pseudo-science, to rationalize policies involving actual or potential mass killing; the involvement of highly-educated professionals in the enterprise; and the facilitating roles of bureaucratic organization, euphemistic language, and a variety of psychological defense mechanisms, such as psychic numbing and doubling. The authors devote a chapter to the question of victims of the Holocaust and potential victims of nuclear war. They conclude with a call for further development of a gradually emerging "species mentality," that is, "full consciousness of ourselves as members of the human species, a species now under threat of extinction...a sense of self that identifies with the entire human species." (p.258)

* 7.103 *
Markusen, Eric. "Genocide and Total War: A Preliminary Comparison." In *Genocide and the Modern Age*. Ed. by Isidor Wallimann and Michael Dobkowski. New York; Greenwood Press, 1987. LC 86-9978. ISBN 0-313-24198-8.

Markusen identifies a number of psychological, organizational, and technological factors common to both genocide and total war and concludes that "Warfare in the twentieth century has become increasingly genocidal, and several genocides...resemble military campaigns and utilize military forces in the killing process." (p.118)

* 7.104 *
Markusen, Eric. "Genocide, Total War, and Nuclear Omnicide." In *Genocide: A Critical Bibliographic Review, V. II*. Ed. by Israel W. Charny. London: Mansell and New York: Facts on File, 1991. ISBN 0-7201-2053-5 (Mansell).

Includes a discussion of genocide, total war, and the capacity for nuclear war as national security policies, as well as an analysis of organizational loyalty as an important psychosocial facilitating factor in several types of governmental mass killing.

* 7.105 *
Markusen, Eric, and David Kopf. *The Holocaust and Strategic Bombing: Genocide and Total War in the Twentieth Century*. Boulder, CO: Westview Press. Forthcoming.

The authors make a comparative analysis of genocide and war as two forms of state-sanctioned mass killing that focuses on the Holocaust as an exemplary case of genocide and the British and American strategic bombing campaigns of World War II as an exemplary case of total war. They analyze the two cases in terms of a conceptual framework of psychological, organizational, and technological facilitating factors, and then apply the framework to the nuclear arms race. Finally, they examine the implications of the study for other twentieth century wars and genocides.

* 7.106 *
Mason, Henry L. "Imponderables of the Holocaust." *World Politics* 34, no. 3 (1981): 90-113.

* 7.107 *
Mason, Henry L. "The Fate of the Earth and the Fate of the Jews: Responses to Holocaust." Unpublished manuscript. 124p. 1986.

* 7.108 *
Mason, Henry L. "Implementing the Final Solution: The Ordinary Regulating of the Extraordinary." *World Politics* 40, no. 4 (1988): 543-569.

All three of these works contribute important insights not only to the understanding of the Holocaust, but of genocide and other forms of mass killing as well, particularly with respect to ideological and institutional aspects. The 1986 monograph is a comparative analysis of the Holocaust and the capacity for nuclear omnicide. Mason is a Professor in the Department of Political Science at Tulane University, New Orleans, Louisiana 70118.

* 7.109 *
Merton, Robert K. "Bureaucratic Structure and Personality." In *Social Theory and Social Structure*. Ed. by Robert K. Merton. New York: The Free Press, 1957. LC 56-10581.

Merton's is a concise, classic analysis of the nature of bureaucracy and the multiple effects of bureaucracies on individuals working within them. Of particular relevance are his discussions of "trained incapacities" and "the stress on the depersonalization of relationships."

* 7.110 *
Nash, Henry T. "The Bureaucratization of Homicide." *Bulletin of the Atomic Scientists* 36, no. 4 (1980): 22-27.

In this very significant article, Nash, a former intelligence analyst in the Air Targets Division of the U.S. Air Force, explains how the bureaucratic nature of his working environment made it possible "calmly to plan to incinerate vast numbers of unknown human beings without any sense of moral revulsion." (p.22) Among factors Nash discusses are the preoccupation with technique and puzzle-solving at the expense of moral-ethical concerns and the use of euphemistic language that mutes the full reality of the work being done.

* 7.111 *
Opotow, Susan, ed. "Moral Exclusion and Injustice." *Journal of Social Issues* 46, no. 1 (1990): 1-99.

Among the most noteworthy articles in this valuable collection are "Psychological Roots of Moral Exclusion," by Morton Deutsch; "Selective Activation and Disengagement of Moral Control," by Albert Bandura; and "Moral Exclusion, Personal Goal Theory, and Extreme Destructiveness," by Evrin Staub.

* 7.112 *
Peattie, Lisa. "Normalizing the Unthinkable." *Bulletin of the Atomic Scientists* 40, no. 3 (1984): 32-36.

Peattie explicitly compares the Holocaust to the preparations for nuclear war. She suggests that "There appears to be no situation so abnormal, experientially, socially, morally, that human beings, if not totally stunned out of all reactivity, will not at least strive to assimilate it to normal practice..." (p.32) She then analyzes how the division of labor in both enterprises contributed importantly to the process of normalization.

* 7.113 *
Sanford, Nevitt, Craig Comstock, and Associates, eds. *Sanctions for Evil*. San Francisco, CA: Jossey-Bass, 1971. LC 79-129769. ISBN 0-87589-077-6.

This is a pioneering collection of essays on social and psychological processes that facilitate collective violence and mass killing. The titles of only a few of the chapters will give a hint of the range of issues that are examined: "Conditions for Guilt-Free Massacre," by Troy Duster; "Groupthink Among Policymakers," by Irving Janis; "Authoritarianism and Social Destructiveness" by Nevitt Sanford; "Evil and the American Ethos," by Robert Bellah; "Existential Evil," by Robert Jay Lifton; and "Resisting Institutional Evil from Within," by Jan Howard and Robert Somers.

* 7.114 *
Staub, Ervin. *Roots of Evil: The Origins of Genocide and Other Group Violence*. Cambridge and New York: Cambridge University Press, 1989. LC 89-32632. ISBN 0-521-35407-2.

An authority on altruism grapples with the problem of mass killing in this valuable book. In the first part, Staub develops a conceptual framework of psychological and social factors that account for how "a subgroup of society...comes to be mistreated and destroyed by a more powerful group or government." (p.4) In the middle two parts, he tests the applicability of his conceptual framework by comparatively analyzing four cases of genocide and mass killing: the Holocaust, the Turkish genocide of the Armenians, the Cambodian "autogenocide" from 1975 through 1978, and the "disappearances" and murders of civilians in Argentina during the 1970s. Finally, in the fourth part, he discusses the origins of war and then applies the lessons from the comparative analysis, as well as his earlier work on prosocial and altruistic behavior, to the problem of creating "a world of nonaggression, cooperation, caring, and human connection." (p.283)

* 7.115 *
Weber, Max. "Bureaucracy." In *From Max Weber: Essays in Sociology*. Ed. by H.H. Gerth and C. Wright Mills. New York: Oxford University Press, 1946. LC 46-5298.

The classic analysis of the characteristics of bureaucracies.

Chapter 8

EARLY WARNING, INTERVENTION, AND PREVENTION OF GENOCIDE

by **Israel W. Charny**

The record of governments on the prevention of, or intervention in, genocide has always been very poor. Even those states that can be called the bastions of democracy, such as the United States and Israel, have deeply tarnished records. In part to counterbalance the performance of governments, it is urgently necessary to make individuals far more aware than they have been of their responsibility to guard against the intrusion of attitudes that promote genocide. Charny analyzes various key indicators that new genocidal threats may be taking shape. Governments should immediately give their support to several international initiatives for the prevention of genocide, such as the creation of an International Genocide Bureau or a World Genocide Tribunal.

The Foreseeability of Genocide

After a genocide has occurred, there are many people all around the world who care very much about the fates of the victims, the unbearable pain of the survivors and their extended families, and the survival of their national, ethnic, or religious group. However, human society has thus far failed, one can say almost completely, to take strong and effective stands against *ongoing* events of genocide or genocide which threatens to occur in the *foreseeable future*.

It can be argued that some or perhaps even much of the Holocaust could have been prevented had the world taken notice of the information that was coming in about the incredible murders of the Jews. To this day, for example, there are many who are critical of both the United States and British governments at the time for failing to commit any military resources to bombing the supply lines to Auschwitz, if not sections of Auschwitz itself—as Jews had requested of the Allied governments at the time. Similarly, there are many criticisms of the International Red Cross, which maintained silence about its knowledge of Hitler's death camps.[1] There are even criticisms of Zionist organizations, in the United States and in the Jewish community of then-Palestine, for failing to take sufficient actions against Hitler in the 1930s, the years when the discriminatory Nuremberg laws were being passed and persecutions were occurring daily, even before the actual full-blown death machinery was launched. In each of these cases, the parties who *could* have helped had their own "good reasons" for not offering the help they could have given.

No Cooperation with Mass Killers

In each case, there was a "reasonable" argument why Hitler could not be opposed more openly because of what it would have "cost" to do so: America and England needed their full resources for the war effort and did not want to "waste" one soldier or one bomb on missions that weren't critical to the war effort; the International Red Cross was concerned not to be barred by Hitler from rendering its important services to other people in need in the various countries of Europe that Hitler occupied; and the Zionists were concerned before the outbreak of the war about getting out as many Zionist Jews as they could from Germany and Europe, and wanted the cooperation of the Nazi officials for this purpose.

To fight genocide, one has to have a conviction that, at no point in history and despite any self-interest, one must never cooperate with any form of mass killing, genocidal massacre, or genocide.

It is interesting that in personal situations of murder, most people would not hesitate to choose the principle that murder must be opposed even if it costs them something. Would you agree to be paid off to remain silent about the murder of your neighbor? Would you agree to "forget" a murder that you saw in your community in order to protect yourself from the retaliations of the murderer against yourself and your family?

Somehow when the patterns of murder are larger, involving thousands and millions of people, it is easier to persuade people to watch out for their own interests and to avoid the risks of intervention.

The Record of Governments Is Very Poor

The record of governments on genocide is often, if not virtually always, very poor. At the level of international government, following the sincere hopes of much of humankind in creating the UN and in passage of the United Nations Convention on Genocide in the wake of World War II, the real record, as described by Professor Leo Kuper of UCLA in *The Prevention of Genocide*,[2] is a sorry one of indifference, cynicism, impotence, and most outrageous manipulations by member nations. Thus, former Amnesty America President David Hawk has done intrepid research on the genocide in Cambodia and created a Cambodia Documentation Commission which undertook to prepare a legal brief to bring charges against the government of Cambodia before the World Court in fulfillment of the procedures of the UN Genocide Convention. After several years of arduous work in preparing the necessary legal materials, the Commission found that it could enlist no country in the world which was a member state of the United Nations to formally bring the charges.[3]

There are two reasons why even governments of democratic societies do so poorly. The first is that, insofar as a government itself is a perpetrator of genocide, its reflex reaction is to defend itself from scrutiny and criticism, and therefore correction becomes unlikely. In the case of totalitarian governments, the intention of the government from the outset will be to deceive everyone including its own people and suppress protest and opposition to its genocidal policy.

The second major obstacle is that the overwhelming consideration of governments is, always, one of pragmatic self-interest and realism, which, of course, is what we mean by ***Realpolitik***. This situation is not unlike that of major tobacco companies that go on promoting their products in the face of the overwhelming scientific evidence that smoking brings death to millions of people.

Governments have been known to rationalize their policies of "playing ball" with other genocidal nations on the basis of every possible consideration: business needs, protection of one's own nationals, even the idea that maintaining a presence in the genocidal country will make it more possible to moderate the genocidal policy sometime in the future! Almost invariably, the truth is that underlying these policies of collaboration with a genocidal nation we will find a) a value system that places cynical realism and ambition above any consideration of genuine ethical or spiritual commitments to other peoples' lives, and b) indifference, if not contempt, for the minority that is being victimized.

Ugly Behaviors in the Bastions of Democracy

In this essay, I use examples particularly from the two countries in which I am privileged to be at home and about which I care deeply. Both are proudly committed to the deepest democratic values: one is the greatest power on earth today, the United States; the other is a struggling tiny nation built on the ashes of the most severe instance of genocide in human history, Israel. The ugly behaviors and values that surface even in these outstanding bastions of democracy teach us that the evolutionary challenge for people and nations to commit themselves to genuine protection of all human life is a huge task that basically is still far beyond our Earth-civilization.

The U.S. and Pol Pot

Government complicity in mass murders is far from ancient history.[4] In our times, we have the continuing example of the United States maintaining diplomatic recognition of Pol Pot and his Khmer Rouge party as the legitimate ruling authority of the nation of Cambodia. This situation would be akin to the United States continuing to recognize Hitler and his Nazi party, had he lived following World War II. Why did America continue to recognize Pol Pot? America could not bear the alternative of recognizing the Communist regime installed in Cambodia by the government of Vietnam, which is the hated Communist government that America had been unable to defeat in the Vietnam war. The parallel to this situation in the World War II scenario would have been that America had chosen to continue recognizing Hitler in order to avoid doing any kind of business with the Soviet-installed Communist rulers of East Germany. Pol Pot and his Khmer Rouge party had killed between 1 and 3 million Cambodian people out of a population of 7 million—cruelly, bizarrely, as was described so vividly in the movie "The Killing Fields." Was there any justification whatsoever for continuing to recognize him, even if it did "cost us something?" As this article was being written, there were more than a few indications that Pol Pot may yet reconquer Cambodia and create a new ruling government.[5] If he does so, it will be due in no small part to American recognition and actual material support given him these many years despite his despicable crimes.

The U.S., Israel, and China

The nations of the world today face the same question with regard to the People's Republic of China. In July 1989, the government of China massacred an estimated five thousand students in Tiananmen Square in Peking. Within a week, *the government of China was denying that a massacre had taken place*. China has given the world a living example of how governments deny their actions and then rewrite history.[6] In the year that followed, it is reported that ten thousand people have been jailed for their participation or sympathy with the students' movement that had been demanding greater freedom. Yet there are nations today that are cultivating relations with China, and the United States is one of these. Even though Congress insisted that the U.S. suspend relations with China, President Bush used his executive authority to renew cordial relations with them. Israel is another country that has cultivated contact with China in its eagerness to gain recognition from this mammoth power and to cultivate with it economic relationships that would strengthen her security.

Israel, the U.S., and the Armenian Genocide

Perhaps the most troubling example today of the inherent tendency of government as a bureaucratic organizational process to cultivate indifference to victims is found in certain actions of the Israeli government. Many of us would have expected this government to be the outstanding exception in our era because of the Jewish people's profound awareness of the horrors of massacre, the dangers of corrupt government, and its own outrage at the indifference of nations when Jewish victims were being led to their deaths in the Holocaust.

Yet Israel's Foreign Ministry ordered its diplomatic staff in the United States to lobby in 1989 against passage of legislation in the U.S. Senate introducing a commemorative day for the Armenian genocide.[7] The government of Turkey bitterly opposes such legislation and any public confirmation of the Ottoman Turkish genocide of the Armenians in 1915-1922, and even threatens to withdraw from NATO if such legislation is passed. Both the Reagan administration and the Bush administration have bowed completely to the Turks; in fact Bush did so after having given a pledge to the Armenian community during his campaign to support such legislation. Israel's explanation is that it must protect its interests with its nearby Moslem neighbor, Turkey, that Israel is a small nation, and Jews have learned from history that they must take care of themselves.

Another explanation that has been reported in the press, which to the credit of Israeli society roundly criticized the government position, is that "we don't want other nations like the Armenians and the Cambodians comparing their genocides to the Holocaust," meaning that nobody else's genocidal tragedy should be allowed to be compared with the unique tragedy of the Holocaust of the Jewish people—an argument which I have heard myself from a senior Foreign Ministry official when we were arguing back in 1982 over the ministry's demands that we remove any papers on the Armenian genocide from the agenda of the International Conference on the Holocaust and Genocide which we were convening in Tel Aviv.[8]

The Responsibility of Individuals

Both the United States and the State of Israel obviously should know better about doing *any* kind of business with mass killers, no matter how "practical" it may be. I hope this article will inspire some readers to choose to stand up and demand that their government take consistent ethical actions against any genocide. The responsibility of individuals also includes taking a stand against human rights violations and dehumanization of any people, and having the courage to refuse to follow any orders, even when one serves in a military organization, that call for the murders of innocent people. It also means refusing to accept assignments to plan such actions for the future. Some years ago, a graduate of one of America's great military academies was ordered to prepare plans for preemptive strikes against the cities of the Soviet Union and refused; he was ordered to quarters, courtmartialled, and then given a dishonorable discharge from the military. In the context of the fears America held of Soviet nuclear attacks, it was ostensibly legitimate for the United States military to be planning scenarios of defense against a possible enemy, but this young military officer knew that the planning of self-defense cannot include preparations for murdering hundreds of thousands and millions of civilians. He was prepared to pay a price for standing up for what he knew to be a true principle of American democracy, the universal principle of respect for human life.

The Courage to Withstand One's Own Nation

There is no easy way for an individual to make an enduring commitment against genocide. For when the time comes, if we are citizens of a state that is committing genocide, it means that we must have the courage to stand up against our own nation, society, perhaps even our own families.

This was the choice Germans had to make during World War II, whether to follow the orders to commit the murders that Hitler and his staff demanded of them or to defy those orders and attempt to circumvent their own government. Interestingly enough, in recent years a study has been reported of some hundred Germans who did refuse to follow orders, and to everyone's surprise it has turned out that the majority were not made to pay for their refusal.[9] But of course it is not always possible to count on this. On the contrary, the choice of standing for principle has to include thinking about whether or not one would be prepared to make the ultimate sacrifice of oneself rather than participate in killing innocent others. All the information we have from public opinion studies and social science studies suggests that the majority of Americans, and the majority of all human beings in this world, *would* do what they were told if they were commanded by their superior officers in the military, or their government officials, to go and kill masses of helpless men, women, and children of another people.[10] I want this essay to raise the question for you the reader *whether you are the kind of person who is willing to be different in principle*. The chart on page 154 indicates what a willingness to be different entails.

Proposal for a World Genocide Early Warning System Foundation[10a]

The concept of a Genocide Early Warning System has been published in a variety of articles and chapters, and has earned strong positive reviews from human rights specialists, social scientists, and some national leaders. Willie Brandt, former Chancellor of West Germany, wrote, "Your plan to develop concepts and proposals for disseminating the information on the genocide and human rights data bank sounds fascinating. I would like to assure you that I am ready to give my moral support." A former U.S. Deputy Assistant Secretary of State for Human Rights, Roberta Cohen, says, "Your proposal to establish a Genocide Early Warning System is an excellent idea. Had such a system operated effectively in the past, countless lives might have been saved in many parts of the world."

The purpose of the Genocide Early Warning System is to collect information on three levels. First and foremost, it is to assemble information of ongoing genocides and massacres in the world on a regular, authoritative basis. Second, it is to maintain a continuous monitoring of information on human rights violations. Third, it is to be the basis for a series of researches to understand more of the patterns through which massacre, mass murder, and genocide build up in a society, so that we will learn how to predict and alert people to the increasing dangers of mass murders in different societies well before they happen.

There is no data bank for human rights information in the world today. Moreover, there is no responsible ongoing information source for the news of severe conditions of massacre and mass murder. What happens characteristically is that the information is reported episodically in certain newspapers. At the time of these reports they are often, characteristically, described as "unconfirmed" or "alleged." In any case, having printed the news, these newspapers tend *not* to follow up with many subsequent stories because, after all, the story has already been printed! In other words, from the point of view of the news that "makes news," once a massacre has been reported, even its continuation may not be that "interesting" to those news sources that see themselves as having to provide a kind of entertainment quality with "new" stories for their readers.

The problem goes deeper, however. Even if the news tracking is more complete—as happens when some country or area of the world seizes the imagination of the rest of the world—the reader still is left with an experience of learning that something terrible has happened that he or she can do nothing about. Such experiences often produce feelings of despair or cynicism or both for readers.

The purpose of creating a Genocide Early Warning System Foundation is to help to develop a center that not only will receive, house, and make available on a continuous basis information of ongoing massacres in the world, but also that will be an international agency on behalf of human society as it speaks for the intention of humankind to care about and protect human life. The informations to be delivered to society by the early warning system are not only to maintain updated factual information, but also to convey the presence of an international agency that represents the evolution of a humane society which intends to keep a spotlight on the wrongdoings of mass murder. Sadly, the millions of words written about genocides to date represent essentially crying after the task is over. The real purpose of early warnings of genocide is to help the world develop new energies and new forms for attacking mass murder long before the murderers have completed their horrible task.

The Genocide Early Warning System we have planned is built on a conceptual structure that assembles information over a long term about the basic processes in each society which *support human life* and those which are moving towards the *destruction of human life*. Both processes are known to be present in all societies. An equal balance of these processes favors the protection of human life as the desired hallmark of a society which will be unavailable to engage in mass murder. Clearly, in some societies long before any mass murder has been executed, the balance in some societies is very much tipped towards destruction of human life.

The Genocide Early Warning System identifies *ongoing processes* as differentiated from *critical incidents*, which are also recorded; the first refers to, for instance, the degree of protection of free speech, or the degree of discrimination of minorities, while the second refers to dramatic events such as a major turn in policy as a result of the emergence of a new leader, the impact of going to war, or economic breakdown.

Another level of analysis assembles informations about *societal processes* as a whole such as previously described in the way of a free press, or the role of law, along with the roles of *leadership* or the major decisions and implementations by presidents, prime ministers, dictators, church leaders, and heads of states or cultures.

These levels of information are studied along a time continuum that begins with the ongoing situation in a culture long before there may have developed what we call *the genocidal fantasy or ideology*. The monitoring continues by tracking when an idea of genocide begins to be widely proposed and approved in a society, and gains political support of groups of people who actually try to organize to implement the genocidal plan. Thus, when Hitler speaks of destroying the Jews long before actual Holocaust events have come into reality, these moments are tracked by the Genocide Early Warning System as dangerous moments that already go beyond underlying historic patterns of antisemitism in the society. When even in the great American democracy, an ethnic religious leader such as Louis Farrakhan openly celebrates with his black community the burning of Jews in the ovens, this is a category of information that signals increased danger in the Genocide Early Warning System. The early warning system is responsive to any ideas that refer to keeping other groups of people "in their places," "kicking out" an ethnic, national, or religious group from the society, and certainly any ideas about eliminating them in a "final solution." Even in a society under siege from its obvious enemies, such as Israel which is surrounded by several Arab states that have a long history of intention and have never given up the idea of destroying the Jewish state, plans that are proposed in the Israeli society for getting rid of the Arabs in a forced migration or "transfer" will be registered in the early warning system as a formulation of a genocidal fantasy or ideology that has to be watched carefully.[11]

The Genocide Early Warning System continues by observing any events in a society which can become triggers or precipitants for further escalations of the destructive trends and genocidal fantasies present in that society. Often these involve rumors of terrorist events that have been directed at one's people which understandably fan the retaliatory instincts of the population. This is the classic prescription of pogroms throughout history; for example, rumors that Jews killed a Christian sparked many pogroms or violent massacre of Jews. What are *natural* feelings of revenge are taken as a basis for unleashing the virulent genocidal mentality that has been awaiting in the society—as ultimately it awaits in *all* human societies at this point in our evolution as a species.

Finally, the Genocide Early Warning System tracks those situations and events where actual legalization and institutionalization of genocide in a given society begin to take place: the military give orders to kill the targeted group; the legal system justifies those who do the killing; the church system ignores or trains students to applaud the killing. In this manner the various institutions of society are coopted and corrupted as supporters of genocide.

As the accompanying typology shows, the Genocide Early Warning System has identified ten major early warning processes which are studied along the axes described above.

Chart: Taking a Stand Against Genocide

Tasks	Past	Present	Future
Knowing about genocide	Knowing about genocides that have taken place	Knowing about genocides that are taking place today or are imminent	Knowing about ethnic hatred and major human rights violations and other early warnings of possible development of genocide
	Combatting denials of genocide ("There were no gas chambers in the so-called Holocaust." There was no Armenian genocide.")		
Preparing to take a moral stand as an individual	Honoring memorials of past genocides	Refusing to participate in, approve, or allow prejudice, intolerance, dehumanization, human rights violations, and violence toward others	
		Refusing to follow social norms or to obey direct instructions or orders to commit genocide	
Taking a stand against in collective political responses to one's government and in other collective areas such as work and church	Supporting public commemoration of past genocides out of respect to the victim people and to establish more positive traditions of "man's greater humanity to man"	Opposing, through public protests, nonviolent resistance or revolution, legal genocide or any policy of mass murder or genocide	

Early Warning Processes

Early Warning Process 01. The Valuing of Human Life. The valuing of human life refers to the basic norms in any given society with respect to the degree to which human life is to be valued or not. Life is cheap in totalitarian societies. It can also be held cheap in other ways, such as in societies that provide medical and rehabilitative services indifferently or callously, after a nuclear accident. The respect and value which are placed on human life are important aspects of a society when it must face the possibility of being drawn into committing mass murders of a target group.

Early Warning Process 02. Concern with the Quality of Human Experience. The second indicator is the concern that a society shows for the quality of human experience, and whether and to what extent the norms of society are that people should be given the opportunity to live out their lives as comfortably as possible with respect to basic shelter, food, medical treatment, opportunity to work, freedom from oppression, free speech, and so forth. Societies that do not care about their own people are hardly likely to care about others.

Early Warning Process 03. The Valuing of Power. This early warning indicator refers to the ways in which power is valued in a society. Power in the sense of self-affirmation is necessary to work the engines of life of both individuals and groups, but when the goals of power are to gain control over other people, dominate them, enslave them, and exploit them, such a power orientation is inherently a harbinger of policies of torture, disappearance, execution, and genocidal massacres.

Early Warning Process 04. Machinery for Managing Escalations of Threat. This early warning process refers to the development of a machinery for managing escalations of threat. Objective threats are omnipresent in human life, but there are also dangers of subjective exaggerations and distortions in the human experiences of threats, so that there is a serious need for cross-checking of information and checks-and-balances on the powers of decision makers who formulate the policies of responding to dangers. Thus, there were American military and political leaders who called earnestly for pre-emptive nuclear strikes against the population centers of the Soviet Union in the years before *Glasnost* and *Perestroika*. What a tragedy that would have been.

Early Warning Process 05. Orientation Towards Force for Self-defense and in Solution of Conflicts. A society's orientation towards force for self-defense in its solution of conflicts is the next early warning process. It is, of course, a continuation of the previous indicator since the question now is how much force should be used in response to varying degrees of threat aimed towards one's people. It is human to want to destroy our enemies completely, but there are dangers of misjudging threats; the use of force in self-defense in itself may be excessively brutal and destructive, and no longer for defense as it is for brutality, sadism, and murder. The preservation of life is no less a continuing moral goal when one has to use force in self-defense than it is in times before the crisis.

Early Warning Process 06. Overt Violence and Destructiveness. This early warning process involves a society's use of overt violence and destructiveness. Some societies are concerned that their police, army, and population at large not be inherently violent, so that, for example, police do not kill even when they are doing their duty to stop criminals and enemies. The unarmed English bobby with his night stick was a symbol for many years of this kind of police power which is intended to minimize undue escalation and use of violence. The degree to which violence is heralded, rehearsed, and taught on American television is obviously connected to the very real dangers too many Americans face from assault and murder in many cities across their great continent. A society that limits exposure to violence in its media, and develops more mature attitudes in its journalistic reports of actual events of violence, can also be expected to be less susceptible to being drawn into genocidal violences towards others.

Early Warning Process 07. Dehumanization of a Potential Victim Target Group. This early warning process refers to dehumanization of a potential victim target group. "Polok jokes" and "nigger jokes" that may seem like innocuous humor can become the basis in the anxious times of societies for assigning target groups of peoples a status as *less-than-human* or *non-human*, and therefore not deserving of the protections that human society gives to its bonafide members.

Every person and every society must decide how much to curtail the natural humor of ethnic differences, especially when these become manifestly prejudicial statements openly devaluing and degrading another group. When in a society there develops an actual choice of whether or not to attack and exterminate a given minority group, the extent to which that minority previously has been assigned a role of sub-human or non-human will play an important role even in the readiness of the soldiers on the front line to execute such a policy.

Early Warning Process 08. Perception of Victim Group as Dangerous. This early warning process is the perception of the potential victim group as dangerous. Incongruously, many of the minority groups who have been targeted as less-than-us or not-human at the same time are treated as if they were a most dangerous force that threatens to wipe out an entire society. In other words, the dehumanized are also invested with super-human powers. As groups they are alleged to have physical, economic, religious, or racial powers to destroy us, and this situation naturally means that it is proper to invoke self-defense mechanisms against them, and to seek to "destroy them before they destroy us." The fact that these people also have been defined as not-human then allows one to be cruel and brutal to them. Genocide is now fully possible.

Early Warning Process 09. Availability of Victim Group. The early warning system continues with a dimension of the availability of the victim group. This topic is very difficult to speak about. There is no justification for any degree of excusing victimizers as if their victims were "asking for it" or were in any way to blame for being available to be victimized. Responsibility for the victimization by the perpetrator stands in its own right and must be totally condemned. However, without losing respect for the victims or empathy for their plight, it has to be noted that groups and nations that are, to begin with, defenseless, weak, naive, and susceptible to being bullied and terrorized do make the victimization process more possible. Thus, the State of Israel represents a necessary historical corrective process by which the Jewish people have moved from being naive scholars of the Bible and romantic believers in the goodness of God to being a strong nation with an excellent army that will, legitimately, never again allow Jews to be killed en masse. The fact also is that, when former victim-peoples become strong, they must also learn not to overuse their power as other nations have done to them.

Early Warning Process 10. Legitimation of Victimization by Leadership Individuals and Institutions.

This indicator refers to an advanced stage in development of genocide when a society's leadership actually endorses and ratifies the mass destruction. The strongmen of the government or the cabinet authorize and praise the killing of the targeted victim-people. The courts dismiss or simply do not bring charges against perpetrators, the churches bless in the names of their gods, and so on.

Other Proposals for Preventing Genocide

A variety of thinkers and groups have made similar proposals for early warnings of genocides. Speaking for the Baha'i International Community, a great faith that holds as a cardinal principle the oneness of humankind, in an address given in London in March 1982, Gerald Knight called for the development of an International Genocide Bureau.[12] He said then what is still true today:

At the moment there is no focus, no central clearing house for cases of genocide. No agency exists for concentrating world attention specifically on genocide. A Genocide Bureau would pay particular attention to countries during times of national crises—war, revolution, political conflict, economic emergency—because genocide is especially likely to be attempted under the cover of nationwide disorder and confusion and when international attention is focused on other issues. As soon as genocide was suspected, the Genocide Bureau would immediately investigate.

Secrecy is the greatest ally of any government involved in genocide, and one of the functions of the Genocide Bureau would be to mobilize public opinion and put pressure on the guilty government by exposing its activities.

Attorney Luis Kutner[13] created a proposal for what he called a *World Genocide Tribunal*. Political scientists Louis Beres[14] and Barbara Harff[15] have written, independently, about the need for legal principles that would justify *humanitarian intervention* by one nation into situations when another nation has entered into a policy of mass killings of a targeted people. As noted earlier, David Hawk created the *Cambodia Documentation Commission* and has attempted to create a legal brief to bring charges against the government of Cambodia.

International Alert

Leo Kuper of UCLA, the doyen of scholarship on genocide in the world today, proposed some years ago creating a new organization, *International Alert*, which has since come into being.[16] The first secretary-general of International Alert in London was Martin Ennals, a former secretary-general of Amnesty International for many years, who believes now that the time has come to begin dealing not only with government imprisonment and torture of individuals which is what Amnesty specializes in (although it is also concerned with some broader aspects of extra-judicial executions by governments), but also with governments committing mass murder and genocide. International Alert seeks to intervene at the level of government and the international system as soon as possible after news of mass murders arises. It is also noteworthy that the United States Department of State issues an annual report on human rights in countries around the world, and increasingly the European Parliament takes stands on violations of human rights.

Conclusions

There is no question but that a variety of people and institutions are groping towards articulating a new worldwide awareness of human rights and genocide, but most of these initiatives are in their infancy, and are highly irregular, relatively unsupported, and unsystemized. It is not yet clear if any of them will be able to generate a momentum that will support the development of a permanent system for monitoring genocide in this world.

Our proposal of a Genocide Early Warning System was hailed by *Choice*, a library review magazine, as "brilliant." It was noted by the *New York Times Book Review* as a "noteworthy contribution to thinking about the condition of humanity on the earth." And it has been recognized and hailed by a United Nations study on genocide, which wrote as follows:

Many welcome the establishment of early warning systems of potential genocide situations in order to prevent recurrence of the crime. Intelligent anticipation of potential cases could be based on the databank of continuously updated information, which might enable remedial, deterrent or avert measures to be planned ahead. Reliable information is the essential oxygen for human rights: this could be facilitated by the development of the United Nations satellite communications network. The Institute on the Holocaust and Genocide in Israel has proposed such a body.

A Lutheran minister, Pastor Niemoeller, who was a victim of the Nazis, spoke out about the importance of all of us caring about all other people. The beautiful poetic statement attributed to him has become a profound source of inspiration. It is a statement that goes to the heart of what the proposal to monitor genocide in the world involves:

> First they came for the Jews
> and I did not speak out—
> because I was not a Jew.
>
> Then they came for the communists
> and I did not speak out—
> because I was not a communist.
>
> Then they came for the trade unionists
> and I did not speak out—
> because I was not a trade unionist.
>
> Then they came for me—
> and there was no one left
> to speak out for me.

NOTES

1. Arieh Ben-Tov, *Facing the Holocaust in Budapest: The International Committee of the Red Cross and the Jews in Hungary, 1943-1945* (Geneva: Henry Dunant Institute; Dordrecht: Martinus Nijhoff, 1988).

2. Leo Kuper, *Genocide: Its Political Use in the Twentieth Century* (London: Penguin Books, 1981).

3. David Hawk, "The CDC [Cambodia Documentation Commission] View of the UN Peace Plan for Cambodia," *Newsletter of the Institute for the Study of Genocide* no. 7 (1991): 11-12. See also "Campaign to Bring Khmer Rouge to Trial," *Internet on the Holocaust and Genocide* Issue 10 (June 1987): 1; "In Cambodia It Can Happen Again," *Internet on the Holocaust and Genocide* Issue 23 (November 1989): 4; Hurst Hannum, "International Law and Cambodia Genocide: The Sounds of Silence," *Human Rights Quarterly* 11 (1989): 82-138.

4. Israel W. Charny, "A Proposal for a New Encompassing Definition of Genocide, Including New Legal Categories of Accomplices to Genocide and Genocide as a Result of Ecological Destruction and Abuse," presented to the First Raphael Lemkin Symposium on Genocide, Yale University Law School, February 1991.

5. "Fears of Khmer Rouge in Cambodia Mount," *Internet on the Holocaust and Genocide* Issue 18 (December 1988): 1-2 and "In Cambodia It Can Happen Again," 4.

6. "China Gives Contemporary Example of Government Denial of Genocidal Massacre," *Internet on the Holocaust and Genocide* Issue 22 (September 1989): 1.

7. "Government Opposition to Armenian Genocide Bill Provokes Widespread Protest in Israel," *Internet on the Holocaust and Genocide* Issue 23 (November 1989): 2.

8. Israel W. Charny and Shamai Davidson, eds., *The Book of the International Conference on the Holocaust and Genocide* (Tel Aviv: Institute of the International Conference on the Holocaust and Genocide, 1983).

9. David H. Kitterman, "Those Who Said 'No': Germans Who Refused to Execute Civilians During World War II," *German Studies Review* 11, no. 2 (1988): 241-254.

10. Ron Jones, "The Third Wave," in *Experiencing Social Psychology*, ed. by Ayala Pines and Christina Maslach (New York: Alfred A. Knopf, 1984); Herbert C. Kelman and V. Lee Hamilton, *Crimes of Obedience: Toward a Social Psychology of Authority and Responsibility* (New Haven, CT, and London: Yale University Press, 1989); Stanley Milgram, *Obedience to Authority* (New York: Harper & Row, 1974).

10a. The concept of a Genocide Early Warning System was formulated by me some years ago and then developed in detail in collaboration with Chanan Rapaport, then director of the Szold National Institute for Behavioral Sciences in Jerusalem.

11. Israel W. Charny and Daphna Fromer, "The Readiness of Health Profession Students to Comply with a Hypothetical Program of Forced Migration of a Minority Population," *American Journal of Orthopsychiatry* 60, no. 4 (1990): 486-495.

12. Gerald Knight, "A Genocide Bureau" (Editor's title). Text of a talk delivered at the Symposium on Genocide, London, 20 March 1982. Mimeographed, 14p.

13. Luis Kutner and Ernest Katin, "World Genocide Tribunal: A Proposal for Planetary Preventive Measures Supplementing a Genocide Early Warning System," in *Toward the Understanding and Prevention of Genocide*, ed. by Israel W. Charny (Boulder, CO: Westview Press, 1984).

14. Louis Rene Beres, "Genocide, State and Self," *Denver Journal of International Law and Policy* 18, no. 1 (1989): 37-57.

15. Barbara Harff, "Humanitarian Intervention," in *Genocide: A Critical Bibliographic Review* V.2., ed. by Israel W. Charny (London: Mansell Publishing Ltd. and New York: Facts on File, 1991).

16. Leo Kuper, *Prevention of Genocide* (New Haven, CT: Yale University Press, 1985). International Alert, "Early Warning and Conflict Resolution," report by Rudolfo Stavenhagen, Rapparteur of the Consultation on Early Warnings (Geneva: August 1989), pamphlet, 10p.; International Alert, "Early Warning and Conflict Resolution." 2nd Annual Consultation, report by Sandy Coleven (Geneva: August 1990), pamphlet, 20p.

CHAPTER 8: ANNOTATED BIBLIOGRAPHY

* 8.1 *
Bar-On, Dan. *Legacy of Silence: Encounters with Children of the Third Reich*. Cambridge, MA: Harvard University Press, 1989. LC 89-7484. ISBN 0-674-52185-4.

An Israeli psychologist, the son of a German-Jewish physician who fled Germany at the beginning of the Holocaust, returned to his father's homeland to conduct his research on the children of Nazis who had been active in the Holocaust. Bar-On's findings show that most of the children of perpetrators not only were protected by their families from knowing the truth about their parents in the Holocaust, as was German society as a whole even from knowing about the Holocaust, but that they themselves also set up walls of denial of the truth so that between parent and child there were "double walls" of denial. This study has important implications for those who want to create educational or preventive programs against genocide.

* 8.2 *
Bardakjian, Kevork B. *Hitler and the Armenian Genocide*. Cambridge, MA: Zoryan Institute, 1985. LC 85-52406. ISBN 0-916431-18-5.

The rhetorical question, "Who remembers the Armenians?" has been widely attributed to Hitler, speaking to his officers on the eve of World War II. Bardakjian provides the documentary substantiation that Hitler indeed did address his officers in this way. The failure of the world to punish the perpetrators of the Armenian genocide, including the Allies who had pledged to try the Turkish leaders of the Armenian genocide but then set them free, was a grave injustice against the Armenian people which also set the stage for the Holocaust.

* 8.3 *
Butz, Arthur R. *The Hoax of the Twentieth Century: The Case Against the Presumed Extermination of European Jewry*. Torrance, CA: Institute for Historical Review, 1976, 1983. NUC 86-78331. ISBN 0-911038-23-X.

Butz, a tenured professor of engineering at Northwestern University, has written an ugly, poisonous book that, in part because of its powerful title, has become one of the flagships of the "revisionist" movement, which denies that there ever was a Holocaust. Many Americans have demanded that Northwestern revoke Butz' tenure on the grounds of his flagrant violation of the basic standards of intellectual integrity and truth, but the university and many others believe the damage that would be done to academic freedom would be greater if he were dismissed. It is relevant to recall that, increasingly, many countries, and the courts in many countries, are creating and enforcing laws which make it illegal to deny the Holocaust or another known genocide.

* 8.4 *
Chalk, Frank, and Kurt Jonassohn. *The History and Sociology of Genocide: Analyses and Case Studies*. New Haven, CT: Yale University Press, 1990. LC 89-27381. ISBN 0-300-04445-3.

Historian Frank Chalk and sociologist Kurt Jonassohn have collaborated for many years in co-teaching a pioneer college course on the history and sociology of genocide. This is their comprehensive collection and analysis of case histories throughout human history.

* 8.5 *
Charny, Israel W. "April 2018, Intergalactic Associated Press." *Internet on the Holocaust and Genocide* Double Issue 25/26 (April 1990): 13-14. Special Issue on the 75th Anniversary of the Armenian Genocide.

In a satire based on predictive references to the future in 2018, Charny speculates that by then the universe will have seen not only continued instances of genocide as we know it but also of *planeticide* and *attempted planeticide*. He examines the follies of attempts to restrict current-day definitions of genocide to pure or ideal terms and to exclude various instances of mass death from equal consideration.

* 8.6 *

Charny, Israel W., ed. *Genocide: A Critical Bibliographic Review*, V. 2. London: Mansell Publishing Ltd. and New York: Facts on File, 1991. ISBN 0-7201-2053-5 (Mansell).

The second volume of this definitive series contains a special section on denials of the Holocaust and the Armenian Genocide, including a chapter by Vahakn Dadrian on documentation of the Armenian genocide in Turkish sources. Other sections cover law and genocide; education about the Holocaust and genocide; other topics include the language of genociders, total war, and genocide; the roles of professions and professionals in genocide; righteous gentiles in the Holocaust; and museums and memorials of the Holocaust and genocide.

* 8.7 *

Charny, Israel W., ed. *Genocide: A Critical Bibliographic Review*. London: Mansell Publishing Limited and New York: Facts on File, 1988. ISBN 0-7201-186-X (Mansell).

This important collection, the first in a series, contains encyclopedic-like essays and critical annotated bibliographies. It presents several cases of genocide—including the Holocaust, Armenian genocide, Cambodian genocide, Ukrainian famine, and many other genocides in the twentieth century—and the long-term history and sociology of genocide, and also treats several fields of the study of genocide—including the development of scholarship in genocide and its prevention; the psychology of genocidal destructiveness; the philosophical study of genocide and especially nuclear dangers; and the literature, art and film of the Holocaust, other genocides, and the future of nuclear and other "futuristic destruction." Hailed as brilliant and pace-setting, the book has also been adopted as a text for college courses.

* 8.8 *

Charny, Israel W. "Genocide: The Ultimate Human Rights Problem." *Social Education: Special Issue on Human Rights* 24 (1985): 448-452. Reprinted in *Social Science Record* 24, no. 2 (1987): 4-7.

Charny proposes a **humanistic** definition of genocide rather than a restrictive or legalistic particularization: any organized killing of masses of human beings in non-combat situations, whether on the basis of religious, national, political, or any other basis of differentiation of people, as if such and such people deserve to be victims of mass death.

* 8.9 *

Charny, Israel W. *How Can We Commit the Unthinkable?: Genocide, the Human Cancer*. Boulder, CO: Westview Press, 1982. LC 81-19784. ISBN 0-86531-358-X.

This is a seminal book on the psychology of genocide in the individual, its origins in family psychology and in collective processes, and especially the psychology of peoples' readiness to sacrifice other humans. Second, it is a seminal book because it formulates a major proposal for a World Genocide Early Warning System. The press, political officials, and social scientists have hailed the proposal as capable of saving human lives.

* 8.10 *

Charny, Israel W. "How To Avoid (Legally) Conviction for Crimes of Genocide: A One-Act Reading." *Social Science Record* 24, no. 2 (1987): 89-93. Reprinted in *Internet on the Holocaust and Genocide* Issue 16 (June 1988).

In a satirical playlet—which can be read-performed on stage as well as read quietly—Charny shows how genociders will always seek to "get away" with their actions. Hitler, Stalin, Pol Pot, Talaat, and Idi Amin are seen going together to consult a group of international lawyers, "Satan, Conformist and Whore," on how they could hope to avoid prosecution for genocide as international law against mass murder expands. They are advised to consider taking advantage of the biggest loophole in present law by killing many different peoples including their most desired victims all together, so that it may be possible for them to conceal the specific intentional target of their genocide.

* 8.11 *

Charny, Israel W. "The Psychology of Denial of Unknown Genocides." In *Genocide: A Critical Bibliographic Review*, V. 2. Imprint the same as 8.19.

An incredible number of people as well as organizations and governments in many different countries around the world devote themselves, and huge financial resources, to denying that one or another known genocide ever took place—examples include Turkish insistence that there never was an Armenian genocide and neo-Nazi and anti-Semitic claims that there never was a Holocaust. In this comprehensive study of the forms and dynamics of such denials, the author also calls for more concentrated attacks against those who deny known genocides for their obvious incitements to horrible new acts of violence against still further victims.

* 8.12 *
Charny, Israel W., ed. *Toward the Understanding and Prevention of Genocide: Proceedings of the International Conference on the Holocaust and Genocide*. Boulder, CO, and London: Westview Press, 1984. LC 84-15241. ISBN 0-86531-843-3.

The historic first International Conference on Holocaust and Genocide was held in Tel Aviv in 1982. This selective volume of its proceedings contains key papers, including reports and reactions to government efforts to stop the conference from taking place. Also included are case studies and analyses, including Soviet Union genocide, and the Nazi genocide of the Gypsies, dynamics of genocide and its prediction, education about genocide, and prevention. It is a widely used source-book and college text.

* 8.13 *
Charny, Israel W., and Chanan Rappaport. "A Genocide Early Warning System."*The Whole Earth Papers* 14 (1980): 28-35.

Charny and Rappaport provide a concise but detailed outline of the purposes and major content categories of a proposed Genocide Early Warning System. They include summary charts of ten Early Warning Processes.

* 8.14 *
Charny, Israel W., David Lisbona, and Marc Sherman. *Holocaust and Genocide Bibliographic Database, 1980-1990*. Draft 1.1. Jerusalem: Institute on the Holocaust and Genocide, 1991. The institute's address is POB 10311, 91102 Jerusalem, Israel.

Under a grant from the United States Institute of Peace, a U.S. government agency in Washington, DC, the Institute on the Holocaust and Genocide in Jerusalem has assembled a worldwide team of scholars to create a first computerized bibliographic database on Holocaust and genocide, largely for the period 1980-1990. The first product of the Institute should be available through the Library of USIP [1550 M Street, NW, Washington, DC 20005] in 1992, and may also be available for direct purchase on IBM diskettes from the Institute on the Holocaust and Genocide. The institute is also advancing in its work towards creating a first thesaurus of Holocaust and genocide terms.

* 8.15 *
Chorover, Stephen L. *From Genesis to Genocide: The Meaning of Human Nature and the Power of Behavior Control*. Cambridge, MA: MIT Press, 1979. LC 78-21107. ISBN 0-262-03068-3.

Chorover has created a chilling document on behavior control and fascism. His book is an excellent starting place for anyone who is unfamiliar with the Nazi traditions of superiority and philosophy of genetic improvement of the species, and with the bloodcurdling history of the Nazis, first program of actual mass destruction, namely of the mentally ill and mentally defective as well as many handicapped children.

* 8.16 *
Dadrian, Vahakn N. "The Anticipation and Prevention of Genocide in International Conflicts: Some Lessons from History." *International Journal Group Tensions* 18, no. 3 (1988): 205-214.

An intrepid researcher of the Armenian genocide turns his attention to the prediction and prevention of future genocides of any of the many peoples of our world. Dadrian proposes that the sources of potential genocide are in: a) the type of the groups locked in conflict and their standard relationship to each other; b) the nature and history of the conflict; and c) the degree of disparity of power relations between these groups.

* 8.17 *
Dimensions: A Publication of the Anti-Defamation League. 1985-. 3/yr. ISSN 0882-1240.

Published by B'nai B'rith's Anti-Defamation League, this very readable magazine about the Holocaust generally chooses a thematic focus for an issue such as journalistic reports of the Holocaust or the rescuers of Holocaust victims. It also presents excellent short and long reviews of books and articles on the Holocaust and genocide.

* 8.18 *
Eitinger, Leo, and Robert Krell with Miriam Rieck. *The Psychological and Medical Effects of Concentration Camps and Related Persecutions on Survivors of the Holocaust: A Research Bibliography*. Vancouver: University British Columbia Press, 1985. LC 86-120224. ISBN 0-7748-0220-0.

Professor Leo Eitinger of Oslo was one of the first European physicians to describe the terrible impacts of the concentration camp syndrome following World War II. Joined by Canadian psychiatrist, Robert Krell, he provides a systematic bibliography of the literature about victims of the Holocaust through 1984.

* 8.19 *
Fein, Helen. "Scenarios of Genocide." In *Toward the Understanding and Prevention of Genocide*. Ed. by Israel W. Charny. Imprint the same as 8.14.

By removing the actual names of the victimizer and victim peoples, and also the names of countries and geographic locales of each genocidal case history, and then substituting unfamiliar made-up names for all of the above, Fein generates a series of templates or basic scenarios for how genocide has come about and how it can come about in a wide variety of historical, political, and ethnic circumstances. Hers is a brilliant pedagogical tool as well as a worthwhile collection for scholars and researchers of generic forms or scenarios of genocide.

* 8.20 *
Fein, Helen. "Genocide: A Sociological Perspective." *Current Sociology* 38, no. 1 (1990) Whole Number.

In this 104-page monograph, Fein provides a comprehensive review of the field of genocide study, which she follows with a 225-item bibliography of the main literature of the field, accompanied by numerous brief critical annotations. Fein is a passionate spokesperson for a precise and rigorous definition of genocide. She is also the author of an award-winning study of the differential outcomes of the Holocaust in different cultures, *Accounting for Genocide* (New York: Free Press, 1979).

* 8.21 *
Fromm, Erich. *For the Love of Life*. Ed. by Hans Durgen Schultz. Trans. from the German by Robert and Rita Kimber. New York: Free Press, 1988. LC 85-20518. ISBN 0-02-910930-2. Based on radio interviews in the late 1970s.

"If you begin your resistance to a Hitler, only after he has won his victory, then you've lost before you've even begun. For to offer resistance you've got to have an inner core, a conviction. You have to have faith in yourself to be able to think critically, to be an independent human being, a human being and not a sheep." (p.133) "Anyone who takes this path will learn to resist not only the great tyrannies, like Hitler's, but also the 'small tyrannies,' the creeping tyrannies of bureaucratization and alienation in everyday life." (p133)

* 8.22 *
Gibson, Janice T., and Mika Haritos-Fatouros. "The Education of a Torturer." *Psychology Today* 20, no. 11 (1986): 50-58.

Using the step-by-step method, the authors analyze the sequence of desensitization through which people are trained to be members of a secret police (in this case in Greece) who are prepared to torture and cruelly kill their victims. Their findings are consistent with earlier observations of how the Nazis trained their feared SS Deathhead squads.

* 8.23 *
Glaser, K., and S.T. Possony. *Victims of Politics: The State of Human Rights*. New York: Columbia University Press, 1979. LC 78-5591. ISBN 0-231-04442-9.

The authors survey forced migrations or forced transfers of populations and provide details of the tremendous losses of life that *inevitably* accompany such steps.

* 8.24 *
Harff, Barbara. *Genocide and Human Rights*. Denver, CO: Graduate School of International Studies, University of Denver, 1984. ISBN 0-87940-074-9 pa. NUC 86-70567.

Harff, a political scientist, has written a poignant, caring monograph about natural law as well as the evolving technical legal basis for humanitarian intervention of one nation in another's affairs for the specific purposes of stopping genocide. Such intervention can be without exploitation for national gain.

* 8.25 *
Harff, Barbara, and Ted Robert Gurr. "Genocides and Politicides since 1945: Evidence and Anticipation." *Internet on the Holocaust and Genocide* Special Issue 13 (December 1987).

Political scientists Harff and Gurr are pioneering in the development of computerized empirical informations on two critical aspects of genocide: Harff reports on a databank of politicides, or mass killings on the basis of political identity since World War II; Gurr reports on a databank about minorities around the world and monitors the extent to which they are at risk of mounting persecution and genocide.

* 8.26 *
Holocaust and Genocide Studies. 1986-. Q. Pergamon Press Journals. Headington Hill Hall, Oxford OX3 0BW, England. Editor-in-Chief: Yehudah Bauer. Chairman of the Editorial Board: Elie Wiesel. ISSN 8756-6583.

This is probably the flagship scholarly journal in the field of Holocaust and genocide studies, although it is heavily biased towards scholarship primarily of the Holocaust and towards "purist definitions" of the Holocaust. It publishes much less about the genocides of other people.

* 8.27 *
Horowitz, Irving Louis. *Genocide: State Power and Mass Murder*. New Brunswick, NJ: Transaction, 1976. LC 76-2276. ISBN 0-87855-191-3. Revised edition issued under the title *Taking Lives* in 1980.

Horowitz' typology is a useful starting point for the examination of the roles and functions of bureaucracy, government organization, and national policy in the making of genocide. His is a classic work on the nature of government in genocidal societies.

* 8.28 *
Hovannisian, Richard G., ed. *The Armenian Genocide in Perspective*. New Brunswick, NJ, and Oxford: Transaction Books, 1987. LC 85-29038. ISBN 0-88738-096-4.

Hovannisian has brought together an outstanding collection of papers on the Armenian genocide. In addition to historical analysis of the genocide, there is consideration of the impact of the events on literature, the psychosocial sequelae for survivors and their families, a study of oral histories of survivors, and an analysis of the Turks' unending efforts to deny the Armenian genocide.

* 8.29 *
International Conference on the Holocaust and Genocide (lst: 1982): Tel Aviv, Israel. *The Book of the International Conference on the Holocaust and Genocide: Book One. The Conference Program and Crisis*. Ed. by Israel W. Charny and Shamai Davidson. Tel Aviv: Institute of the International Conference on the Holocaust and Genocide, 1983. NUC 87-126011.

Book One is a photocopy-printed softcover book that includes the full program, abstracts of papers, evaluations of participants, and comments by the world press. It also contains extensive reports of the crisis that erupted when the governments of Turkey and Israel sought to censor reports of the Armenian genocide, if not to close down the entire conference.

* 8.30 *
Internet on the Holocaust and Genocide. 1985-. 6/yr. Institute on the Holocaust and Genocide, POB 10311, 91102 Jerusalem, Israel.

This invaluable newsletter reports studies, projects, and developments around the world relating to genocide and its prevention. It is distributed on a voluntary subscription basis by the Institute, which is interested in making the publication available to younger scholars who have limited funds.

* 8.31 *
Jones, Ron. "The Third Wave." In *Experiencing Social Psychology*. Ed. by Ayala Pines and Christina Maslach. New York: Alfred A. Knopf, 1984. LC 83-16277. ISBN 0-394-33547-7 pa.

An American high-school history teacher succeeds superbly in teaching his students about how the Holocaust came about by creating a parallel process of group identification with power, conformity, and ideology in the classroom and high school. The written report has been followed by a video film, *The New Wave*, which is an excellent instructional tool for students, community groups, teachers, and even professional scholars for genocide.

* 8.32 *
Kelman, Herbert C., and V. Lee Hamilton. *Crimes of Obedience: Toward a Social Psychology of Authority and Responsibility*. New Haven, CT, and London: Yale University Press, 1989. LC 88-5049. ISBN 0-300-04184-5.

In an important study, Kelman and Hamilton analyze the crucial issue of conformity and obedience to norms of destruction. Even after Lt. Calley had been convicted for his role as commander of the U.S. forces at My Lai, 67 percent of Americans replied to a research questionnaire that they believed most people would follow orders, and 51 percent said that had they themselves been at My Lai, they too would have obeyed orders to slaughter the villagers (see also 7.99).

* 8.33 *
Knight, Gerald. "A Genocide Bureau." [Editor's title]. Text of talk delivered at the Symposium on Genocide, London, 20 March 1982. Available from The Baha'i International Community, 866 United Nations Plaza, New York, NY 10017. Mimeographed. 14p.

In this beautiful address, a representative of the Baha'i International Community proposed an international mechanism for monitoring and responding to signals, threats, and reports of genocide. Although the paper can be difficult to locate, it is such a thoughtful and creative proposal that I believe it is well worth trying to access. Baha'i International later created International Alert.

* 8.34 *
Kren, George, and Leon Rappoport. *The Holocaust and the Crisis of Human Behavior*. New York: Holmes & Meier, 1980. LC 79-23781. ISBN 0-8419-0544-4.

Collatorators Kren, a historian, and Rappoport, a psychologist, claim in this excellent book that human life can never again be the same after the Holocaust.

Thus, they argue that no field of human inquiry and scholarship remains relevant or meaningful unless it inquires into how and why the bizarre destruction of human life that took place in the Holocaust came about.

* 8.35 *

Kren, George M. "The Holocaust and the Foundations of Moral Judgment." *Journal of Value Inquiry* 21 (1987): 55-64.

Kren is an articulate analyst of the ethical implications of the Holocaust. Among his important observations, he notes the following: "There is something very strange and odd in the fact that almost all of the perpetrators of what arguably is the most radical horror of this century, while awaiting execution, argued, with obvious sincerity, that they had done no wrong. A recurring theme found in all the trial records of individuals who had participated in mass killing is the indignant surprise they express that anyone should blame them for their actions, since they were only doing their duty." (p. 56)

* 8.36 *

Kuper, Leo. *Genocide: Its Political Use in the Twentieth Century*. New Haven, CT, and London: Yale University Press, 1981. LC 81-16151. ISBN 0-300-02795-0.

Kuper's is the single most comprehensive and important assembly of case histories of genocide in the field.

* 8.37 *

Kuper, Leo. *International Action Against Genocide*. Report no. 53. London: Minority Rights Group, 1982. ISSN 0305-6552. 17p.

The Minority Rights Group in London is an organization that has pioneered in the study of the ethnic histories and conflicts of minority groups around the planet. This pamphlet is an excellent brief introduction to definitions of different types of genocide and to concepts of international intervention.

* 8.38 *

Kuper, Leo. *The Prevention of Genocide*. New Haven, CT, and London: Yale University Press, 1985. LC 85-40465. ISBN 0-300-03418-0.

In a critically honest analysis of the history of international intervention in cases of genocide, especially by the United Nations, Kuper concludes that the UN has been virtually a total failure. He analyzes which basic revisions will be needed in the UN Convention on Genocide—many of which were later adopted by the UN Whitaker Commission. Based on his realistic view of the international system, Kuper proposes strengthening and expanding non-governmental international organizations. He also proposes a new organization, *International Alert*, which has since come into being. For more information, write to International Alert, Box 259, 1015 Gayley Ave., Los Angeles, CA 90024.

* 8.39 *

Kutner, Luis, and Ernest Katin. "World Genocide Tribunal: A Proposal for Planetary Preventive Measures Supplementing a Genocide Early Warning System." In *Toward the Understanding and Prevention of Genocide*. Ed. by Israel W. Charny. Imprint the same as 8.14.

The authors are attorneys who are concerned with developing legally correct procedures for reviewing allegations and early reports of massacres according to proper rules of evidence, but at the same time they are courageously concerned with creating an international agency that will respond quietly and meaningfully to emergency situations of genocide. Luis Kutner is well known for legal work on a principle of international habeas corpus. He has been nominated several times for the Nobel Peace Prize.

* 8.40 *

Lemkin, Raphael. *Axis Rule in Occupied Europe*. New York: Columbia University Press, 1944. LC 44-47388.

Raphael Lemkin was the originator of the concept of **genocide**, and certainly the person who can be credited almost singlehandedly with proposing and gaining the acceptance of the UN of the U.N. Convention on Genocide. A Polish-Jewish attorney with a prominent post in the Polish Prosecutor's Office before World War II, he was the only member of his family to escape the Holocaust. Arriving in the U.S., he devoted his entire being to the push for the adoption of the Convention. Not long after its adoption, he died, sick and penniless for having given his life to this immense cause. *Axis Rule in Occupied Europe* is Lemkin's monumental summary of the reign of the arch fascist regime.

In the coming years, several of Lemkin's exciting unpublished manuscripts, including his autobiography, *Uncommon Warrior*, which was rejected by several U.S. publishers in his lifetime on the grounds that it would not sell, will be edited by Rabbi Steven Jacobs. The first volume is scheduled for publication by Edwin Mellen Press.

* 8.41 *
Lifton, Robert J., and Eric Markusen. *The Genocidal Mentality: Nazi Holocaust and Nuclear Threat.* New York: Basic Books, 1990. LC 89-43101. ISBN 0-465-02662-1.

In this intelligent and humane book, psychiatrist Robert Lifton and sociologist Eric Markusen collaborate in calling for a new step in the *evolution of our species*, that we exercise our capacity to choose and shape our lives towards a *life-caring mentality* as opposed to a *genocidal mentality*.

* 8.42 *
Lifton, Robert Jay. *The Nazi Doctors: Medical Killing and the Psychology of Genocide.* New York: Basic Books, 1986. LC 85-73874. ISBN 0-465-04904-4.

The fact that so many *healers* were ready to kill teaches us all how many of us human beings can be corrupted by the lust or opportunity to have power, maim, and kill others. In this study, Lifton originates new concepts of "doubling" and "healing-killing" which are certain to become basic new conceptual tools in the field. For other interpretations, see annotations 2.30 and 7.27.

* 8.43 *
Milgram, Stanley. *Obedience to Authority.* New York: Harper & Row, 1974. LC 71-138748. ISBN 0-06-012938-7.

In perhaps the single most important social science experiment of our times, Milgram demonstrates that a *majority* of human beings, from all walks of life, are available to do serious, possibly lethal harm to others. The context of the study is a simulation of a psychological experiment in learning where actors play the role of subjects who must memorize nonsense syllables, while the real subjects of the study are instructed to assist the researcher by giving progressively stronger electric shocks up to dangerous lethal doses, when the learning subject makes an error. No actual shock is given, but because the actors pretend to be hurt, the teaching subjects are not aware that their pain is simulated. It is worth mentioning that the crucial point Milgram makes has been amplified and supplemented in other essays and studies of which the following two entries are examples.

* 8.44 *
Mansson, H.H. "Justifying the Final Solution." *Omega* 3, no. 2 (1977): 79-87.

In this study college students manifest a readiness to agree to the execution of mental defectives. See also the next item.

* 8.45 *
Charny, Israel W., and Daphna Fromer. "The Readiness of Health Profession Students to Comply with a Hypothetical Program of Forced Migration of a Minority Population." *American Journal of Orthopsychiatry* 60, no. 4 (1990): 486-495.

Charny and Fromer examine the readiness of students in the Israeli health professions to participate, as professionals, in a government plan for forced migration of the Arabs out of Israel.

* 8.46 *
Perec, Georges. *W or the Memory of Childhood.* Trans. from the French by David Bellos. New York: David R. Goodine, 1988. LC 88-45291. ISBN 0-87923-756-2.

In a brilliant fictional treatment, Perec satirizes a nation where Sport is King and where citizens are forced into life-and-death competitions, and losers are punished, tortured, and murdered. Perec has creative insight into the tragically common possibilities of madness in societies—and the absurdity of the definitional basis for identifying target groups as deserving of legal extermination. See 8.19 for Fein's fictionalized but very real historical scenarios of genocide.

* 8.47 *
Porter, Jack Nusan, ed. *Genocide and Human Rights: A Global Anthology.* Washington, DC: University Press of America, 1982. LC 81-40580. ISBN 0-8191-2289-0.

Porter's important collection of studies of genocide includes his own excellent analysis of the conditions under which genocide is most and least likely to occur; for example, genocide is likely when a minority group is an outsider, when there is a racist ideology. The contributors make an outstanding effort to define genocide and to summarize the conditions that facilitate its occurrence and conditions which work against genocide taking place.

* 8.48 *
Rapoport, Anatol. "Preparation for Nuclear War: The Final Madness." *American Journal of Orthopsychiatry* 54, no. 4 (1984): 524-529.

Rapoport, a renowned philosopher of science, warns against the ultimate madness where seemingly rational people will yet undertake and justify the use of nuclear weapons which threaten to destroy our very species. "The planners of nuclear war—that is, primarily the personnel of the military establishments of both superpowers and their political entourages—satisfy two criteria for madness: they are immersed in an imaginary world of their own making, dissociated from reality, and their activities constitute a clear menace to humanity." (p. 525)

* 8.49 *
Roiphe, Anne. *A Season for Healing: Reflections on the Holocaust*. New York: Summit Books, 1988. LC 88-21537. ISBN 0-671-66753-X.

"Roiphe courageously concludes that it may be time to stop particularizing the Jewish experience and begin to generalize it because to insist forever on its unique exclusivity deepens rifts among nations, religions and individuals. To admit that the monstrous lessons of the Holocaust have a universal application in no way diminishes the horror. In fact, that acknowledgment may be the first step toward a broader and deeper humanity...Roiphe's book can be read as a reminder that humanity itself has become an endangered species." From a review by Elaine Kendall in the *Los Angeles Times Book Review* (27 November 1988).

* 8.50 *
Salk, Jonas. *Man Unfolding*. New York: Harper & Row, 1972. LC 74-181642. ISBN 0-06-073739-8.

Salk calls for humankind to move forward in evolution by adopting new values and new ethics. "The essential requirement for such a value system would seem to be the creation of an *identity* of interest rather than a *conflict* of interest, between the individual and the species, between the citizen and society, and between nations and mankind. This basic issue must be faced lest men in their greedy competition...destroy themselves and their planet." (p. 101) Salk is the world-renowned creator of the Salk vaccine for polio.

* 8.51 *
San Jose Conferences on the Holocaust (1977-1978). *The Holocaust: Ideology, Bureaucracy, and Genocide*. Ed. by Henry Friedlander and Sybil Milton. Millwood, NJ: Kraus International Publications, 1980. LC 80-16913. ISBN 0-527-63807-2.

This seminal and relatively early post-Holocaust work contains the most inclusive effort ever made to look at the roles of professionals in a series of fields—universities, law, medicine, physical sciences, technology, government, and the church—in participating in or collaborating and enabling the Holocaust to take place. Much more research is still needed on this subject today even many years later, but the book is still well worth reading for the integrity of its effort to bring together these important subjects.

* 8.52 *
Shofar: Inter-disciplinary Journal of Jewish Studies. 1982-. Q. Purdue University Research Foundation. Ed.: Joseph Haberer. ISSN 0882-8539.

Shofar is an excellent all-around review of contemporary Jewish thought that includes long and briefer annotated reviews of the literature on the Holocaust.

* 8.53 *
Staub, Ervin. *The Roots of Evil: The Origins of Genocide and Other Group Violence*. Cambridge: Cambridge University Press, 1989. ISBN 0-521-35407-2.

Staub theorizes that individuals and collectives such as nations move in a continuum of steps towards becoming genocidal destroyers. He analyzes four case histories, with an impressive combination of psychological and historical detail. The four cases are the Holocaust, the Armenian genocide, the Cambodian genocide, and disappearances in Argentina. Staub, who as a child was rescued from the Holocaust by gentiles, writes with special eloquence about human beings' potentials for caring and rescuing.

* 8.54 *
Taylor, Cecil P. *Good: A Tragedy*. London: Methuen Ltd., 1982. ISBN 0-413-52130-3.

Taylor's wonderful play shows the "becoming" of a vicious Nazi. The protagonist is a pleasant, friendly academician whose closest friend is a Jewish psychiatrist, but power corrupts more and more, and he becomes more and more self-serving, charged up by his growing power. Ultimately he is transformed into a willing destroyer. The bad in him has won out over the good.

* 8.55 *
Tec, Nechama. *When Light Pierced the Darkness: Christian Rescue of Jews in Nazi-Occupied Lands*. New York: Oxford University Press, 1986. ISBN 0-19-503643-3.

Tec, herself a Holocaust survivor who became a sociologist in America, reports on studies of gentiles who saved Jews in the Holocaust. She found any number who did not like Jews, even disliked them, yet had no question about their responsibility to save them, despite great personal risk, simply because they were fellow human beings. For another interpretation, see 2.80.

* 8.56 *
Thompson, John L.P. "Genocide as Boundary-Crossing Behavior." *Internet on the Holocaust and Genocide* Special Issue 21 (1989).

In this research, Thompson studies the history of violence in Ireland, but the larger significances of his work are these: 1) theoretically, he conceives of violence as a continuum that extends to genocide and must be monitored against development into genocide; and 2) in the process of the research he creates and works with original measures of violence, such as the degree of public outrage at various types and degrees of cruelty and violence, that can be useful to other researchers of genocide.

* 8.57 *
Totten, Samuel, and William S. Parsons, eds. "Teaching about Genocide." *Social Education* 55, no. 2 (February 1919): 84-133.

"Teaching and learning about genocide is not easy, for it is both a complex and horrific subject," write Parsons and Totten in this special issue. "However, if teachers across the globe taught their students about genocide and helped them to understand their responsibility in our global village, they could possibly make a major contribution to humanity."

* 8.58 *
Whitaker, Ben. *Revised and Updated Report on the Question of the Prevention and Punishment of the Crime of Genocide.* Report prepared for United Nations. Economic and Social Council. Commission on Human Rights. Sub-Commission on the Prevention of Discrimination and Protection of Minorities. 6th sess., 1985. E/CN.4/ Sub.2/1985/6, 2 July 1985.

This is an admirable hard-hitting proposal by a formal UN research group for revision and expansion of the UN Convention on Genocide. In the process of this formal report, the document presents a remarkably vivid and comprehensive overview of the history of genocide, and the emergence of international governmental and non-governmental policies and initiatives towards punishment, intervention, and prevention of genocide.

The Whitaker Report is also deserving of special commendation for its formal correction of earlier UN denial of the history of the Armenian genocide. Whitaker succeeded in stewarding his report, which affirms the Armenian genocide, through a maze of Turkish and other government efforts at denial. The Whitaker Report is the second full-scale investigation by the UN of genocide and of UN law on genocide since the inception of the world body. An earlier report was submitted by Nicodeme Rusashyankiko in 1973 and revised in final draft in 1978, following which the commission chairperson returned to his native Rwanda and is reported never to have been heard from again. See also the following entry.

* 8.59 *
Internet on the Holocaust and Genocide (January-February 1985). Special Double Issue on the Whitaker Report to the UN.

This special issue of *Internet* provides a step-by-step summary as well as interpretive essays on the major conclusions of the Whitaker Report.

* 8.60 *
Wiesel, Elie. *The Oath.* New York: Random House, 1973. LC 73-5042. ISBN 0-394-48779-6.

Elie Wiesel is a child-survivor of the Holocaust whose autobiographical novels, such as *Night* and *Dawn*, have shaken the world, and whose inspiring ethical orientation to protesting past and future dangers of genocide to *all* peoples have earned him the awesome Nobel Peace Prize. In *The Oath*, using the form of a novel, Wiesel describes the brewing of a fictional genocidal massacre in a village. The story is a gripping small-scale parable of the development of the Holocaust.

APPENDIX:
CHRONOLOGY OF GENOCIDE

by Michael Dobkowski

Country	Dates	Perpetrators	Victims	Estimated Nos.
Melos	416 B.C.E.	Athenians	Melians	Unknown
Carthage	146 B.C.E.	Romans	Carthaginians	150,000
Southern France	1208-1226	Papacy and French Catholics	Albigensian Cathars	Unknown
China	1211-34	Chingis Khan and Mongols	Chinese, Muslims, Persians, and others	Unknown
The Americas	1492-1789	Spanish, Portuguese, British, and French	Indians	Unknown but in the millions
Japan	1587-1610	Japanese	Christians in Japan	285,000
New England	1630-38	Puritans	Pequot Indians	50,000 100,000
Australia	1800-50	European Settlers	Aboriginal Peoples	30,000 - 50,000
Southern Africa	1818-28	Shaka and the Zulus	Ndwandwe	40,000
Appalachia to Oklahoma	1838-39	U.S. Government	Cherokee Indians	4,000 - 15,000
Northern California	1856-60	Settlers in California	Yuki Indians	3,000 - 3,500
German S.W. Africa	1904	German Troops	Herero	65,000
Ottoman Empire	1915-22	Young Turks and Kurds	Armenians	1,000,000 - 1,500,000
Soviet Union	1932-37	Stalin and Soviet Regime	Ukrainians	4 - 10 Million
Germany	1939-45	Germans and Collaborators	Jews Gypsies	5.8 million 50,000

Country	Dates	Perpetrators	Victims	Estimated Nos.
Sudan	1955-72	Sudanese Army	Southern Sudanese	500,000
Indonesia	1965-67	Vigilantes	Communists	200,000 - 600,000
Nigeria	1966-70	Other Nigerians	Ibos	2-3 Million
Paraguay	1968-72	Paraguayans	Aché Indians	1,000
Bangladesh	1971	East Pakistan Army	Bengalis	1.3 - 3 Million
Burundi	1972	Tutsis	Hutus	100,000 - 200,000
East Timor	1975	Indonesian Army	Timorese	60,000 - 100,000
Cambodia	1975-79	Khmer Rouge	Cambodians	1 - 2.5 Million
Uganda	1976-78	Ugandan Army	Ugandans	500,000
Bangladesh	1971 to the present	Bangladeshi Army and Bengali settlers	Non-Bengali tribal peoples of the Chittagong Hill Tracts of south-eastern Bangladesh	200,000

Author Index

Aaby, Peter 1.35
Abella, Irving 2.83
Ablin, David 1.1
Abzug, Robert H. 2.50
Adalian, Rouben 5.A
Adams, James 7.32
Adelson, Alan 2.36
Ahmad, Eqbal 1.2
Ainsztein, Reuben 2.105
Alexander, Edward 2.123
Allworth, Edward 6.1
Ankara University 5.18
Appelfeld, Aharon 2.109, 2.110, 2.111
Arad, Yitzchak 2.37, 2.51
Arendt, Hannah 2.15, 3.1
Arens, Richard 1.4, 1.5
Aronson, Ronald 7.83
Askenasy, Hans 7.84
Ataöv, Türkkaya 5.20, 5.21
Axelrod, Daniel 7.68
Baker, Leonard 2.38
Ball, Desmond 7.59
Bar-On, Dan 4.13, 8.1
Barabas, Alicia 1.6
Bardakjian, Kevork B. 8.2
Bartolomé, Miguel 1.6
Bauer, Yehuda 2.84, 2.85, 3.2, 3.3,
..... 3.4, 3.5, 3.6
Bauman, Zygmunt 2.16, 7.86
Baumel, Judith Tydor 2.86
Bedau, Hugo Adam 7.85
Bellis, Paul 6.17
Berenbaum, Michael 3.7
Berglund, Staffan 1.7
Bergmann, Martin S. 4.14
Berkovits, Eliezer 2.139, 2.140
Bettelheim, Bruno 2.17
Bettelheim, Charles 6.18
Bierman, John 2.70
Blatter, Janet 2.124
Bodley, John H. 1.8, 1.9
Bor, Josef 2.39
Borkin, Joseph 2.52
Borowski, Tadeusz 2.112
Braham, Randolph L. 2.1, 2.125
Branford, Sue 1.10
Breitman, Richard 2.18, 2.94
Brenner, Robert Reeve 4.1
Brintnall, Douglas E. 1.11
Bryce, Viscount 5.G

Budiardjo, Carmel 1.12, 1.13
Bundy, McGeorge 7.60
Burger, Julian 1.14
Butz, Arthur R. 8.3
Cargas, Harry James 2.141
Carr, Edward Hallett 6.19
Carrere d'Encausse, Helene 6.20
Carroll, Berenice A. 7.33
Carter, Ashton 7.61
Carynyk, Marco 6.21
Chalk, Frank 2.19, 6.22, 7.10, 8.4
Charny, Israel W. 7.11, 7.12, 7.13, 7.87, 7.88,
..... 8.5, 8.6, 8.7, 8.8, 8.9, 8.10,
..... 8.11, 8.12, 8.13, 8.14, 8.45
Chodziesner, Gertrud 2.116
Chorover, Stephen L. 2.20, 8.15
Churchill, Ward 7.14
Coates, Kenneth 1.28
Cohen, Arthur 2.142
Colchester, Marcus 1.16
Colletta, Nat J. 1.17
Collins, Randall 7.89
Comstock, Craig 7.113
Conquest, Robert 1.18, 1.19, 6.2, 6.3
Corsun, Andrew 5.17
Coser, Lewis 7.90
Costanza, Mary S. 2.126
Council on Turkish-American
  Relations 5.6
Dadrian, Vahakn N. 3.8, 5.B, 5.C, 7.15,
..... 7.16, 7.17, 7.18, 8.16
Dando, William A. 7.1
Dargyay, Eva K. 1.20
Davies, R.W. 6.19, 6.23
Davis, Robert 1.21
Davis, Shelton H. 1.22
Dawidowicz, Lucy 2.2, 3.9
Delbo, Charlotte 2.57
Des Pres, Terrence 2.53
Deutscher, Isaac 3.10
Devalle, Susana B.C. 1.23
Dimsdale, Joel E. 4.2
Dinnerstein, Leonard 2.87
Dmytryshyn, Basil 6.24
Dobkowski, Michael M. 7.31
Dobroszycki, Lucjan 2.40
Dolot, Miron 6.4
Donat, Alexander 2.58
Dorstal, W. 1.24
Dower, John W. 7.35

Dwork, Deborah	2.21
Dyer, Gwynne	7.34
Eckhardt, A. Roy	2.143, 3.11, 3.12, 3.13
Eckhardt, Alice L.	2.143, 3.12, 3.13
Eckhardt, William	7.2, 7.36
Eckman, Lester	2.107
Edib, Halide (Adivar)	5.4
Editors of *Life*, The	5.7
Edwards, Coral	1.26
Eitinger, Leo	8.18
Elder, James F.	1.25
Eliach, Yaffa	2.144
Elliot, Gil	7.3
Ellison, Herbert J.	6.25
Emin, Ahmed	5.5
Epstein, Helen	4.3
Ervin, Alexander M.	1.27
Ezrahi, Sidra Dekoven	2.127
Fackenheim, Emil	2.145, 3.14, 3.15, 3.16, 3.17
Falconi, Carlo	2.88
Falk, Richard	7.74, 7.91
Farrar, Marjorie	7.37
Feig, Konnilyn	2.54
Feigl, Erich	5.27
Fein, Helen	2.22, 7.19, 8.19, 8.20
Feingold, Henry L.	2.89, 3.18, 3.19
Fenelon, Fania	2.59
Ferencz, Benjamin B.	2.55
Fetter, Steve	7.38
Feuer, Lewis S.	3.20
Fine, Ellen S.	2.128
Fisher, Robin	1.28
Fleming, Gerald	2.3
Flender, Harold	2.71
Flinker, Moshe	2.60
Ford, Daniel	7.62
Foreign Policy Institute	5.25
Fox, John P.	3.21
Frank, Anne	2.61
Frankl, Viktor E.	2.23, 4.15
Freeman, Michael	3.22
Frey, Robert S.	3.25
Friedlander, Henry	3.23
Friedländer, Saul	2.90, 3.24, 4.16
Friedman, Philip	2.24, 2.72, 3.26
Friedman, Saul S.	2.91
Fromer, Daphna	8.45
Fromm, Erich	8.21
Fuller, J.F.C.	7.39
Gabriel, Richard	7.40
Gailey, Christine Ward	1.29
Gander, T.J.	7.41
Gault, William Barry	7.92
Gay, William C.	7.63, 7.64
Geis, Miep	2.73
Gibson, Janice T.	8.22
Gilbert, Martin	1.30, 2.4, 2.92
Gill, Anton	4.17
Glaser, K.	8.23
Glock, Oriel	1.10
Goldberg, Hillel	3.27
Gols, Alison Leslie	2.73
Goodman, Michael Harris	1.31
Green, Gerald	2.129
Greenberg, Irving	2.147
Grossman, David	2.113
Group for the Advancement of Psychiatry	7.93
Gunter, Michael M.	5.15
Gurr, Ted Robert	7.20, 8.25
Gürün, Kâmuran	5.22
Gutman, Yisrael	2.41
Haas, Aaron	4.4
Habermas, Jürgen	3.28
Hallie, Philip	2.74
Halperin, Morton	7.65
Hamilton, V. Lee	7.99, 8.32
Hancock, Ian	3.29
Harff, Barbara	7.20, 8.24, 8.25
Haritos-Fatouros, Mika	8.22
Harkin, Tom	7.66
Hart, Hornell	7.94
Hartigan, Richard Shelly	7.42
Hartman, Geoffrey	2.25
Hauptman, Laurence M.	1.32
Heinemann, Marlene	2.130
Heller, Celia Stopnicka	2.5
Heller, Mikhail	6.26
Herken, Gregg	7.67
Hernandez, Deborah Pacini	1.33
Heuser, Beatrice	3.30
Heyen, William	2.114, 2.115
Hilberg, Raul	2.6, 2.42, 3.31, 3.32
Hillesum, Etty	2.62
Hochhuth, Rolf	2.93
Hong, Evelyne	1.34
Hood, Marlowe	1.1
Horowitz, Irving Louis	7.21, 8.27
Hovannisian, Richard G.	5.D, 8.28
Huberband, Shimon	2.148
Hughes, Everett C.	7.95
Huttenbach, Henry R.	7.22
Hvalkof, Soren	1.35
Insdorf, Annette	2.131
Institute for Ataturk's Principles and the History of Turkish Renovation	5.13
Institute for the Study of Turkish Culture	5.26

International Conference on the Holocaust and Genocide (1st: 1982): Tel Aviv, Israel ... 8.29
International Symposium on the Holocaust, Cathedral of St. John the Divine ... 2.146
Jäckel, Eberhard ... 3.33
Jagendorff, Siegfried ... 2.43
Jakobovits, Immanuel ... 3.34
Jaspers, Karl ... 2.26
Johnson, Robert ... 7.96
Jonassohn, Kurt ... 2.19, 6.22, 7.10, 8.4
Jones, Ron ... 8.31
Jucovy, Milton ... 4.14
Kaku, Michio ... 7.68
Kaplan, Chaim ... 2.44
Kaplan, Fred ... 7.69
Katin, Ernest ... 8.39
Katz, Steven T. ... 3.36, 7.23, 7.97
Kedourie, Elie ... 5.8
Keegan, John ... 7.43
Kelman, Herbert C. ... 7.99, 8.32
Kemal, Mustafa Ataturk ... 5.3
Kennett, Lee ... 7.44
Kermisz, Josef ... 2.42
Kewley, Vanja ... 1.37
Kingston-Mann, Esther ... 6.5
Kirschner, Robert ... 2.149
Klein, Gerda ... 2.63
Kliot, N. ... 1.38
Kloian, Richard D. ... 5.E
Knight, Gerald ... 8.33
Knopp, Josephine Z. ... 2.132
Koestler, Arthur ... 6.6
Kohler, Gernot ... 7.2
Kolkowicz, Roman ... 7.70
Koonz, Claudia ... 2.7
Kopf, David ... 7.105
Korczak, Janusz ... 2.45
Kordan, Bohdan S. ... 6.21
Kovel, Joel ... 7.71
Kramer, Ronald C. ... 7.72
Kravchenko, Victor ... 6.7
Krell, Robert ... 8.18
Kren, George ... 8.34
Kren, George M. ... 2.27, 3.37, 3.38, 8.35
Krystal, Henry ... 4.5
Kulka, Otto Dov ... 3.39
Kuper, Leo ... 3.40, 7.24, 7.25, 7.100, 8.36, 8.37, 8.38
Kurtz, Lester R. ... 7.73
Kutner, Luis ... 8.39
Lang, Berel ... 2.28, 7.26, 7.98
Langer, Lawrence ... 4.6, 4.7
Langer, Lawrence L. ... 2.133, 2.134, 2.135

Lanzmann, Claude ... 2.8, 3.41
Lapides, Robert ... 2.36
Laqueur, Walter ... 2.94, 2.95
Lazar, Chaim ... 2.107
Legters, Lyman H. ... 1.39, 6.8
Leitner, Isabella ... 2.64, 2.65
Lemkin, Raphael ... 8.40
Levi, Primo ... 2.66, 4.8, 4.18
Leviton, Daniel ... 7.4
Lewin, M. ... 6.9
Lewis, Norman ... 1.40
Lewy, Guenter ... 2.96
Lifton, Robert Jay ... 2.29, 2.30, 7.27, 7.45, 7.74, 7.101, 7.102, 8.41, 8.42
Liong, Liem Soei ... 1.12, 1.13
Lipstadt, Deborah E. ... 2.97
Lisbona, David ... 8.14
Littell, Franklin H. ... 2.150
Lizot, Jaques ... 1.41
Lopez, George A. ... 7.8, 7.46
Lowry, Heath W. ... 5.14
Luciuk, Luyblubomyr Y. ... 6.21
Luel, Steven A. ... 4.19
Mace, James E. ... 6.10, 6.11, 6.12
Maksudov, S. ... 6.13
Mansson, H.H. ... 8.44
Marcus, Paul ... 4.19
Mark, Ber ... 2.106
Markus, Andrew ... 1.42
Markusen, Eric ... 2.29, 7.28, 7.102, 7.103, 7.104, 7.105, 8.41
Marrus, Michael R. ... 2.9, 2.31
Marrus, Michael Robert ... 3.42
Marullo, Sam ... 7.72
Mason, Henry L. ... 7.106, 7.107, 7.108
Mattingley, Christobel ... 1.43
Mayer, Arno J. ... 2.10
Mazian, Florence ... 7.29
McCarthy, Carolyn ... 5.33
McCarthy, Justin ... 5.10, 5.33
McLean, Scilla ... 7.75
McLoughlin, William G. ... 1.44
McNeely, Jeffrey A. ... 1.45
Medvedev, Roy A. ... 6.14
Mendelsohn, Ezra ... 2.11
Merton, Robert K. ... 7.109
Michaelis, Meir ... 2.75
Milgram, Stanley ... 8.43
Millar, James R. ... 6.27
Miller, Judith ... 2.32
Milner, Clyde A. ... 1.46
Milton, Sybil ... 2.124
Mitrany, David ... 6.15
Moody, Roger ... 1.47
Morgan, Sally ... 1.48

Morgenthau, Henry 5.F
Morse, Arthur D. 2.98
Morse, Jonathan 2.136
Moskovitz, Sarah 4.9
Muller, Filip 2.67
Munzel, Mark 1.49
Nash, Henry T. 7.110
Neher, André 2.151
Nekrich, Aleksander M. 6.26
Neterowicz, Eva M. 1.50
Neusner, Jacob 3.43
Newson, Linda A. 1.51
Nolan, Janne E. 7.47
Nolte, Ernst 3.44, 3.45
Nomberg-Przytyk, Sara 2.68
O'Connell, Robert L. 7.48
Ohland, Klaudine 1.52
Oliner, Pearl M. 2.76
Oliner, Samuel P. 2.76
Olson, James S. 1.53
Opotow, Susan 7.111
Orel, Şinasi 5.23
Ortiz, Roxanne Dunbar 1.54
Oshry, Ephraim 2.152
Ottoman Archives 5.28
Paine, Robert 1.55
Papazian, Pierre 3.46
Parsons, William S. 8.57
Pasha, Djemal 5.2
Pasha, Talaat 5.1
Paxton, Robert O. 2.9
Pawelczynska, Anna 2.56
Pearson, Michael 7.63
Peattie, Lisa 7.112
Penkower, Monty N. 2.99
Perec, Georges 8.46
Permanent Peoples' Tribunal Session
 of the Philippines 1.56
Pipes, Richard 6.16
Pitt, David 1.45
Porat, Dina 2.100
Porter, Jack Nusan 4.20, 8.47
Possony, S.T. 8.23
Price, David 1.57
Rabinowitz, Dorothy 4.21
Ramos, Alicida R. 1.58
Rapoport, Anatol 8.48
Rappaport, Chanan 7.87, 8.13
Rappaport, Leon 2.27, 3.38, 8.34
Read, Peter 1.26, 1.59
Reitlinger, Gerald Roberts 2.12
Retboll, Torben 1.60
Reynolds, Henry 1.61
Rhodes, Richard 7.5, 7.76
Richelson, Jeffrey 7.59

Rieck, Miriam 8.18
Ringelblum, Emmanuel 2.46
Roberts, Jan 1.62
Roiphe, Anne 8.49
Rosenbaum, Irving J. 2.153
Rosenberg, Alan 3.48
Rosenfeld, Alvin H. 2.137
Rosenfeld, Harvey 2.77
Rosensaft, Menachem 3.49
Ross, Robert W. 2.101
Rotenstreich, Nathan 3.50
Rubenstein, Richard L. 2.33, 2.34, 2.154,
. . . . 3.51, 7.6, 7.30
Ruether, Rosemary Radford 2.155
Rummel, R.J. 7.7a, 7.7b
Sachs, Nelly 2.117
Sagan, Carl 7.77
Sahaydak, Maksym 1.63
Salk, Jonas 8.50
Sallagar, Frederick 7.49
San Jose Conferences on the
 Holocaust (1977-1978) 8.51
Sanford, Nevitt 7.113
Santoni, Ronald E. 7.64
Schaffer, Ronald 7.50
Schleunes, Karl 2.13
Schneider, Robin 1.52
Schorsch, Ismar 3.52
Sederberg, Peter C. 7.78
Sereny, Gita 2.35
Sevilla-Casas, Elias 1.64
Shaw, Ezel Kural 5.9
Shaw, Stanford J. 5.9
Sherman, Marc 8.14
Sherry, Michael S. 7.51
Sichrovsky, Peter 4.10, 4.22
Sigal, John J. 4.11
Şimşir, Bilâl N. 5.32
Smith, Richard Chase 1.65
Solomon, Susan Gross 6.28
Somerville, John 7.79
Sonyel, Salâhi R. 5.11, 5.16,
. . . . 5.29, 5.30, 5.31
Spector, Leonard S. 7.80
Spiegelman, Art 2.118, 2.119
Stambler, Eric 7.54
Staron, Stanislaw 2.42
Staub, Ervin 7.114, 8.53
Stedman, Raymond William 1.66
Stein, Richard A. 3.53
Steinberg, Arlene 4.23
Steinbrunner, John D. 7.61
Steiner, George 3.54
Steinitz, Lucy Y. 4.24
Stewart, Desmond 5.7

Stockholm International Peace
    Research Institute 7.52
Stohl, Michael 7.8
Suhl, Yuri 2.108
Szonyi, David M. 4.24
Talmon, J.L. 3.55
Tapp, Nicholas 1.67
Taylor, Cecil P. 8.54
Taylor, Kenneth 1.58
Tec, Nechama 2.78, 2.79, 2.80, 8.55
Terzani, Tiziano 1.68
The Assembly of Turkish American
    Associations 5.24
Thomas, C.E. 7.66
Thompson, John L.P. 8.56
Thornton, Russell 1.69
Tory, Avraham 2.47
Totten, Samuel 8.57
Toynbee, Arnold Joseph 5.G
Treece, David 1.70
Troper, Harold 2.83
Trunk, Isaiah 2.48
Turco, Richard 7.77
Turnbull, Colin 1.71
Tushnet, Leonard 2.49
UNESCO 1.72
United States. President's Commission
    on the Holocaust 3.47
Uras, Esat 5.12
Valkeapaa, Nils-Aslak 1.73
Van Creveld, Martin 7.53
Viola, Lynne 6.29
Walker, Paul 7.54
Wallace, David 7.55
Wallimann, Isidor 7.31
Walter, Lynn 1.74
Wasserstein, Bernard 2.102
Weber, Max 7.115
Weinfeld, Morton 4.11
Wells, Leon 2.69
Wertham, Frederic 3.57
Westing, Arthur H. 7.9
Wheelon, Albert D. 7.47
Whitaker, Ben 8.58
White, Ralph K. 7.81
Whitten, Norman E., Jr. 1.75
Wiesel, Elie 2.120, 2.121, 4.12,
. . . . 4.25, 8.60
Wiesenthal, Simon 2.122
Williams, Peter 7.55
Willis, Robert E. 3.58
Wilson, Raymond 1.53
World Bank 1.77
Wright, Gordon 7.57
Wright, Quincy 7.58
Wyman, David S. 2.103, 2.104
Yahil, Leni 2.14, 2.81
Young, James E. 2.138, 4.26
Zannis, Mark 1.21
Zimmels, H.J. 2.156
Zraket, Charles A. 7.61
Zuccotti, Susan 2.82
Zuckerman, Edward 7.82

TITLE INDEX

The Abandonment of the Jews: America
   and the Holocaust, 1941-1945 .... 2.103
"Acceleration in Social Change" 7.94
"Accommodation and Adjustment to
   Ethnic Demands: The Mediterranean
   Framework" 1.38
Accounting for Genocide: National
   Responses and Jewish Victimization
   during the Holocaust 2.22
The Ache Indians: Genocide in Paraguay ... 1.49
Act and Idea in the Nazi Genocide 2.28
After Auschwitz: Radical Theology and
   Contemporary Judaism 2.154
"Against Mystification" 3.2
"Against Relativism: A Comment on
   the Debate on the Uniqueness of
   the Shoah" 3.53
Against the State of Nuclear Terror 7.71
The Age of Triage: Fear and Hope in an
   Overcrowded World 2.33, 7.6
The Age of Wonders 2.109
All but My Life 2.63
The Altruistic Personality: Rescuers of
   Jews in Nazi Europe 2.76
Ambassador Morgenthau's Story 5.F
America and the Survivors of
   the Holocaust 2.87
"The 'American Genocide' Pathologies of
   Indian-White Relations" 1.39
American Jewry and the Holocaust 2.84
"...and the Dirty Little Weapons" 7.54
Andonian "Documents" Attributed
   to Talaat 5.20
Anne Frank Remembered 2.73
"The Anticipation and Prevention of
   Genocide in International Conflicts:
   Some Lessons from History" 7.18, 8.16
"April 2018, Intergalactic Associated
   Press" 8.5
The Architect of Genocide: Himmler and the
   Final Solution 2.18
Are We All Nazis? 7.84
Armenian Allegations: Myth and Reality,
   a Handbook of Facts and Documents 5.24
"Armenian Deportations: A Reappraisal
   in the Light of New Documents" 5.11
An Armenian Falsification 5.21
The Armenian File: The Myth of
   Innocence 5.22
The Armenian Genocide in Perspective 8.28

The Armenian Genocide in the U.S.
   Archives, 1915-1918 .... 5.A
The Armenian Genocide: News Accounts
   from the American Press, 1915-1922 .... 5.E
The Armenian Holocaust: a Bibliography
   Relating to the Deportations, Massacres,
   and Dispersion of the Armenian People,
   1915-1923 .... 5.D
The Armenian Issue in Nine Questions
   and Answers 5.25
"Armenian Terrorism: A Profile" 5.17
The Armenians in History and the Armenian
   Question 5.12
Armenians in the Ottoman Empire and
   Modern Turkey (1912-1926) 5.13
Art of the Holocaust 2.124
The Artists of Terezin 2.129
Auschwitz and the Allies 2.92
Auschwitz: Beginning of a New Era?
   Reflections on the Holocaust 2.146
Auschwitz: True Tales from a Grotesque
   Land 2.68
Axis Rule in Occupied Europe. 8.40
Badenheim 1939 .... 2.110
"Ballistic Missiles and Weapons of
   Mass Destruction: What Is the Threat?
   What Should Be Done?" 7.38
Before the Bulldozer 1.57
Behind the Forbidden Door 1.68
Belzec, Sobibor, Treblinka: The
   Operation Reinhard Death Camps 2.51
The Best Sons of the Fatherland; Workers
   in the Vanguard of Soviet
   Collectivization 6.29
"Between Historical Myth and Revisionism?:
   The Third Reich from the Perspective
   of 1980" 3.44
Beyond Belief: The American Press
   and the Coming of the Holocaust,
   1933-1945 .... 2.97
Bitburg in Moral and Political
   Perspective 2.25
The Blue and the Yellow Stars of David:
   The Zionist Leadership in Palestine
   and the Holocaust, 1939-1945 .... 2.100
The Book of the International Conference
   on the Holocaust and Genocide:
   Book One. The Conference Program
   and Crisis 8.29
Born Guilty: Children of Nazi Families 4.10

Title	Ref
Bound in Misery and Iron: The Impact of the Grande Carasjas Program on the Indians of Brazil	1.70
Breaking the Silence	2.94
A Brief Glance at the "Armenian Question"	5.20
Britain and the Jews of Europe, 1939-1945	2.102
British Documents on Ottoman Armenians, Volume I (1856-1880), Volume II (1880-1890)	5.19
The Broken Connection: On Death and the Continuity of Life	7.101
"Bureaucracy"	7.115
"Bureaucratic Structure and Personality"	7.109
"The Bureaucratization of Homicide"	7.110
The Button: The Pentagon's Command and Control System	7.62
By Words Alone: The Holocaust in Literature	2.127
The Cambodian Agony	1.1
"Categories without Culture: Structuralism, Ethnohistory and Ethnocide"	1.29
The Catholic Church and Nazi Germany	2.96
Cherokees and Missionaries, 1789-1839	1.44
Children of the Holocaust: Conversations with Sons and Daughters of Survivors	4.3
Children with a Star	2.21
China's Bloody Century: Genocide and Mass Murder since 1900	7.7b
The Chittagong Hill Tracts	1.15
Chronicle of the Lodz Ghetto, 1941-1944	2.40
"Civilian Deaths in Wartime"	7.36
Class Struggles in the USSR; Second Period: 1923-1930	6.18
"'Cloud of Smoke, Pillar of Fire': Judaism, Christianity, and Modernity after the Holocaust"	2.147
Communism and the Dilemmas of National Liberation: National Communism in Soviet Ukraine, 1918-1933	6.10
"Concerning Authentic and Unauthentic Responses to the Holocaust"	3.14
The Conduct of War, 1789-1961	7.39
"Confessing God after Auschwitz: A Challenge for Christianity"	3.58
"The Convergent Aspects of the Armenian and Jewish Cases of Genocide: A Reinterpretation of the Concept of Holocaust"	3.8, 7.17
Counsels of War	7.67
The Crime and Punishment of I. G. Farben	2.52
Crimes of Obedience: Toward a Social Psychology of Authority and Responsibility	7.99, 8.32
The Crucifixion of the Jews	2.150
Culture and Conservation	1.45
The Cunning of History: The Holocaust and the American Future	2.34, 3.51, 7.30
Dam a River, Damn a People?	1.55
Danger and Survival: Choices About the Bomb in the First Fifty Years	7.60
Dark Soliloquy	2.116
Dawn	2.120
The Day after World War III	7.82
Days of Sorrow and Pain	2.38
Death Brigade	2.69
Death in Life: Survivors of Hiroshima	7.45
Deaths Caused by Disease in Relation to the Armenian Question	5.21
"The Decision to Collectivize Agriculture"	6.25
Decline of an Empire; the Soviet Socialist Republics in Revolt	6.20
The Deportees of Malta and the Armenian Question	5.32
The Deputy	2.93
The Destruction of the European Jews	2.6
"Determining the Uniqueness of the Holocaust: The Factor of Historical Valence"	3.18
The Dialectics of Disaster: A Preface to Hope	7.83
The Dialectics of Domination in Peru	1.65
The Diary of a Young Girl	2.61
Dimensions: A Publication of the Anti-Defamation League	8.17
Displacement of the Armenians Documents	5.30
Dispossession	1.61
"Documentation of the Armenian Genocide in Turkish Sources"	5.B
Documents on the Armenian Question: Forged and Authentic	5.21
Documents on Ottoman-Armenians	5.34
A Double Dying: Reflections on Holocaust Literature	2.137
The Drowned and the Saved	4.8
Dry Tears: The Story of a Lost Childhood	2.78
East Timor, Indonesia and the Western Democracies	1.60
The Eastern Question: Imperialism and the Armenian Community	5.26
The Echo of the Nazi Holocaust in Rabbinic Literature	2.156
"Ecocide, Genocide, and the Nuremberg Tradition of Individual Responsibility"	7.91
Economic Development and Tribal Peoples	1.77
"The Education of a Torturer"	8.22
Eichmann in Jerusalem: A Report on the Banality of Evil	2.15, 3.1
An End to Laughter	1.16
Engines of War: Merchants of Death and the New Arms Race	7.32
Environmental Warfare: A Technical, Legal, and Policy Appraisal	7.9

"Epilogue: The Nuclear Arms Race
   and Genocide" 7.100
Erika: Poems of the Holocaust 2.114
"Essay: On the Place of the Holocaust in
   History; In Honour of Franklin H. Littell" .. 3.3
"Essay: Quantity and Interpretation—Issues
   in the Comparative Historical Analysis
   of the Holocaust" 7.23
Ethnicity, Economy and the State in Ecuador . 1.74
Ethnocide of Ukrainians in the U.S.S.R.
   An Underground Journal from the Soviet
   Ukraine, Spring 1974 .... 1.63
"European History—Seedbed of the Holocaust" 3.55
Execution by Hunger; the Hidden Holocaust .. 6.4
The Exile of the Word: From the Silence of
   the Bible to the Silence of Auschwitz ... 2.151
Eyewitness Auschwitz 2.67
The Face of Battle 7.43
"The Fact Behind the Telegrams Attributed
   to Talaat Pasha by the Armenians" 5.23
Faith after the Holocaust 2.139
The Faith and Doubt of Holocaust Survivors .. 4.1
Faith and Fratricide: Theological Roots
   of Anti-Semitism 2.155
"'Faith Ethics and the Holocaust': Some
   Personal, Theological, and Religious
   Responses to the Holocaust" 3.34
"Famine and Nationalism in Soviet Ukraine" . 6.11
"The Fate of the Earth and the Fate of the
   Jews: Responses to Holocaust" 7.107
Final Solution 2.12
Five Minutes to Midnight: Why the Nuclear
   Threat Is Growing Faster Than Ever 7.66
Flight and Rescue 2.85
"The Folk Culture and Development: Cultural
   Genocide or Cultural Revitalization?" 1.17
For the Love of Life 8.21
The Foreign Office and the Famine:
   British Documents on Ukraine
   and the Great Famine 6.21
The Forest Indians in Stroessner's Paraguay:
   Survival or Extinction? 1.4
The Forgotten Victim: A History of
   the Civilian 7.42
The Formation of the Soviet Union;
   Communism and Nationalism 1917-1923 .. 6.16
Foundation of a Planned Economy, 1926-1929
   Vol. 1, Parts 1 and 2, of A History of
   Soviet Russia 6.19
Fragments of Isabella:
   A Memoir of Auschwitz 2.64
From Bergen-Belsen to Jerusalem:
   Contemporary Implications
   of the Holocaust 3.15
From Genesis to Genocide 2.20

From Genesis to Genocide:
   The Meaning of Human Nature
   and the Power of Behavior Control 8.15
"From the Holocaust to the Holocaust" 3.41
Gender and Destiny: Women Writers and
   the Holocaust 2.130
Generations of the Holocaust 4.14
The Genocidal Mentality: Nazi Holocaust
   and Nuclear Threat 2.29, 8.41, 7.102
"Genocidal Process: The German Genocide
   Against Jews" 3.40
Genocide: A Critical Bibliographic Review,
   vol.1 .... 7.12, 8.7
Genocide: A Critical Bibliographic Review,
   vol.2 .... 7.13, 8.6
"Genocide: A Sociological Perspective" 7.19, 8.20
Genocide and Human Rights 8.24
Genocide and Human Rights:
   A Global Anthology 8.47
"Genocide and Omnicide: Technology at
   the Limits" 7.98
"Genocide and Social Science" 3.22
Genocide and the Modern Age: Etiology and
   Case Studies of Mass Death 7.31
"Genocide and Total War: A Preliminary
   Comparison" 7.103
"Genocide as a Problem of National and
   International Law: The World War I
   Armenian Case and its Contemporary
   Legal Ramifications" 5.C
"Genocide as Boundary-Crossing Behavior" .. 8.56
"A Genocide Bureau" 8.33
"A Genocide Early Warning System" 8.13
Genocide in Paraguay 1.5
"Genocide in Vietnam?" 7.85
Genocide: Its Political Use in the
   Twentieth Century 7.24, 8.36
The Genocide Machine in Canada 1.21
Genocide: State Power and Mass Murder ... 8.27
"Genocide: The Ultimate Human
   Rights Problem" 8.8
"Genocide, Total War,
   and Nuclear Omnicide" 7.104
"Genocide: Toward a Functional Definition" . 7.14
"Genocides and Politicides since 1945:
   Evidence and Anticipation" 8.25
The Geography of Famine 7.1
"German Motivations for the Destruction
   of the Jews" 3.31
Ghetto Diary 2.45
Ghetto in Flames 2.37
"Good People and Dirty Work" 7.95
Good: A Tragedy 8.54
Governing Savages 1.42

Government Violence and Repression:
   An Agenda for Research 7.8
The Great Terror, A Reassessment 1.18, 6.2
Greetings from Lappland 1.73
"The Gulf War: Not So Clean" 7.46
The Harvest of Sorrow: Soviet
   Collectivization and the Terror-Famine 1.19, 6.3
Hassidic Tales of the Holocaust 2.144
"The Historikerstreit: Uniqueness and
   Comparability of the Holocaust" 3.30
The History and Sociology of Genocide 6.22, 7.10
The History and Sociology of Genocide:
   Analyses and Case Studies 2.19, 8.4
A History of Strategic Bombing 7.44
"History of the Ottoman Empire and
   Modern Turkey, vol. 1, Empire of the
   Gazis: The Rise and Decline of the
   Ottoman Empire 1280-1808, vol. 2,
   Reform, Revolution, and Republic: The
   Rise of Modern Turkey 1808-1975 . . . . . . 5.9
History, Structure and Survival:
   A Comparison of the Yuki (Ukmno'm)
   and Tolowa (Hush) Indians of
   Northern California" 1.69
Hitler and the Armenian Genocide 8.2
Hiltler and the "Armenian Question" 5.20
Hitler and the Final Solution 2.3
Hitler's Death Camps:
   The Sanity of Madness 2.54
The Hmong of Thailand 1.67
The Hoax of the Twentieth Century: The
   Case Against the Presumed Extermination
   of European Jewry 8.3
The Holocaust 2.14
The Holocaust: A History of the Jews of
   Europe during the Second World War 2.4
"The Holocaust: A 'Non-Unique' Event for
   All Humanity?" 3.21
Holocaust and Genocide Bibliographic
   1980-1990 . . . . 8.14
Holocaust and Genocide Studies 8.26
The Holocaust and Halakha 2.153
"The Holocaust and Jewish Survival" 3.52
"The Holocaust and Philosophy" 3.16
The Holocaust and Strategic Bombing:
   Genocide and Total War in the
   Twentieth Century 7.105
The Holocaust and the Crisis of
   Human Behavior 2.27, 3.38, 8.34
"The Holocaust and the Enigma of
   Uniqueness: A Philosophical Effort
   at Practical Clarification" 3.12
"The Holocaust and the Foundations of
   Moral Judgment" 8.35

The Holocaust and the Literary
   Imagination 2.133
"The Holocaust as a Unique
   Historical Event" 3.50
"The Holocaust: History as Aberration" . . . 3.49
The Holocaust: Ideology, Bureaucracy,
   and Genocide 8.51
The Holocaust in History 2.31
"The Holocaust in Perspective" 3.42
The Holocaust Kingdom: A Memoir 2.58
"The Holocaust: Some Unresolved Issues" . . 3.37
"Holocaust Survivors and Their Children:
   A Review of the Clinical Literature" 4.23
Holocaust Testimonies 2.134
Holocaust Testimonies:
   The Ruins of Memory 4.6
"Holocaust Theology: The Survivors
   Statement—Part I" 3.27
"Holocaust Theology: The Survivors
   Statement—Part II" 3.28
Horrendous Death, Health, and Well-Being . . . 7.4
"How Armenian Propaganda Nurtured a
   Gullible Christian World in Connection
   with the Deportations and 'Massacres'" . . 5.29
How Can We Commit the Unthinkable?:
   Genocide, the Human Cancer 7.87, 8.9
How Nuclear Weapons Decisions Are Made . 7.75
"How to Avoid (Legally) Conviction for
   Crimes of Genocide: A One-Act Reading" . 8.10
"How Unique Is the Holocaust?" 3.19
A Hundred Years War 1.59
Hydraulic Development and Ethnocide:
   The Mazatec and Chinantec People of
   Oaxaca, Mexico 1.6
I Chose Freedom: The Personal and
   Political Life of a Soviet Official 6.7
If This Is a Man 2.66
"The Impact of Total War" 7.57
"Implementing the Final Solution: The
   Ordinary Regulating of the Extraordinary" 7.108
"Imponderables of the Holocaust" 7.106
In the Lion's Den:
   The Life of Oswald Rufeisen 2.79
In the Shadow of the Holocaust:
   The Second Generation 4.4
Incendiary Weapons 7.52
Indefensible Weapons: The Political and
   Psychological Case Against Nuclearism . . 7.74
Indelible Shadows: Film and the Holocaust . 2.131
Indian Survival in Colonial Nicaragua 1.51
Indians of the Americas 1.54
Indigenous Peoples 1.36
The Indigenous Voice 1.47

The Industrialization of Soviet Russia, Vol. 1, The Socialist Offensive; the Collectivization of Soviet Agriculture, 1929-1930, and Vol. 2, The Soviet Collective Farm, 1929-1930 .... 6.23
Informe Final: Reunion de Expertos sobre Etnodesarrollo y Etnocidio en America Latina, 7-11 de Diciembre de 1981; FLACSO, San Jose, Costa Rica N. SS-82/WS/32 .... 1.72
The Informed Heart: Autonomy in a Mass Age 2.17
Inside the Vicious Heart: Americans and the Liberation of Nazi Concentration Camps 2.50
"Institutions and the Promotion of Violence" . 7.96
International Action Against Genocide 8.37
Internet on the Holocaust and Genocide 8.30, 8.59
An Interrupted Life: The Diaries of Etty Hillesum 2.62
Into That Darkness: An Examination of Conscience 2.35
The Iroquois Struggle for Survival 1.32
Is God an American? An Anthropological Perspective of the Missionary Work of the Summer Institute of Linguistics ... 1.35
"Is the Holocaust Explicable" 3.4
"Is the Holocaust Unique?" 3.11
"Is There a Survivors' Syndrome?" 4.20
"Issues in Post-Holocaust Christian Theology" 3.25
The Italians and the Holocaust: Persecution, Rescue and Survival 2.82
Jagendorf's Foundry: Memoir of the Romanian Holocaust, 1941-1944 .... 2.43
A Jew Today 4.25
Jewish Resistance in Nazi-occupied Eastern Europe 2.105
The Jewish Resistance 2.107
The Jewish Return into History 2.145
"The Jewish Tragedy and the Historian" 3.10
"Jewish Values in the Post-Holocaust Future: A Symposium" 3.35
The Jews of East Central Europe Between the World Wars 2.11
The Jews of Warsaw, 1939-1943: Ghetto, Underground, Revolt 2.41
The Jews Were Expendable: Free World Diplomacy and the Holocaust 2.99
The Journey Back from Hell 4.17
Judenrat: The Jewish Councils in Eastern Europe under Nazi Occupation ... 2.48
"Justifying the Final Solution" 8.44

Kiddush Hashem: Jewish Religious and Cultural Life in Poland during the Holocaust 2.148
The Last Dalai Lama 1.31
The Last Frontier; Fighting over Land in the Amazon 1.10
Legacy of Night: The Literary Universe of Elie Wiesel 2.128
Legacy of Silence: Encounters with Children of the Third Reich 4.13, 8.1
Lenin and the Problem of Marxist Peasant Revolution 6.5
Less Than Slaves: Jewish Forced Labor and the Quest for Compensation 2.55
Lest Innocent Blood Be Shed 2.74
Let History Judge; the Origins and Consequences of Stalinism 6.14
Lethal Politics: Soviet Genocide and Mass Murder since 1917 .... 7.7a
Living after the Holocaust: Reflections by Children of Survivors Living in America .. 4.24
The Living Witness; Art in Concentration Camps and Ghettos 2.126
"Locating the Holocaust on the Genocide Spectrum: Towards a Methodology of Definition and Categorization" 7.22
Lodz Ghetto: Inside a Community under Siege 2.36
The Logic of Nuclear Terror 7.70
"The Long Life of Metaphor—a Theological-Metaphysical Approach to the Shoah" ... 3.54
A Long Night's Journey into Day; A Revised Retrospective on the Holocaust 2.143, 3.13
"Looking at Potatoes from Below" 3.57
"Losses Suffered by the Population of the USSR in 1918-1958" 6.13
The Lost Children 1.26
Love Despite Hate: Child Survivors of the Holocaust and Their Adult Lives 4.9
The Macmillan Atlas of the Holocaust 1.30
The Making of the Atomic Bomb 7.76
Man Unfolding 8.50
Man's Search for Meaning: An Introduction to Logotherapy 2.23, 4.15
"Man-Made Death: A Neglected Mortality" ... 7.5
"The Man-Made Famine of 1933 in the Soviet Ukraine: What Happened and Why?" 6.12
Managing Nuclear Operations 7.61
Marx Against the Peasant; a Study in Social Dogmatism 6.15
Marxism and the U.S.S.R.; the Theory of Proletarian Dictatorship and the Marxist Analysis of Soviet Society 6.17

"Mass Collectivization and the
   Contribution of Soviet Agriculture
   to the First Five Year Plan" 6.27
Massacres to Mining 1.62
Massive Psychic Trauma 4.5
Maus II: A Survivor's Tale and Here
   My Troubles Began 2.119
Maus: A Survivor's Tale 2.118
Memoirs of Halide Edib 5.4
Memories of a Turkish Statesman, 1913-1919 . 5.2
"Minorities" 5.8
"The Miserable Practice of the Insinuators:
   The Uniqueness of the National-Socialist
   Crimes Cannot Be Denied" 3.33
The Missionaries 1.40
Modernity and the Holocaust 2.16, 7.86
"Moral Exclusion and Injustice" 7.111
Moscow and the Ukraine, 1917-1953 ...... 6.24
Mothers in the Fatherland: Women, the
   Family, and Nazi Politics 2.7
The Mountain People 1.71
Multi-Ethnicity in India: The Adivasi
   Peasants of Chota Nagpur and Santal
   Parganas 1.23
Muslims and Minorities: The Population
   of Ottoman Anatolia and the End of
   the Empire 5.10
Mussolini and the Jews: German-Italian
   Relations and the Jewish Question
   in Italy 2.75
My Place 1.48
A Myth of Terror. Armenian Extremism:
   Its Causes and Its Historical Context 5.27
The National Integration of Mapuche 1.7
National Revolution and Indigenous Identity .. 1.52
Native Americans in the Twentieth Century .. 1.53
Natives of Sarawak: Survival in
   Borneo's Vanishing Forests 1.34
The Nazi Doctors: Medical
   Killing and the
   Psychology of Genocide 2.30, 7.27, 8.42
The New Conservatism: Cultural Criticism
   and the Historians' Debate 3.28
New Lives: Survivors of the Holocaust
   Living in America 4.21
Night 2.121, 4.12
No Haven for the Oppressed 2.91
None Is Too Many 2.83
None of Us Will Return 2.57
"Normalizing the Unthinkable" 7.112
Notes from the Warsaw Ghetto: The
   Journal of Emmanuel Ringelblum 2.46
"Nuclear 'War' Is Omnicide" 7.79
The Nuclear Arms Race 7.63

The Nuclear Cage: A Sociology of
   the Arms Race 7.73
Nuclear, Chemical, and Biological Warfare .. 7.41
The Nuclear Fallacy: Dispelling the Myth
   of Nuclear Strategy 7.65
Nuclear Winter, Deterrence and the
   Prevention of Nuclear War 7.78
O the Chimneys 2.117
The Oath 8.60
Obedience to Authority 8.43
"Ocean Mining and Cultural
   Genocide in Guam" 1.3
Of Arms and Men: A History of War,
   Weapons, and Aggression 7.48
On the Edge of Destruction 2.5
"On the Possibility of the Holocaust:
   An Approach to a Historical Synthesis" .. 3.24
On the Road to Tribal Extinction:
   Depopulation, Deculturation, and
   Maladaptation among the Bartak of
   the Philippines 1.25
One by One, by One: Facing the Holocaust .. 2.32
The Ottoman Armenians: Victims of Great
   Power Diplomacy 5.31
Out of the Backyard; Readings on
   Canadian Native History 1.28
The Painful Field: The Psychiatric
   Dimension of Modern War 7.40
Paper Walls 2.104
Pasha Are Forgeries! 5.20
A Past That Will Not Pass Away—A Speech It
   Was Possible to Write, But Not to Present" 3.45
A Path Where No Man Thought:
   Nuclear Winter and the
   End of the Arms Race 7.77
The Pavement of Hell 2.49
Philippines, Repression and Resistance 1.56
"Philosophy and Contemporary Faces of
   Genocide: Multiple Genocide and
   Nuclear Destruction" 7.64
"Philosophy and the Holocaust" 7.26
Pius XII and the Third Reich 2.90
"The Place of the Holocaust in Contemporary
   History" 3.5
Playing for Time 2.59
The Politics of Genocide 2.1
The Politics of Rescue: The Roosevelt
   Administration and the Holocaust,
   1939-1945 .... 2.89
"Posthumous Memoirs of Talaat Pasha" ... 5.1
"Preparation for Nuclear War:
   The Final Madness" 8.48
The Prevention of Genocide 7.25, 8.38
"Professions, Professionals, and Genocide" .. 7.28

Title	Ref
Psychiatric Aspects of the Prevention of Nuclear War	7.93
Psychoanalytic Reflections on the Holocaust	4.19
The Psychological and Medical Effects of Concentration Camps and Related Persecutions on Survivors of the Holocaust: A Research Bibliography	8.18
Psychology and the Prevention of Nuclear War: A Book of Readings	7.81
"The Psychology of Denial of Unknown Genocides"	8.11
"The Public Relations of Ethnocide"	1.2
The Question of German Guilt	2.26
Rabbinic Responsa of the Holocaust Era	2.149
Raoul Wallenberg, Angel of Rescue	2.77
"The Readiness of Health Profession Students to Comply with a Hypothetical Program of Forced Migration of a Minority Population"	8.45
"The Reasoning of Holocaust Theology"	3.20
Reflections of the Holocaust in Art and Literature	2.125
Report from the Frontier	1.14
Report to the President	3.47
Rescue in Denmark	2.71
The Rescue of Danish Jewry: Test of a Democracy	2.81
The Resonance of Dust	2.123
Resource Development and Indigenous People	1.33
Responsa from the Holocaust	2.152
A Review of the Acculturation Approach in Anthropology with Special Reference to Recent Change in Native Alaska"	1.27
Revised and Updated Report on the Question of the Prevention and Punishment of the Crime of Genocide	8.58
Revolt Against the Dead	1.11
Righteous Gentile	2.70
"'Righteous Gentiles' in the Nazi Era"	3.26
The Rise of American Air Power: The Creation of Armageddon	7.51
The Road to Total War	7.49
Roads to Extinction: Essays on the Holocaust	2.24
The Roots of Evil: The Origins of Genocide and Other Group Violence	7.114, 8.53
Russian Peasants and Soviet Power, a Study of Collectivization	6.9
Sacha Runa: Ethnicity and Adaptation of Ecuadorian Jungle Quicha	1.75
Sanctions for Evil	7.113
Saving the Fragments: From Auschwitz to New York	2.65
"Scenarios of Genocide"	8.19
Scroll of Agony	2.44
A Season for Healing: Reflections on the Holocaust	8.49
See Under: Love	2.113
Shadows of Auschwitz: A Christian Response to the Holocaust	2.141
Shadows of the Indian	1.66
Shoah: An Oral History of the Holocaust	2.8
Shofar: Inter-disciplinary Journal of Jewish Studies	8.52
"The Significance of the Holocaust"	3.32
The Silence of Pius XII	2.88
"Singularity and Its Relativization: Changing Views in German Historiography on National Socialism and the 'Final Solution'"	3.39
The Situation of the Indian in South America	1.24
So It Was True: The American Protestant Press and the Nazi Persecution of the Jews	2.101
"Some Remarks on Slaughter"	7.92
The Soviet Agrarian Debate; a Controversy in Social Science, 1923-1929	6.28
"The Soviet Gulag: Is It Genocidal?"	6.8
"Soviet Myth and Reality"	6.6
Soviet Nationality Problems	6.1
A Speech Delivered by Ghazi Mustapha Kemal, October 1927	5.3
'Statement' Wrongly Attributed to Mustafa Kemâl Atatürk	5.20
Stranger at Home: "The Holocaust," Zionism, and American Judaism	3.43
Strangers in Their Own Land	4.22
Strategic Nuclear Targeting	7.59
"Structural and Armed Violence in the 20th Century: Magnitudes and Trends"	7.2
A Study of War	7.58
The Sunflower	2.122
Survival in Auschwitz: The Nazi Assault on Humanity	4.18
Survival in Our Own Land	1.43
Surviving the Holocaust: The Kovno Ghetto Diary	2.47
The Survivors: An Anthology of Life in the Death Camps	2.53
Survivors, Victims, and Perpetrators: Essays on the Nazi Holocaust	4.2
The Swastika Poems	2.115
Symposium on International Terrorism: Armenian Terrorism, Its Supporters, the Narcotic Connection, the Distortion of History	5.18
Taking Lives: Genocide and State Power	7.21
"Teaching about Genocide"	8.57
"Technology and Genocide: Technology as a 'Form of Life.'"	7.97

Title	Ref
Technology and War: From 2000 B.C. to the Present	7.53
The Terezin Requiem	2.39
The Terrible Secret: Suppression of the Truth about Hitler's "Final Solution"	2.95
Their Brothers' Keepers	2.72
"A Theoretical Model of Genocide with Particular Reference to the Armenian Case"	7.16
They Fought Back: The Story of Jewish Resistance in Nazi Europe	2.108
"Thinking about the Six Million: Facts, Figures, Perspectives"	3.9
"The Third Wave"	8.31
"Third World Ballistic Missiles"	7.47
This Way to the Gas, Ladies and Gentlemen	2.112
"Three Faces of Cruelty: Towards a Comparative Sociology of Evil"	7.89
Tibet: Behind the Ice Curtain	1.37
Tibetan Village Communities: Structure and Change	1.20
To Mend the World: Foundations of Future Jewish Thought	3.17
To Win a Nuclear War: The Pentagon's Secret War Plans	7.68
"'Total War,' the Self-Fulfilling Prophecy?"	7.33
"Toward a Methodology of Teaching about the Holocaust"	3.23
"Toward a Sociology of Nuclear Weapons"	7.72
"Toward Empirical Theory of Genocides and Politicides: Identification and Measurement of Cases since 1945"	7.20
Toward the Understanding and Prevention of Genocide: Proceedings of the International Conference on the Holocaust and Genocide	7.11, 8.12
The Tragedy of Tibet	1.50
Trauma and Rebirth: Intergenerational Effects of the Holocaust	4.11
The Treatment of Armenians in the Ottoman Empire, 1915-1916; Documents Presented to Viscount Grey of Fallodan, Secretary of State for Foreign Affairs	5.G
The Treaty with Turkey: Why It Should Be Ratified	5.6
The Tremendum	2.142
The Trial of Judaism in Contemporary Jewish Writing	2.132
Tribal People and Development Issues	1.8
The Turco-Armenian 'Adana Incidents' in the Light of Secret British Documents (July 1908-December 1909)	5.16
Turkey	5.7
"Turkey and the Armenians"	5.15
Turkey in the World War	5.5
Turks and Armenians: A Manual on the Armenian Question	5.33
Twentieth Century Book of the Dead	7.3
The Twisted Road to Auschwitz	2.13
"A Typology of Genocide"	7.15
Tzili: The Story of a Life	2.111
"The U.S. Congress and Adolf Hitler on the Armenians"	5.14
The Undeclared Bomb: The Spread of Nuclear Weapons, 1987-88	7.80
"Understanding the Psychology of Genocidal Destructiveness"	7.88
Unfulfilled Promise: Rescue and Resettlement of Jewish Refugee Children in the United States 1934-1945	2.86
"The 'Unique' Intentionality of the Holocaust"	3.36
"A 'Unique Uniqueness?'"	3.46
"The Uniqueness and Universality of the Holocaust"	3.7
"Uniqueness, Gypsies and Jews"	3.29
Unit 731: Japan's Secret Biological Warfare in World War II	7.55
Uprising in the Warsaw Ghetto	2.106
Utopia in Power; the History of the Soviet Union from 1917 to the Present	6.26
Values and Violence in Auschwitz: A Sociological Analysis	2.56
Versions of Survival: The Holocaust and the Human Spirit	2.135, 4.7
Vichy France and the Jews	2.9
Victims of Politics: The State of Human Rights	8.23
Victims of Progress	1.9
Victims of the Miracle	1.22
"The Visibility of Evil"	7.90
W or the Memory of Childhood	8.46
War	7.34
The War Against East Timor	1.12
The War Against the Jews, 1933-1945	2.2
War without Mercy: Race and Power in the Pacific War	7.35
The Warsaw Diary of Adam Czerniakow	2.42
"Was the Holocaust Unique? A Peculiar Question?"	3.48
"Was the Holocaust Unique?: Responses to Pierre Papazian"	3.56
West Papua: The Obliteration of a People	1.13
Western Expansion and Indigenous Peoples	1.64
When Light Pierced the Darkness: Christian Rescue of Jews in Nazi-Occupied Poland	2.80
When Light Pierced the Darkness: Christian Rescue of Jews in Nazi-Occupied Lands	8.55

When Memory Comes	4.16
While Six Million Died: A Chronicle of American Apathy	2.98
"Whose Holocaust?"	3.6
Why Did the Heavens Not Darken?	2.10
Why Genocide: The Armenian and Jewish Experiences in Perspective	7.29
Wings of Judgement: American Bombing in World War II	7.50
With God in Hell: Judaism in the Ghetto and Deathcamps	2.140
With Good Intentions: Quaker Work among the Pawnees, Otos, and Omahas in the 1870s	1.46
Witness to Cultural Genocide. First-Hand Reports on Rumania's Minority Policies Today	1.76
The Wizards of Armageddon	7.69
Word by Word: The Language of Memory	2.136
"World Genocide Tribunal: A Proposal for Planetary Preventive Measures Supplementing a Genocide Early Warning System"	8.39
World Military and Social Expenditures	7.56
"World War II as Total War"	7.37
Writing and Rewriting the Holocaust	2.138
Writing and Rewriting the Holocaust: Narrative and the Consequences of Interpretation	4.26
The Yanomami in Brazil	1.58
The Yanomami in the Face of Ethnocide	1.41
Yildiz Collection: The Armenian Question, Talori Incidents	5.28
Young Moshe's Diary	2.60

8669